THE PLOUGHSHARES READER:
NEW FICTION FOR THE EIGHTIES

THE PLOUGHSHARES READER:
NEW FICTION FOR THE EIGHTIES

Edited and with an introduction by
DeWitt Henry

published by THE PUSHCART PRESS

Library of Congress Card Number: 84-062095
ISBN 0-916366-30-8

Second Printing July, 1985

Manufactured in The United States of America by
Ray Freiman & Company, Stamford, Connecticut

This book is dedicated to
the editors of *Ploughshares:*

Anne Bernays
Frank Bidart
Henry Bromell
Rosellen Brown
Raymond Carver
Andre Dubus
George Garrett
Lorrie Goldensohn
David Gullette
Donald Hall
Paul Hannigan
Seamus Heaney
Fanny Howe
Justin Kaplan
George Kimball
Thomas Lux
Gail Mazur
James Alan McPherson
Jay Neugeboren
Tim O'Brien
Joyce Peseroff
Jayne Anne Phillips
James Randall
Lloyd Schwartz
Jane Shore
Richard Tillinghast
Ellen Bryant Voigt
Dan Wakefield
Ellen Wilbur
Alan Williamson;

and to my co-director,
Peter O'Malley

Acknowledgments

The following works are reprinted by permission of the publishers and authors.

"A Compassionate Leave" © 1981 by Richard Yates. Reprinted from LIARS IN LOVE by Richard Yates. Published by Delacorte/Seymour Lawrence.

"Going After Cacciato" © 1976 by Tim O'Brien

"A Small, Good Thing" © 1980 by Raymond Carver. Reprinted from CATHEDRAL by Raymond Carver. © 1983 by Alfred Knopf Co.

"Lily" © 1982 by T. Alan Broughton

"Duck Season" © 1978 by T. Alan Broughton

"Household" © 1981 by Susan Engberg

"Davidson Among The Chosen" © 1978 by Philip Damon

"Uncle Nathan" © 1978 by Jay Neugeboren

"All Sorts of Impossible Things" © 1980 by John McGahern

"Works of the Imagination" © 1982 by Gina Barriault. Excerpted from THE INFINITE PASSION OF EXPECTATION, © 1982 by Gina Berriault. Published by North Point Press and reprinted by permission. All Rights Reserved.

"At St. Croix" © 1979 by Andre Dubus. From FINDING A GIRL IN AMERICA by Andre Dubus. Copyright © 1980 by Andre Dubus. Reprinted by permission of David R. Godine, Publisher, Boston.

"El Paso" © 1978 by Jayne Anne Phillips. Reprinted from BLACK TICKETS by Jayne Anne Phillips. © 1980 by Jayne Anne Phillips. Reprinted by permission of Dell Publishing Co., Inc.

"Ollie, Oh..." © 1982 by Carolyn Chute

"Bunco" © 1980 by Marilyn Jean Conner

"The Intruders of Sleepless Nights" © 1982 by Pamela Painter

"Bijou" © 1981 by Stuart Dybek

"West" © 1980 by Maxine Kumin. Reprinted from WHY CAN'T WE LIVE TOGETHER LIKE CIVILIZED HUMAN BEINGS by Maxine Kumin. Published by Viking Penguin, Inc. and reprinted by permission.

"The Legacy of Beau Kremel" © 1978 by Stephen Wolf

"Fathers" © 1984 by Robley Wilson, Jr.

"The Pilot Messenger" © 1981 by Eve Shelnutt. Reprinted from THE LOVE CHILD. Published by Black Sparrow Press and reprinted by permission of John Martin.

"Minnie the Moocher's Hair" © 1982 by Jack Pulaski

"Winterblossom Garden" © 1982 by David Low

"Offices of Instruction" © 1983 by Jocelyn Hausmann

"Static Discharge" © 1978 by Lew McCreary

"Age" © 1982 by Janet Desaulniers

"White Boy" © 1981 by Ivy Goodman. Reprinted from HEART FAILURE. Published by University of Iowa Press, 1983.

"Expensive Gifts" © 1980 by Sue Miller

"Island" © 1983 by Edward P. Jones

"Trespass" © 1983 by Sandra Scofield

"The Eighth Day" © 1983 by Max Apple. Reprinted from FREE AGENTS by Max Apple. Published by Harper and Row.

"The Carved Table" © 1980 by Mary Peterson

"Moonlight" © 1981 by Richard Wertime

"The Coggios" © 1981 by Sharyn Layfield

Contents

DeWitt Henry

Introduction

Where most "new" or "best" story anthologies are drawn
from single author collections or from all magazines or all
literary magazines in a given year, this *Reader* attempts to represent the best from a single literary quarterly during its first
fifteen, improbable years. I hope readers will be challenged by
the variety and range of stories included, by authors known
and unknown, and convinced by the integrity of standards
they represent.

Ploughshares was founded in Cambridge, Massachusetts,
in 1970 by a round-table of younger poets and writers, including Iowa Writers' Workshop veterans, New York School/
Bowery veterans, one Dubliner, Harvard graduate assistants,
and Black Mountain descendents. We disagreed heatedly
about what writing was worthwhile, let alone best, but agreed
on the richness and diversity of our literary generation, and on
the abundance of work for which there was, at least locally, no
attractive, energetic, caring, discriminating outlet, and hadn't
been for some time. We set out to redress that lack with a
quarterly devoted to new poetry and fiction, and one that
would embody the spirit of our debates in its editorial policy.
Each issue would be edited by a different writer as a kind of
statement, turning the series itself into a forum for contrasting
viewpoints and ideas. The progress, vitality and coherence of
this forum would be shaped by Peter O'Malley and myself as
permanent "directors," acting on the advice of previous editors, contributors, and local trustees. We sought to give different factions and elements of the writing community access and

editorial "justice," to challenge provincialisms of taste, theory and acquaintance, and to demand both of readers and editors a purity of original regard. There would be no name dropping, no trading of favors, no indulgence of personal as opposed to literary friendships, no self-advancement, and no lowering of standards for the sake of some theoretical "correctness." Each editor would be held to task by the quality of work he or she was rejecting as well as accepting, and by regard for the other editors and for the audience won by our collective efforts. Against the odds, not the least of which has been a prolonged dependence on volunteerism in lieu of cash, this system has worked well, building on strengths, attracting new writers as editors, and resulting in a series richer than the sum of its parts.

The thirty-three stories included here were selected from issues edited by Tim O'Brien, Rosellen Brown, Andre Dubus, Seamus Heaney, Jay Neugeboren, Jayne Anne Phillips, James Randall, Alan Williamson, Dan Wakefield, Donald Hall, Raymond Carver, George Garrett and myself. None, to my knowledge, came originally from agents. Six were solicited from writers the editors admired. The rest were unsolicited. Roughly one third were the author's first publication. Though most of our fiction editors would differ more fundamentally from the editors, say, of *TriQuarterly* during these years than from each other, at least in refusing to make "value judgements on the question of modality" (as Seymour Epstein puts it in *Ploughshares 3/1*), each has introduced different writers and interests to the magazine, and none would choose the same thirty-three stories from the one hundred and seventy-five we have published, nor even agree probably on as many as six or seven. This selection is my own; among possible bests, I have chosen, finally, according to my own vision, stories worthy of each other, stories that enlarge and strengthen the whole, stories that have withstood, compelled and grown with my rereading and remain permanently new, and that suggest the mix of subjects, sensibilities, and approaches characteristic of the magazine.

They are stories for the Eighties, not because of their concern with timely social issues or the transitory surface of our culture, but because of their stubborn focus, in a time of accelerating change, on human themes. They seek, through the discipline of their art, in Thoreau's words, "to drive life into a corner and reduce it to its lowest terms, and, if it proved mean, why then to get the whole and genuine meanness of it, and publish its meanness to the world; or if it were sublime, to know it by experience." They bring realities to mind. Speaking of death, love, sex, comings of age, age itself, the family, justice, communication and its lack, courage, compassion, prejudice, fear of life, strength of life, they speak from felt experience in a world of human events and relationships, and, in most cases, in a "transparent" way. Most, not all, labor to get the writer's performing self out of the way and to direct the language, by image and evocation, to a character's speaking voice; to a smellable, noisy, touchable, surrounding world; to the drama of people, what they do to each other and what happens to them. The deeper that drama is explored — into questions about personality, relationship, experience — the stronger the story. All are objective art. Each bears, in Jay Neugeboren's words, "evidence of a single, unique mind working freely." All progress through risk as the means to vision rather than to sport. They are also stories that illuminate each other, inviting comparison in different ways.

In otherwise dissimilar stories by Richard Yates, Andre Dubus, Gina Berriault and Janet Desaulniers, for instance, the main character is emotionally paralyzed and must find or rediscover courage and humanity in love for a sister, children, mankind, a father, a daughter. Berriault and Dybek differently raise the question of compassion and art; in one, imagination involves an acceptance of personal mortality with the awakening to "everyone else on earth"; while in the other, the angry attempt of an avant-garde imagination to awaken its audience calls more attention to the art than to its subject and permits indifference to "the myriad names of the dead" — Dybek, or course, does not, and the reader can't help but feel moved. Eight stories, including two by T. Alan Broughton, highlight the problem of attempting an opposite sex point of view (where gender may stand for age, class, race and all the other differences) and remind us, as did Rosellen Brown's entire issue on this topic, that you needn't be one to render one, but that you do need talent and craft. Still another problem shared by Philip Damon and Marilyn Jean Conner is the use of comic butts: sympathy for the injured fool may swing judgment against the "us" being affirmed.

Where the specialty of *Ploughshares* has been discovery and rediscovery, often against the grain of popular, academic, and critical fashions, I hope this collection may win wider readership for the lesser known writers represented, thirteen of whom have yet to publish first books. I also hope that satisfied readers will subscribe to the continuing anthology that is the magazine itself, available for $14 a year from Ploughshares, Inc., Box 529, Cambridge, MA 02139.

The point, finally, is not that commercial publishers have abandoned their literary purpose; nor that small presses and literary magazines must now provide due access for a whole new generation of writers, remarkable for their differences of direction.

The point is that the work exists. That fiction, as Roger Sale argued in our pages, "seems now to be enjoying something very much like a golden age." That our classics, our generation's Joyces, Hemingways, Fitzgeralds, Woolfs, are emerging, and that *Ploughshares* has been privileged to publish more than our share of these writers, often early, often with their very best work, as we hope to in the future.

Lastly, our thanks to The Pushcart Press for its support, and good luck with the new series of *Readers* from other jour-

INTRODUCTION

nals this publication leads off.

Thanks, also, to the Massachusetts Council on the Arts and Humanities, the National Endowment for the Arts, the Coordinating Council of Literary Magazines, Emerson College, and our patrons for their continuing support.

Richard Yates

A Compassionate Leave

Nothing ever seemed to go right for the 57th Division. It had come overseas just in time to take heavy casualties in the Battle of the Bulge; then, too-quickly strengthened with masses of new replacements, it had plodded through further combat in eastern France and in Germany, never doing badly but never doing especially well, until the war was over in May.

And by July of that year, when service with the Army of Occupation had begun to give every promise of turning into the best time of their lives — there were an extraordinary number of unattached girls in Germany then — all the men of the luckless 57th were loaded into freight trains and hauled back to France.

Many of them wondered if this was their punishment for having been indifferent soldiers. Some of them even voiced that question, during the tedious ride in the boxcars, until others told them to shut up about it. And there was little hope of welcome or comfort in their destination: the people of France were famous, at the time, for detesting Americans.

When the train carrying one batallion came to a stop at last in a sunny field of weeds near Rheims, which nobody even wanted to learn how to pronounce, the men dropped off and struggled with their equipment into trucks that drove them to their new place of residence — an encampment of olive-drab squad tents hastily pitched a few days before, where they were told to stuff muslin mattress covers with the clumps of straw provided for that purpose, and to cradle their empty rifles upside down in the crotches formed by the crossed wooden legs of their canvas cots. Captain Henry R. Widdoes, a gruff and hard-drinking man who commanded "C" company, explained everything the next morning when he addressed his assembled men in the tall yellow grass of the company street.

"Way I understand it," he began, taking the nervous little backward and forward steps that were characteristic of him, "this here is what they call a Redeployment camp. They got a good many of 'em going up all through this area. They'll be moving men out of Germany according to the Point System and bringing 'em through these camps for processing on their way home. And what we're gonna do, we're gonna do the whaddyacallit, the processing. We're the permanent party here. I don't know what our duties'll be, mostly supply work and clerical work, I imagine. Soon as I have more information I'll let you know. Okay."

Captain Widdoes had been awarded the Silver Star for leading an attack through knee-deep snow last winter; the attack had gained him an excellent tactical advantage and lost him nearly half a platoon. Even now, many of the men in the company were afraid of him.

A few weeks after their arrival in the camp, when their straw mattresses had flattened-out and their rifles were beginning to speckle with rust from the dew, there was a funny incident in one of the squad tents. A buck sergeant named Myron Phelps, who was thirty-four but looked much older, and who had been a soft-coal miner in civilian life, delicately tapped the ash from a big PX cigar and said "Ah, I wish you kids'd quite talking about Germany. I'm tired of all this Germany, Germany, Germany." Then he stretched out on his back, causing his flimsy cot to wobble on the uneven earth. He folded one arm under his head to suggest a world of peace, using the other to gesture lazily with the cigar. "I mean what the hell would you be doing if you *was* in Germany? Huh? Well, you'd be out getting laid and getting the clap and getting the syphilis and getting the blue-balls, that's all, and you'd be drinking up all that schnapps and getting soft and getting out of shape. Right? Right? Well, if you ask me, this here is a whole lot better. We got fresh air, we got shelter, we got food, we got discipline. This is a *man's* life."

And at first everybody thought he was kidding. It seemed to take at least five seconds, while they gaped at Phelps and then at each other and then at Phelps again, before the first thunderclap of laughter broke.

"Jee-sus *Christ*, Phelps, 'a man's life'," somebody cried, and somebody else called "Phelps, you're an asshole, You've always *been* an asshole."

Phelps had struggled upright under the attack; his eyes and mouth were pitiably angry, and there were pink blotches of embarrassment in both cheeks.

". . . How about your fucking *coal* mine, Phelps? Was that 'a man's life' too?. . ."

He looked helpless, trying to speak and not being heard, and soon he began to look wretched. It was clear in his face that he knew the phrase "a man's life" would now be passed around to other tents, to other explosions of laughter, and that it would haunt him as long as he stayed in this company.

Private First Class Paul Colby was still laughing along with the others when he left the tent that afternoon, on his way to an appointment with Captain Widdoes, but he wasn't sorry when the laughter dwindled and died behind him. Poor old Myron Phelps had made buck sergeant because he'd been one of the only two men left in his squad last winter, and he would almost certainly lose the stripes soon if he went on making a fool of himself.

And there was more to it than that. Whether Paul Colby was quite able to admit it to himself or not, he had agreed with at least one element in Phelps' outburst: he too had come to like the simplicity, the order and the idleness of life in these tents in the grass. There was nothing to prove here.

Colby had been one of the replacements who joined the company last January, and the few remaining months of the war had taken him through pride and terror and fatigue and dismay. He was nineteen years old.

At Captain Widdoes's desk in the orderly room tent, Colby came to attention, saluted, and said "Sir, I want to request permission to apply for a compassionate leave."

"For a what?"

"For a compassionate —"

"At ease."

"Thank you, sir. The thing is, back in the States you could sometimes get a compassionate leave if you had trouble at home — if there'd been a death, or if somebody was very sick or something like that. And now over here, since the war ended, they've been giving them out for guys just to visit close relatives in Europe — I mean nobody has to be sick or anything."

"Oh, yeah?" Widdoes said. "Yeah, I think I read that. You got relatives here?"

"Yes, sir. My mother and my sister, in England."

"You English?"

"No, sir, I'm from Michigan; that's where my father lives."

"Well, then, I don't get it. How come your —"

"They're divorced, sir."

"Oh." And Widdoes' frown made clear that he still didn't quite get it, but he began writing on a pad. "Okay, uh, Colby," he said at last, "Now, you write down your — you know — your mother's name here, and her address, and I'll get somebody to put the rest of the shit together. You'll be informed it if comes through, but I better tell you, all the paperwork's so fucked-up throughout this area I don't think you better count on it."

So Colby decided not to count on it, which brought a slight easing of pressure in his conscience. He hadn't seen his mother or sister since he was eleven, and knew almost nothing of them now. He had applied for the leave mostly from a sense of duty, and because there had seemed no alternative. But now there were two possibilities, each mercifully beyong his control:

If it came through there might be ten days of excessive politeness and artificial laughter and awkward silences, while they all tried to pretend he wasn't a stranger. There might be slow sightseeing tours of London in order to kill whole afternoons; they might want to show him "typically English" things to do, like nibbling fish-and-chips out of twisted newspaper, or whatever the hell else it was that typically English people did, and there would be repeated expressions of how nice everything was while they all counted the days until it was over.

If it didn't come through he might never see them again; but then he had resigned himself to that many years ago, when it had mattered a great deal more — when it had, in fact, amounted to an almost unendurable loss.

"Well, your mother was one of these bright young English girls who come over to America thinking the streets are paved with gold," Paul Colby's father had explained to him, more than a few times, usually walking around the living room with a drink in his hand. "So we got married, and you and your sister came along, and then pretty soon I guess she started wondering, well, where's the great promise of this country? Where's all the happiness? Where's the gold? You follow me, Paul?"

"Sure."

"So she started getting restless — damn, she got restless, but I'll spare you that part of it — and pretty soon she wanted a divorce. Well, okay, I thought, that's in the cards, but then by Jesus she said 'I'll take the children.' And I told her, I said 'Way-*hait* a minute.' I said 'Hold your *horses* a minute here, Miss Queen of England; let's play *fair*.'

"Well, fortunately, I had this great friend of mine at the time, Earl Gibbs, and Earl was a crackerjack lawyer. He told me 'Fred, she wouldn't have a leg to stand on in a custody dispute.' I said 'Earl, just get me the kids.' I said 'Let me have the kids, Earl, that's all I ask.' And he tried. Earl did his best for me, but you see by then she'd moved down to Detroit and she had both of you there with her, so it wasn't easy. I went down there once to take you both to a ball game, but your sister said she didn't like baseball and wasn't feeling very well anyway — Christ, what grief a little thing like that can cause! So it was just you and me went out to Briggs Stadium that day and watched the Tigers play — do you remember that? Do you remember that, Paul?"

"Sure."

"And then afterwards I brought you back up here to stay with me. Well, your mother threw a fit. That's the only word for it. She was wholly irrational. She already had boat tickets to England, you see, for the three of you, and she came storming up here in this rattletrap little Plymouth that she didn't even know how to drive, and she started yelling and screaming that I'd 'kidnapped' you. Do you remember?"

"Yes."

"Well, that was one God-awful afternoon. Earl Gibbs and his wife happened to be here with me at the time, and that saved the day — or half-saved it, I guess. Because once we'd all managed to get your mother calmed down a little, Earl went to her and talked to her for a long time, and in the end he said 'Vivien, count your blessings. Settle for what you can get.'

"So you see, she had no choice. She drove away in that crummy car with your sister riding beside her, and I guess a couple weeks later they were in London, and that was it. That was it.

"Well, but the point I'm trying to make here, Paul, is that things did work out pretty much for the best after all. I was fortunate enough to meet your stepmother, and we're right for each other. Anybody can see we're right for each other, right? As for your mother, I know she was never happy with me. Any man, Paul — *any* man — oughta know when a woman isn't happy with him. And what the hell, life's too short: I forgave her long ago for the pain she caused me as my wife. There's only one thing I can't forgive her for. Ever. She took away my little girl."

Paul Colby's sister Marcia was almost exactly a year younger than he. At five she had taught him how to blow steady bubbles in bathwater; at eight she had kicked over his electric train in order to persuade him that paper dolls could be more entertaining, which was true; a year or so after that, trembling in fear together, they had dared each other to jump from a high limb of a maple tree, and they'd done it, though he would always remember that she went first.

On the afternoon of their parents' hysteria, and of the lawyer's sonorous entreaties for order in the living room, he had watched Marcia from the house as she waited in the passenger's seat of the mud-spattered Plymouth in the driveway. And because he was fairly sure nobody would notice his absence, he went out to visit with her.

When she saw him coming she rolled down her window and said "What're they doing in there, anyway?"

"Well, they're — I don't know. There's a lot of — I don't really know what they're doing. I guess it'll be okay, though."

"Yeah, well, I guess so too. Only, you better get back inside, Paul, okay? I mean I don't think Daddy'd want to see you out here."

"Okay." On his way to the house he stopped and looked back, and they exchanged quick, shy waves.

At first there were frequent letters from England — jolly, sometimes silly, hastily written ones from Marcia; careful and increasingly stilted ones from his mother.

During the "Blitz" of 1940, when every American radio news commentator implied that all London was in rubble and on fire, Marcia wrote at some length to suggest that perhaps the reports might be exaggerated. Things were certainly terrible in the East End, she said, which was "cruel" because that was where most of the poor people lived, but there were "very extensive areas" of the city that hadn't been touched. And the suburb where she and their mother were, eight miles out, had been "perfectly safe." She was thirteen when she wrote that, and it stayed in his mind as a remarkably intelligent, remarkably thoughtful letter for someone of that age.

Over the next few years she drifted out of the habit of writing, except for Christmas and birthday cards. But his mother's letters continued with dogged regularity, whether he'd answered the last one or not, and it became an effort of will to read them — an effort even to open the flimsy blue envelopes and unfold the note-paper. Her strain in the writing was so clear that it could only make for strain in the reading; her final, pointedly cheerful paragraph always came as a relief, and he could sense her own relief at having brought it off. She had married again within a year or two after going back to England; she and her new husband soon had a son, "your little half-brother," of whom she said Marcia was "enormously fond." In 1943 she wrote that Marcia was "with the American Embassy in London now, " which seemed a funny thing to say about a sixteen-year-old girl, and there were no supporting details.

He had written to his sister from Germany once, managing to work in a few deft references to his combat infantry service, and had received no reply. It could have been because military mail was unreliable at the time, but it could also have meant she'd simply neglected to write back — and that had left a small, still-open wound in his feelings.

Now, after leaving the orderly room, he wrote a quick letter to his mother explaining his helplessness in the matter of the leave; when it was done and mailed he felt he could easily afford to stretch out on his cot in the drowsing, mildewed, half-deserted tent. He wasn't far across the aisle of trampled dirt from where poor old Myron Phelps lay sleeping off his shame — or, more likely, still ashamed and so pretending to sleep.

The big news of the following month was that three-day passes to Paris would now be issued in "C" company, a few at a time, and the tents began to ring with shrill and lubricious talk. Sure, the French hated Americans — everybody knew that — but everybody knew what "Paris" meant, too. All you had to do in Paris, it was said, was walk up to a girl on the street — well-dressed, high-class-looking, *any* kind of girl — and say "Are you in business, baby?" If she wasn't she'd smile and say no; if she was — or maybe even if she wasn't but just sort of happened to feel like it — then oh, Jesus God.

Paul Colby arranged to take his pass with George Mueller, a quiet, thoughtful boy who had become his best friend in the rifle squad. Several nights before they went to Paris, in one of the soft-voiced conversations that were characteristic of their friendship, he haltingly confided to George Mueller what he'd never told anyone else and didn't even want to think about: he had never gotten laid in his life.

And Mueller didn't laugh. He'd been a virgin too, he said, until one night in a bunker with a German girl a week before the war ended. And he wasn't even sure if that counted: the girl had kept laughing and laughing — he didn't know what the hell she was laughing about — and he'd been so nervous that he didn't really get inside her before he came, and then she'd pushed him away.

Colby assured him that it did count — it certainly counted a great deal more than any of his own dumb fumblings. And he might have told Mueller about a few of those, but decided they were better kept to himself.

Not long before they'd left Germany, "C" Company had been placed in charge of two hundred Russian "Displaced Persons" — civilian captives whom the Germans had put to work as unpaid laborers in a small-town plastics factory. On Captain Widdoes' orders, the newly freed Russians were soon quartered in what looked like the best residential section of town — neat, attractive houses on a hill well away from the factory — and the Germans who'd lived up there (those, at least, who hadn't fled the advancing army days or weeks before) were assigned to the barracks in the old slave-laborers' compound.

There wasn't much for the riflemen to do in that pleasant, partially bombed-out town but stroll in the gentle spring weather and make occasional gestures at keeping things, as Widdoes said, "under control." Paul Colby was on guard duty alone at the very top of the residential hill one afternoon at sunset when a Russian girl came out and smiled at him, as though she'd been watching him from a window. She was seventeen or so, slim and pretty, wearing the kind of cheap, old, wash-ruined cotton dress that all the Russian women wore, and her breasts looked as firm and tender as ripe nippled peaches. Apart from knowing he would absolutely have to get his hands on her, he didn't know what to do. Far down the hill, and on either side, there was no one else in sight.

He made what he hoped was a courtly little bow and shook hands with her — that seemed an appropriate opening for an acquaintance that would have to take place without language — and she gave no sign of thinking it silly or puzzling. Then he bent to put his rifle and helmet on the grass, straightened up again and took her in his arms — she felt marvelous — and kissed her mouth, and there was a thrilling amount of tongue in the way she kissed back. Soon he had one splendid breast naked in his hand (he fondled it as impersonally as if it *were* a nippled peach) and blood was flowing heavily in him; but then the old, inevitable shyness and the terrible awkwardness set in, as they'd set in with every girl he had ever touched.

And as always before, he was quick to find excuses: he

couldn't take her back into the house because it would be crowded with other Russians — or so he imagined — and he couldn't have her out here because someone would be sure to come along; it was almost time for the guard truck to pick him up anyway.

There seemed nothing to do, then, but release the girl from their clasping embrace and stand close beside her, one arm still around her, so they could gaze together down the long hill at the sunset. It occurred to him, as they lingered and lingered in that position, that they might make an excellent scene for the final fadeout of some thunderous Soviet-American movie called *Victory Over the Nazis*. And when the guard truck did come for him, he couldn't even lie to himself that he felt anger and frustration: he was relieved.

There was a taciturn, illiterate rifleman in the second squad named Jesse O. Meeks — one of the four or five men in the platoon who had to mark "X" instead of signing the payroll every month — and within two days after the fadeout of the great Soviet-American movie, Jesse O. Meeks took full possession of that sweet girl.

"Ain't no use lookin' around for old Meeks tonight," somebody said in the platoon quarters. "No use lookin' for him tomorra, either, or the day after that. Old Meeks got himself shacked-up re-eal fine."

But here in France, on a morning bright with promise, Colby and George Mueller presented themselves at the First Sergeant's desk to claim their three-day passes. At the left-hand edge of the desk, on a metal base screwed into the wood, stood an ample rotary dispenser of linked, foil-wrapped condoms: you could reel off as many as you thought you might need. Colby let Mueller go first, in order to watch how many he took — six — then he self-consciously took six himself and stuffed them into his pocket, and they set out together for the motor pool.

They wore their brand-new Eisenhower jackets, with their modest display of ribbons and the handsome blue-and-silver panels of their Combat Infantry Badges, and they had carefully darkened and shined their combat boots. They walked clumsily, though, because each of them carried two cartons of stolen PX cigarettes inside his trouserlegs: cigarettes were said to bring twenty dollars a carton on the Paris black market.

Coming into the city was spectacular. The Eiffel Tower, the Arch of Triumph — there it all was, just the way it looked in *Life* magazine, and it went on for miles in all directions: there was so much of it that you couldn't stop turning and looking, turning and looking again.

The truck let them off at the American Red Cross club, which would serve as a homely base of operations. It provided dormitories and showers and regular meals, and there were rooms for ping-pong and for drowsing in deep upholstered chairs. Only some kind of a twerp would want to spend much time in this place, when there was such a wealth of mystery and challenge beyond its doors, but Colby and Mueller agreed to have lunch here anyway, because it was lunchtime.

And the next thing, they decided, was to get rid of the cigarettes. It was easy. A few blocks away they met a small, tight-faced boy of about fourteen who led them upstairs to a triple-locked room that was packed to the ceiling with American cigarettes. He was so intimidating in his silence and so impatient to conclude the deal, paying them off from a huge roll of lovely French banknotes, as to suggest that in three or four more years he might be an important figure in the European underworld.

George Mueller had brought his camera and wanted snapshots to send to his parents, so they took a guided bus tour of major landmarks that went on until late in the afternoon.

"We ought to have a map," Mueller said when they were rid of the boring, chattering tour guide at last. "Let's get a map." There were shabby old men everywhere selling maps to soldiers, as if selling toy balloons to children; when Colby and Mueller opened the many folds of theirs and spread it flat against the granite side of an office building, jabbing their forefingers at different parts of it and both talking at once, it was their first discord of the day.

Colby knew, from having read *The Sun Also Rises* in high school, that the Left Bank was where everything nice was most likely to happen. Mueller had read that book too, but he'd been listening to the guys in the tent for weeks, and so he favored the area up around the Place Pigalle.

"Well, but it's all prostitutes up there, George," Colby said. "You don't want to settle for some prostitute right away, do you? Before we've even tried for something better?" In the end they reached a compromise: they would try the Left Bank first — there was plenty of time — and then the other.

"Wow," Mueller said in the Metro station; he had always been good at figuring things out. "See how this works? You push the button where you are and the one where you want to go, and the whole fucking route lights up. You'd have to be an idiot to get lost in this town."

"Yeah."

And Colby soon had to admit that Mueller was right about the Left Bank. Even after a couple of hours its endless streets and boulevards failed to suggest that anything nice might happen. You could see hundreds of people sitting bright with talk and laughter in each of the long, deep side-walk cafes, with plenty of good-looking girls among them, but their cool and quickly-averted glances established at once their membership in the majority of French who detested Americans. And if you did occasionally see a pretty girl walking alone and tried to catch her eye, however bashfully, she looked capable of pulling a police whistle out of her purse and blowing it, hard, on being asked if she was in business.

But oh, Jesus God, the area up around the Place Pigalle.

It throbbed in the new-fallen darkness with the very pulse of sex; it had a decidedly sinister quality too, in the shadows and in the guarded faces of everyone you saw. Steam rose from iron manhole lids in the street and was instantly turned red and blue and green in the vivid lights of gas and electric signs. Girls and women were everywhere, walking and waiting, among hundreds of prowling soldiers.

Colby and Mueller took their time, watching everything, seated at a cafe table and nursing highballs of what the waiter had promised was "American whiskey." Dinner was out of the way — they had made a quick stop at the Red Cross to wash up and to eat, and Mueller had left his camera there (he didn't want to look like some tourist tonight) — so there was nothing to do for a while but watch.

"See the girl coming out of the door with the guy across the street?" Mueller inquired, narrowing his eyes. "See 'em? The girl in the blue? And the guy's walking away from her now?"

"Yeah."

"I swear to God it wasn't five minutes ago I saw them going *in* that door. Son of a bitch. She gave him five minutes — *less* than five minutes — and she probably charged him twenty bucks."

"Jesus." And Colby took a drink to help him sort out a quick profusion of ugly pictures in his mind. What could be accomplished in five minutes? Wouldn't it take almost that long just to get undressed and dressed again? How miserably premature could a premature ejaculation be? Maybe she had blown him, but even that, according to exhaustive discourse in the tent, was supposed to take a hell of a lot longer than five minutes. Or maybe — this was the possibility that brought a chill around his heart — maybe the man had been stricken with panic up there in the room. Maybe, watching her get ready, he had suddenly known he couldn't do what was expected — known it beyond all hope of trying or even of pretending to try — and so had blurted some apology in high-school French and shoved money into her hands, and she'd followed him closely downstairs talking all the way (Coarse? Contemptuous? Cruel?) until they were free to separate in the street.

For himself, Colby decided it would be best not to go with a streetwalker — even one he might spend a long time choosing for qualities of youth and health and the look of a gentle nature. The thing to do was find a girl in a bar — this bar or one of the others — and talk with her for a while, however brokenly, and go through the pleasant ritual of buying drinks. Because even if the girls in the bars *were* only streetwalkers at rest (or could they be whores of a higher calibre, with higher prices? And how could you possibly find out about distinctions like that?) — even so, you might at least have some sense of acquaintance before arriving at the bed.

It took him a minute or two to catch the waiter's eye for another round, and when he turned back he found George Mueller conversing with a woman who sat alone at the next table, a few inches away. The woman — you couldn't call her a girl — was trim and pleasant-looking, and from the stray phrases Colby overheard she seemed to be speaking mostly in English. Mueller had turned his chair away for talking, so his face was partly obscured, but Colby could see the heavy blush of it and the tense, shy smile. Then he saw the woman's hand moving slowly up and down Mueller's thigh.

"Paul?" Mueller said when he and the woman got up to leave. "Look: I may not see you again tonight, but I'll see you back in the whaddycallit in the morning, okay? The Red Cross. Or maybe not in the morning, but you know. We'll work it out."

"Sure; that's okay."

In no other bar of the entire area around the Place Pigalle could a girl or a woman be found sitting alone. Paul Colby made certain of that because he tried them all — tried several of them twice or three times — and he drank so much in the course of his search that he wandered miles from where he'd started. He was in some wholly separate part of Paris when the sound of a rollicking piano brought him in off the street to a strange little American-style bar. There he joined five or six other soldiers, most of them apparently strangers to one another; they stood with their arms around each others' Eisenhower jackets and sang all ten choruses of "Roll Me Over" at the top of their lungs, with the piano thumping out the melody and the flourishes. Somewhere in the sixth or seventh verse it struck him that this might be considered a fairly memorable way to conclude your first night in Paris, but by the time it ended he knew better — and so, plainly, did all the other singers.

George Mueller had said you would have to be an idiot to get lost in this town, but Paul Colby stood for half an hour in some Metro station, pushing buttons, making more and more elaborate route patterns light up in many colors, until a very old man came along and told him how to get to the Red Cross club. And there, where everybody knew that only some kind of a twerp would want to spend much time, he crawled into his dormitory bed as if it were the last bed in the world.

Things were even worse the next day. He was too sick with hangover to get his clothes on until noon; then he crept downstairs and looked into each of the public rooms for George Mueller, knowing he wouldn't find him. And he walked the streets for hours, on sore feet, indulging himself in the bleak satisfactions of petulance. What the hell was supposed to be so great and beautiful about Paris, anyway? Had anybody ever had the guts to say it was just another city like Detroit or Chicago or New York, with too many pale, grim men in business suits hurrying down the sidewalks, and with too much noise and gasoline exhaust and too much plain damned uncivilized rudeness? Had anybody yet confessed to being dismayed and bewildered and bored by this whole fucking place, and lonely as a bastard too?

Late in the day he discovered white wine. It salved and

dispelled his hangover; it softened the rasp of his anger into an almost pleasant melancholy. It was very nice and dry and mild and he drank a great deal of it, slowly, in one quietly obliging cafe after another. He found various ways to compose himself at the different tables, and soon he began to wonder how he must look to casual observers; that, for as long as he could remember, had been one of his most secret, most besetting, least admirable habits of mind. He imagined, as the white wine wore on and on, that he probably looked like a sensitive young man in wry contemplation of youth and love and death — an "interesting" young man — and on that high wave of self-regard he floated home and hit the sack again.

The final day was one of stunted thought and shriveled hope, of depression so thick that all of Paris lay awash and sinking in it while his time ran out.

Back in the Place Pigalle at midnight and drunk again — or more likely feigning drunkenness to himself — he found he was almost broke. He couldn't afford even the most raucous of middle-aged whores now, and he knew he had probably arranged in his secret heart for this to be so. There was nothing left to do but make his way to the dark part of the city where the Army trucks were parked.

You weren't really expected to make the first truck; you could even miss the last truck, and nobody would care very much. But those unspoken rules of conduct no longer applied to Paul Colby: he was very likely the only soldier in Europe ever to have spent three days in Paris without getting laid. And he had learned beyond question now that he could no longer attribute his trouble to shyness or awkwardness; it was fear. It was worse than fear: it was cowardice.

"How come you didn't pick up my messages?" George Mueller asked him in the tent the next day. Mueller had left three notes for Colby on the Red Cross message board, he said — one on the morning after they'd split up that first night, and two others later.

"I guess I didn't even notice there was a message board."

"Well, Christ, it was right there in the front room, by the desk," Mueller said, looking hurt. "I don't see how you could've missed it."

And Colby explained, despising himself and turning away quickly afterwards, that he hadn't really spent all that much time in the Red Cross club.

Less than a week later he was summoned to the orderly room and told that the papers for his compassionate leave were ready. And a very few days after that, abruptly deposited somewhere in London, he checked into a murmurous, echoing Red Cross club that was almost a duplicate of the one in Paris.

He spent a long time in the shower and changed meticulously into his other, wholly clean uniform — stalling and stalling; then, with his finger trembling in the dial of a cumbersome British coin telephone, he called his mother.

"Oh, my dear," her voice said. "Is this really you? Oh, how very strange. . ."

It was arranged that he would visit her that afternoon, "for tea," and he rode out to her suburb on a clattering commuters' train.

"Oh, well, how nice!" she said in the doorway of her tidy, semi-detached house. "And how fine you are in your marvelous American uniform. Oh, my dear; oh, my dear." As she pressed the side of her head against the ribbons and the Combat Badge she seemed to be weeping, but he couldn't be sure. He said it certainly was good to see her too, and they walked together into a small living room.

"Well, my goodness," she said, having apparently dried her tears. "How can I possibly hope to entertain a great big American soldier in a scruffy little house like this?"

But soon they were comfortable — at least as comfortable as they would ever be — sitting across from each other in upholstered chairs while the clay filaments popped and hissed and turned blue and orange in a small gas fireplace. She told him her husband would soon be home, as would their son, who was now six and "dying" to meet him.

"Well, good," he said.

"And I did try to reach Marcia on the phone, but I was a fraction of a second too late at the Embassy switchboard; then later I rang her flat but there was no answer, so I expect they're both out. She's been sharing a flat with another girl for a year or so now, you see —" and here his mother sniffed sharply through one nostril and turned her face partly away, a mannerism that brought her suddenly alive from his memory — "she's quite the young woman of the world these days. Still, we can try again later in the evening, and perhaps we'll —"

"No, that's okay," he said. "I'll call her tomorrow."

"Well, whatever you wish."

And it was whatever he wished for the rest of that rapidly darkening afternoon, even after her husband had come home — a drained-looking man in middle age whose hat left a neat ridge around the crown of his flat, well-combed hair, and who ventured almost no conversational openings; and their little boy, who seemed far from dying to meet him as he peered from hiding and stuck out his tongue.

Would Paul like another bread-and-butter sandwich with his tea? Good. Would he like a drink? Oh, good. And was he sure he wouldn't stay a while longer and have some sort of scrappy little supper with them — baked beans on toast sort of thing — and spend the night? Because really, there was plenty of room. It was whatever he wished.

He could hardly wait to get out of the house, though he kept assuring himself, on the train back into town, that he hadn't been rude.

And he awoke barely able to face breakfast in his nervousness about calling the American Embassy.

"Who?" said a switchboard operator. "What department is that, please?"

"Well, I don't know; I just know she works there. Isn't there some way you can —"

"Just a moment. . .yes, here: we do have a Miss Colby, Marcia, in Disbursements. I'll connect you." And after several buzzings and clickings, after a long wait, a voice came on the line as clear as a flute and happy to hear from him — a sweet-sounding English girl.

". . . Well, that'd be marvelous," she was saying. "Could you come 'round about five? It's the first building over from the main one, just to the left of the F.D.R. statue if you're coming up from Berkeley Square; you can't miss it; and I'll be there in half a minute if you're waiting, or — you know — I'll be waiting there if you're late."

It took him a while to realize, after hanging up the phone, that she hadn't once spoken his name; she had probably been shy too.

There was an overheated shop in the Red Cross basement where two sweating, jabbering Cockneys in undershirts would steam-press your whole uniform for half a crown, while many soldiers waited in line for the service, and Colby chose to kill part of the afternoon down there. He knew his clothes didn't really need pressing, but he wanted to look nice tonight.

Then he was coming up from Berkeley Square, trying in every stride to perfect what he hoped would be a devil-may-care kind of walk. There was the F.D.R. statue, and there was her office building; and there in the corridor, straggling alone behind a group of other women and girls, came a hesitant, large-eyed, half-smiling girl who could only have been Marcia.

"Paul?" she inquired. "Is it Paul?"

He rushed forward and enwrapped her in a great hug, pinning her arms and nuzzling her hair, hoping to swing her laughing off her feet — and he brought it off well, probably from his self-tutelage in the devil-may-care walk; by the time her shoes hit the floor again she *was* laughing, with every sign of having liked it.

"...Well!" she said. "Aren't you something."

"So are you," he said, and offered her his arm for walking.

In the first place they went to, which she'd described as "a rather nice, smallish pub not far from here," he kept secretly congratulating himself on how well he was doing. His talk was fluent — once or twice he even made her laugh again — and his listening was attentive and sympathetic. Only one small thing went wrong: he had assumed that English girls liked beer, but she changed her order to "pink gin," which made him feel dumb for having failed to ask her; apart from that he couldn't find anything the matter with his performance.

If there had been a mirror behind the bar he would certainly have sneaked a happy glance into it on his way to the men's room; he had stamped twice on the old floor in the regulation manner for making his trouserlegs "blouse-down" over his boots, then walked away from her through the smoke-hung crowd in the new devil-may-care style, and he hoped she was watching.

"...What does 'Disbursements' mean?" he asked when he got back to their table.

"Oh, nothing much. In a business firm I suppose you'd call it the payroll office. I'm a payroll clerk. Ah, I know," she said then, with a smile that turned wittily sour, "Mother's told you I'm 'with the American Embassy.' God. I heard her saying that to people on the phone a few times when I was still living there; that was about the time I decided to move out."

He had been so concerned with himself that he didn't realize until now, offering a light for her cigarette, what a pretty girl she was. And it wasn't only in the face; she was nice all the way down.

"...I'm afraid our timing's been rather awkward,

Paul," she was saying. "Because tomorrow's the last day before my vacation and I had no idea you were coming, you see, so I arranged to spend the week with a friend up in Blackpool. But we can get together again tomorrow night, if you like — could you come up to the flat for supper or something?"

"Sure. That'd be fine."

"Oh, good. Do come. It won't be much, but we can sort of fortify ourselves by having a real dinner tonight. Jesus, I'm hungry, aren't you?" And he guessed that a lot of English girls had learned to say "Jesus" during the war.

She took him to what she called "a good black-market restaurant," a warm, closed-in, upstairs room that did look fairly clandestine; they sat surrounded by American officers and their women, forking down rich slices of what she told him was horsemeat steak. They were oddly shy with each other there, like children in a strange house, but soon afterwards, in the next pub they visited, they got around to memories.

"It's funny," she said. "I missed Daddy terribly at first, it was like a sickness, but then it got so I couldn't really remember him very well. And lately, I don't know. His letters seem so — well, sort of loud and empty. Sort of vapid."

"Yeah. Well, he's a very — yeah."

"And once during the war he sent me a Public Health Service pamphlet about venereal disease. That wasn't really a very tactful thing to do, was it?"

"No. No, it wasn't."

But she remembered the electric train and the paper dolls. She remembered the terrifying jump from the maple tree — the worst part, she said, was that you had to clear another horrible big branch on the way down — and yes, she remembered waiting alone in the car that afternoon while their parents shouted in the house. She even remembered that Paul had come out to the car to say goodbye.

At the end of the evening they settled into still another place, and that was where she started talking about her plans. She might go back to the States and go to college next year — that was what their father wanted her to do — but then there was also a chance that she might go back and get married.

"Yeah? No kidding? Who to?"

The little smile she gave him then was the first disingenuous look he had seen in her face. "I haven't decided," she said. "Because you see there've been any number of offers — well, *almost* any number." And out of her purse came a big, cheap American wallet of the kind with many hinged plastic frames for photographs. There was one smiling or frowning face after another, most of them wearing their overseas caps, a gallery of American soldiers.

"...and this is Chet," she was saying, "he's nice; he's back in Cleveland now. And this is John, he'll be going home soon to a small town in east Texas; and this is Tom; he's nice; he's..."

There were probably five or six photographs, but there seemed to be more. One was a decorated 82nd Airborne man who looked impressive, but another was a member of service and support personnel — a "Blue-Star Commando" — and Colby had learned to express a veiled disdain for those people.

"Well, but what does that matter?" she inquired. "I don't care what he 'did' or didn't 'do' in the war; what's *that* got to do with anything?"

"Okay; I guess you're right," he said while she was putting the wallet away, and he watched her closely. "But look: are you in love with any of these guys?"

"Oh, well, certainly, I suppose so," she said. "But then, that's easy, isn't it?"

"What is?"

"Being in love with someone, if he's nice and you like him."

And that gave him much to think about, all the next

day.

The following night, when he'd been asked to "come up for supper or something," he gravely inspected her white, ill-furnished apartment and met her roommate, whose name was Irene. She looked to be in her middle thirties, and it was clear from her every glance and smile that she enjoyed sharing a place with someone so much younger. She made Colby uneasy at once by telling him what a "nice-looking boy" he was; then she hovered and fussed over Marcia's fixing the drinks, which were a cheap brand of American blended whiskey and soda, with no ice.

The supper turned out to be even more perfunctory than he'd imagined — a casserole of Spam and sliced potatoes and powdered milk — and while they were still at the table Irene laughed heartily at something Colby said, something he hadn't meant to be all that funny. Recovering, her eyes shining, she turned to Marcia and said, "Oh, he's sweet, your brother, isn't he — and d'you know something? I think you're right about him. I think he *is* a virgin."

There are various ways of enduring acute embarrassment: Colby might have hung his blushing head, or he might have stuck a cigarette in his lips and lighted it, squinting, looking up at the woman with still-narrowed eyes and saying "What makes you think that?" but what he did instead was burst out laughing. And he went on laughing and laughing long after the time for showing what a preposterous assumption they had made; he was helpless in his chair; he couldn't stop.

"...*Irene!*" Marcia was saying, and she was blushing too. "I don't know what you're *talking* about — *I* never said that."

"Oh, well, sorry; sorry; my fault," Irene said, but there was still a sparkle in her eye across the messy table when he pulled himself together at last, feeling a little sick.

Marcia's train would leave at nine, from some station far in the north of London, so she had to hurry. "Look, Paul," she said over the hasty packing of her suitcase, "there's really no need for you to come along all that way; I'll just run up there by myself."

But he insisted — he wanted to get away from Irene — and so they rode nervously together, without speaking, on the Underground. But they got off at the wrong stop — "Jesus, that was foolish," she said; "now we'll have to walk" — and when they were walking they began to talk again.

"I'll never know what possessed Irene to say such a silly thing," she said.

"That's okay. Forget it."

"Because I only said you seemed very young. Was that such a terrible thing to say?"

"I guess not."

"I mean who ever minded being *young*, for God's sake — isn't that what everyone wants to be?"

"I guess so."

"Oh, you guess not and you guess so. Well, it's true — everyone does want to be young. I'm eighteen now, and sometimes I wish I were *six*teen again."

"Why?"

"Oh, so I could do things a little more intelligently, I suppose; try not to go chasing after uniforms quite so much — British *or* American; I don't know."

So she had been laid at sixteen, either by some plucky little R.A.F. pilot or some slavering American, and probably by several of both.

He was tired of walking and of carrying the suitcase; it took an effort of will to remind himself that he was an infantry soldier. Then she said "Oh, look: we've made it!" and they ran the last fifty yards into the railroad station and across its echoing marble floor. But her train had gone, and there wasn't another one due to leave for an hour. They sat uncomfortably on an old wooden bench for a while; then they went out to the street again to get the fresh air.

She took the suitcase from him, placed it against the

base of a lamppost and seated herself prettily on it, crossing her nice legs. Her knees were nice too. She looked thoroughly competent and composed. She would leave tonight knowing he was a virgin — she would know it forever, whether she ever saw him again or not.

"Paul?" she said.

"Yeah?"

"Look, I was only sort of teasing you about those boys in the photographs — I don't know why I did that, except to be silly."

"Okay. I knew you were teasing." But it was a relief to hear her say it, even so.

"They were just boys I met when I used to go to the Red Cross dances at Rainbow Corner. None of them ever really did propose to me except Chet, and that was only a kidding-around sort of thing because he said I was pretty. If I ever took him up on it he'd die."

"Okay."

"And it was silly just now to tell you about chasing uniforms when I was sixteen — God, I was *terrified* of boys at sixteen. Have you any idea what it is that makes people of our age want to claim more knowledge of — of sex and so forth than they really have?"

"No. No, I don't." He was beginning to like her more and more, but he was afraid that if he let her go on she might soon insist she was a virgin too, to make him feel better; that would almost certainly be a condescending lie, and so would only make him feel worse.

"Because I mean we have our whole *lives*," she said, "isn't that right? Take you: you'll be going home soon and going to college and there'll be girls coming in and out of your life for years; then eventually you'll fall in love with someone, and isn't that what makes the world go around?"

She was being kind to him; he didn't know whether to be grateful or to sink even further into wretchedness.

"And then me, well, I'm in love with someone now,"

she said, and this time there appeared to be no teasing in her face. "I've wanted to tell you about him ever since we met, but there hasn't been time. He's the man I'm going up to spend the week with in Blackpool. His name is Ralph Kovacks and he's twenty-three. He was a waist-gunner on a B-17 but he only flew thirteen missions because his nerves fell apart and he's been in and out of hospitals ever since. He's sort of small and funny-looking and all he wants to do is sit around in his underwear reading great books, and he's going to be a philosopher and I've sort of come to think I can't live without him. I may not go to the States at all next year; I may go to Heidelberg because that's where Ralph wants to go; the whole question is whether or not he'll let me stay with him."

"Oh," Colby said. "I see."

"What d'you mean, you 'see'? You really aren't much of a conversationalist, you know that? You 'see.' What can you possibly 'see' from what little I've told you? Jesus, how can you see anything at all with those big, round, virginal eyes of yours?"

He was walking away from her, head down, because there seemed nothing else to do, but he hadn't gone far before she came running after him, her little high-heeled shoes clicking on the sidewalk. "Oh, Paul, don't go away," she called. "Come back; please come back. I'm terribly sorry."

So they went back together to where the suitcase stood against the lamppost, but this time she didn't sit down. "I'm terribly sorry," she said again. "And look, don't come to the train with me; I want to say goodbye here. Only, listen. Listen. I know you'll be all right. We'll both be all right. It's awfully important to believe that. Well; God bless."

"Okay, and you too," he said. "You too, Marcia."

Then her arms went up and around his neck and the whole slender weight of her was pressed against him for a moment, and in a voice broken with tears she said "Oh, my brother."

He walked a great distance alone after that, and there wasn't anything devil-may-care about it. The heels of his boots came down in a calm, regular cadence, and his face was set in the look of a practical young man with a few things on his mind. Tomorrow he would telephone his mother and say he'd been called back to France, "for duty," a phrase she would neither understand nor ever question; then all that would be finished. And with seven days left in this vast, intricate, English-speaking place, there was every reason to expect he would have a girl.

Tim O'Brien

Going After Cacciato

It was a bad time. Billy Boy Watkins was dead, and
so was Frenchie Tucker. Billy Boy had died of fright,
scared to death on the field of battle, and Frenchie Tucker
had been shot through the neck. Lieutenants Sidney
Martin and Walter Gleason had died in tunnels. Pederson
was dead and Bernie Lynn was dead. Buff was dead. They
were all among the dead. The war was always the same,
and the rain was part of the war. The rain fed fungus that
grew in the men's socks and boots, and their socks rotted,
and their feet turned white and soft so that the skin could
be scraped off with a fingernail, and Stink Harris woke up
screaming one night with a leech on his tongue. When it
was not raining, a low mist moved like sleep across the
paddies, blending the elements into a single gray
element, and the war was cold and pasty and rotten. Lieutenant Corson, who came to replace Lieutenant Martin,
contracted the dysentery. The tripflares were useless.
The ammunition corroded and the foxholes filled with
mud and water during the nights, and in the mornings
there was always the next village and the war was always
the same. In early September Vaught caught an infection.
He'd been showing Oscar Johnson the sharp edge on his
bayonet, drawing it swiftly along his forearm and peeling
off a layer of mushy skin. "Like a Gillette blueblade,"
Vaught had grinned. It did not bleed, but in a few days
the bacteria soaked in and the arm turned yellow, and
Vaught was carried aboard a Huey that dipped perpen-
dicular, blades clutching at granite air, rising in its own
wet wind and taking Vaught away. He never returned to
the war. Later they had a letter from him that described

Japan as smoky and full of bedbugs, but in the enclosed snapshot Vaught looked happy enough, posing with two sightly nurses, a long-stemmed bottle of wine rising from between his thighs. It was a shock to learn that he'd lost the arm. Soon afterward Ben Nystrom shot himself in the foot, but he did not die, and he wrote no letters. These were all things to talk about. The rain, too. Oscar said it made him think of Detroit in the month of May. "Not the rain," he liked to say. "Just the dark and gloom. It's Number One weather for rape and looting. The fact is, I do ninety-eight percent of my total rape and looting in weather just like this." Then somebody would say that Oscar had a pretty decent imagination for a nigger.

That was one of the jokes. There was a joke about Oscar. There were many jokes about Billy Boy Watkins, the way he'd collapsed in fright on the field of glorious battle. Another joke was about the lieutenant's dysentery, and another was about Paul Berlin's purple biles. Some of the jokes were about Cacciato, who was as dumb, Stink said, as a bullet, or, Harold Murphy said, as an oyster fart.

In October, at the end of the month, in the rain, Cacciato left the war.

"He's gone away," said Doc Peret. "Split for parts unknown."

The lieutenant didn't seem to hear. He was too old to be a lieutenant, anyway. The veins in his nose and cheeks were shattered by booze. Once he had been a captain on the way to being a major, but whiskey and the fourteen dull years between Korea and Vietnam had ended all that, and now he was just an old lieutenant with the dysentery. He lay on his back in the pagoda, naked except for green socks and green undershorts.

"Cacciato," Doc Peret repeated. "He's gone away. Split, departed."

The lieutenant did not sit up. He held his belly with both hands as if to contain the disease.

"He's gone to Paris," Doc said. "That's what he tells Paul Berlin, anyhow, and Paul Berlin tells me, so I'm telling you. He's gone, packed up and gone."

"Paree," the lieutenant said softly. "In France, Paree? *Gay* Paree?"

"Yes, sir. That's what he says. That's what he told Paul Berlin, and that's what I'm telling you. You ought to cover up, sir."

The lieutenant sighed. He pushed himself up, breathing loud, then sat stiffly before a can of Sterno. He lit the Sterno and cupped his hands around the flame and bent down, drawing in the heat. Outside, the rain was steady. "Paree," he said wearily. "You're saying Cacciato's left for gay Paree, is that right?"

"That's what he said, sir. I'm just relaying what he told to Paul Berlin. Hey, really, you better cover yourself up."

"Who's Paul Berlin?"

"Right here, sir. This is Paul Berlin."

The lieutenant looked up. His eyes were bright blue, oddly out of place in the sallow face. "You Paul Berlin?"

"Yes, sir," said Paul Berlin. He pretended to smile.

"Geez, I thought you were Vaught."

"Vaught's the one who cut himself, sir."

"I thought that was you. How do you like that?"

"Fine, sir."

The lieutenant sighed and shook his head sadly. He held a boot to dry over the burning Sterno. Behind him in the shadows sat the crosslegged, roundfaced Buddha, smiling benignly from its elevated perch. The pagoda was cold. Dank and soggy from a month of rain, the place smelled of clays and silicates and old incense. It was a single square room, built like a pillbox with a flat ceiling that forced the soldiers to stoop and kneel. Once it might have been an elegant house of worship, neatly tiled and painted and clean, candles burning in holders at the Buddha's feet, but now it was bombed-out junk.

Sandbags blocked the windows. Bits of broken pottery lay
under chipped pedestals. The Buddha's right arm was
missing and his fat groin was gouged with shrapnel. Still,
the smile was intact. Head cocked, he seemed interested
in the lieutenant's long sigh. "So. Cacciato's gone away,
is that it?"

"There it is," Doc Peret said. "You've got it now."

Paul Berlin smiled and nodded.

"To gay Paree," the lieutenant said. "Old Cacciato's
going to Paree in France." He giggled, then shook his
head gravely. "Still raining?"

"A bitch, sir."

"You ever seen rain like this? I mean, ever?"

"No, sir," Paul Berlin said.

"You Cacciato's buddy, I suppose?"

"No, sir," Paul Berlin said. "Sometimes he'd tag
along, but not really."

"Who's his buddy?"

"Vaught, sir. I guess Vaught was, sometime."

"Well," the lieutenant said, dropping his nose inside
the boot to smell the sweaty leather, "well, I guess we
should just get Mister Vaught in here."

"Vaught's gone, sir. He's the one who cut himself —
gangrene, remember?"

"Mother of Mercy."

Doc Peret draped a poncho over the lieutenant's
shoulders. The rain was steady and thunderless and
undramatic. Though it was mid-morning, the feeling was
of endless dusk.

"Paree," the lieutenant murmured. "Cacciato's
going to gay Paree — pretty girls and bare ass and Frogs
everywhere. What's wrong with him?"

"Just dumb, sir. He's just awful dumb, that's all."

"And he's walking? He says he's walking to gay
Paree?"

"That's what he says, sir, but you know how Cacciato
can be."

"Does he know how far it is?"

"Six thousand eight hundred statute miles, sir. That's what he told me — six thousand eight hundred miles on the nose. He had it down pretty well. He had a compass and fresh water and maps and stuff."

"Maps," the lieutenant said. "Maps, flaps, schnaps. I guess those maps will help him cross the oceans, right? I guess he can just rig up a canoe out of those maps, no problem."

"Well, no," said Paul Berlin. He looked at Doc Peret, who shrugged. "No, sir. He showed me on the maps. See, he says he's going through Laos, then into Thailand and Burma, and then India, and then some other country, I forget, and then into Iran and Iraq, and then Turkey, and then Greece, and the rest is easy. That's exactly what he said. The rest is easy, he said. He had it all doped out."

"In other words," the lieutenant said, lying back, "in other words, fuckin AWOL."

"There it is," said Doc Peret. "There it is."

The lieutenant rubbed his eyes. His face was sallow and he needed a shave. For a time he lay very still, listening to the rain, hands on his belly, then he giggled and shook his head and laughed. "What for? Tell me — what the fuck for?"

"Easy," Doc said. "Really, you got to stay covered up, sir, I told you that."

"What for? I mean, what for?"

"Shhhhhhh, he's just dumb, that's all."

The lieutenant's face was yellow. He laughed, rolling onto his side and dropping the boot. "I mean, why? What sort of shit is this — walking to fucking gay Paree? What kind of bloody war is this, tell me, what's wrong with you people? Tell me — what's *wrong* with you?"

"Shhhhhh," Doc purred, covering him up and putting a hand on his forehead. "Easy does it."

"Angel of Mercy, Mother of Virgins, what's wrong

with you guys? Walking to gay Paree, what's *wrong*?"

"Nothing, sir. It's just Cacciato. You know how Cacciato can be when he puts his head to it. Relax now and it'll be all fine. Fine. It's just that rockhead, Cacciato."

The lieutenant giggled. Without rising, he pulled on his pants and boots and a shirt, then rocked miserably before the blue Sterno flame. The pagoda smelled like the earth, and the rain was unending. "Shoot," the lieutenant sighed. He kept shaking his head, grinning, then looked at Paul Berlin. "What squad you in?"

"Third, sir."

"That's Cacciato's squad?"

"Yes, sir."

"Who else?"

"Me and Doc and Eddie Lazzutti and Stink and Oscar Johnson and Harold Murphy. That's all, except for Cacciato."

"What about Pederson and Buff?"

"They're the dead ones, sir."

"Shoot." The lieutenant rocked before the flame. He did not look well. "Okay," he sighed, getting up. "Third Squad goes after Cacciato."

Leading to the mountains were four clicks of level paddy. The mountains jerked straight out of the rice, and beyond those mountains and other mountains was Paris.

The tops of the mountains could not be seen for the mist and clouds. The rain was glue that stuck the sky to the land.

The squad spent the night camped at the base of the first mountain, then in the morning they began the ascent. At mid-day Paul Berlin spotted Cacciato. He was half a mile up, bent low and moving patiently, steadily. He was not wearing a helmet — surprising, because Cacciato always took great care to cover the pink bald spot at the crown of his skull. Paul Berlin spotted him, but it was

Stink Harris who spoke up.

Lieutenant Corson took out the binoculars.

"Him, sir?"

The lieutenant watched while Cacciato climbed toward the clouds.

"That him?"

"It's him. Bald as an eagle's ass."

Stink giggled. "Bald as Friar Tuck — it's Cacciato, all right. Dumb as a dink."

They watched until Cacciato was swallowed in the rain and clouds.

"Dumb-dumb," Stink giggled.

They walked fast, staying in a loose column. First the lieutenant, then Oscar Johnson, then Stink, then Eddie Lazzutti, then Harold Murphy, then Doc, then, at the rear, Paul Berlin. Who walked slowly, head down. He had nothing against Cacciato. The whole episode was silly, of course, a dumb and immature thing typical of Cacciato, but even so he had nothing special against him. It was just too bad. A waste of time in the midst of infinitely wider waste.

Climbing, he tried to picture Cacciato's face. The image came out fuzzed and amorphous and bland — entirely compatible with the boy's personality. Doc Peret, an acute observer of such things, hypothesized that Cacciato had missed Mongolian idiocy by the breadth of a single, wispy genetic hair. "Could have gone either way," Doc had said confidentially. "You see the slanting eyes? The pasty flesh, just like jelly, right? The odd-shaped head? I mean, hey, let's face it — the guy's fuckin ugly. It's only a theory, mind you, but I'd wager big money that old Cacciato has more than a smidgen of the Mongol in him."

There may have been truth to it. Cacciato looked curiously unfinished, as though nature had struggled long and heroically but finally jettisoned him as a hopeless cause, not worth the diminishing returns. Open-faced, round, naive, plump, tender-complected and boyish, Cacciato lacked the fine detail, the refinements and final touches that maturity ordinarily marks on a boy of seventeen years. All this, the men concluded, added up to a case of simple gross stupidity. He wasn't positively disliked — except perhaps by Stink Harris, who took instant displeasure with anything vaguely his inferior — but at the same time Cacciato was no one's friend. Vaught, maybe. But Vaught was dumb, too, and he was gone from the war. At best, Cacciato was tolerated. The way men will sometimes tolerate a pesky dog.

It was just too bad. Walking to Paris, it was one of those ridiculous things Cacciato would do. Like winning the Bronze Star for shooting a dink in the face. Dumb. The way he was forever whistling. Too blunt-headed to know better, blind to the bodily and spiritual dangers of human combat. In some ways this made him a good soldier. He walked point like a boy at his first county fair. He didn't mind the tunnel work. And his smile, more decoration than an expression of emotion, stayed with him in the most lethal of moments — when Billy Boy turned his last card, when Pederson floated face-up in a summer day's paddy, when Buff's helmet overflowed with an excess of red and gray fluids.

It was sad, a real pity.

Climbing the mountain, Paul Berlin felt an odd affection for the kid. Not friendship, exactly, but — real pity.

Not friendship. Not exactly. Pity, pity plus wonder. It was all silly, walking away in the rain, but it was something to think about.

They did not reach the summit of the mountain until mid-afternoon. The climb was hard, the rain sweeping down, the mountain oozing from beneath their feet. Below, the clouds were expansive, hiding the paddies and the war. Above, in more clouds, were more mountains.

Oscar Johnson found where Cacciato had spent the

first night, a rock formation with an outcropping ledge as a roof, a can of burnt-out Sterno, a chocolate wrapper, and a partly burned map. On the map, traced in red ink, was a dotted line that ran through the paddyland and up the first small mountain of the Annamese Cordillera. The dotted line ended there, apparently to be continued on another map.

"He's serious," the lieutenant said softly. "The blockhead's serious." He held the map as if it had a bad smell.

Stink and Oscar and Eddie Lazzutti nodded.

They rested in Cacciato's snug rock nest. Tucked away, looking out on the slate rain toward the next mountain, the men were quiet. Paul Berlin laid out a game of solitaire. Harold Murphy rolled a joint, inhaled, then passed it along, and they smoked and watched the rain and clouds and wilderness. It was peaceful. The rain was nice.

No one spoke until the ritual was complete.

Then, in a hush, all the lieutenant could say was, "Mercy."

"Shit," was what Stink Harris said.

The rain was unending.

"We could just go back," Doc Peret finally said. "You know, sir? Just head on back and forget him."

Stink Harris giggled.

"Seriously," Doc kept on, "we could just let the poor kid go. Make him MIA, strayed in battle, the lost lamb. Sooner or later he'll wake up, you know, and he'll see how insane it is and he'll come back."

The lieutenant stared into the rain. His face was yellow except for the network of broken veins.

"So what say you, sir? Let him go?"

"Dumber than a rock," Stink giggled.

"And smarter than Stink Harris."

"You know *what*, Doc."

"Pickle it."

"Who's saying to pickle it?"

"Just pickle it," said Doc Peret. "That's what."

Stink giggled but he shut up.

"What do you say, sir? Turn back?"

The lieutenant was quiet. At last he shivered and went into the rain with a wad of toilet paper. Paul Berlin sat alone, playing solitaire in the style of Las Vegas. Pretending, of course. Pretending to pay thirty thousand dollars for the deck, pretending ways to spend his earnings.

When the lieutenant returned he told the men to saddle up.

"We turning back?" Doc asked.

The lieutenant shook his head. He looked sick.

"I knew it!" Stink crowed. "Damn straight, I knew it! Can't hump away from a war, isn't that right, sir? The dummy has got to learn you can't just hump your way out of a war." Stink grinned and flicked his eyebrows at Doc Peret. "I knew it. By golly, I knew it!"

Cacciato had reached the top of the second mountain. Standing bareheaded, hands loosely at his sides, he was looking down on them through a blur of rain. Lieutenant Corson had the binoculars on him.

"Maybe he don't see us," Oscar said. "Maybe he's lost."

"Oh, he sees us. He sees us fine. Sees us real fine. And he's not lost. Believe me, he's not."

"Throw out smoke, sir?"

"Why not?" the lieutenant said. "Sure, why not throw out pretty smoke, why not?" He watched Cacciato through the glasses while Oscar threw out the smoke. It fizzled for a time and then puffed up in a heavy cloud of lavender. "Oh, he sees us," the lieutenant whispered. "He sees us fine."

"The bastard's *waving*!"

"I can see that, thank you. Mother of Saints."

As if stricken, the lieutenant suddenly sat down in a puddle, put his head in his hands and began to rock as the lavender smoke drifted up the face of the mountain. Cacciato was waving both arms. Not quite waving. The arms were flapping. Paul Berlin watched through the glasses. Cacciato's head was huge, floating like a balloon in the high fog, and he did not look at all frightened. He looked young and stupid. His face was shiny. He was smiling, and he looked happy.

"I'm sick," the lieutenant said. He kept rocking. "I tell you, I'm a sick, sick man."

"Should I shout up to him?"

"Sick," the lieutenant moaned. "Sick, sick. It wasn't this way on Pusan, I'll tell you that. Sure, call up to him — I'm sick."

Oscar Johnson cupped his hands and hollered, and Paul Berlin watched through the glasses. For a moment Cacciato stopped waving. He spread his arms wide, as if to show them empty, slowly spreading them out like wings, palms up. Then his mouth opened wide, and in the mountains there was thunder.

"What'd he say?" The lieutenant rocked on his haunches. He was clutching himself and shivering. "Tell me what he said."

"Can't hear, sir. Oscar —?"

There was more thunder, long lasting thunder that came in waves from deep in the mountains. It rolled down and moved the trees and grasses.

"Shut the shit up!" The lieutenant was rocking and shouting at the rain and wind and thunder. "What'd the dumb fucker say?"

Paul Berlin watched through the glasses, and Cacciato's mouth opened and closed and opened, but there was only more thunder. Then his arms began flapping again. Flying, Paul Berlin suddenly realized. The poor kid was perched up there, arms flapping, trying to fly. Fly! Incredibly, the flapping motion was smooth and practiced and graceful.

"A chicken!" Stink squealed. "Look it! A squawking chicken!"

"Mother of Children."

"Look it!"

"A miserable chicken, you see that? A chicken!"

The thunder came again, breaking like Elephant Feet across the mountains, and the lieutenant rocked and held himself.

"For Christ sake," he moaned, "what'd he say? Tell me."

Paul Berlin could not hear. But he saw Cacciato's lips move, and the happy smile.

"Tell me."

So Paul Berlin, watching Cacciato fly, repeated it. "He said goodbye."

In the night the rain hardened into fog, and the fog was cold. They camped in the fog, near the top of the mountain, and the thunder stayed through the night. The lieutenant vomited. Then he radioed that he was in pursuit of the enemy.

"Gunships, Papa Two-Niner?" came the answer from far away.

"Negative," said the old lieutenant.

"Arty? Tell you what. You got a real sweet voice, Papa Two-Niner. No shit, a lovely voice." The radio-voice paused. "So, here's what I'll do, I'll give you a bargain on the arty — two for the price of one, no strings and a warranty to boot. How's that? See, we got this terrific batch of new 155 in, first class ordinance, I promise you, and what we do, what we do is this. What we do is we go heavy on volume here, you know? Keeps the prices low."

"Negative," the lieutenant said.

"Well, geez. Hard to please, right? Maybe some nice illum, then? Willie Peter, real boomers with some genuine sparkles mixed in. We're having this close-out sale, one time only.''

"Negative. Negative, negative, negative.''

"You'll be missing out on some fine shit.''

"Negative, you monster.''

"Okay,'' the radio-voice said, disappointed-sounding, "but you'll wish . . . No offense, Papa Two-Niner. Have some happy hunting.''

"Mercy,'' said the lieutenant into a blaze of static.

The night fog was worse than the rain, colder and more saddening. They lay under a sagging lean-to that seemed to catch and hold the fog like a net. Oscar and Harold Murphy and Stink and Eddie Lazzutti slept anyway, curled around one another like lovers. They could sleep and sleep.

"I hope he's moving,'' Paul Berlin whispered to Doc Peret. "I just hope he keeps moving. He does that, we'll never get him.''

"Then they'll chase him with choppers. Or planes or something.''

"Not if he gets himself lost,'' Paul Berlin said. "Not if he hides.''

"What time is it?''

"Don't know.''

"What time you got, sir?''

"Very lousy late,'' said the lieutenant from the bushes.

"Come on.''

"Four o'clock. O-four-hundred, which is to say a.m. Got it?''

"Thanks.''

"Charmed.'' His ass, hanging six inches from the earth, made a soft warm glow in the dark.

"You okay, sir?''

"I'm wonderful. Can't you see how wonderful I am?''

"I just hope Cacciato keeps moving,'' Paul Berlin whispered. "That's all I hope — I hope he uses his head and keeps moving.''

"It won't get him anywhere.''

"Get him to Paris maybe.''

"Maybe,'' Doc sighed, turning onto his side, "and where is he then?''

"In Paris.''

"No way. I like adventure, too, but, see, you can't walk to Paris from here. You just can't.''

"He's smarter than you think,'' Paul Berlin said, not quite believing it. "He's not all that dumb.''

"I know,'' the lieutenant said. He came from the bushes. "I know all about that.''

"Impossible. None of the roads go to Paris.''

"Can we light a Sterno, sir?''

"No,'' the lieutenant said, crawling under the lean-to and lying flat on his back. His breath came hard. "No, you can't light a fucking Sterno, and no, you can't go out to play without your mufflers and galoshes, and no, kiddies and combatants, no, you can't have chocolate sauce on your broccoli. No.''

"All right.''

"No!''

"You saying no, sir?''

"No,'' the lieutenant sighed with doom. "It's still a war, isn't it?''

"I guess.''

"There you have it. It's still a war.''

The rain resumed. It started with thunder, then lightning lighted the valley deep below in green and mystery, then more thunder, then it was just the rain. They lay quietly and listened. Paul Berlin, who considered himself abnormally sane, uncluttered by high ideas or lofty ambitions or philosophy, was suddenly struck between the eyes by a vision of murder. Butchery, no less. Cacciato's right temple caving inward, a moment of black silence, then the enormous explosion of outward-going brains. It was no metaphor; he didn't think in metaphors. No, it was a simple scary vision. He tried to reconstruct the thoughts that had led to it, but there was nothing to be found — the rain, the discomfort of mushy flesh. Nothing to justify such a bloody image, no origins. Just Cacciato's round head suddenly exploding like a pricked bag of helium: boom.

Where, he thought, was all this taking him, and where would it end? Murder was the logical circuit-stopper, of course; it was Cacciato's rightful, maybe inevitable due. Nobody can get away with stupidity for-ever, and in war the final price for it is always paid in purely biological currency, hunks of toe or pieces of femur or bits of exploded brain. And it *was* still a war, wasn't it?

Pitying Cacciato with wee-hour tenderness, and pity-ing himself for the affliction that produced such visions, Paul Berlin hoped for a miracle. He was tired of murder. Not scared by it — not at that particular moment — and not awed by it, just fatigued.

"He did some awfully brave things," he whispered. Then realized that Doc was listening. "He did. The time he dragged that dink out of his bunker, remember that."

"Yeah."

"The time he shot the kid in the kisser."

"I remember."

"At least you can't call him a coward, can you? You can't say he ran away because he was scared."

"You can say a lot of other shit, though."

"True. But you can't say he wasn't brave. You can't say that."

"Fair enough," Doc said. He sounded sleepy.

"I wonder if he talks French."

"You kidding, partner?"

"Just wondering. You think it's hard to learn French, Doc?"

"Cacciato?"

"Yeah, I guess not. It's a neat thing to think about, though, old Cacciato walking to Paris."

"Go to sleep," Doc Peret advised. "Remember, pal, you got your own health to think of."

They were in the high country.

It was country far from the war, high and peaceful country with trees and thick grass, no people and no dogs and no lowland drudgery. Real wilderness, through which a single trail, liquid and shiny, kept taking them up.

The men walked with their heads down. Stink at point, then Eddie Lazzutti and Oscar, next Harold Murphy with the machine gun, then Doc, then the lieutenant, and last Paul Berlin.

They were tired and did not talk. Their thoughts were in their legs and feet, and their legs and feet were heavy with blood, for they'd been on the march many hours and the day was soggy with the endless rain. There was nothing symbolic, or melancholy, about the rain. It was simple rain, everywhere.

They camped that night beside the trail, then in the morning continued the climb. Though there were no signs of Cacciato, the mountain had only one trail and they were on it, the only way west.

Paul Berlin marched mechanically. At his sides, balancing him evenly and keeping him upright, two canteens of Kool-Aid lifted and fell with his hips, and the hips rolled in their ball-and-socket joints. He respired and sweated. His heart hard, his back strong, up the high country.

They did not see Cacciato, and for a time Paul Berlin thought they might have lost him forever. It made him feel better, and he climbed the trail and enjoyed the scenery and the sensations of being high and far from the real war, and then Oscar found the second map.

The red dotted line crossed the border into Laos.

Farther ahead they found Cacciato's helmet and armored vest, then his dogtags, then his entrenching tool and knife.

"Dummy just keeps to the trail," the lieutenant moaned. "Tell me why? Why doesn't he leave the trail?"

"It's the only way to Paris," Paul Berlin said.

"A rockhead," said Stink Harris. "That's why."

Liquid and shiny, a mix of rain and red clay, the trail took them higher.

Cacciato eluded them but he left behind the wastes of his march — empty tins, bits of bread, a belt of golden ammo dangling from a dwarf pine, a leaking canteen, candy wrappers and worn rope. Clues that kept them going. Tantalizing them on, one step then the next — a glimpse of his bald head, the hot ash of a breakfast fire, a handkerchief dropped coyly along the path.

So they kept after him, following the trails that linked one to the next westward in a simple linear direction without deception. It was deep, jagged, complex country, dark with the elements of the season, and ahead was the frontier.

"He makes it that far," Doc Peret said, pointing to the next line of mountains, "and we can't touch him."

"How now?"

"The border," Doc said. The trail had leveled out and the march was easier. "He makes it to the border and it's bye-bye Cacciato."

"How far?"

"Two clicks maybe. Not far."

"Then he's made it," whispered Paul Berlin.

"Maybe so."

"By God!"

"Maybe so," Doc said.

"Boy, lunch at Tour d'Argent! A night at the old opera!"

"Maybe so."

The trail narrowed, then climbed, and a half-hour later they saw him.

He stood at the top of a small grassy hill, two

hundred meters ahead. Loose and at ease, smiling, Cacciato already looked like a civilian. His hands were in his pockets and he was not trying to hide himself. He might have been waiting for a bus, patient and serene and not at all frightened.

"Got him!" Stink yelped. "I knew it! Now we got him!"

The lieutenant came forward with the glasses.

"I knew it," Stink crowed, pressing forward. "The blockhead's finally giving it up — giving up the old ghost, I knew it!"

"What do we do, sir?"

The lieutenant shrugged and stared through the glasses.

"Fire a shot?" Stink held his rifle up and before the lieutenant could speak he squeezed off two quick rounds, one a tracer that turned like a corkscrew through the mist. Cacciato smiled and waved.

"Look at him," Oscar Johnson said. "I do think we got ourselves a predicament. Truly a predicament."

"There it is," Eddie said, and they both laughed, and Cacciato kept smiling and waving.

"A true predicament."

Stink Harris took the point, walking fast and chattering, and Cacciato stopped waving and watched him come, arms folded and his big head cocked as if listening for something. He looked amused.

There was no avoiding it.

Stink saw the wire as he tripped it, but there was no avoiding it.

The first sound was that of a zipper suddenly yanked up; next, a popping noise, the spoon releasing and primer detonating; then the sound of the grenade dropping; then the fizzling sound. The sounds came separately but quickly.

Stink knew it as it happened. With the next step, in one fuzzed motion, he flung himself down and away, rolling, covering his skull, mouth open, yelping a funny, trivial little yelp.

They all knew it.

Eddie and Oscar and Doc Peret dropped flat, and Harold Murphy bent double and did an oddly graceful jackknife for a man of his size, and the lieutenant coughed and collapsed, and Paul Berlin, seeing purple, closed his eyes and fists and mouth, brought his knees to his belly, coiling, and let himself fall.

Count, he thought, but the numbers came in a tangle without sequence.

His belly hurt. That was where it started. First the belly, a release of fluids in the bowels next, a shitting feeling, a draining of all the pretensions and silly hopes for himself, and he was back where he started, writhing. The lieutenant was beside him. The air was windless — just the misty rain. His teeth hurt. Count, he thought, but his teeth hurt and no numbers came. I don't want to die, he thought lucidly, with hurting teeth.

There was no explosion. His teeth kept hurting and his belly was floating in funny ways.

He was ready, steeled. His lungs hurt now. He was ready, but there was no explosion. Then came a fragile pop. Smoke, he thought without thinking, smoke.

"Smoke," the lieutenant moaned, then repeated it, "fucking smoke."

Paul Berlin smelled it. He imagined its velvet color, purple, but he could not open his eyes. He tried, but he could not open his eyes or unclench his fists or uncoil his legs, and the heavy fluids in his stomach were holding him down, and he could not wiggle or run to escape. There was no explosion.

"Smoke," Doc said softly. "Just smoke."

It was red smoke, and the message seemed clear. It was all over them. Brilliant red, thick, acid-tasting. It spread out over the earth like paint, then began to climb against gravity in a lazy red spiral.

"Smoke," Doc said. "Smoke."

Stink Harris was crying. He was on his hands and knees, chin against his throat, bawling and bawling. Oscar and Eddie had not moved.

"He had us," the lieutenant whispered. His voice was hollowed out, senile sounding, almost a reminiscence. "He could've had all of us."

"Just smoke," Doc said. "Lousy smoke is all."

"The dumb fucker could've had us."

Paul Berlin could not move. He felt entirely conscious, a little embarrassed but not yet humiliated, and he heard their voices, heard Stink weeping and saw him beside the trail on his hands and knees, and he saw the red smoke everywhere, but he could not move.

"He won't come," said Oscar Johnson, returning under a white flag. "Believe me, I tried, but the dude just won't play her cool."

It was dusk and the seven soldiers sat in pow-wow.

"I told him all the right stuff, but he won't give it up. Told him it was crazy as shit and he'd probably end up dead, and I told him how he'd end up court-martialed at the best, and I told him how his old man would shit when he heard about it. Told him maybe things wouldn't go so hard if he just gave up and came back right now. I went through the whole spiel, top to bottom. The dude just don't listen."

The lieutenant was lying prone, Doc's thermometer in his mouth, sick-looking. It wasn't his war. The skin on his arms and neck was loose around deteriorating muscle.

"I told him — I told him all that good shit. Told him it's ridiculous, dig? I told him it won't work, no matter what, and I told him we're fed up. Fed up."

"You tell him we're out of rations?"

"Shit, yes, I told him that. And I told him he's gonna starve his own ass if he keeps going, and I told him we'd have to call in gunships if it came to it."

"You tell him he can't walk to France?"

Oscar grinned. He was black enough to be indistinct in the dusk. "Maybe I forgot to tell him that."

"You should've told him."

The lieutenant slid a hand behind his neck and pushed against it as if to relieve some spinal pressure. "What else?" he asked. "What else did he say?"

"Nothing, sir. He said he's doing okay. Said he was sorry to scare us with the smoke."

"The bastard." Stink kept rubbing his hands against the black stock of his rifle.

"What else?"

"Nothing. You know how he is, sir. Just a lot of smiles and stupid stuff. He asked how everybody was, so I said we're fine, except for the scare with the smoke boobytrap, and then he said he was sorry about that, so I told him it was okay. What can you say to a dude like that?"

The lieutenant nodded, pushing against his neck. He was quiet awhile. He seemed to be making up his mind. "All right," he finally sighed. "What'd he have with him?"

"Sir?"

"Musketry," the lieutenant said. "What kind of weapons?"

"His rifle. That's all, his rifle and some bullets. I didn't get much of a look."

"Claymores?"

Oscar shook his head. "I didn't see none. Maybe so."

"Grenades?"

"I don't know. Maybe a couple."

"Beautiful recon job, Oscar. Real pretty."

"Sorry, sir. He had his stuff tight, though."

"I'm sick."

"Yes, sir."

"Dysentery's going through me like coffee. What

you got for me, Doc?''

Doc Peret shook his head. "Nothing, sir. Rest."

"That's it," the lieutenant said. "What I need is rest."

"Why not let him go, sir?"

"Rest," the lieutenant said, "is what I need."

Paul Berlin did not sleep. Instead he watched Cacciato's small hill and tried to imagine a proper ending.

There were only a few possibilities remaining, and after what had happened it was hard to see a happy end to it. Not impossible, of course. It could still be done. With skill and boldness, Cacciato might slip away and cross the frontier mountains and be gone. He tried to picture it. Many new places. Villages at night with barking dogs, people whose eyes and skins would change in slow evolution and counterevolution as Cacciato moved westward with whole continents before him and the war far behind him and all the trails connecting and leading toward Paris. It could be done. He imagined the many dangers of Cacciato's march, treachery and deceit at every turn, but he also imagined the many good times ahead, the stinging feel of aloneness, and new leanness and knowledge of strange places. The rains would end and the trails would go dry and be baked to dust, and there would be changing foliage and great expanses of silence and songs and pretty girls in straw huts and, finally, Paris.

It could be done. The odds were like poison, but it could be done.

Later, as if a mask had been peeled off, the rain ended and the sky cleared and Paul Berlin woke to see the stars.

They were in their familiar places. It wasn't so cold. He lay on his back and counted the stars and named those that he knew, named the constellations and the valleys of the moon. It was just too bad. Crazy, but still sad. He should've kept going — left the trails and waded through streams to rinse away the scent, buried his feces, swung from the trees branch to branch; he should've slept through the days and ran through the nights. It might have been done.

Toward dawn he saw Cacciato's breakfast fire. He heard Stink playing with the safety catch on his M-16, a clicking noise like a slow morning cricket. The sky lit itself in patches.

"Let's do it," the lieutenant whispered.

Eddie Lazzutti and Oscar and Harold Murphy crept away toward the south. Doc and the lieutenant waited a time then began to circle west to block a retreat. Stink Harris and Paul Berlin were to continue up the trail.

Waiting, trying to imagine a rightful and still happy ending, Paul Berlin found himself pretending, in a vague sort of way, that before long the war would reach a climax beyond which everything else would become completely commonplace. At that point he would stop being afraid. All the bad things, the painful and grotesque things, would be in the past, and the things ahead, if not lovely, would at least be tolerable. He pretended he had crossed that threshold.

When the sky was half-light, Doc and the lieutenant fired a red flare that streaked high over Cacciato's grassy hill, hung there, then exploded in a fanning starburst like the start of a celebration. Cacciato Day, it might have been called. October something, in the year 1968, the year of the Pig.

In the trees at the southern slope of the hill Oscar and Eddie and Harold Murphy each fired red flares to signal their advance.

Stink went into the weeds and hurried back, zipping up his trousers. He was very excited and happy. Deftly, he released the bolt on his weapon and it slammed hard into place.

"Fire the flare," he said, "and let's go."

Paul Berlin took a long time opening his pack.

But he found the flare, unscrewed its lid, laid the firing pin against the primer, then jammed it in.

The flare jumped away from him. It went high and fast, rocketing upward and taking a smooth arc that followed the course of the trail, leaving behind a dirty wake of smoke.

At its apex, with barely a sound, the flare exploded in a green dazzle over Cacciato's hill. It was a fine, brilliant shade of green.

"Go," whispered Paul Berlin. It did not seem enough. "Go," he said, and then he shouted, "Go."

Raymond Carver

A Small, Good Thing*

Saturday afternoon she drove to the bakery in the shopping center. After looking through a loose-leaf binder with photographs of cakes taped onto the pages, she ordered chocolate, the child's favorite. The cake she chose was decorated with a space ship and launching pad under a sprinkling of white stars at one end of the cake, and a planet made of red frosting at the other end. His name, SCOTTY, would be in raised green letters beneath the planet. The baker, who was an older man with a thick neck, listened without saying anything when she told him the child would be eight years old next Monday. The baker wore a white apron that looked like a smock. Straps cut under his arms, went around in back and then to the front again where they were secured under his heavy waist. He wiped his hands on his apron as he listened to her. He kept his eyes down on the photographs and let her talk. He let her take her time. He'd just come to work and he'd be there all night, baking, and he was in no real hurry.

She gave the baker her name, Ann Weiss, and her telephone number. The cake would be ready on Monday morning, just out of the oven, in plenty of time for the child's party that afternoon. The baker was not jolly. There were no pleasantries between them, just the minimum exchange of words, the necessary information. He made her feel uncomfortable, and she didn't like that. While he was bent over the counter with the pencil in his hand, she studied his coarse features and wondered if he'd ever done anything else with

* This story is expanded and revised from *What We Talk About When We Talk About Love*.

his life besides be a baker. She was a mother and thirty-three years old, and it seemed to her that everyone, especially someone the baker's age — a man old enough to be her father — must have children who'd gone through this special time of cakes and birthday parties. There must be that between them, she thought. But he was abrupt with her, not rude, just abrupt. She gave up trying to make friends with him. She looked into the back of the bakery and could see a long, heavy wooden table with aluminum pie pans stacked at one end, and beside the table a metal container filled with empty racks. There was an enormous oven. A radio was playing country-western music.

The baker finished printing the information on the special order card and closed up the binder. He looked at her and said, "Monday morning." She thanked him and drove home.

On Monday morning, the birthday boy was walking to school with another boy. They were passing a bag of potato chips back and forth and the birthday boy was trying to find out what his friend intended to give him for his birthday that afternoon. Without looking, he stepped off the curb at an intersection and was immediately knocked down by a car. He fell on his side with his head in the gutter and his legs out in the road. His eyes were closed, but his legs began to move back and forth as if he were trying to climb over something. His friend dropped the potato chips and started to cry. The car had gone a hundred feet or so and stopped in the middle of the road. A man in the driver's seat looked back over his shoulder. He waited until the boy got unsteadily to his feet. They boy wobbled a little. He looked dazed, but okay. The driver put the car into gear and drove away.

The birthday boy didn't cry, but he didn't have anything to say about anything either. He wouldn't answer when his friend asked him what it felt like to be hit by a car. He walked home, and his friend went on to school. But after

the birthday boy was inside his house and was telling his
mother about it, she sitting beside him on the sofa, holding
his hands in her lap, saying, "Scotty, honey, are you sure you
feel all right, baby?" thinking she would call the doctor
anyway, he suddenly lay back on the sofa, closed his eyes,
and went limp. When she couldn't wake him up, she hurried
to the telephone and called her husband at work. Howard
told her to remain calm, remain calm, and then he called an
ambulance for the child and left for the hospital himself.

Of course, the birthday party was cancelled. The child
was in the hospital with a mild concussion and suffering from
shock. There'd been vomiting, and his lungs had taken in
fluid which needed pumping out that afternoon. Now he
simply seemed to be in a very deep sleep — but no coma,
Doctor Francis had emphasized; no coma, when he saw the
alarm in the parents' eyes. At eleven o'clock that Monday
night when the boy seemed to be resting comfortably enough
after the many X-rays and the lab work, and it was just a
matter of his waking up and coming around, Howard left the
hospital. He and Ann had been at the hospital with the child
since that morning, and he was going home for a short while
to bathe and to change clothes. "I'll be back in an hour," he
said. She nodded. "It's fine," she said. "I'll be right here."
He kissed her on the forehead, and they touched hands. She
sat in a chair beside the bed and looked at the child. She was
waiting for him to wake up and be all right. Then she could
begin to relax.

Howard drove home from the hospital. He took the wet,
dark streets very fast, then caught himself and slowed down.
Until now, his life had gone smoothly and to his satisfaction
— college, marriage, another year of college for the advanced
degree in business, a junior partnership in an investment
firm. Fatherhood. He was happy and, so far, lucky — he
knew that. His parents were still living, his brothers and his
sister were established, his friends from college had gone out
to take their places in the world. So far he had kept away

from any real harm, from those forces he knew existed and that could cripple or bring down a man, if the luck went bad, if things suddenly turned. He pulled into the driveway and parked. His left leg began to tremble. He sat in the car for a minute and tried to deal with the present situation in a rational manner. Scotty had been hit by a car and was in the hospital, but he was going to be all right. He closed his eyes and ran his hand over his face. In a minute, he got out of the car and went up to the front door. The dog was barking inside the house. The telephone rang and rang while he unlocked the door and fumbled for the light switch. He shouldn't have left the hosptial, he shouldn't have. "God dammit!" he said. He picked up the receiver and said, "I just walked in the door!"

"There's a cake here that wasn't picked up," the voice on the other end of the line said.

"What are you saying?" Howard asked.

"A cake," the voice said. "A sixteen dollar cake."

Howard held the receiver against his ear, trying to understand. "I don't know anything about a cake," he said. "Jesus, what are you talking about?"

"Don't hand me that," the voice said.

Howard hung up the telephone. He went into the kitchen and poured himself some whiskey. He called the hospital. But the child's condition remained the same; he was still sleeping and nothing had changed there. While water poured into the tub, Howard lathered his face and shaved. He'd just stretched out in the tub and closed his eyes when the telephone began to ring. He hauled himself out, grabbed a towel, and hurried through the house, saying, "Stupid, stupid," for having left the hospital. But when he picked up the receiver and shouted, "Hello!" there was no sound at the other end of the line. Then the caller hung up.

He arrived back at the hospital a little after midnight. Ann still sat in the chair beside the bed. She looked at

Howard, and then she looked back at the child. The child's eyes stayed closed, the head was still wrapped in bandages. His breathing was quiet and regular. From an apparatus over the bed hung a bottle of glucose with a tube running from the bottle to the boy's arm.

"How is he?" Howard said. "What's all this?" waving at the glucose and the tube.

"Doctor Francis's orders," she said. "He needs nourishment. He needs to keep up his strength. Why doesn't he wake up, Howard? I don't understand, if he's all right."

Howard put his hand against the back of her head. He ran his fingers through her hair. "He's going to be all right. He'll wake up in a little while. Doctor Francis knows what's what."

After a time he said, "Maybe you should go home and get some rest. I'll stay here. Just don't put up with this creep who keeps calling. Hang up right away."

"Who's calling?" she asked.

"I don't know who, just somebody with nothing better to do than call up people. You go on now."

She shook her head. "No," she said, "I'm fine."

"Really," he said. "Go home for a while, and then come back and spell me in the morning. It'll be all right. What did Doctor Francis say? He said Scotty's going to be all right. We don't have to worry. He's just sleeping now, that's all."

A nurse pushed the door open. She nodded at them as she went to the bedside. She took the left arm out from under the covers and put her fingers on the wrist, found the pulse, and then consulted her watch. In a little while she put the arm back under the covers and moved to the foot of the bed where she wrote something on a clipboard attached to the bed.

"How is he?" Ann said. Howard's hand was a weight on her shoulder. She was aware of the pressure from his fingers.

"He's stable," the nurse said. Then she said, "Doctor will be in again shortly. Doctor's back in the hospital. He's making rounds right now."

"I was saying maybe she'd want to go home and get a little rest," Howard said. "After the doctor comes," he said.

"She could do that," the nurse said. "I think you should both feel free to do that, if you wish." The nurse was a big Scandinavian woman with blond hair. There was the trace of an accent in her speech.

"We'll see what the doctor says," Ann said. "I want to talk to the doctor. I don't think he should keep sleeping like this. I don't think that's a good sign." She brought her hand up to her eyes and let her head come forward a little. Howard's grip tightened on her shoulder, and then his hand moved to her neck where his fingers began to knead the muscles there.

"Doctor Francis will be here in a few minutes," the nurse said. Then she left the room.

Howard gazed at his son for a time, the small chest quietly rising and falling under the covers. For the first time since the terrible minutes after Ann's telephone call to him at his office, he felt a genuine fear starting in his limbs. He began shaking his head, trying to keep it away. Scotty was fine, but instead of sleeping at home in his own bed he was in a hospital bed with bandages around his head and a tube in his arm. But this help was what he needed right now.

Doctor Francis came in and shook hands with Howard, though they'd just seen each other a few hours before. Ann got up from the chair. "Doctor?"

"Ann," he said and nodded. "Let's just first see how he's doing," the doctor said. He moved to the side of the bed and took the boy's pulse. He peeled back one eyelid and then the other. Howard and Ann stood beside the doctor and watched. Then the doctor turned back the covers and listened to the boy's heart and lungs with his stethescope. He pressed his fingers here and there on the abdomen. When he was finished he went to the end of the bed and studied the chart. He noted the time, scribbled something on the chart, and then looked at Howard and Ann.

"Doctor, how is he?" Howard said. "What's the matter with him exactly?"

"Why doesn't he wake up?" Ann said.

The doctor was a handsome, big-shouldered man with a tanned face. He wore a three-piece suit, a striped tie, and ivory cuff-links. His grey hair was combed along the sides of his head, and he looked as if he had just come from a concert. "He's all right," the doctor said. "Nothing to shout about, he could be better, I think. But he's all right. Still, I wish he'd wake up. He should wake up pretty soon." The doctor looked at the boy again. "We'll know some more in a couple of hours, after the results of a few more tests are in. But he's all right, believe me, except for that hair-line fracture of the skull. He does have that."

"Oh, no," Ann said.

"And a bit of a concussion, as I said before. Of course, you know he's in shock," the doctor said. "Sometimes you see this in shock cases."

"But he's out of any real danger?" Howard said. "You said before he's not in a coma. You wouldn't call this a coma then, would you, doctor?" Howard waited. He looked at the doctor.

"No, I don't want to call it a coma," the doctor said and glanced over at the boy once more. "He's just in a very deep sleep. It's a restorative, a measure the body is taking on its own. He's out of any real danger, I'd say that for certain, yes. But we'll know more when he wakes up and the other tests are in. Don't worry," the doctor said.

"It's a coma," Ann said. "Of sorts."

"It's not a coma yet, not exactly," the doctor said. "I wouldn't want to call it coma. Not yet anyway. He's suffered shock. In shock cases this kind of reaction is common enough; it's a temporary reaction to bodily trauma. Coma. Well, coma is a deep, prolonged unconsciousness that could go on for days, or weeks even. Scotty's not in that area, not as far as we can tell anyway. I'm certain his condition will show improvement by morning. I'm betting that it will anyway. We'll know more when he wakes up, which shouldn't be long now. Of course, you may do as you like, stay here or go home for a time. But by all means feel free to leave the hospital for a while if you want. This is not easy, I know." The doctor gazed at the boy again, watching him, and then he turned to Ann and said, "You try not to worry, little mother. Believe me, we're doing all that can be done. It's just a question of a little more time now." He nodded at her, shook hands with Howard again, and then he left the room.

Ann put her hand over her child's forehead. "At least he doesn't have a fever," she said. Then she said, "My God, he feels so cold though. Howard? Is he supposed to feel like this. Feel his head."

Howard touched the child's temples. His own breathing had slowed. "I think he's supposed to feel this way right now," he said. "He's in shock, remember?" That's what the doctor said. The doctor was just in here. He would have said something if Scotty wasn't okay."

Ann stood there a while longer, working her lip with her teeth. Then she moved over to her chair and sat down.

Howard sat in the chair next to her chair. They looked at each other. He wanted to say something else and reassure her, but he was afraid too. He took her hand and put it in his lap, and this made him feel better, her hand being there. He picked up her hand and squeezed it. Then he just held her hand. They sat like that for a while, watching the boy and not talking. From time to time he squeezed her hand. Finally, she took her hand away.

"I've been praying," she said.

He nodded.

She said, "I almost thought I'd forgotten how, but it came back to me. All I had to do was close my eyes and say, 'Please, God, help us, — help Scotty'; and then the rest was easy. The words were right there. Maybe if you prayed too," she said to him.

"I've already prayed," he said. "I prayed this afternoon, yesterday afternoon, I mean, after you called, while I was driving to the hospital. I've been praying," he said.

"That's good," she said. For the first time now, she felt they were together in it, this trouble. She realized with a start it had only been happening to her and to Scotty. She hadn't let Howard into it, though he was there and needed all along. She felt glad to be his wife.

The same nurse came in and took the boy's pulse again and checked the flow from the bottle hanging above the bed.

In an hour another doctor came in. He said his name was Parsons, from Radiology. He had a bushy moustache. He was wearing loafers, a western shirt, and a pair of jeans.

"We're going to take him downstairs for more pictures," he told them. "We need to do some more pictures, and we want to do a scan."

"What's that?" Ann said. "A scan?" She stood between this new doctor and the bed. "I thought you'd already taken all your X-rays."

"I'm afraid we need some more," he said. "Nothing to be alarmed about. We just need some more pictures, and we want to do a brain scan on him."

"My God," Ann said.

"It's perfectly normal procedure in cases like this," this new doctor said. "We just need to find out for sure why he isn't back awake yet. It's normal medical procedure, and nothing to be alarmed about. We'll be taking him down in a few minutes." this doctor said.

In a little while two orderlies came into the room with a gurney. They were black-haired, dark-complexioned men in white uniforms, and they said a few words to each other in a foreign tongue as they unhooked the boy from the tube and moved him from his bed to the gurney. Then they wheeled him from the room. Howard and Ann got on the same elevator. Ann stood beside the gurney and gazed at the child. She closed her eyes as the elevator began its descent. The orderlies stood at either end of the gurney without saying anything, though once one of the men made a comment to the other in their own language, and the other man nodded slowly in response.

Later that morning, just as the sun was beginning to lighten the windows in the waiting room outside the X-Ray department, they brought the boy out and moved him back up to his room. Howard and Ann rode up on the elevator with him once more, and once more they took up their places beside the bed.

They waited all day, but still the boy did not wake up. Occasionally one of them would leave the room to go downstairs to the cafeteria to drink coffee and then, as if suddenly remembering and feeling guilty, get up from the table and hurry back to the room. Doctor Francis came again that afternoon and examined the boy once more and then left after telling them he was coming along and could wake up any minute now. Nurses, different nurses than the night before, came in from time to time. Then a young woman from the lab knocked and entered the room. She wore white slacks and a white blouse and carried a little tray of things which she put on the stand beside the bed. Without a word to them, she took blood from the boy's arm. Howard closed his eyes as the woman found the right place on the boy's arm and pushed the needle in.

"I don't understand this," Ann said to the woman.

"Doctor's orders," the young woman said. "I do what I'm told to do. They say draw that one, I draw. What's wrong with him, anyway?" she said. "He's a sweetie."

"He was hit by a car," Howard said. "A hit and run."

The young woman shook her head and looked again at the boy. Then she took her tray and left the room.

"Why won't he wake up?" Ann said. "Howard? I want some answers from these people."

Howard didn't say anything. He sat down again in the chair and crossed one leg over the other. He rubbed his face. He looked at his son and then he settled back in the chair, closed his eyes, and went to sleep.

Ann walked to the window and looked out at the parking lot. It was night and cars were driving into and out of the parking lot with their lights on. She stood at the window with her hands gripping the sill and knew in her heart that they were into something now, something hard. She was afraid, and her teeth began to chatter until she tightened her jaws. She saw a big car stop in front of the hospital and someone, a woman in a long coat, got into the car. For a minute she wished she were that woman and somebody, anybody, was driving her away from here to somewhere else, a place where she would find Scotty waiting for her when she stepped out of the car, ready to say *Mom* and let her gather him in her arms.

In a little while Howard woke up. He looked at the boy again, and then he got up from the chair, stretched, and went over to stand beside her at the window. They both stared out at the parking lot. They didn't say anything. But they seemed to feel each other's insides now, as though the worry had made them transparent in a perfectly natural way.

The door opened and Doctor Francis came in. He was wearing a different suit and tie this time. His gray hair was combed along the sides of his head, and he looked as if he had just shaved. He went straight to the bed and examined the boy. "He ought to have come around by now. There's just no good reason for this," he said. "But I can tell you we're all convinced he's out of any danger. We'll just feel better when he wakes up. There's no reason, absolutely none, why he shouldn't come around. Very soon. Oh, he'll have himself a dilly of a headache when he does, you can count on that. But all of his signs are fine. They're as normal as can be."

"Is it a coma then?" Ann asked.

The doctor rubbed his smooth cheek. "We'll call it that for the time being, until he wakes up. But you must be worn out. This is hard. Feel free to go out for a bite," he said. "It would do you good. I'll put a nurse in here while you're gone, if you'll feel better about going. Go and have yourselves something to eat."

"I couldn't eat," Ann said. "I'm not hungry."

"Do what you need to do, of course," the doctor said. "Anyway, I wanted to tell you that all the signs are good, the tests are positive, nothing at all negative, and just as soon as he wakes up he'll be over the hill."

"Thank you, doctor," Howard said. He shook hands with the doctor again. The doctor patted Howard's shoulder and went out.

"I suppose one of us should go home and check things," Howard said. "Slug needs to be fed, for one thing."

"Call one of the neighbors," Ann said. "Call the Morgans. Anyone will feed a dog if you ask them to."

"All right," Howard said. After a while he said, "Honey why don't you do it? Why don't you go home and check on things, and then come back? It'll do you good. I'll be right here with him. Seriously," he said. "We need to keep up our strength on this. We'll want to be here for a while even after he wakes up."

"Why don't you go?" she said. "Feed Slug. Feed yourself."

"I already went," he said. "I was gone for exactly an hour and fifteen minutes. You go home for an hour and freshen up. Then come back. I'll stay here."

She tried to think about it, but she was too tired. She closed her eyes and tried to think about it again. After a time she said, "Maybe I will go home for a few minutes. Maybe if I'm not just sitting right here watching him every second he'll wake up and be all right. You know? Maybe he'll wake up if I'm not here. I'll go home and take a bath and put on clean clothes. I'll feed Slug. Then I'll come back."

"I'll be right here," he said. "You go on home, honey, and then come back. I'll be right here keeping an eye on things." His eyes were bloodshot and small, as if he'd been drinking for a long time. His clothes were rumpled. His beard had come out again. She touched his face, and then she took her hand back. She understood he wanted to be by himself for a while, to not have to talk or share his worry for a time. She picked up her purse from the nightstand, and he helped her into her coat.

"I won't be gone long," she said.

"Just sit and rest for a little while when you get home," he said. "Eat something. Take a bath. After you get out of the bath, just sit for a while and rest. It'll do you a world of good, you'll see. Then come back down here," he said. "Let's try not to worry. You heard what Doctor Francis said."

She stood in her coat for a minute trying to recall the doctor's exact words, looking for any nuances, any hint of something behind his words other than what he had said. She tried to remember if his expression had changed any when he bent over to examine the child. She remembered the way his features had composed themselves as he rolled back the child's eyelids and then listened to his breathing.

She went to the door where she turned and looked back. She looked at the child, and then she looked at the father. Howard nodded. She stepped out of the room and pulled the door closed behind her.

She went past the nurses' station and down to the end of the corridor, looking for the elevator. At the end of the corridor she turned to her right where she found a little waiting room where a Negro family sat in wicker chairs. There was a middle-aged man in a khaki shirt and pants, a baseball cap pushed back on his head. A large woman wearing a house dress and slippers was slumped in one of the chairs. A teenaged girl in jeans, hair done in dozens of little braids, lay stretched out in one of the chairs smoking a cigarette, her legs crossed at the ankles. The family swung their eyes to her as she entered the room. The little table was littered with hamburger wrappers and styrofoam cups.

"Franklin," the large woman said as she roused herself. "Is about Franklin?" Her eyes widened. "Tell me now, lady," the woman said. "Is about Franklin?" She was trying to rise from her chair, but the man had closed his hand over her arm.

"Here, here," he said. "Evelyn."

"I'm sorry," Ann said. "I'm looking for the elevator. My son is in the hospital, and now I can't find the elevator."

"Elevator is down that way, turn left," the man said as he aimed a finger.

The girl drew on her cigarette and stared at Ann. Her eyes were narrowed to slits, and her broad lips parted slowly as she let the smoke escape. The Negro woman let her head fall on her shoulder and looked away from Ann, no longer interested.

"My son was hit by a car," Ann said to the man. She seemed to need to explain herself. "He has a concussion and a little skull fracture, but he's going to be all right. He's in shock now, but it might be some kind of coma too. That's what really worries us, the coma part. I'm going out for a little while, but my husband is with him. Maybe he'll wake up while I'm gone."

"That's too bad," the man said and shifted in the chair. He shook his head. He looked down at the table, and then he looked back at Ann. She was still standing there. He said, "Our Franklin, he's on the operating table. Somebody cut him. Tried to kill him. There was a fight where he was at. At this party. They say he was just standing and watching. Not bothering nobody. But that don't mean nothing these days. Now he's on the operating table. We're just hoping and praying, that's all we can do now." He gazed at her steadily.

Ann looked at the girl again, who was still watching her, and at the older woman who kept her head down, but whose eyes were now closed. Ann saw the lips moving silently, making words. She had an urge to ask what those words were. She wanted to talk more with these people who were in the same kind of waiting she was in. She was afraid, and they were afraid. They had that in common. She would have liked to have said something else about the accident, told them more about Scotty, that it had happened on the day of his birthday, Monday, and that he was still unconscious. Yet she didn't know how to begin. She stood there looking at them without saying anything more.

She went down the corridor the man had indicated and found the elevator. She stood for a minute in front of the closed doors, still wondering if she was doing the right thing. Then she put out her finger and touched the button.

She pulled into the driveway and cut the engine. She closed her eyes and leaned her head against the wheel for a minute. She listened to the ticking sounds the engine made as it began to cool. Then she got out of the car. She could hear the dog barking inside the house. She went to the front door, which was unlocked. She went inside and turned on lights and put on a kettle of water for tea. She opened some dog food and fed Slug on the back porch. The dog ate in hungry little smacks. It kept running into the kitchen to see that she was going to stay. As she sat down on the sofa with her tea, the telephone range.

"Yes!" she said as she answered. "Hello!"

"Mrs. Weiss," a man's voice said. It was five o'clock in the morning, and she thought she could hear machinery or equipment of some kind in the background.

"Yes, yes! What is it?" she said. "This is Mrs. Weiss. This is she. What is it, please?" She listened to whatever it was in the background. "Is it Scotty, for Christ's sake?"

"Scotty," the man's voice said. "It's about Scotty, yes. It has to do with Scotty, that problem. Have you forgotten about Scotty?" the man said. Then he hung up.

She dialed the hospital's number and asked for the third

floor. She demanded information about her son from the nurse who answered the telephone. Then she asked to speak to her husband. It was, she said, an emergency.

She waited, turning the telephone cord in her fingers. She closed her eyes and felt sick to her stomach. She would have to make herself eat. Slug came in from the back porch and lay down near her feet. He wagged his tail. She pulled at his ear while he licked her fingers. Howard was on the line.

"Somebody just called here," she said. She twisted the telephone cord. "He said, he said it was about Scotty." She cried.

"Scotty's fine," Howard told her. "I mean he's still sleeping. There's been no change. The nurse has been in twice since you've been gone. They're in here every thirty minutes or so. A nurse or else a doctor. He's all right."

"Somebody called, he said it was about Scotty," she said.

"Honey, you rest for a little while, you need the rest. Then come back here. It must be that same caller I had. Just forget it. Come back down here after you've rested. Then we'll have breakfast or something."

"Breakfast," she said. "I don't want any breakfast."

"You know what I mean," he said. "Juice, something, I don't know. I don't know anything, Ann. Jesus, I'm not hungry either. Ann, it's hard to talk now. I'm standing here at the desk. Doctor Francis is coming again at eight o'clock this morning. He's going to have something to tell us then, something more definite. That's what one of the nurses said. She didn't know any more than that. Ann? Honey, maybe we'll know something more then. At eight o'clock. Come back here before eight. Meanwhile, I'm right here and Scotty's all right. He's still the same," he added.

"I was drinking a cup of tea," she said, "when the telephone rang. They said it was about Scotty. There was a noise in the background. Was there a noise in the background on that call you had, Howard?"

"I don't remember," he said. "Maybe the driver of the car, maybe he's a psychopath and found out about Scotty somehow. But I'm here with him. Just rest like you were going to do. Take a bath and come back by seven or so, and we'll talk to the doctor together when he gets here. It's going to be all right, honey. I'm here, and there are doctors and nurses around. They say his condition is stable."

"I'm scared to death," she said.

She ran water, undressed, and got into the tub. She washed and dried quickly, not taking the time to wash her hair. She put on clean underwear, wool slacks, and a sweater. She went into the living room where the dog looked up at her and let its tail thump once against the floor. It was just starting to get light outside when she went out to the car.

She drove into the parking lot of the hospital and found a space close to the front door. She felt she was in some obscure way responsible for what had happened to the child. She let her thoughts move to the Negro family. She remembered the name "Franklin" and the table that was covered with hamburger papers, and the teenaged girl staring at her as she drew on her cigarette. "Don't have children," she told the girl's image as she entered the front door of the hospital. "For God's sake, don't."

She took the elevator up to the third floor with two nurses who were just going on duty. It was Wednesday morning, a few minutes before seven. There was a page for a Doctor Madison as the elevator doors slid open on the third floor. She got off behind the nurses, who turned in the other direction and continued the conversation she had interrupted when she'd gotten into the elevator. She walked down the corridor to the little alcove where the Negro family had been waiting. They were gone now, but the chairs were scattered in such a way that it looked as if people had just jumped from them the minute before. The table top cluttered with the same cups and papers, the ashtray was filled with cigarette butts.

She stopped at the nurses' station just down the corridor from the waiting room. A nurse was standing behind the counter, brushing her hair and yawning.

"There was a Negro man in surgery last night," Ann said. "Franklin was his name. His family was in the waiting room. I'd like to inquire about his condition."

A nurse who was sitting at a desk behind the counter looked up from a chart in front of her. The telephone buzzed and she picked up the receiver, but she kept her eyes on Ann.

"He passed away," said the nurse at the counter. The nurse held the hairbrush and kept on looking at her. "Are you a friend of the family or what?"

"I met the family last night," Ann said. "My own son is in the hospital. I guess he's in shock. We don't know for sure what's wrong. I just wondered about Mr. Franklin, that's all. Thank you." She moved down the corridor. Elevator doors the same color as the walls slid open and a gaunt, bald man in white pants and white canvas shoes pulled a heavy cart off the elevator. She hadn't noticed these doors last night. The man wheeled the cart out into the corridor and stopped in front of the room nearest the elevator and consulted a clipboard. Then he reached down and slid a tray out of the cart. He rapped lightly on the door and entered the room. She could smell the unpleasant odors of warm food as she passed the cart. She hurried past the other station without looking at any of the nurses and pushed open the door to the child's room.

Howard was standing at the window with his hands behind his back. He turned around as she came in.

"How is he?" she said. She went over to the bed. She dropped her purse on the floor beside the nightstand. She seemed to have been gone a long time. She touched the child's face. "Howard?"

"Doctor Francis was here a little while ago," Howard said. She looked at him closely and thought his shoulders were bunched a little.

"I thought he wasn't coming until eight o'clock this morning," she said quickly.

"There was another doctor with him. A neurologist."

"A neurologist," she said.

Howard nodded. His shoulders were bunching, she could see that. "What'd they say, Howard? For Christ's sake, what'd they say? What is it?"

"They said they're going to take him down and run more tests on him, Ann. They think they're going to operate, honey. Honey, they are going to operate. They can't figure out why he won't wake up. It's more than just shock or concussion, they know that much now. It's in his skull, the fracture, it has something, something to do with that, they think. So they're going to operate. I tried to call you, but I guess you'd already left the house."

"Oh, God," she said. "Oh, please, Howard, please," she said, taking his arms.

"Look!" Howard said then. "Scotty! Look, Ann!" He turned her toward the bed.

The boy had opened his eyes, then closed them. He opened them again now. The eyes stared straight ahead for a minute, then moved slowly in his head until they rested on Howard and Ann, then traveled away again.

"Scotty," his mother said, moving to the bed.

"Hey, Scott," his father said. "Hey, son."

They leaned over the bed. Howard took the child's hand in his hands and began to pat and squeeze the hand. Ann bent over the boy and kissed his forehead again and again. She put her hands on either side of his face. "Scotty, honey, it's mommy and daddy," she said. "Scotty?"

The boy looked at them, but without any sign of recognition. Then his eyes scrunched closed, his mouth opened, and he howled until he had no more air in his lungs. His face seemed to relax and soften then. His lips parted as his last breath was puffed through his throat and exhaled gently through the clenched teeth.

The doctors called it a hidden occlusion and said it was a one-in-a-million circumstance. Maybe if it could have been detected somehow and surgery undertaken immediately, it could have saved him. But more than likely not. In any case, what would they have been looking for? Nothing had shown up in the tests or in the X-rays. Doctor Francis was shaken. "I can't tell you how badly I feel. I'm so very sorry, I can't tell you," he said as he led them into the doctors' lounge. There was a doctor sitting in a chair with his legs hooked over the back of another chair, watching an early morning TV show. He was wearing a green delivery room outfit, loose green pants and green blouse, and a green cap that covered his hair. He looked at Howard and Ann and then looked at Doctor Francis. He got to his feet and turned off the set and went out of the room. Doctor Francis guided Ann to the sofa, sat down beside her and began to talk in a low, consoling voice. At one point he leaned over and embraced her. She could feel his chest rising and falling evenly against her shoulder. She kept her eyes open and let him hold her. Howard went into the bathroom, but he left the door open. After a violent fit of weeping, he ran water and washed his face. Then he came out and sat down at the little table that held a telephone. He looked at the telephone as though deciding what to do first. He made some calls. After a time, Doctor Francis used the telephone.

"Is there anything else I can do for the moment?" he asked them.

Howard shook his head. Ann stared at Doctor Francis as if unable to comprehend his words.

The doctor walked them to the hospital's front door. People were entering and leaving the hospital. It was eleven o'clock in the morning. Ann was aware of how slowly, almost reluctantly she moved her feet. It seemed to her that Doctor Francis was making them leave, when she felt they should stay, when it would be more the right thing to do, to stay. She gazed out into the parking lot and then turned around and looked back at the front of the hospital. She began shaking her head. "No, no," she said. "I can't leave him here, no." She heard herself say that and thought how unfair it was that the only words that came out were the sort of words used on TV shows where people were stunned by violent or sudden deaths. She wanted her words to be her own. "No," she said, and for some reason the memory of the Negro woman's head lolling on the woman's shoulder came to her. "No," she said again.

"I'll be talking to you later in the day," the doctor was saying to Howard. "There are still some things that have to be done, things that have to be cleared up to our satisfaction. Some things that need explaining."

"An autopsy," Howard said.

Doctor Francis nodded.

"I understand," Howard said. Then he said, "Oh, Jesus. No, I don't understand, Doctor. I can't, I can't. I just can't."

Doctor Francis put his arm around Howard's shoulders. "I'm sorry. God, how I'm sorry." He let go of Howard's shoulders and held out his hand. Howard looked at the hand, and then he took it. Doctor Francis put his arms around Ann once more. He seemed full of some goodness she didn't understand. She let her head rest on his shoulder, but her eyes stayed open. She kept looking at the hospital. As they drove out of the parking lot, she looked back at the hospital once more.

At home, she sat on the sofa with her hands in her coat pockets. Howard closed the door to the child's room. He got the coffee maker going and then he found an empty box. He had thought to pick up some of the child's things. But instead he sat down beside her on the sofa, pushed the box to one side, and leaned forward, arms between his knees. He began to weep. She pulled his head over into her lap and patted his shoulder. "He's gone," she said. She kept patting his shoulder. Over his sobs she could hear the coffee maker hissing in the kitchen. "There, there," she said tenderly. "Howard, he's gone. He's gone and now we'll have to get used to that. To being alone."

In a little while Howard got up and began moving aimlessly around the room with the box, not putting anything into it, but collecting some things together on the floor at one end of the sofa. She continued to sit with her hands in her coat pockets. Howard put the box down and brought coffee into the living room. Later, Ann made calls to relatives. After each call had been placed and the party had answered, Ann would blurt out a few words and cry for a minute. Then she would quietly explain, in a measured voice, what had happened and tell them about arrangements. Howard took the box out to the garage where he saw the child's bicycle. He dropped the box and sat down on the pavement beside the bicycle. He took hold of the bicycle awkwardly so that it leaned against his chest. He held it, the rubber pedal sticking into his chest. He gave the wheel a turn.

Ann hung up the telephone after talking to her sister. She was looking up another number, when the telephone rang. She picked it up on the first ring.

"Hello," she said, and she heard something in the background, a humming noise. "Hello!" she said. "For God's sake," she said. "Who is this? What is it you want?"

"Your Scotty, I got him ready for you," the man's voice said. "Did you forget him?"

"You evil bastard!" she shouted into the receiver. "How can you do this, you evil son of a bitch?"

"Scotty," the man said. "Have you forgotten about Scotty?" Then the man hung up on her.

Howard heard the shouting and came in to find her with her head on her arms over the table, weeping. He picked up the receiver and listened to the dial tone.

Much later, just before midnight, after they had dealt with many things, the telephone rang again.

"You answer it," she said. "Howard, it's him, I know." They were sitting at the kitchen table with coffee in front of them. Howard had a small glass of whisky beside his cup. He answered on the third ring.

"Hello," he said. "Who is this? Hello! Hello!" The line went dead. "He hung up," Howard said. "Whoever it was."

"It was him," she said. "That bastard. I'd like to kill him," she said. "I'd like to shoot him and watch him kick," she said.

"Ann, my God," he said.

"Could you hear anything?" she said. "In the background? A noise, machinery, something humming?"

"Nothing, really. Nothing like that," he said. "There wasn't much time. I think there was some radio music. Yes, there was a radio going, that's all I could tell. I don't know what in God's name is going on," he said.

She shook her head. "If I could, could get, my hands, on him." It came to her then. She knew who it was. Scotty, the cake, the telephone number. She pushed the chair away from the table and got up. "Drive me down to the shopping center," she said. "Howard."

"What are you saying?"

"The shopping center. I know who it is who's calling. I know who it is. It's the baker, the son-of-a-bitching baker, Howard. I had him bake a cake for Scotty's birthday. That's who's calling. That's who has the number and keeps calling us. To harass us about the cake. The baker, that bastard."

They drove out to the shopping center. The sky was clear and stars were out. It was cold, and they ran the heater in the car. They parked in front of the bakery. All of the shops and stores were closed, but there were cars at the far end of the lot in front of the cinema. The bakery windows were dark, but when they looked through the glass they could see a light in the back room and, now and then, a big man in an apron moving in and out of the white, even light. Through the glass she could see the display cases and some little tables with chairs. She tried the door. She rapped on the glass. But if the baker heard them he gave no sign. He didn't look in their direction.

They drove around behind the bakery and parked. They got out of the car. There was a lighted window too high up for them to see inside. A sign near the back door said, "The Pantry Bakery, Special Orders." She could hear faintly a radio playing inside and something — an oven door? — creak as it was pulled down. She knocked on the door and waited. Then she knocked again, louder. The radio was turned down and there was a scraping sound now, the distinct sound of something, a drawer, being pulled open and then closed.

Someone unlocked the door and opened it. The baker stood in the light and peered out at them. "I'm closed for business," he said. "What do you want at this hour? It's midnight. Are you drunk or something?"

She stepped into the light that fell through the open door. He blinked his heavy eyelids as he recognized her.

"It's you," he said.

"It's me," she said. "Scotty's mother. This is Scotty's father. We'd like to come in."

The baker said, "I'm busy now. I have work to do."

She had stepped inside the doorway anyway. Howard came in behind her. The baker moved back. "It smells like a bakery in here. Doesn't it smell like a bakery in here, Howard?"

"What do you want?" the baker said. "Maybe you want your cake? That's it, you decided you want your cake. You ordered a cake, didn't you?"

"You're pretty smart for a baker," she said. "Howard, this is the man who's been calling us. This is the baker man." She clenched her fists. She stared at him fiercely. There was a

deep burning inside her, an anger that made her feel larger
than herself, larger than either of these men.

"Just a minute here," the baker said. "You want to pick
up your three day old cake? That it? I don't want to argue
with you, lady. There it sits over there, getting stale. I'll give
it to you for half of what I quoted you. No. You want it? You
can have it. It's no good to me, no good to anyone now. It
cost me time and money to make that cake. If you want it,
okay, if you don't, that's okay too. I have to get back to
work." He looked at them and rolled his tongue behind his
teeth.

"More cakes," she said. She knew she was in control of
it, of what was increasing her. She was calm.

"Lady, I work sixteen hours a day in this place to earn a
living," the baker said. He wiped his hands on his apron. "I
work night and day in here, trying to make ends meet." A
look crossed Ann's face that made the baker move back and
say, "No trouble now." He reached to the counter and picked
up a rolling pin with his right hand and began to tap it
against the palm of his other hand. "You want the cake or
not? I have to get back to work. Bakers work at night," he
said again. His eyes were small, mean-looking, she thought,
nearly lost in the bristly flesh around his cheeks. His neck was
thick with fat.

"We know bakers work at night," Ann said. "They make
phone calls at night too. You bastard," she said.

The baker continued to tap the rolling pin against his
hand. He glanced at Howard. "Careful, careful," he said to
Howard.

"My son's dead," she said with a cold, even finality. "He
was hit by a car Monday morning. We've been waiting with
him until he died. But of course, you couldn't be expected to
know that, could you? Bakers can't know everything. Can
they, Mr. Baker? But he's dead. He's dead, you bastard!" Just
as suddenly as it had welled in her the anger dwindled, gave
way to something else, a dizzy feeling of nausea. She leaned

against the wooden table that was sprinkled with flour, put her hands over her face and began to cry, her shoulders rocking back and forth. "It isn't fair," she said. "It isn't, isn't fair."

Howard put his hand at the small of her back and looked at the baker. "Shame on you," Howard said to him. "Shame."

The baker put the rolling pin back on the counter. He undid his apron and threw it on the counter. He looked at them, and then he shook his head slowly. He pulled a chair out from under a card table that held papers and receipts, an adding machine and a telephone directory. "Please sit down," he said. "Let me get you a chair," he said to Howard. "Sit down now, please." The baker went into the front of the shop and returned with two little wrought-iron chairs. "Please sit down you people."

Ann wiped her eyes and looked at the baker. "I wanted to kill you," she said. "I wanted you dead."

The baker had cleared a space for them at the table. He shoved the adding machine to one side, along with the stacks of note paper and receipts. He pushed the telephone directory onto the floor, where it landed with a thud. Howard and Ann sat down and pulled their chairs up to the table. The baker sat down too.

"I don't blame you," the baker said, putting his elbows on the table. "First. Let me say how sorry I am. God alone knows how sorry. Listen to me. I'm just a baker. I don't claim to be anything else. Maybe once, maybe years ago I was a different kind of human being, I've forgotten, I don't know for sure. But I'm not any longer, if I ever was. Now I'm just a baker. That don't excuse my offense, I know. But I'm deeply sorry. I'm sorry for your son, and I'm sorry for my part in this. Sweet, sweet Jesus," the baker said. He spread his hands out on the table and turned them over to reveal his palms. "I don't have any children myself, so I can only imagine what you must be feeling. All I can say to you now is that I'm sorry. Forgive me, if you can," the baker said. "I'm not an evil man, I don't think. Not evil, like you said on the phone. You got to understand that what it comes down to is I don't know how to act anymore, it would seem. Please," the man said, "let me ask you if you can find it in your hearts to forgive me?"

It was warm inside the bakery. In a minute, Howard stood up from the table and took off his coat. He helped Ann from her coat. The baker looked at them for a minute and then nodded and got up from the table. He went to the oven and turned off some switches. He found cups and poured coffee from an electric coffee maker. He put a carton of cream on the table, and a bowl of sugar.

"You probably need to eat something," the baker said. "I hope you'll eat some of my hot rolls. You have to eat and keep going. Eating is a small, good thing in a time like this," he said.

He served them warm cinnamon rolls just out of the oven, the icing still runny. He put butter on the table and knives to spread the butter. Then the baker sat down at the table with them. He waited. He waited until they each took a roll from the platter and began to eat. "It's good to eat something," he said, watching them. "There's more. Eat up. Eat all you want. There's all the rolls in the world in here."

They ate rolls and drank coffee. Ann was suddenly hungry, and the rolls were warm and sweet. She ate three of them, which pleased the baker. Then he began to talk. They listened carefully. Although they were tired and in anguish, they listened to what the baker had to say. They nodded when the baker began to speak of loneliness, and the sense of doubt and limitation that had come to him in his middle years. He told them what it was like to be childless all these years. To repeat the days with the ovens endlessly full and endlessly empty. The party food, the celebrations he'd worked over. Icing knuckle-deep. The tiny wedding couples stuck into cakes. Hundreds of them, no, thousands by now.

Birthdays. Just imagine all those candles burning. He had a necessary trade. He was a baker. He was glad he wasn't a florist. It was better to be feeding people. This was a better smell anytime than flowers.

"Smell this," the baker said, breaking open a dark loaf. "It's a heavy bread, but rich." They smelled it, then he had them taste it. It had the taste of molasses and coarse grains. They listened to him. They ate what they could. They swallowed the dark bread. It was like daylight under the fluorescent trays of light. They talked on into the early morning, the high pale cast of light in the windows, and they did not think of leaving.

T. Alan Broughton

Lily

"Do you mind if I take my teeth out?"

He grinned from the bathroom doorway. Lily leaned against the padded headboard, a fringe of green sheet draped across her breasts.

"I try to be a gentleman at all times." His grin broadened to a leer.

He would have pinched her buttock again. The left one was mottled with bruises, and she was trying to figure which side of the bed to lie on.

"They get loose sometimes when I'm worked up. You wouldn't mind?"

She shrugged. The sheet slipped. He stared.

"Suit yourself, buster."

As he turned his gut swayed over the top of his boxer shorts, hand prying in his mouth. "Ah 'on't ee a 'inute."

When he closed the door all light was blocked. Under the door to the hallway came the muffled sounds of her son and the rest of his band in the living room, lolling stoned after that night's engagement. If she lay on the right of the bed and turned on her left side, only her right buttock would be accessible. She did not know if he was a squeezer or biter or sucker. She slid down in the middle of the bed and stared at the ceiling. The beer was settling in her belly as if it had rolled there in its own barrel.

I'm not unhappy, she had said to her son Burt that week. *It's just that sometimes this life sucks*. To which she added now, watching the ceiling raise and lower itself in billows, *Get a hold of yourself, Lily*.

Only a Saturday night like any other in the long winter.

Nothing on TV, Burt out with his band, the cold creeping up
her ankles, going for her knees and thighs until she wanted
to stand on a chair and scream at the goddamn floor. So
down to The Spread Eagle, a drink or two, quarters in some
slot — jukebox or bumper pool — and sometimes, like
tonight, a good Joe with money on his way north to sell this
or that in Montreal. Hell, it was different in July. More
people around, summer folks, as if the town were a big house
with all its rooms filled at last. What they saw in a village
with a dying mine, talc dust from the ore trucks coating the
maple leaves gray, she could not understand. Supposedly the
fishing. But at least in summer there was none of this rattling
around with nothing but wind, groans of the mining
machines, or a trailer truck you could hear for twenty miles
coming, twenty miles going.

When Burt twanged a note on the electric guitar, she
jolted out of a doze. The water had been running for a long
time. She sat up dizzily. Cut his wrists? Sudden remorse. A
family man. Couldn't face the loneliness anymore. She
struggled out of the covers, tangled for a moment, swung
free but off balance so that she stiff-armed the door. It
cracked back against the wall. He turned from the bathtub
where he was standing up to his bowed calves in water, face
gaping. He was still wearing his shorts.

"Jesus, lady."

"What the hell are you doing?"

His lips sucked in and puckered out over his gums. "I
don't like to offend," he mumbled. "My feet smell bad."

She did not like seeing her own bare and drooping body
in the hard fluorescence of the mirror. Her hand waved.
"You smell fine. But I'll be dead asleep soon."

As she turned away he was lifting one leg unsteadily
over the rim. When was the last time she'd had a man
without a paunch? Not that she didn't have her own. But
she'd worked on that recently. Cut out desserts at lunch.
Those candy bars at coffee breaks.

He settled on her like a sack of meal, lips blowing and flapping against her neck. But he had the right equipment, and it worked, and for all his beefy eagerness he took his time and did not pinch anymore. "Oh Jesus, oh Jesus," she rasped, settling into a solid punch and counterpunch of hips. He was not a talker either, and she liked that, the way he rolled off, slapped her once on the thigh with a lazy flipper and eased quickly into a slow puffing doze. Nothing to talk about anyway. The best part was always the languid silence afterwards, all those good muscles rippling down in slow billows into peace. She hated the ones who had to chatter on like little monkeys picking at their fleas.

She thought sleep would come easily. She was still numb with beer and whiskey chasers. Burt and his friends had settled into a stupor with only desultory jags of conversation, more like shared moans. She yawned deeply, turned on her side as she always did in preparation for that long, lazy glide to morning. In front of her but not touching was the snoring body of someone whose name she could not recall. He sold wool. She had been shown the samples of fleece in the back of the car. *Feel them. Merino. Australian. What a muff.* Burt was laughing in the other room, voice suddenly as tight as one of the strings of his guitar. She did a slow arc around the silence afterwards. The boy needed to get out of Mineville. Dead end playing for bars and graduations. Cut a record in Boston. Get into a real group somewhere, not these deadbeats. Knock it off, baby. Sleep. And she saw him in front of lean Arty on the drums, curved over that guitar as if someone had slammed it flat into his gut and he had lost all his breath, yelping *Knock it off, baby, knock it off.*

But she did not sleep. A fact could be important. You never knew. You lose a name, you lose the face, the day, the year even that you saw the face, and when it was thrust at you later, the mind stammered, went blank. She bore down hard. He sold wool. He lived in Dedham. One of his best customers was in Montreal. He rooted for the Patriots for

years but had switched to Buffalo. His wife had a hysterectomy last week and he said it was about time. Should have
done it thirty years ago. Too many mouths to feed. His name
was. Name was.

She turned on her back, angry now. She did not care
what this man's name was. But the principle counted. She
might never see him again, unless he passed through later,
and then he would have to take his chances because there
might be something better going on that night. Or she
might not need him or anyone. Hysterectomy of the mind.
No. Not enough. How did you cut out the impulse? And
anyway he usually went through northern Vermont, some
woolen mill there, but too much snow this week.

Maybe if she could recall this one's name she could trace
back through all the others to remember the faces, figures,
even circumstances around the man who had written a letter
to her just this week. She had his name, but not his face. But
The Spread Eagle, so known to her that she could even now
count the mugs on the wall, list the exact sequence of beer
labels on the knobs of the taps, would not give up any of its
own concreteness to the man. And the jukebox would be
howling as if to mock her, *Ah'm jes' yo lonesum luvsum
buddy fo' tonigh'*.

She pushed herself up slowly to sit with her back against
the cold naugahyde. Gently. Not to wake him. So randy he
would probably want her again and she was in no mood for
that. Jim Guyette's voice started whirling around in the other
room, up, spiraling down. He was always on some pill that
pushed him high when the others were gliding low, and he
would fly off like a bat, plunging against the walls, the screen
door until a sufficient opening was there for him to skitter
into dawn in his father's battered truck. She groped in the
drawer of the bedside table, swung her legs slowly over the
edge and lifted herself from the bed. His snore cut off, he
floundered sideways with a moan, then began breathing
steadily again. She padded to the bathroom.

The nightlight was strong enough to let her read and leave her body as only a vague presence in the mirror and chrome. His teeth made a crescent gleam on the counter. She skipped the first part, about how none of the managers would buy chocolate turtles anymore now that some lady in Poughkeepsie was suing because she had bitten into one and found the first joint of a finger, flesh and bone mummified in nougat. Used to be the basic item on Shammalian Company's list. But in the long last paragraph the handwriting became very small, not just because the bottom of the page was approaching, but as if the words, so quickly, loosely scrawled above, were being picked up, held by thumb and forefinger, then carefully pinned in place.

Well, I guess you're wondering why I'm writing all this. Maybe you get lots of letters from guys like me, if you don't take that bad because I don't mean to imply you sleep with anybody that comes along. What I'm trying to say is, you're not just anybody to me. Like it says in the old song, I can't get you off my mind. I been thinking a lot. My life has been a mess a long time now. Always on the road, a marriage that got busted years ago and a kid I never see because she ran off with a Allied Moving man, had his own rig, day after the divorce. There's lots more to say about that but I won't. And I won't keep it from you that I try to enjoy myself on the road. But things don't give me the same kick anymore. I just about puked in Buffalo. At myself, I mean, waking up the next day and thinking about where I was, who I'd been for all these years. It wasn't her fault. Now I been sleeping alone ever since. So you see, I had to write. Do you think you could drop me a line? I'd kind of like to see you on my next trip through. Maybe you feel the same way. Course, maybe you don't remember. I'd hate to make a real fool of myself. But I'd sure like to get a handle on things.
  Lots of love,
      Crandal
  P.S. Call me Cran, like you did.

Her stomach knotted. *Cran, like you did.* She pressed her fingers against her eyelids so hard that small white dots sparked wildly. The afternoon the letter came she had been amused. By dinner she was getting worried. She had assumed that sometime when she was not trying to think of him directly, he would pop out, like a word you wanted for a letter and woke up yelling in the middle of the night long after you had dropped the poor substitute in the mailbox. She had waited four days. Nothing was coming. Could that mean her mind was going? She had held the strainer over the sink, staring at her neighbor's bathtub virgin until the spaghetti was hopelessly congealed. Then she was angry at that Cran, Crandal, C. Denton on the envelope. What right did he have to go making something simple so complicated? But *to get a handle on things* was the phrase that stuck with her. Burt had pushed his plate aside. *Geesum, Mom, what's wrong with you lately? This stuff tastes like soapsuds.* She lifted her fork. No wonder. Instead of the parmesan beside it on the counter, she had sprinkled Comet.

"Hon', you in there?"

The door gave slightly toward her. His paw curled around the side of it. For one mean moment, she imagined shoving the door with her foot, crushing the fingers against the jamb.

"I gotta pee." He cleared his throat.

Hell, it wasn't his fault that even as she'd gone through the usual motions at the bar that night — let him buy her drinks, laid off on the bumper pool so he wouldn't lose all the games — she had sensed herself standing away from it all, watching her motions. *Things don't give me the same kick anymore.* Goddamn the pushy little candyman anyway. Who'd he think he was writing out of nowhere, making other people feel their lives were a mess?

The voice coughed. "You OK in there?"

She stood, put the letter in the medicine cabinet and flushed the toilet. When she pulled the door he was leaning against the jamb, everything drooping — his eyelids and lower lip, sagging shoulders and belly that slung down nearly concealing the black furze. His face tried to gather some expression.

"Thanks. Gotta go you gotta go."

"What's your name?" she said flatly as he sidled past.

"Abe."

"Abe what?"

"Cronk."

When he came back to bed she was still sitting up. He lay on his back and put one hand onto the top of her thigh but that was all.

"They never sleep out there, do they?"

She could tell he had put his teeth in.

"Sleeps all day," she muttered, sorry she had not bought a pack of cigarettes before they left the bar. He smoked cigars. But she was trying to give up smoking.

He breathed in slowly through his nose. "I smell good stuff."

She was used to the odor of burning hemp. All day it clung to the padded furniture, mingled with her cooking smells.

"You wouldn't be able to get me some now? I'd pay. I sleep like a log when I have one."

"I don't mess around in Burt's life."

"So who's messing?"

"I mean I don't use the stuff myself. I don't much approve, I guess."

"I could go out, see if he would. Save you the trouble."

He rose on one elbow. She imagined him in his trousers only, belt unbuckled, Guyette hooting around him. She flung back the covers and groped in the closet for her bathrobe, tied it tightly and clutched the collar to her neck. "You hold still."

Their limbs and pale faces were lifted out of the dark by swatches of purple from the streetlight. The only thing moving was the slim trail of smoke, a spark in someone's face, passed on to an outstretched hand.

"Hi, Mom. Can't sleep?"

She could hardly breathe in the heavy air and her eyes watered as she blinked into the dark.

"You guys are going to suffocate. Don't you want to crack the door open?"

"Too frigging cold." That was Guyette, more mellow than she had expected.

"Don't want to waste a puff. Your well-insulated room saves lots of cash."

"Is that Donny Cates?" She looked at the unlaced boots where the voice had come from.

"Yes'm. Back from Mex. We're celebrating. Brought my pals a gift."

"I wish you'd quit corrupting my son," she said without expression, and even Burt hooted. She crossed her arms tightly because the nylon was too cool. "Can I see you for a minute, Burt?"

He heaved up from the couch, once again that unrecognizable hulk, no longer a boy except in her persistent ability to call up his childhood from memory. Not seeing his face, just those rolled shoulders, the permanent stoop from having outgrown his companions at every age, the shock of hair at the peak of his head that never lay flat except after a shower, she too easily saw his father who would have been sleeping it off on the couch, would have heaved up in the same way at dawn if she had stormed out of their bedroom furious with a night of waiting for him to relent and come to bed. She would have been risking his fists, and if he had his boots on, bruises that would show black on her thighs for a month. But usually there would be the gruff curse, a lamp toppling in the wake of his stagger, sound of his motorcycle exploding against whatever peace it would chase all the way down the highway to the mines. And once, so far beyond that he never came back.

"You coming?"

He was in the kitchen waiting for her. She shook her head. Asleep on her feet?

She did not turn on the light. "What time is it?"

"Must be about three."

She paused, but the image of Abe, persisting and padding out into this other world with his dumb face and oily ways, shoved her on.

"Listen, could you give me a joint? I mean sell me one."

He breathed in sharply, and when his voice said, "Huh?" it was as if she had booted him in the gut.

"He says it helps him sleep."

"Hold on." Burt's palm came down on the counter and he leaned forward. "You want me to go in there and get one for you guys?"

Wrong. She knew it. But now she was defensive. "What's the matter with that? He'll pay for it."

"The matter? Gees, Mom. What the hell do you want my pals to think?"

"Oh, forget it." She was genuinely ashamed. It mattered to him and she should have known. "Look. He might come out and try to buy one. He's not too swift."

"Who does the joker think he is? You tell him to stay in there if he knows what's good for him."

"He's my guest. He can go where he wants."

"Well, I got guests too. And I don't care to have my guests meet your guests."

They stood absolutely still. She wanted to say *You don't talk to your mother like that. This is my goddamn house, who pays the bills?* But the same fear that had checked her again and again all year cut off her anger. He talked too often about leaving, really leaving, not just those gigs for a few days, not even a long stay in Boston, but gone, as far as Chicago, California, God knew where. He and the group had stayed in Montreal for two weeks. Toward the end she had not been able to sleep, as if sleep depended on half-waking at night to hear them stumbling in, Burt saying, *Cool it, cool it,* the sound from time to time of the refrigerator opening, slamming shut when someone went for a beer.

"Sorry, Burt. I'll tell him it's all used up."

"Shit, Mom. You oughto know better. What would they think?" His voice rose, reminding her of those first years of adolescence, the wheedling reprimands.

"I said I'm sorry."

"Forget it. Look, maybe I can sneak . . ."

"Don't. Close up soon, will you? I just want the guy to sleep it off."

His hand, that beefy, always slightly moist but gentle hand, rested on her shoulder as they turned back to the other room. They had argued often but never struck each other, not even when he was a child. He stopped before they reached the living room. Donny was muttering some endless story about a bust in Mexico.

"Mom, you gotta start to get a handle on things. What's going to happen when I go? Now, don't get all worked up on me, but lately, things are getting pretty screwy."

Her pulse jumped. He had never talked to her like that. Now what? Weirdoes writing letters, her own son saying her life was a mess. She wanted to tell him about the letter, but he had started walking and she followed to stay under the hand.

"'Night, Mrs. Shackett," Arty's voice said as Burt sloughed off to his place on the couch. "We'll keep it real quiet."

She could not find her voice to answer, waved an arm, and shut the door behind her. He was sleeping so deeply that he did not even stir when she slipped under the covers.

He was like all the others when they woke. Yes, sure, some coffee would be great. Don't go to no trouble, now. Looked bleary, did not quite focus on her, shoveled down some eggs and toast, probably burned his lips on the coffee, said something grinning about *Swell time, some gal, we'll be in touch,* and all the time Lily stared at him intensely but not really concentrating on his features or gestures. She was trying to see if he could be dissolved and regrouped in the shape of Crandal Denton. Once when he paused to sneeze, his face gaping, hand held ready, she had a flash of detail, a nose or chin or maybe it was a scarred cheek, but she could not keep the image in mind. " 'Scuse," he muttered, picking the end of his tie off the plate.

Only after he left did she get around to reading the folded note from Burt stuck with the beetle magnet on the refrigerator door.

> Mom,
>   Don't wake me till next month.
> Sorry for last night. Maybe if we talk soon.
> Anyway, forgot to say Gramps had the nursing home call. Wants to see you tomorrow, hell, today, I mean Sunday.
> Me and the guys decided we almost got enough loot to try a few weeks on the road. Maybe Memphis? Friend of Donny's Dad owns a bar there. We'll talk.

She cleared the table, started to rinse dishes, saw the slow straight drop of big snowflakes, and turned away from the sink and window. She drove the eighty miles to Greendale Rest Haven with the radio on so loud that even the passing trailer trucks did not cut through the mat of sounds. Her own son would give her advice? Lily sang when she knew the words, hummed when she did not, but not out of joy.

"They're trying to kill me again," he whispered in her ear, his unblinking eye in its heavy folds staring wide, and then he pushed her away, face dead because a nurse had swished into the room. She stooped to lift the blanket that had slipped from his knees, white cloth stretching across the expanse of her shapeless buttocks.

"Accusing us again, Mr. Mongeon? Now is that any way to talk about your friends?"

"Spy," he hissed, pulling the blanket up to his neck.

The nurse winked at Lily. Lily stared back. She did not believe her father, but she did not care for the nurse's condescension. Both father and daughter were silent until the nurse had finished her quick tour of the room, neatening the bed, dropping some used tissue in the wastebasket. Lily suspected the whole thing was done for her since she had never seen more than one nurse on duty at a time in the rambling wood-frame house. She probably dozed somewhere and waited for a relative to arrive. As for Mr. Briggs, the director, Lily saw him only on holiday occasions. He seemed to spend most of the winter in Florida.

Left alone with him, Lily said, "They won't kill you."

He looked at her with half-closed eyes. "How do you know?"

"Intercepted messages. Orders from the president. He has planted a taster in the kitchen."

"Ah-ha." His hand came down on his knee, his face thrust toward her. "He remembered."

"How could he forget, Pops? You and Bob Hope and Anita Bryant and all the others doing their duty for the boys."

"Still, they're mean here," he said querulously. "Couldn't we just go home?"

She shook her head. "Can't guarantee your safety there."

He looked sadly at the door as if he could see someone standing beyond it. "That bad. Well, I guess we all have our duties. Dull here, though. I'd rather be entertaining the troops."

Suddenly his hands, palms up, were snatching at the air, and she could almost see the balls, weights, cups, even glasses that he sometimes juggled in his act. And he could do it with a ball balanced on his nose. The hands stopped abruptly and he folded them in his lap, turned that other face to her — old, tired, but not harried.

"How's Burt?"

She talked, he listened. It had taken her years to move so easily with his different lives, but now they did it like two experienced dancers and she even thought sometimes of Fred Astaire and some lithe partner swooping in elegant arcs, switching with ease from adagio to jazzy presto. She kept a close look on his face. She could tell almost immediately when some vein or artery back there switched off or flooded open. His eyes would narrow, that cagey smile would take his lips, and they would be back in a world of troops and enemies, spies in the closet.

"I wish I could hear his band. But I suppose they make noise like some of that monkey chatter we see on TV here. Is he ugly now like them too?"

She cleaned Burt up in the next sentence or two, made him into a regular Lawrence Welk. She paused, groping for a new center of conversation, but before she could start talking about her fuel bill he had dozed, head sliding forward like an abandoned puppet. She sat back. Depending on how long he slept, she would stay or go. He did not seem to mind that, never referred to her vanishing. She was certain that often he did not know whether she was really there anyway, and it was eerie to think that at times she was there for him when she was actually elsewhere.

She had brought the letter and it stiffly shaped the pocket of her coat. Not that she would have shared it with him, but she wanted to stop somewhere on the way home, read it again over a cup of coffee, or maybe having it sitting there would be a reminder. But Crandal Denton did not rise. She shifted nervously, her foot half asleep.

The sunlight found a long seam between gray plates of cloud and as if flicked on, it struck the windowsill, the arm of his chair, and ended on the palm, a half-circle of motionless hand. The fingers were laxly spread, joints swollen so that they touched, but what she saw were the spaces between where the light passed through. They were the hands of magic. In his black cutaway, the starched white shirt, he would be the only person visible on the stage, silver and red balls weaving and flashing in air, an elegant pattern of atoms that the hands did not even seem to touch as they shaped their own dance. The sun was cut off. For a moment her eyes still saw the lit impression of a hand, and the dulled image slowly taking its place was worn like a glove. She stood quietly, took one last look at his bowed head, and walked away.

She did not stop on the way home, partly because the clouds merged, snow began falling in small flakes, dense and unblown so she knew this was no flurry. But also she could not remember in time that she wanted to pause, so all the usual diners and bars rose, streaked by, lifting a small regret, reminding her to stop at the next one, but then she would sink into a nearly blank daze of humming wheels, occasional cigarette, and snow making separate trees and bushes unfamiliar. She tried the radio, but it would not work, jolted it with the heel of her hand, but even that did not produce the usual yelp back into voice or music. The Mineville sign was caked with new snow. It was dusk and no one was on the road. A cluster of houses swept by, the turn-off to the mine, the street to her own house, and she kept driving all the way to the junction before she stopped at the Highway Department depot, made a U-turn, and let the car idle by the side of the road. She leaned her head on the back of the seat and stared at the ceiling. Her hands were trembling in her lap.

The house was dark. She listened to the slight ticking of the engine as it cooled. No footsteps in the snow to the front porch. She paused in the kitchen to write a note. *Tired. Going to sleep. Keep it quiet.* Who wanted to eat or talk? She was relieved he was out. She did not turn on any lights and when she was safely in her bedroom, she flung disheveled sheets and blankets into some sort of layered order, discarded her clothes, and curled into the center of the bed, falling asleep as soon as her body stopped shivering.

She had forgotten to set the alarm and woke late, her body lunging out of bed in shocked reflex. Although she had not waked at all in the night, she was unrested, certain she had gained weight in the past hours. She groped for her clothes. No coffee. She noticed Burt's door was open, his bed still made, but she did not have time to think about that. The car lights shone palely against the dull morning. She had left them on, and by now the battery was too weak to turn the cold engine. She cursed, stepped out and slammed the car door, locking her keys inside. For a moment she stood perfectly still, clutching the collar of her coat tightly to her neck, staring straight down at the toes of her boots, and then she closed her eyes and breathed deeply through her open mouth, letting the metallic air sear her throat and lungs.

The office was only a short walk anyway. She would have to get hold of Burt, tell him to leave the house door open, maybe pry the car window. What if you did that to yourself when you were miles away from anywhere? She imagined herself on a deserted highway, snow falling heavily around her. She had walked off the road for a moment. Now she could not even find her way back to the useless car. There was only snow, a rough stubble of weed and brambles poking through, and she did not have any gloves.

She pulled the cover off her typewriter. The half-finished letter was there. It would have to be flattened when she took it out. She reached for the earphones.

"You're late." Cliff's voice from his office. For the first time since she had stumbled in, she noticed that the two easy chairs and magazine table where clients were supposed to sit and wait were gone. The carpet had dusty squares where they had been sitting.

"Car wouldn't start." She held the earphones in her lap. It was the first time she had spoken that morning and her voice was thick and drowsy.

"For two hours?"

"What time is it?"

"Ten."

His figure was in the doorway to his office but she kept staring away toward the blank space where even the lamp was gone.

"Repossessed," he said dully. "You look awful."

"When?"

"Early this morning. Luckily no one else was here. They were waiting when I came. Of course, if someone had been here, we'd still have the furniture, I guess."

"I thought that vice president from the mines was going to call you this weekend."

"He did."

"No go?"

Cliff was tall, but he always seemed taller because of a slight forward stoop that made him look as if he were afraid of clobbering his head on low pipes in a cellar. His eyes never quite focussed together and in spite of working for him for five years, even of grappling with him on desktops and beds during the first year until he went back to his wife, Lily could never remember which eye was really looking at her.

"Didn't like my plans. Or his wife didn't. She said the kitchen was on the wrong side of the house. Wanted to see the mountain from her sink window. I said that was a waste. He said he understood my feelings but they had found some-one else she could work with more closely. I said I didn't want to get close to her anyway. He hung up. You look a mess."

She pulled the letter, balled it up, prepared to disconnect the tapes. "No need to type that, then."

"No need." He was lighting the next cigarette from the butt that dashed a white trail down his tie.

"How long do we have before the next phase?" she asked.

"I have two weeks, the bank says. One contract is all they need."

"Prospects?"

"I haven't heard the phone ring yet."

The mammoth gray trucks began their day-long rumble through town, loads of talc on their way to processing. In winter it was more bearable with the snow to muffle the weighted pounding of tires, to hold down the clouds of pale dust left in the swirl of wake.

"And me?"

"I should have called, but I chickened out."

"That bad?"

He stooped to grind the butt on the side of her wastebasket. "Noon."

He kept grinding well past the necessary point. His hair was not thinning up there anymore, it was gone. He went to the window to stand with his back to her. The jacket rode awkwardly up one hip. His wife always bought him ill-fitting clothes to exaggerate his dowdier qualities.

"I've got a check for the whole day for you, though. And unemployment can be arranged for a while."

"Thanks. Loads."

"Might be temporary, you know."

But she had watched the spiraling descent for two years since the branch of a large architectural firm had opened in nearby Pine Grove.

"Mind if I use the typewriter for a while?"

The shoulders shrugged. "Don't jam it. They'll be coming for that this afternoon."

She laughed harshly, a bark. He turned, hands in his back pockets. His face drooped, shoulders slumped, elbows out, he looked a total loser. But he always had. Someone in the bar once had explained it to her. *Look, that guy's face, you see?* He had pointed at Jack Semple who was sitting in a daze over a sudsy mug. *It's the way their eyes, eyebrows, lips, go down. I'm telling you. I studied up on it in a book I bought at the Grand Union. It's called the art of physiognomy. A face like that is doomed. All the signs say down, down, down.* She had argued. In bed that night he had read her face and foreseen good times, much pleasure, no hang-ups. The next day she had looked at Cliff and seen nothing but down.

"Don't make it harder on me."

"Who is? I won't jam it."

"I'll take you to lunch."

"No thanks."

Another truck tromped by, jabbing its airbrakes with a squeal.

"Fucking talc," he muttered., "I've got powder up my ass," and he half-closed the door to his office.

She cranked in the paper, their best with the elegant watermark. She could cross out the business heading, put her own address. The typewriter hummed at her.

Dear Crandal Denton.

She ripped it out, lifted another sheet.

Dear Cran,

You've got some nerve, writing a woman out of the blue like that. What do I know about you? Why do you think I'd remember you after so much time? You treat someone like a one-night stand and then you expect them to be sitting around waiting? Well, I haven't been. You weren't the last, you know.

There. That's what pisses me most. I always say what I feel so there's no getting misunderstood later. But maybe I don't see what you're after, and if you didn't mean it that way, like above, then I'm sorry. You don't sound too hot. Actually I understand that plenty. My life's on the bum right now too. I'm sitting at my desk here at work for the last time. Laid off. Hah. If I'm not laid on, I'm laid off. I saw it coming for some time, but what can you do? There's no jobs in this f-ing town and the mine dropped half its people in the fall too. On top of that my car's dead and the keys are locked in it and I don't know where the hell my son was last night. Maybe you met him. Burt. Electric guitar.

Tell the truth, I don't remember you and that bugs the hell out of me. I used to remember all the faces, most of the names. I wish you hadn't written because now I'm wondering — what the hell's going on, Lily? Is it the booze, the late nights, or just getting old or worrying too much about where the next pork chop comes from? Maybe we ought to get together some time. Cry over some beers. Jesus.

It's worse than all that, though. Sometimes . . .

Lily paused. Her fingers had done a steady jig, her eyes not even focussing to check if it was coming out right. But she could usually feel the mistakes before she saw them, a jammed key or a finger poking the wrong letter. Now the words appeared and she had to read because she really was not sure what she was about to say.

. . . I get scared. Sometimes I feel like I'm walking around in the woods where the old mines used to be and I don't see the red signs that say Danger — Abandoned Shaft. Sometimes hunters don't see them in snowstorms. They just fall in.

She pulled the letter out slowly, took the pen and signed it *Lily* on the bottom. She did not want to proofread it. On the envelope she typed the address, copying it off the letter she still carried in her pocket, and then she took a stamp from the dispenser. She thought about pocketing the rest of the roll, but did not.

"I'm going to the P.O. and home." She put on her coat. No answer. "You send me the check."

His chair squeaked. "Lily?" The voice was so quiet she had to lean toward the opening.

"What?"

"I'm sorry."

She waited, but that was all.

"Not your fault, buddy. It hurts you more than it hurts me."

A sigh. The squeak. He would be leaning back with his hands meshed on his belly, face as down as a basset's.

She walked the street to the post office, past the row of boutiques, shuttered and closed until summer. She stayed across the street from the grocery store because she did not want to be trapped into small talk. In the post office where the heat had fogged all the windows, air heavy with Gertrude Mack's acrid sweat and her dim bulk moving like a slow cow grazing behind the stacks of little windows, Lily slipped her letter through the slot and then checked her own box. The oil bill. She stuffed that in her pocket without opening it. Already she was two months behind. A letter. Holiday Inn. Crandal Denton.

She moved away from the boxes to the writing counter where she could spread out the letter and read with her back to the door. She breathed once deeply, staring at the triple shots of the Wanted whose eyes were always shut off even though they stared directly forward.

Dear Lily Shackett,
If I could of, I would of taken back the letter and I am hoping it didn't cause you to think I am too crazy or something. Actually, I am, but that is no reason to go getting crazy with someone you hardly know. So since I did mail the last letter, I got to face the facts and try to apologize at least and hope you'll let me tell you maybe how come I got sort of crazy.
You see, here's what happened.

Lily heard the door swinging open, shut, open, shut, voices, a cold draft of air by her ankles, but she did not look around. For a moment she also could not proceed. Why was her heart beating so fast, a knotting across her chest as if she were furious or terribly sad?

When I wrote you, something big was about to happen to me and I guess I couldn't face it. My kid was coming to see me. He's sixteen and when I got to the motel here there was this message from his mother that I was supposed to call her. I lied a little about all that. She did run off, and I never see the kid, but I write and sometimes my ex lets me know how the boy is doing. It's just that I'm careful never to get the route that takes me to Houston because I'm scared what I'd do if I saw the bugger she married. I mean, there just never was any other woman for me but her.

She'd traced me down thru the company. Seems my son put it to her. Either he was going to get to see me, or he was going to run off from home and bum around the country looking for me. She decided better she should let him see me than he should go off on his own into a world where nothing good is waiting for most people, especially kids. Christ, it freaked me. Hearing her voice. Knowing the next day Ben, that's his name, would be at the airport.

What I wrote was true. You come back to me often, and right then like a hot flash. See, I remembered you had a kid and how I wished I could of talked to him more than to say hello-goodbye when I got up in the night. And you had a swell way with him. I listened through the door when you had to tell him and his friends to cool it. I wanted to ask you what it was like to live alone with the kid like that, bringing him up without a dad. But we had too much else to do and it was fun.

"Hello, Lily."

She snapped her head around. Pud, the barman. She waved. He grinned, did not come over. The face straight ahead of her was heavily jowled, one ear asymmetrically lower than the other. He seemed adenoidal, mouth slightly open. Shot two policemen in Moline. Hijacking and kidnapping.

Anyway, I went to the airport. She'd forgot to tell me which flight, and I couldn't call back, afraid I'd get that goddamned homebreaker on the line. I met all the planes from Houston. I didn't think clearly till I got there how I hadn't seen him for ten years and he wouldn't look like he did when he was a little kid. It got so I was wandering around stopping everyone that looked his age. Most of them thought I was a pervert or moony or something. I figured I ought to wear a sign. About ten that night I hadn't eaten and I was going crazy. I kept seeing him when he was five getting off a plane and being lost and it would all be my fault. I never been so lonely in my life.

I found him though. Or he found me. I'd about given up. I felt this hand on my shoulder and I looked up and a guy about six-three was looking down at me. "You're my dad, aren't you?" It was some shock. For a minute I thought he was the meanest looking thing I'd ever seen. Big jaw, scruffy hair on his face, a kind of caved-in looking nose because he plays basketball and some kid in the championship last year tried to put an elbow through his head. But soon I felt good. If my ex had kept a picture of me all that time, maybe she still had a little buzz for me somewhere.

Well, I won't go on. We're getting along great now and I feel lots better. Suddenly that night in the middle of a talk we were having (he didn't like that asshole his mom married either, says he cheats all the time on her) I thought of how I mailed that letter to you. I jumped up. It was like I could see how stupid it all was, you getting a letter from some guy you had one night of fun with, going on about how he couldn't forget you and you probably having a good laugh. I deserved that, so I don't mind. But I wanted to explain. Feels like things are changing for better. I've got my son now, and I'm going to keep him if he wants. Who knows, maybe me and Clair will even have a talk before long.

It wasn't crazy, Lily, because I do remember you, and you are something special. But you're right to think Big Deal, who does he think he is? Anyway, I promise I won't embarrass you like the letter said I would. They changed my route to the West Coast so I'm going to live in San Diego and I won't be back your way. I'm thinking of taking Ben to Hawaii first.

Thanks for listening, Cran.

She put her palm flat over the top of the letter, not slapping but pressing down as if she could shove it under water. *Son of a bitch, son of a bitch*, a voice was saying in her, and she could not see the kidnapper clearly anymore. She strode to the window.

"Gert."

The broad heap of flesh in its sack of clothes turned slowly from the mailbag. She trundled to the window, unexpressive eyes and tiny mouth lost in the jowled melon of her head.

"I dropped a letter in the slot. Could you give it back? Forgot something I want to add."

Somewhere under all that flesh was a neck because the face swiveled slightly from side to side. "No way. Regala-shuns."

"What regulations? It's got my name on the outside. Not postmarked yet. It's mine."

"Can't do it, Lily." An asthmatic voice came out of the barely parted lips, but it was deep, firm. "Fed'rul regala-shuns. Once it's in the box, it's mailed. You can fill out a request and I'll hold the letter till the super up to the Forks OK's it."

The bag to Gertrude's right was clipped to its wheeled bin under the slot, and Lily was certain that was her envelope on top.

"Oh, c'mon, Gert. It's just me."

But the head was shaking. Suddenly Lily was intensely aware of the great dark blotches of sweat around the under-arms of the woman's smock, of the way her body sloped out-ward on all sides from the neckless head, and Lily's own body was swelling, all her organs crushed by the leaden weight of proliferating cells.

"Forget it," she said weakly and stumbled toward the door as fast as she could.

The Gordon's Office Supply truck was already outside Cliff's when she walked by. She should have stopped at the grocery store, but the thought of food nauseated her. From the end of the street she could see the distant driveway, her car tucked close to the porch. Might as well let it sit. She would not have the money to feed it with gas for a while. Pops would have to fight the enemy alone or discuss strategy with her at long distance. She wished she could recall Denton's face so she could give it a swift kick and punt it out of sight forever. Not seeing him made it impossible to dismiss the whole stupid business.

The front door was unlocked. She paused in the kitchen. Burt was bumping around in his bedroom.

"Burt?"

The noise stopped. His head and shoulders appeared at the far end of the hall. "Dressing. I been looking for you. Gotta hurry. They're coming for me."

She could not breathe. She had always feared he and his friends would be busted for something. She would see a three-headed Burt on the post office wall glaring out at her. A lot of it would be her fault.

"What have you done?" she wailed.

He came out buckling his pants, shoes untied. "Done? What the hell's the matter?"

"Who's coming for you?"

"Roy, Arty. We've swung the deal, Mom. Chicago. Ten days engagement if the first two nights go good. Maybe more."

She sat heavily at the kitchen table. "Christ. Thanks for the warning."

His grin was dying fast. "Aw, c'mon. How did I know? This guy phoned Arty, was trying to get him all yesterday. Chrissake, it's a big break. The Ramrods got their start there. Agents keep an eye on the place, and . . ."

"What the hell am I supposed to do without you? This big place, the fucking winter, goddamn snow, goddamn idiot town." She stopped. Her voice was rising steadily in pitch and volume as if on the increasing velocity of her heartbeat. His face had gathered into a truculent pucker. "And where were you last night?"

"I thought you'd understand. I thought you'd be proud. We might make it. And we celebrated at the Forks, slept at Arty's place."

"Make it. Make what? Bumming around for the rest of your life from joint to joint, and I mean both kinds. Shoveling that freaking garbage to a bunch of drunk pigs? How are you going to meet some nice gal, how can I watch you burn out your head with the stuff that goes in and out of it night after night?"

She had never liked their rock, always told him they might at least go legitimate, get into Country-Western. But even she knew she was not saying anything she meant now, and her anger was gone before he could push back at her.

"I'm sorry. Pack up and go. You're old enough to look out for yourself."

She watched the angry responses melt away in his breathing, the few hesitant attempts to start a sentence that halted until he said simply, "I gotta hurry," and turned back to his bedroom.

She sat for a while, listening to the furnace go on and off, thinking of how it was guzzling the oil out of her half-empty tank. Of course it was true that Burt had hardly travelled out of Mineville at all, not like her childhood with Pops, those tours with the little circuses to fair after fair all summer long. She remembered the relief when at last she was old enough to say no, she wasn't coming, she only wanted to stay in Mineville and he could come back when he wanted. *Little Mom*, he called her then, and always came back.

Burt flushed the toilet, reappeared dragging his backpack, the sinisterly misshapen guitar case. He stood awkwardly between the two objects.

"It won't be long. I'll call."

She breathed deeply. "Just don't get in trouble, will

you? I didn't bring you up for trouble."

But he was not listening. "Cliff told me."

She shrugged. "It was a long time coming."

"Maybe we'll hit the chips, Mom. I could send you some cash."

She looked at him hard. "I'm on my own. No son of mine is going to pay my unemployment."

They both heard the car rattle in, horn honking. She did not stand. He lifted his pack and guitar.

"Tell Gramps to hang in."

"No one tells Gramps what to do."

He grinned. "You too."

The door swung open, Arty grabbed the sack, yelled, " 'Lo, Miz Shackett. Come on, you spastic," Burt turned as if he were being whirled off by the current of a flooded river, his face wide-eyed and mouth open, and the door closed as the blast of cold air reached her.

For a long time she sat hardly moving, so weary that she was certain she was not even thinking except for thinking about how she was not thinking. Then she dozed. When she began to move around the house the rooms were already dusky. She had left the porch light on all day. In the living room she touched the television switch but did not turn it. Finally she went to her bureau, groped for the wallet tucked between layers of pantyhose. Four hundred dollars. Enough to get by. She would go down to the mine office tomorrow. See if there was anything doing.

With cold fury she remembered the key in the locked car. She had no talent for wheedling the window with hangers, was angry at Burt as if he should have known, then at the car itself. She took the flashlight and stood in the driveway shining it through the window at the keys where the ignition held one embedded, the rest hanging in their case. Like a scrotum without balls, she thought, remembering some traveller years ago who had joked with her about that and had sung a dirty song at her with a nasal whine, *I'm gonna stick my key in, baby, and turn you on.*

Her hands were cold but her body flared back at the frozen air. She walked stiffly into the house, went to the tool
chest by the cellar door and plucked out the hammer. Back
by the car she paused, then lifted and swung. The head plunged through. The glass cracked and hazed in an intricate
web. She swung again, slow, methodical strokes until the
whole side window had shattered in and pieces of it hung
meshed toward the seat. Then she reached in, yanked out the
keys, and clutched them in her fist. She stood by the sink,
shivering uncontrollably until she was warm again. She put
the hammer in the dishdrainer and went to change her
clothes.

Lily ate two dill pickles and a bowl of Pud's soup which
was always the same. They called it the Pud Muddle because
before the pot was empty he added to it. He liked to call it
Century Soup. Then she settled in for a night of serious
drinking which meant slow, steady consumption, none of
that nervous gulping she could get into on nights when she
came late and had too much catching up to do. Hardly anyone was there. Monday night, and only the steadys would
drift in. But there was always the shift at the mine which
meant one group stopping on their way to work, the other on
their way home. She knew most of the men, and some women were among them now too. On winter nights like this
they tended to stay longer before going home to sleep as if
the house was another kind of shaft, not much warmer and
full of its own hazards.

She talked with Pud when he wanted, talked with Wilbur the town "Idiot" who only looked dumb but was smart
enough to get a free ride all his life, listened to Monty Davis
who had been demoted to the bulldozer and wanted someone to help unload his bile. All the time like a gentle hum
her mind droned on, telling her things were looking bad.
But she was not about to complain. The pickles were arguing
with her soup. She sent more whiskey to quiet things down.

At about nine she noticed the man three stools down the bar where it turned — big-boned, lean, and tall enough so he tended to hunch over his drink and still look bigger than anyone around him. She closed her eyes. Knew him from two, three years ago. But not his name, or what he did. Jesus. What if that were Crandal Denton? She opened her eyes. He was looking at her. The beaked, rocky face let out a single wide grin and then extinguished it. No. Not Denton. But whoever he was, he had been all right. Didn't have a paunch.

They went through the usual "remember me's?" the drinks, yeh, he was still working for Adelphia Fasteners, our motto, "Get a Good Grip on Yourself," and she didn't look a day older, never had forgotten that night two, three years ago, raining in mid-January and he'd coasted sideways all the way out of town. Sure, she'd have some drinks, and after that, who knew — free as a bird, a fucking spread eagle, no a vulture, who cared, but it was great being up so high and shitting on the rest of the world. He laughed. Pud laughed. She started drinking too fast, and her head would not stop humming. "It's a long way down from up here," she said hazily, and Glen, that was his name, looked at Pud and both of them looked at her and she shrugged as if they were too dumb to understand.

They were halfway through their tenth game of bumper pool when she came down with a thump, all the wind knocked out of her. She leaned on the table. Glen played with severe concentration, his seamed brow greased with sweat. He was waiting for her to move away.

"I remember," she said out loud to the small square of patched green.

"My shot." He was elbowing her away because she had left a sweet set-up.

"No, wait. I remember the son of a bitch."

He looked at her with dazed eyes, leaning into the cone of light.

"Who?

Denton was wearing a Red Sox baseball cap on the back of his head. When he smiled he looked like Mickey Rooney, a kid, and not much bigger than that. He had a nervous hitch with one shoulder, even in his sleep, and when he made love to her he paddled over her body, all flippers and flukes and deep dives followed by leaps for air. She had laughed the whole time, felt as if someone were tickling her all over and she were rolling, rolling in grass to get away from all the pokes and jiggles. She started laughing now, had to lean her butt on the table, nearly doubled up. When she stood straight, wiping her eyes, he was staring down at her.

"Oh, never mind," she moaned.

Pud too was staring, his rag on the counter, and Wilbur, eyes crossed, hoping to get the joke.

"My shot," he said doggedly.

She started to stand away, looked over her shoulder at the table, the brightly polished balls. He was arching his hand on spider legs, pumping the cue. But before he could shoot she had lifted the cue ball, then two more. They were heavy and cold where she cradled them against her gut.

"What the shit are you doing? That was a set-up for me."

"Watch, buster."

She stood away from the table, looked up quickly to be certain there was all the space she needed. She weighed the first ball tentatively in one hand, held the other two ready in the other. Then it was launched, coming down, another up, the third, and she kept her eyes on the three glistening arcs, letting her hands move as Pops had always told her to, concentrating, concentrating, cutting out everything else in the world but the round smooth objects, believing they were all connected by the same force that brought them inevitably down to her waiting hand. She had lain for hours on the patchy green of the back yard, Sunday afternoons, Pops practicing in the sun with his shirt off, so many things flying around him at once that if she squinted she thought she and the house and tree and Pops himself were being juggled by unseen hands in wide swoops of dazzling air.

But she missed one, the other struck hard against her wrist and she was left holding the cue ball in her right hand.

"He taught me that," she said quietly to the space where old mugs squatted in rows above the booze. "Pops taught me that." But she was not thinking about Pops any longer. The man she had remembered could not be Crandal Denton. Too long ago, and maybe the man with the baseball cap was only a dream.

Pud's voice, admiring. "Her dad. Greatest juggler I've ever seen. He could juggle cats and dogs if he wanted. Toured with Bob Hope once and . . ."

"That's shit," she said flatly, staring now at the cue ball. No one was talking. "He never did. He just said that."

"C'mon, Lily. He told me. Always said he was going to bring in photos he had."

"No photos. Just words, Pud. He could throw up a lot of them at the same time too."

In the silence she heard the humming again. The mugs, each with a name but untouched for years, looked smug in their dust.

"The hell with it." Lily drew back her arm and threw the ball in a perfect arc. It shattered three mugs and sent six more on either side toppling off in lesser explosions. She stood with one arm stiff on the bar where her body had stepped forward with the toss. The humming had stopped. She would not inquire further. As far as she was concerned, the man she had recalled would be Crandal Denton from now on, and forgotten.

"What the hell'd you do that for?" Pud sounded more hurt than angry. Glen was hulking close.

She did not say much. Glen offered to pay, but Pud would not take it, said he had planned on throwing them out soon anyway, but maybe she'd better go on home now be-

cause he couldn't take more of that in one night, and Chrissake, Lily, that was no way to treat old friends. He was
sweeping when she came around the bar and took his arm in
both hands and stared at him and said, "We're going home,
but I'm real sorry, I *am* sorry. I just had to." He dropped his
broom and took one pass with his free hand through her hair
and said, "That bad?" but as she was walking off, she turned,
her smile numb as if she had not used those muscles for days,
and said, "It was. But not now. C'mon, Big Bird," and Glen
hardly had time to get his jacket.

As they pulled into her driveway behind the dead car he
turned the engine off and said, "You do that often?"

"What?"

"Go out of your head."

She laughed. Jesus, it felt good to get an easy, deep
laugh out, right up from the gut. "When I need to."

"And they treat you that kind? Like Pud did?"

"I do what I like."

"What else do you like?"

"I tell you what I like best. Making love."

He grinned. "That's a mighty high way to put it."

"You know what I mean, buster."

T. Alan Broughton

Duck Season

Gracie turned on her side to look at the clock. She could tell by the way the sun struck the window and glowed through the frozen gauze around the bottom of the pane that a hard frost had come at last, that fall was beginning to be what it should be. All night the wind had shaken and battered the house, ripping out the warm, rainy weather. The leaves would be scattered now all over the lawn and streets. The sun kept dimming and bursting back, and she could smell the cold, cloud-tossed day, smoke from the neighbor's fireplace. Later she would go to the window.

Below, the phone rang and was immediately cut short. They had fixed the one by her bed so it couldn't ring. Someone was up, and they wouldn't be able to keep the kids quiet for long. Except George. They said he'd been sleeping more than usual. Len would be happy about the cold. Duck hunting began soon, and the weather had been so warm that he was afraid the birds would not be flocking in time, like last year when the season was almost over before the flights began, great wedges of geese straggling over the house, ducks skimming across the already frozen pond, but too late. Last week he had been up to the lake with Bert to set up the blind and had described how the boat stuck in the mud, the lake was so low, and he lost a boot trying to push out of the muck.

They had fought for years over the duck hunting. And he never understood how she felt. The whole thing had finally settled into a hostile truce. She couldn't make him understand how obsessed he became, how for all those weeks he would be thinking nothing but ducks, ducks, ducks—not seeing the children, not hearing her. Even when he made love his touches were so vague and remote that she started turning away from him because she'd rather have no lover than be fondled by a spook. Cleaning his guns, getting up at three a.m. to drive off and meet Bert, turning those lovely, bright-feathered creatures into broken-necked and disheveled lumps, their feathers blowing around the lawn for weeks, tracked in by the kids—she'd tried to break him of all that, once even threatened to take the kids and go somewhere else for the whole season, but he set that jaw the way he always did when he was angry, stared with one eyebrow lifted, and said, "Oh, really?"

She turned slowly onto her back, carefully maintaining her numbness. Len thought he was so strong, but he was only damned stubborn. He nearly crushed the house once to avoid taking her advice—cutting down the white pine that died by the fence, and she'd been in the kitchen, looked out the window, and any fool could tell that the limbs were longer toward the house, and more of them too, but there he was chopping as if he thought it would fall the other way. She had gone out on the stoop and told him so, and he'd stared back and then said loud enough so all the neighbors were bound to hear, "It'll damn well fall the way I want it to, woman," and she watched from the kitchen again as the axe beat furiously into the cut. The tree wavered, drifting toward the house, and then there he was, as if he thought he were Samson, right in the way and pushing back against it, and if a burst of wind from the right direction hadn't come he'd have been crushed, but he was lucky and only lost a section of fence. They didn't talk about that at all.

Here he was getting ready to hunt again, as if nothing else were happening. "Your mother's here," he had said. "She can get the kids off to school, and I'm always back by late morning or so." As if it were just any fall. Now that he slept in another room so as not to bother her or not be kept awake by her, she wouldn't see or hear him get up, wouldn't watch through half-sleeping eyes his naked form drawing on layer after layer of clothes, that stealthy way he would pause by her bed before he left as though at least thinking of kissing her, and then he'd be gone. In those days she wouldn't get back to sleep, would worry all morning, the TV kept low so she'd be sure to hear the car popping gravel up in the driveway when he returned—because always the part she couldn't tell him was how she had read about the awful accidents with guns, or people falling out of their boats in the freezing water, and even her father had almost drowned once fishing when his hip boots filled, dragging him down; but that wasn't a fair way to argue, that was weak, and besides she didn't want him to think she cared that much, not about him when he was so stubborn and inconsiderate. Sometimes he wouldn't even come into the house but would stalk off to work at the garage, angry because he hadn't shot anything—angry at her as if she had made it that way.

.   Now the family was beginning to gather, and sometimes she felt sorry that they should have to wait and wait, but at other times she would be angry with them, would want to say as she finally did to her mother one evening, "You shouldn't just sit around like this, it's not good." But nobody wanted to talk about it. There were some things she knew no one in the house, not even she, was allowed to mention. Looking at the clock had become a habit, part of her boredom, but she could not help turning again. Those hands and numbers measured out the light and dark, but only to click off the present, foretelling nothing, and to know where they were going was as impossible as trying to tell the tick from tock. Some nights that was her main pastime.

"Gracie?"

She turned her face to the door. He leaned in, his hand on the doorknob. She could tell he had just shaved by the scoured, pink look to his cheeks, and he was wearing a clean, white shirt, an unknotted tie still dangling loosely from the open collar. Why was he so dressed up, even in his suitpants? He seemed to catch her puzzled glance.

"It's almost time for us to go to church."

"It's Sunday?"

He came all the way in and sat on the edge of the bed.

She could smell the tang of shaving lotion. He had nicked his chin again.

"Yes. Your mother will be here."

"You'll take the kids then?"

"They missed last Sunday. The Father wants . . ." and he hesitated as if he'd thought of something else and then went on, "Father Mulcahey was asking about them."

She knew him well enough to sense he had covered up something in that pause, but the children concerned her now and she went on.

"You woke Georgie? You mustn't let him sleep so late. Mother says he goes to bed early too. Do you think there's something wrong?"

He shook his head and put a hand on hers.

"That shirt's missing a button," she said.

He looked down at his midriff. He was lean and hard-muscled and most of the friends his age, even Bert, bulged out a little at their gut now but he didn't, and she knew he was proud of that.

"Well, it won't show when my jacket's on."

"Oh, Len." She was almost cross. "And for heaven's sake, don't let mother put Betsey into that silly pinafore she gave her. The child just hates it and thinks all her friends are making fun of her."

His hand seemed so heavy and hot and she shifted hers under it.

"You're feeling all right this morning?" he said finally.

That was one of those things she knew everyone had to ask once a day, but long ago it had become rote for all of them, so she just nodded.

"Your mother will be up with some breakfast soon." He stood and paused, looking out the doorway into the hall-way. "The Father was asking if he should stop by maybe. If you'd like a talk a bit with him."

It would please him if she said yes. She tried, but couldn't.

"I don't think so, thanks."

It wasn't *her* religion, after all. She'd done her part by
encouraging her children in it, and going to Mass and learning about it all, but there was one thing she didn't have to
do—she didn't have to believe it.

"You'll be back soon?"

"Oh, yes. Soon as we can," and he stooped so suddenly
to kiss her on the mouth that he was almost gone before she
could kiss him back.

"Len." He paused with his back to her. "I'd love to see
the children all dressed up. If there's a moment."

"Sure."

Then he was gone, and she could hear him calling down
into the hallway below, the clatter and thump as they raced
up the stairs, and suddenly all three were pushing against
each other on the threshold, and she could see the way they
hesitated, a little breathlessly, to enter.

"Georgie, for heaven's sake, brush that hair down
before you go."

He swung in awkwardly, a tie choked up much too tightly
against his throat, those hands and wrists and arms dangling
out of the cuffs of a shirt his body had abruptly outgrown.
He was too tall for a nine-year old, and she knew that made
him awkward, vulnerable.

"Okay," he muttered.

"Come here."

He went to the edge of the bed and stood with his knees
pressing the mattress.

"Now bend down."

He leaned stiffly toward her, his sleepy face sullen. She
put a hand on his brow, ran it over his cheeks.

"Are you feeling all right? Now tell me."

"Yes."

"Then how come you're sleeping so much?"

"I'm tired." He stood straight again.

"He's got Africa sleeping sickness, Gramma says," and
Betsey laughed.

She *was* in that awful pinafore. Gracie felt the old

resentment rise hotly in her, then evaporate. What did it matter? Betsey didn't seem to care. It was just something between her mother and herself.

"Don't be silly," she said. "It's because he's growing very fast."

When Gracie glanced at Adele she could see that her oldest child had decided to be a lady that morning. She had her hair drawn back very tightly and a hint of eyeshade which ordinarily Gracie would have told her to remove immediately, but she knew there wasn't time now, and Len was calling from downstairs.

"Go on," and she saw how almost relieved they were to turn and go. "Georgie."

He paused. She saw his whole figure then on the threshold, the pants hiked up, the shoes turned in slightly at the toes, but also the stark, clear look of his eyes, his mouth open, and she knew why he wasn't sleeping but there was nothing to say, and she remembered once when she had driven past his school and she had seen a child standing at the closed door of the building, obviously waiting for recess to end, not playing with the other children, and suddenly realized that was her child, that bewildered look on his face coming out of a life entirely separate from hers, and she had driven on quickly, hoping he had not seen her.

"Do brush your hair," she murmured. He nodded and was gone.

She liked many things about the church and thought now of that neat, washed sense the people around gave off, the incense, Father Mulcahey's voice which was clear and carried the words well, and even if she kept herself separate from some last part of it, she liked the way Len was solemn, would kneel so totally that she knew he felt a power she couldn't hope to admit with such severity. No, somewhere back of it all for her were those monotonous Sundays when she was a child and living with her grandmother, and they would dress up and go to The Church of the Redeemer, and she knew perfectly well that it was because good families were supposed to do that, and if they lingered afterwards it was only to be certain they had been sufficiently seen. Well, she probably should have let Len tell Father Mulcahey to come, and she almost called him back but heard the door slam and the sound of the truck starting and she thought no, I couldn't, I couldn't pretend anyway, and suddenly she was falling asleep which happened often now, and she didn't try to stop it.

But woke with the pain, remembering she had not taken her pills. She had been dreaming that someone was sawing her in half; she was in the magician's box, and he was stooped somewhere out of sight, groaning slightly as he jerked the saw back and forth, but the trick wasn't working right and the saw was actually beginning to cut into her. Then the magician's voice was her own and she saw her mother standing there.

"The pills," she said, but her mother already had them with a glass of water, and she helped her sit up slightly to swallow them down.

"I didn't know whether to wake you. You were sleeping so peacefully. It seemed a shame."

For a moment Gracie couldn't answer. She was sweating all over, the pain made everything blurred, and she concentrated on not getting sick because then the pills would fail and that would be worse, worse, worse, and they'd have to give her a shot and she was tired of her body being punched and poked. She tried to focus on the hand that stroked her forehead. She tried not to moan. She hated that—it did no good. But she couldn't help it.

After a while it began to ease.

"What's the time?"

"Almost 11:30."

"They should be home."

"Well, they'll be a little late this morning."

"Why?"

"Your father called last night."

Gracie could tell her mother was keeping something from her, but she was too tired to ask what or talk anymore, so she nodded.

"He'll be up next weekend to see you. You know, he has his Fall reunion then too, so he'll stay here in town and drive over to the college."

Next weekend. It seemed so far away. But she could almost laugh. How typical of him to work out everything so practically, conveniently—a visit and his yearly class reunion. He always seemed to need some small excuse to see her.

"Next time he calls, wake me." she said.

Her mother nodded. Gracie knew they wouldn't.

"Some breakfast?"

"No. I can't."

They never argued with her anymore.

"Listen, mother," and she put a hand on her arm. "Promise me something."

Her mother's hand fluttered up, past the glasses that tilted to one side, and jabbed at her hair.

But the phone was ringing downstairs, and her mother left saying, "I'll take it down there."

Of course they weren't going to make any promises. They had their lives to live, and again she resented them bitterly. But she knew it was childish. How she longed to say something fine and noble to Len; she had even made up a whole speech one night to tell him the next day about how it was important for him and the kids that he go on and find another woman and re-marry, and that she wanted him to know that, but damn it all, she couldn't. She had never forgiven him that messing around with Harriet Martin, although he said it was only "funning" because she was in the hospital for a month having difficulties before Betsey was born and he'd gotten lonely. Lonely. Men. As if she hadn't been lonely in that ward with a bunch of women she didn't know because the hospital was way over in New Hampshire, and their insipid yak-yaking from bed to bed all day until she thought she would go mad. She hated women when they got together—all they talked about was kids and gripes and their bodies. Women, women—all her life had been crowded with too many of them: living with her grandmother alone all those years while her father was in the Navy and her mother had run off with another man, her step-mother who had no room for her, back to grandmother, then her own two girls. But thank heavens at last there was Georgie.

Everyone in town knew Len had hung around with that simpering, frizz-haired woman. He even admitted they had gone to bars together, and that night he'd been so drunk and run the truck off the road into Carson's field where he'd gotten mired, Harriet had been with him, and Old Carson had to tow them out with his tractor. Well, thank God, the bitch had moved away. At least he wouldn't marry her; Gracie didn't want someone like that around the kids. But Len always had an eye for women. She would watch him, when they were driving down the street, turn slightly to take in more of some biddy on the sidewalk, and what the hell, if he'd played around some and she didn't know, why should she be so big and brave and make him feel good about moving on? He'd do it anyway if he wanted. He'd do it anyway.

She turned to the clock. Noon. They surely were late. What weren't they telling her? Both Len and her mother had kept something back, something about after church. The windows were rattling again as the wind picked up, and once she was sure she saw some leaves whirl up as high as she was. But the sun was bright, falling now warmly on the end of her bed. All right then, she would let this be her time to get up today.

Slowly, pushing with her hands against the mattress, she eased her back up against the headboard. It was too big a bed for her alone, seemed almost too much to get out of. She tried to toss back the covers but they only folded down halfway, enough to show her bare legs, and she couldn't stand to look at them anymore, almost entirely reduced to bone and sinew. Strange how little bones were when you saw them so clearly. She swung her legs out over the edge, braced herself and put her weight on them, turning so that she could lean with both hands on the bed, and then she worked her way down to the foot where she paused to catch her breath. Groping object by object she made her way to a chair set close to the window for her, and she eased into it. She couldn't sit there long before the edge would begin to bite into her thighs and her legs would go to sleep.

How wild and abandoned the lawn looked! The wind was still gusting, the unmown grass clumped up through the scattered piles of leaves, and a torn, patched light was strewn everywhere. A huge limb of their neighbor's elm had fallen, crushing a length of the fence and almost reaching to the garage. And the children might have been playing there. She had asked the Farnsworths again and again to have the tree cut down, all but dead for two years now, but they kept saying how expensive the job would be and how it was coming down limb by limb anyway. Now Len would have something to say, she hoped, about that. But the wood of the limb would be theirs, having fallen into their property. Not that elm was much good for burning anyway. But it had been a fine tree, tall and bell-shaped, and old Mr. Farnsworth could remember when it was barely ten feet tall.

Trees, trees, she loved them. The nice thing about their house was how even though they were right in the middle of town there were trees everywhere—maples and ash and the big willow cut back that Georgie fell out of two years ago and broke his wrist, and she loved waking at night to hear the wind lash through them before a storm, or in the morning open her eyes to green and the flit of birds. She missed the pine, though, and asked Len to plant another but he never got around to it. Pines had a sound when even the smallest motions of air went through them that was like no other tree. Now, with the leaves almost all stripped off, the other houses nearby were clearly visible: Farnsworth's, and the trailer that the Hodges had set up in the vacant lot. But they had worked hard on it, a decent looking place, and you'd hardly know it was a trailer. Still, she couldn't stand the idea of living in a home without a second story.

There they were. The truck turned in off the dirt road, rolled slowly over the potholes and ridges of their driveway. She could see them crowded into the cab, and of course Georgie would be sitting in the back, pretending he really wasn't cold at all, probably getting some oil or dirt stain all over his new overcoat. She folded her hands. They were there, all there together. But suddenly she wanted to touch or hear them. She sat absolutely still. The truck rocked through a hole and stopped. What if it were like this forever, if when you died it was just a frozen photograph, a picture of the distance going nowhere.

The door swung open, and although the kids tumbled out, Adele and Betsey racing after Georgie who had the newspaper clutched under his arm, another person was in the cab with Len, and for a few moments they sat there, the windshield, mottled by light, concealing their faces, and then he stepped out and came around to help her down and it was Lissy Farnsworth. Slowly the two of them strolled over the lawn to where the fence was broken, Lissy mincing on her toes in high-heeled shoes, and Len took her elbow as she stepped over the debris into her parents' yard. They stood talking for a while. When had Lissy come home? She'd moved to Syracuse at least two years ago.

So that was it. They had all gone to church together, and then probably driven around for a while afterwards, maybe stopped at Russell's for a soda with the kids when they got the paper. And why was Lissy there? Well, it was obvious. He was letting the kids begin to get used to her. She rose slowly, one hand on the windowsill, started to turn away, but couldn't move fast enough. Len glanced up and waved, but she saw nothing on his face to indicate he was at all sorry. Stubborn, stubborn, he'd have his way even in this, and when she reached the bed she could scarcely catch her breath from the exertion. But she was damned if she'd say anything about it to him.

Later she tried to eat the soup Len brought her. She wouldn't say much to him, but agreed the kids should be allowed to go to the movies that afternoon. It was so boring to lift the spoon. She tasted nothing.

"You saw the big limb fall?" he said.

She nodded.

"I guess old man Farnsworth's going to have to listen now."

She stared at him, but he was glancing through the newspaper that he had brought up with him, and from time to time he read her an item.

"That's all I can do," she said weakly, and he took away the half-empty bowl of soup so she could lie down again.

The newspaper rustled, the wind battered, voices of arguing carried up from downstairs, and she dozed again, waking slowly to see one of the girls standing by her bed in a hazy light, and she felt feverish.

"We're going to the movies now, mom. But we don't want to sit with Georgie. Please, will you tell Georgie to sit somewhere else? He's always laughing at the wrong times and saying silly things in the serious parts to show off and . . ."

"Now, Betsey," and her tongue seemed as awkward as the clapper of a bell. "If you just don't pay attention he won't bother you. No, I want you to be patient. You're the oldest and you have to help."

She saw the odd look on her daughter's face; what had she said? What she was saying about George couldn't cause that expression.

"And do wipe off that eyeshade, won't you? I said you could buy it, but not wear it in public. It looks tacky."

"Yes, mother."

That was more like it, the sullen pout, the glance at her father who simply said, "Go on, do what your mother says," and she left, walking heavily.

Gracie turned on her back. "I wasn't too hard on her, was I? I do hate that make-up. She's such a beautiful child," and then she realized she had called her Betsey and yet it was Adele. No wonder she had looked so puzzled. Lord, she couldn't keep anything straight anymore. But there was no more space to think in; like a huge slow wave breaking over her, the pain surged in, not sharp or anything she could cry out against, but a great dull blow that seemed to crush and then scatter her body.

For a long time she hovered about, tossing in a huge wind where she was trying by force of mind to gather the parts of her body. Her body had done this to her, had cut sinew and bones, and scattered into a thousand fragments, and when she reached, either they parted like water before her grasp or else the wind whirled them further away. Even her voice sank like rain into the needles under the pine trees. For a moment she hated her body. Why was it doing this to her? She had been so good to it, and she wanted to cry with frustration, but the wind broke into her gaping mouth, almost taking her mind with it, and so she closed tightly and concentrated, beginning slowly by some force that still lived in the back of her head to bring the parts together again, and as if they were leaves coming down off the trees to her, she made them come, leaves of flesh that were hands and feet and strange cells she did not know, then which she recognized as the ones they had shown her long ago in the slides, sick ones, and yes, if that was necessary to give a little more time, she would even take them.

Dimly she saw the outline of the trunk and branches of a huge tree, diaphanous and silver, its bark shining as if iced with white fire. Then a scraping noise. The tree fell toward her, or was she gently falling into it? Her eyes cleared. Len was bent near the window. He was cleaning his guns and now she could smell the oil. She decided she had never smelled anything so fine, which almost made her laugh—she used to hate the oil because it meant duck season again.

"Len."

He stopped and looked up.

"It was very bad."

He nodded. "Do you want me to have the nurse come?
Do you want a shot?"

"No."

He drew the cloth through again.

"Len."

His hands kept moving but he was looking at her.

"Do you remember that time you took me to the
blind?"

"Sure."

She closed her eyes. They'd had a terrible argument
going there. She had made him take her because she said he
was always away and she wanted to be alone with him and
why didn't he ever take her hunting, why always Bert? Because she couldn't hunt, never used a gun, he'd said, and
that was dangerous. It was dark on the lake, and bitter cold, a
wind knifing at them as they rowed out to the blind, and Len
was stiffly silent, wouldn't even tell her where to sit in the
boat but only pointed with a mittened hand. In the blind she
had no idea what to do, but stood where he told her while he
put out the decoys. Once the wind let up, and off on the
shore a barred owl hooted.

For a moment, just before dawn, she had been much
colder than she ever remembered being, and lonely because
she was sorry, seeing him stand so completely apart from her,
still trying to keep something private. Then, suddenly, it was
dawn, and as if someone had shot the sky open and the light
bled in, guns blasted distantly near the island, and when she
turned the land seemed to have shattered upward, thousands
of dark fragments rising in confusion in the light, raucous
with terror.

"The geese," he said, and slowly they took form, rose
in circles higher and higher, and then wedged off toward the
horizon.

In the near dark she could see the decoys bobbing, so
real that she thought he must shoot now. He stiffened, the
gun rising slowly, although she saw nothing, but then heard
the whistling and flutter. She couldn't catch her breath for a

long time after the gun went off. He spun, his shoulder jolted her, "Get down, dammit," he muttered, and she kneeled against the poles. She didn't know him, this fierce, wheeling block of shadow that loaded and fired, and she plugged her ears with her fingers.

The light was still dim when he stepped down into the boat to retrieve the ducks. She lost sight of him against the black land, hearing for a while the thunk of a bird against the bottom or a slight splash as he stepped out into the shallow water. Then silence, absolute, and a light that seemed to have decided never to increase.

"Len?" she had called tentatively to him across the layers of darkness.

What if out there he had lurched into a deep spot, his boots filling, him struggling silently but dragged down even without a cry? She was going to call again but she shrieked. Something had her by the leg, was pulling her toward the boat slip. She toppled, and he had her, holding her, easing her down into the boat. He was laughing.

"Scared?"

How she hated him for one wild moment, and then his hands held her so tightly, the boat rocked so crazily under them that she began to laugh too, and they had to sit down together, almost tipping over.

"Look," he said. There were ten ducks lumped there, and he held them up one by one. He took out the flask of whiskey he had brought. "That's enough hunting for today."

They climbed back into the blind and sat on the platform. The sun came up into a clear, fall day, and after they finished the bottle she didn't mind the cold at all.

"You won't take George yet, will you?" She wished she could see his face more clearly. It must be late afternoon, almost time to turn the lights on. "He's only nine."

"We'll see."

"Len."

"My dad took me out first when I was five. The sooner

the better. They learn better then.''

She couldn't argue. Maybe tomorrow she would bring it up. But damn it all, why couldn't he just say yes?

"One more year. You could wait till he's ten.''

He didn't answer.

"I'm thirsty.''

She heard him put the gun down, saw his body moving toward the bathroom door, but never remembered having the water because she walked into a curtain of darkness that tangled around her.

But when she woke, although she was too weak to pull herself up in bed, she saw everything clearly—the small lamp on the dresser casting a dim light onto the corners and edges of things, the window shades pulled. She could hear nothing and decided it must be late. Even the wind had stopped. She breathed deeply, in and out. For a moment she wanted nothing to interrupt this peace, afraid even to move again. Finally she looked at the clock. 10:30. They would all be in bed but Len.

She heard the front door close solidly. Probably he would have been outside, looking at the weather. He usually did that before going to bed. But then she remembered the morning. He might have been to see Lissy. She heard him coming slowly up the stairs then down the corridor. She had to decide whether to pretend she was asleep or not. No, she wouldn't. She turned to stare at the door. He came in.

"It's clear as anything.'' He looked so tired. "And there'll be a good frost tonight.''

He sat on the edge of the bed.

"The nurse was here. Do you remember?''

"No.'' But she didn't want to talk about that. "Len.''

"What?''

"Tell me. I want to know. What were you doing this morning?''

She saw the boyish, stubborn look on his face.

"We went to church.''

"No. I mean, why were you so late coming home?''

"We had some things to do."

She couldn't bear it. How could he lie to her, even now? She laughed sharply. "Things? I saw you all, you know. I saw her with you. Len, for God's sake, level with me. I want to know. I have a right to know."

He looked puzzled at first, then his lips drew together. He rose slowly from the bed and walked to the lamp.

"Is there anything you want me to fetch? I'd better be getting some sleep since I promised Jimmy I'd start work on his car early in the morning."

She stared at that set jaw, the heavy, battered hand on the lamp. How she wanted to slap him just once across the face, anything but this.

"Damn, damn. Tell me if it's her. I have a right."

The lamp snapped out.

"I know you were driving around, you all went to church together and that's why you took so long and . . ."

"Stop it. Listen, Gracie, you're wrong. She was just walking back and we gave her a lift. Do you think I could . . ."

"Yes. You know you could. Then what were you doing?"

His voice was low, so low that she had to strain to hear the words that tumbled out.

"We went to see Father Mulcahey. Afterwards. It was the Father's suggestion, you see, he called and said it might be easier and I'd already asked him because I couldn't do it, and your mother couldn't and someone had to explain it, someone had to, Gracie."

"What?"

She felt him moving closer in the dark. His legs touched the bed.

"Tell them you're going to die. I couldn't do it."

She did not answer. She heard him take off his shoes. Then he lay down beside her on the bed and for the first time in months she reached out and his whole body was there and even though it hurt her arm when he lay on it, she made him lie closer and hold her so that his breath was in her ear.

"I'm sorry," she said, but even as she was speaking she heard it and said, "Listen, listen, it's the geese," and they held perfectly still, breathless for a long while, listening to the scattered craking, the high birds calling to each other across the dark, and then he was weeping and she held on with all her strength.

Susan Engberg

Household

Here came Nathalie: forty-one, agile of body, angular of face, with large blue eyes under a flap of greying bangs, dressed at the moment in a woolen bathrobe with threadbare piping, she was carrying her firstborn baby, a daughter, down the upstairs hallway for an early morning nursing. There were paint buckets to be skirted, a folded stepladder, a neatened collection of trays and rollers and brushes, for with characteristic productivity Nathalie was making the most of her confinement. It was late February, six-fifteen; a frosted light filled the windows.

Once again in the big bed she curved her body around her daughter and bared a nipple. A root was tapped, through her to the contented center of the world. Breathing deeply, she closed her eyes beneath the sweep of her mussed hair. Edward turned; she felt his breath, his lips on the crown of her head. He sighed, groped for a baby foot and thus anchored seemed to be setting off again, into a microscopic pattern of decidua, or a laboratory corridor, perhaps a chain of mountains — how could she know? His body twitched. She could not follow, but she heard him, blowing out dream sounds, this youthful husband who had found her in the fullness of time.

Now she herself was sinking into a whitened space where a single sound produced a peacock, fanning out its splendid, iridescent tail. Slowly it pivoted, and Nathalie was drawn down a path between rhododendron and up a hill to a ceremony, a circle of people in white. I can't open my eyes, she apologized; I can't wake up; I am still so tired. With a length of white batiste they swaddled her as she held her baby Caro, swathe after swathe of fine batiste, at first a glory and then a binding fineness, which lo! at the last moment loosened and released her to the air, a flying mummy, trailing white batiste and cradling her baby.

The alarm from the clock broke open a forest of colors. Edward groaned. Nathalie turned, forgetting the peacock, the rhododendron, the white batiste, and the baby received another breast. A crow screamed across the neighborhood. In the nineteenth-century eaves outside the window pigeons cooed rounded, busy mutterings. What, Nathalie wondered, were those red eyes seeing high above the winter street?

Downstairs she and Edward had to speak softly because of Liza, asleep in the living room beneath the ficus tree on Edward's old couch pulled out to make a bed, a lump of taciturn flesh, one plump bare shoulder just visible above the blanket, one wrinkled hiking boot upright on the floor beside the bed, one tipped on its side. The blinds of the living room were closed and for nearly a week for most of each day had remained tight, in spite of the massings of plants: Liza was sleeping, such protracted sleeps as can pull one through times of deep exhaustion or confusion, though whether healing was actually taking place, Nathalie had not been able to judge. She had not even been told the hurt, only that the child — but for goodness' sake no longer in these last few years a child — of her childhood friend was passing through town and needed a bed for one or two nights, which had been extended into four, now six.

"I'm going to try and reach her mother again today," whispered Nathalie to Edward in the kitchen. She poured boiling water onto tea leaves. The kitchen was the one rescued area of the shabby house, now a glowing of refinished wood and fresh paint and new windows: the heart, they had at once agreed, from which all other renovation would spread — slowly, of course, for there was little time, less money.

Edward nodded and continued out the sliding glass door

to the bird feeder with a measure of seeds. Today the air was thick and grey, and there was ice everywhere; a mass of it on a bush looked as if a bucket of cloudy water had been slopped exactly there. Nathalie could make out nothing clearly beyond the first oak and the listing grape arbor, but most certainly Edward, lifting the hinged roof of the feeder, was real, and the baby, strapped into a slanted infant seat on the kitchen counter, flailed arms and legs in pleasure. Caro had learned to smile. She flailed, she smiled; the smiles were evidently connected to the flails. "That's right," said Nathalie softly to the tiny face. "That's my love."

"Murky, but not quite so cold," said Edward, stamping his feet.

"Look, Edward, she's doing it again."

He came to the counter and bent over the baby, who pursed her lips at him and made a sound, miraculous baby.

"Do you hear that?" laughed Edward. "She's trying to talk." He pursed his lips and made an encouraging sound. The baby opened her toothless mouth and smiled. Her feet beat against his thickset chest.

"She's only two months old," said Nathalie. "She can't possibly be talking." But she peered over the top of Edward's head at the infant features that each day were making the smallest, smallest changes.

Edward stood up and put his arms around her. "I'm happy," he said.

The earth, she had discovered, had solid arms after all, need not be conquered or resisted, could answer, concretely. Edward's brown eyes were smiling at her. But was there a slight rasp of weariness in his voice? He was thirty-five. Tenderly she read the crinkles and creases around his eyes and searched into the good-humored lights and wheels of color.

But of course they were both tired; catapulted as they had been into marriage, into parenthood, they had scarcely caught their breaths anyway, and last night Caro had been awake twice past midnight, and Liza had taken to trailing in very late — and though they weren't really responsible, thank heavens, they couldn't help feeling worried — so late last night that Edward had agreed her mother must be reached. What a household, he had said close to Nathalie on the pillow: a newborn infant and an infantile twenty-one year old; what a combination. To say nothing of us, Nathalie had returned. And then they had had to smother their laughter against each other, dazed as they were with fatigue and wonder.

In the kitchen, standing firmly together, they swayed in their embrace, and the baby's feet pushed against their thighs.

"What is it?" he asked. "Your forehead's puckering."

Puckering? She put her fingers to her brow. "It's Liza, I suppose. A puzzlement. She's draining me."

"Send her packing," said Edward. "She's had her sleep. She's not ours. You need to get your own strength up if you're going back to work next month."

"The vagueness is irritating me," said Nathalie. "I have this terrible urge to take her by the shoulders and shake her up."

Nathalie seized Edward by the shoulders and shook; then she shook again, surprised at herself. Edward laughed nd lifted her off her feet. She swayed in the air against him, and her arms relaxed.

Now he was going away to the windowless chambers of the laboratory where all day his giant's eyes would be focusing on arrested bits and pieces of nature, systematically travelling in among the cells, the parts of cells. The prints he brought home from the electron microscope were to Nathalie like the shots coming home from outer space. A segment of tissue, the surface of a planet: human scale had poured itself into the eye of a microscope, the eye of a camera and been translated into patterns, aggregations of bits and pieces of nature, held in place by contrary forces, the force for coming together, the force for going apart, gravity, levity. She said good-bye to Edward. She could not follow.

Now all day her arms alone would hold the baby. One could not shake a baby, no. In the unfilled space of that new mind every incoming gesture, every word must count for ten, a thousand, ten thousand. Gently Nathalie carried her daughter past the darkened living room and up the stairs.

"There's my love," she crooned as she bathed this armful. She wrapped her in a towel, she blew into her navel, she gazed closely into her face and made whatever sounds came into her head. No one else was listening. What clock could possibly measure the vastness of each infant moment? "Love," bubbled Nathalie, "Oh, lova-lova-love." Caro squirmed and smiled and clutched at Nathalie's cheek. From no knowledge of each other, in two months, they had come to this. "That's right," said Nathalie, kissing the tiny fist, "that's right, lova-love."

In the hallway she almost stumbled over Liza, who was sitting on the floor beside the paint cans, still in longjohns and torn satin camisole, examining the valleys between her bare toes.

"Liza! you're awake early."

"I guess I am," admitted Liza, looking up blandly from her round smooth face, her heavy brown fall of hair.

"Well, the bathroom is yours," said Nathalie. "If I had known you were waiting, I wouldn't have dawdled so long."

"Oh, that's all right," said Liza. "I'm in no hurry."

The shower she took while Nathalie nursed and rocked the baby was indeed unhurried. Gallon after gallon of water funneled down through the pipes of the old house. For a moment or two a piece of plaintive song floated above the water, surprisingly buoyant. On the nursery side of the wall Nathalie continued slowly to rock. Her daughter slept in her arms. She should rouse herself, she thought, and change into her painting clothes. She disliked wasting time. She disliked wasting anything. But the stillness of the child seemed to be holding her still.

What she really must do immediately was to try again to
reach Janet before Liza should go off for another afternoon
and evening of wandering. Where did she go? Nathalie had
finally asked. Oh, around town, Liza had answered; sometimes she talked to people. One night she had come home
smelling of beer, unusually cheerful, her heavy body dressed
as usual in layers of clothes — trousers, long skirt, shirts, vest,
scarves, fur-lined leather hat with flaps dangling, clomping
boots. A gypsy, she looked like, or a bedouin, lost from her
tribe. Nathalie, waiting up, making work for herself in the
kitchen, had seized the moment. Ah! how had the town been
tonight? Pretty good, said Liza; she had been talking to one of
the shopkeepers in the arcade; he made jewelry and, look, he
had given her this pretty stone. Quartz? wondered Nathalie.
Quartz it appeared to be; a piece of quartz; why on earth, she
asked herself, but she kept silent. The arcade worried her; the
shops, she had heard, were mere fronts.

But here stood Liza. A midnight snack? A cup of tea, she
had pressed, a banana, an English muffin slathered in butter?
Liza had accepted all three and while she ate Nathalie had
inched closer. Now, what had Liza been saying about her
mother; did Janet still have the same job or was she onto
something else? Liza licked her fingers; she wasn't sure. Well,
did she have the same apartment, the same telephone? Oh
yeah, she still had the same place, Liza had said. And Liza
would be going out there before long, was that the plan?
What were her plans, anyway? Nathalie had bumbled on, unable to stop herself; why, at Liza's age lots of young women
were doing all sorts of interesting things. The possibilities
were enormous. What were Liza's ideas? What was going on?

Then the face had closed down again, the heavy hair had
obscured half the eyes, half the cheeks, and Nathalie had
been saved from saying what was next on her tongue: that at
Liza's age she herself had been well along in design school,
had held scholarships and part-time jobs, had thought she
was learning how to keep herself in hand.

Disastrous, that would have been, a disastrous show of pride, she thought now as she rocked her satisfied baby. Something in Liza's manner had checked her, nothing as extreme as a word, rather an inarticulate arousal, a flicker behind the eyes, but Nathalie had seen it and sensed the source: anger, perhaps even scorn, herself included in the generality of its object, and then something stubborn in herself had risen up in defense of the kitchen, the teapot, the fruit basket, the lithographs on the walls, the woman of forty with her baby, her husband, her work, her energy. She had stopped talking. She had put away the butter and begun to turn out the lights. With nothing to hold to but youth itself, Liza had in a flickering of scrutiny silenced Nathalie's hard-won assertiveness.

She continued to hold the baby, rocking slowly. At last the water was turned off; a hairdryer was turned on; the same song was begun again and abruptly broken off.

Nathalie eased Caro down to the crib and stole past the bathroom to their bedroom, still thick with the atmosphere of night. It would be easy to stretch out under the covers and sink down, but instead she made the bed without wasting a motion. She snapped up the window shade, and pigeons fluttered in alarm from the ledges. Briskly she threw Edward's running shoes into the closet and snatched up the dirty clothes. She was quick; she was efficient; she had always been good at sorting out the necessary from the unnecessary. A proper economy was what distinguished her work in graphics, too: the right amount of free space, the right concentrations of information, the right shapes for each intention. She had an eye; she was reliable; she cared passionately about the finished piece, the look of it in her hands, the paper, the beautiful, defined letters, Sloth she could not abide, nor carelessness; one might as well be tying a stone around one's neck, so heavy were the effects of these attitudes. There! Six minutes and the room was tidy. She felt reestablished.

She pulled the telephone to the bed, lay across the quilt

and dialed the long-distance number she had in this week memorized. Janet was her own age, a friend from grade school days; who had married early; who had quickly produced five children, in almost total unconsciousness she had told Nathalie much later; who had divorced, remarried, divorced, moved here, then there, believed fervently in one after another of various cures of body or spirit.

No answer. Janet had not answered in the evenings; she did not answer in the morning. Nathalie ran her fingers over the blocks of colored fabric on the quilt. She lay back, stretching her body that was now nearly reclaimed from its fantastic expansion into pregnancy. She drummed her fingers in her rigorously flattened abdomen. She was pleased with the firm hold she had been keeping on herself during maternity. Strong mindedness and sensible habits seemed to be seeing her through with extraordinary smoothness.

Surely it shold be easy and reasonable enough to put her arms around this Liza, this child no longer a child, now loose in the world, who had come to lodge in her path and who might have been her own, or even the mother of the baby now asleep down the hall. But what Nathalie wanted to do with the demanding formlessness of the girl was to shake, to shake hard, to rearrange the elements that seemed so irresolutely, so incompetently held together.

She changed her clothes and filled her hands with paint can and brush and took up where she had left off the afternoon before, the trim around the double window in the upstairs hall, each sill, moulding strip, mullion requiring a precise angle of the brush. The paint was white, glossy, steadily redeeming. The view framed was of pine tree, bare oak branches, fog, a suggestion of neighborhood. Liza she could hear now in the kitchen, not clattering, but almost furtively grubbing, rustling. She would let her eat in peace, she decided; she would just finish this window and then go downstairs and casually, mildly inquire into the projected day.

Almost as soon as she had made this resolution of restraint, she set her brush into a jar of solvent, wiped her hands, and went down to the kitchen.

Liza, dressed in Nathalie's dark blue woolen robe, was standing beside the toaster, staring at the slots. For an instant her face looked startled, then slack. Nathalie was both touched and irritated by the free use of the robe.

"All clean?" asked Nathalie. "Your hair looks lovely. Have you found the butter? Do you want to try the new honey? Wonderful stuff. It's local."

"OK," said Liza.

"I see you've boiled water. I'll have another cup of tea with you." Nathalie rolled up the sleeves of her painting shirt and began measuring out tea leaves. "So, you've had a nice shower," she continued. "There's nothing like water. Feeling pretty chipper today?"

"So-so," said Liza.

"You've been tired out."

"Yeah," said Liza. "Real tired out."

"Are you getting rested?"

"I don't know," said Liza. "Maybe."

Nathalie took the teapot to the table near the glass door. A bird book was wedged in the napkin basket; a candle would be lit again that night; honey glowed in the jar: tokens of their love, hers and Edward's; she felt rich. She poured out tea.

"There's plenty of cereal there, Liza, and more bread in the freezer."

"OK," said Liza. "Do you think it would be OK if I had some of that cottage cheese, too?"

"Of course, of course," urged Nathalie. "Take whatever looks good to you. Those bananas are ripe."

Slowly Liza assembled herself a breakfast and carried it to the table. She dipped honey onto her toast and more onto the concoction in her bowl. She took a sip of tea, sighed, tossed back her hair, and began to work her way through the food.

"Did you know I took care of you once when you were a

baby?" asked Nathalie.

"You did? I didn't know that."

"You were a very pretty baby."

"I was?" Liza looked up with her mouth open.

"Yes, you were about a year old, just learning to walk. Janet had come home for her mother's funeral, and I happened to be home, too, from school. Yes, you were adorable. Very pink cheeks, as I remember."

"Were Dick and Hughie there?"

"Oh yes, I had a work-out that afternoon. I think your mother was pregnant then."

"With Jane."

"Yes, it must have been Jane."

"Jane has a baby now."

"That's right. Have you seen Jane's baby?"

"No."

"Well, if you're on your way to see your mother, maybe you could stop at Jane's."

"Maybe."

Liza licked her spoon, pushed her empty cereal bowl away and began to concentrate on toast.

"More tea?" Nathalie asked brightly. She drummed her fingers on the table. She wanted to get that window upstairs finished before the baby should wake up. She wanted to move on later in the day to the taping of the wallboard in her new attic studio. Clearly before her she saw the finished, readied house. It was her excellence, she knew, to draw out orderliness, to improve the surfaces that came beneath her hands. Neither she nor Edward had ever had a house before. It was still a thrill each morning to reenter the well-proportioned spaces, to see their new life framed through a succession of doorways, windows.

Nathalie followed Liza's gaze into the foggy void of the yard. It would be a day of early twilight. She could see herself turning on lamps, moving from room to room with the baby on her shoulder, listening for Edward, cooking supper;

happy.

"So," she said to Liza's soft profile, to her eyes that were the color of the fog, "what are your plans for today?"

"I don't know, Nathalie. I thought maybe I could wash some clothes in your machine."

"Of course. Anything else?"

"I guess I'll go downtown again."

"Goodness, you're going to know more about this town in a week than I've learned in all the time I've been here."

"I like to walk around," said Liza.

"Getting an education?" Nathalie put in and was immediately sorry.

Liza's eyes widened, and in their grey depths Nathalie caught again a flaring up, as if ashes had been stirred. Then the flame dampened. Was it with tears?

Liza said nothing. She smiled faintly and shrugged at Nathalie. Her nose looked red; her full lips were slightly parted.

"Liza, what on earth is going on," said Nathalie as gently as she could. "Are you ill? Are you pregnant?"

"No," said Liza almost inaudibly. "I had some tests."

"Oh, you had tests."

"Yeah." Liza shrugged her shoulders again inside the borrowed robe.

Nathalie took a deep breath and looked out the window; a cardinal, one stroke of red, at that moment alighted on the feeder. "Look there," said Nathalie, "a cardinal." Liza looked.

"Have you been treated badly, Liza?"

"I don't know."

"Do you want to talk?"

"I don't think so."

"Is there anything you want me to do for you?"

"I thought maybe it might be all right if I stayed here for a few more days."

No, no, not the weekend, Nathalie kept herself from saying. She took a sip of tea. Her head felt too full. "When is your mother expecting you?"

"She doesn't know I might come."

"I thought she was expecting you."

"I haven't made up my mind yet."

"Are you going to call her? Do you want to call her from here? Do you want me to call her?"

Liza's eyes widened again. "Do you want me to go away, Nathalie?"

Nathalie rested her chin in her cupped hands and searched Liza's face, where shadows from the subdued daylight seemed to converge. The mouth hung open. Nathalie felt as if her own intelligence were beginning to falter.

"I'm tired," she said abruptly. "I've got a new baby."

"Yeah, that must be real tiring."

"It is."

"Do you want me to wash these dishes?"

Nathalie flicked her eyes over the two cups, the plate, the single bowl. "That would be very nice," she said to Liza, "especially as I think I hear Caro waking up."

"Sure," said Liza, "I don't mind."

"Liza, I wish you would get in touch with your mother. It's all right if you stay here a bit longer, but I think it would be a good idea if you planned your next step."

"Sure, Nathalie, I'll give her a call."

Good luck, thought Nathalie as she ran up the stairs towards the baby. At the landing she paused and brought her fist down on the newel post. Then she sat down on a step and lowered her forehead to her knees. From the other side of the nursery door came the now angry crying of the baby. Nathalie looked at her own long, capable fingers; she spread them on her knees and pressed their tips hard into the paint-splotched fabric. She slowed her breathing and pushed herself up.

"Baby," she said, opening the door to the red-faced infant, "hello, baby. Did you think nobody was at home?"

Her words in the sparely furnished room seemed loud and strained. The day was almost half over. Methodically,

with her lips pressed together, Nathalie peeled sodden layers
of cloth from the baby and the crib mattress. Yesterday at this
time she had been making almost exactly the same motions,
and the day before, almost the same.

In the doorway of the nursery, infant in her arms, she
hesitated, listening, in limbo between the possible levels of
the house. "Let's look over the attic," she whispered to Caro.

Here, beneath the slanted skylights of the altered
dormers, a feasible space was gradually emerging. It was a
pleasure simply to ascend into it. Nathalie's hands had been
instrumental in every layer of the work. "First the insulation
and then the vapor barrier and then the sheetrock and now
the tape and the jointing compound," explained Nathalie as
she walked about the room, jiggling the restive baby. "The
drawing board will go here and the shelves there and the
daybed over there, and then your mother can bring home
work. What do you say? Say something, you funny baby."
She nuzzled her face against the baby's neck. Caro began to
cry again. "What? Hungry? Not so soon!"

She lifted her high in the air beneath one of the skylights
and shook her gently; she sailed her back and forth, a baby
flying, legs dangling, before a backdrop of fog. The crying
mounted. "All right then," said Nathalie somewhat fiercely,
"here we go again," and she sank down into a soiled bean bag
chair, a remnant from her own apartment days, and pulled up
her shirt; "here we go again — my god," and the baby
attached itself to her with ravenous animal pushings. "My
god," said Nathalie, closing her eyes, splaying her legs, giving
way.

When the baby was finished and lay sated against her
forelegs, Nathalie bent to study the self-absorbed face. Milk,
her milk, trembled on the lower lip; the eyes were half-closed
beneath the damp brow. Nathalie lapped the tails of her
painting shirt over the tiny chest. The baby's breath caught
and sighed. I have to stay alive, she thought simply; I have to
stay alive long enough to take care of this child. In the air was

an anticipatory silence.

Far below the telephone was ringing. "Now we have to answer the telephone," she said aloud. "First one thing and then another."

She reached it simultaneously with Liza. "I have it, thank you, Liza," said Nathalie from the bedroom.

"Sure," said Liza.

"Hello, you two," said Edward. "Hello, Liza. How are you today?"

"Oh, pretty good," said Liza.

"How are you, Nathalie?" he asked.

"Living," said Nathalie. "Right here."

"Say, Nathalie," put in Liza, "what does it mean when the washing machine thumps?"

"It means you should turn it off and rearrange the load. Right away."

"Oh. OK, sure," said Liza. "So I guess I'll hang up now. Nice talking to you, Edward."

"Right," said Edward. "Good to hear your voice."

"Bye, Nathalie," said Liza, "I'll hang up now."

"Right-o," said Nathalie. "Thanks."

"That's OK," said Liza. "Bye." There was a pause, a careful click.

"Well," said Edward, "that was a long conversation."

"Yes, there have been a number of words today."

"Anything definitive?"

"We will most likely have a guest for the weekend."

"Ah-ha," said Edward, as if he weren't completely listening. What were her plans for the evening? he wanted to know. Would it be possible for him to bring someone home to dinner? It was that guy he had mentioned to her last night, the one coming in from the West for an interview. A nice fellow, funny as all get out. She would enjoy him.

"Nathalie?" he said. "Are you there?"

Nathalie had stretched across the bed quilt with Caro on her chest. "Right here," she answered as she slipped her fingers beneath the baby's undershirt and lightly stroked the skin of her back, so smooth as scarcely to seem a barrier.

"This fellow John is a gem, you'll enjoy him. And he knows the rivers. He's been canoeing on some of my old trips."

"Another westerner," said Nathalie.

"He's six-four," said Edward. "You should see him."

"Then we'll need a lot of food."

Edward laughed. "Could you shop? I'll get home in time to help cook."

"All right," she said, "I'll go hunt down food."

"Terrific," said Edward and, hey, how was she anyway — and how was the twerp?

"She's right here on my heart," said Nathalie, "twenty-two inches long, visible to the naked eye, undeniable."

"You sound tired. Could you nap?"

"I should take lessons from Liza and Caro."

"That's a thought," said Edward, but now his attention seemed to have shifted again. She was in a room, on a bed, beneath the delicate, piercing weight of a child whose pulse and breath seemed indistinguishable from her own.

"So," said Edward, "I guess that's all. I'm making good progress today on those slides."

"That's good," she said.

"But I'm having more of that same trouble with Maynard. He's throwing his weight around like crazy. I don't know if it's worth it to put up with the politics around here."

"Isn't there enough glory to go around?"

"In a certain light there is. Depends on the point of view."

"I'm sorry you have to deal with that."

"Right. Who needs it?" Edward sighed. "So much for pure research."

Then his voice picked up energy again. " 'Tis but the drama of folly, I'll survive."

Nathalie lay still. She could hear Liza thudding up the

basement stairs; otherwise nothing seemed to be moving.

"Edward, I've got to get out for some air. I'll pick up food."

"Right. I'll get home as soon as I can." He paused, as if thoughts were crowding his speech.

She closed her eyes and saw him leaning against the refrigerator in the cluttered office he shared with Maynard; his sleeves would be rolled up; perhaps he would be scratching his chest, or holding a photographic blow-up at arms length, or running his fingers through his hair. A peacock turned and directed its unwieldly beauty down a rhododendron path. There was a sinking inside the world, then a lifting.

"Edward, I'm falling asleep."

"Go ahead and sleep."

"I'll try to later when Caro takes her real nap."

"Kiss her for me."

"Done. Bye."

"Bye-bye. Nathalie?"

"Edward?"

"No, nothing, I'll tell you later." Now their voices were disconnected.

"Caro," she said, cupping the nearly bald skull with her hand.

"Liza?" she called a few minutes later into the kitchen and then down the stairwell to the basement. "Liza, I'm going to the store. What are your plans? What? I can't hear you. Wait a minute, I'll come down."

With the baby on her hip she went halfway down the steps and found Liza, still dressed in the blue bathrobe, sitting cross-legged on the table in front of the washing machine and reading from a pile of old magazines.

"I'm going to the store," said Nathalie. "Are the machines behaving for you?"

"Pretty good, I guess." Liza stretched and lifted a cascade of hair away from her face.

"You're doing a total cleanup today, aren't you?" asked

Nathalie.

"Really. Soap and water, you know, Nathalie?" She gestured to the machine. "Wow."

"Right," said Nathalie. "Nothing like it. So, what are your plans for today, I mean after your clothes are clean?"

"Today? Oh, I'll be going out, don't worry."

"I'm not worried, I mean, you don't have to go out. Look, Liza, why don't you stay here? Or come back for dinner at least. Edward is bringing a fellow over tonight. We'll have a party."

"Oh, that's all right, Nathalie, I won't bother you."

"Liza," said Nathalie slowly, distinctly, hearing her own voice and not yet knowing who this person was, speaking patiently, a baby slung on her hip, "I would like you to be here tonight. I would like you to come home by six o'clock and be here for the evening."

"Yeah?" Liza looked questioningly across the laundry room.

"Yes," said Nathalie. "Definitely by six o'clock, if not before. You can help us cook."

"I could do that, I guess."

"Yes, you could. We'll see you then."

"I'll try to make it."

"Liza, I'm not saying *try to,* I'm saying *do.*" Her voice rose slightly. "If you're going to continue to camp out here, then I feel Edward and I ought to be able to say something about what sort of schedule you keep."

"Shall I go away? Do you want me to leave?"

"Liza, the point right now is that I want you here by six o'clock tonight. Tomorrow we'll talk about the rest of it."

Liza had crossed her arms over her chest; her hair fell forwards.

"Liza? All right?"

Liza nodded but kept her head lowered.

The washing machine shifted to a new phase, and water gushed into the scrubbing sink. "Liza?" The person holding the baby now went the rest of the way down the stairs and crossed the room and put her hand on Liza's shoulder.

"Liza? What I'm saying is that I've been thinking about you. Will you please come home tonight?"

Liza covered her face with her hands.

"Do you want to talk?" asked Nathalie. "Come on, let's go upstairs and sit down. Come on." She put an arm around Liza's back.

Liza stayed where she was, but she looked at Nathalie through tears.

"Shall I talk?" said Nathalie. "Do you want me to stand here and tell you what I think? I think you should be where you can get some guidance, I mean month after month. Why aren't you in school? Last time I saw you weren't you in school? Weren't you doing some lovely weaving?"

"I've never gone to a school that was any good," said Liza, half crying.

"Even when you were little?"

"Fifth grade was OK. I liked fifth grade."

Nathalie shifted the baby to her shoulder. If she didn't leave for the store now, Caro might be crying before she could get her home. "You liked fifth grade? I did, too. How about high school?"

"Pretty bad."

"And college? You had at least a year, I know."

Liza shrugged. "It was messed up."

"The school was?"

Liza's expression flared up again. "Yeah, Nathalie, even the school was messed up. It was running out of money and the teachers were quitting and most of the time we hardly even had classes, just a lot of meetings. A great big mess."

Nathalie was kissing the downy head of her baby, kissing and tasting and smelling, her body swaying. "I'm sorry," she said.

"Well, it's not as if it's your fault," said Liza.

"Look here, Liza, why don't you put on some clothes and

walk to the store with me? We can talk."

"I can't," said Liza with a flash of triumph. "All my things are in the washing machine."

Gypsy layers of cloth, never for a moment still, floated across Nathalie's mind. "Ah, so they are. All right then," she said, more quickly than she intended, and escaped up the stairs, through the empty kitchen, the hallway. The living room was still darkened, the bed unfolded. "Oh for goodness' sake!" she exclaimed and strode across the room to jerk open the blinds behind the deprived plants. Her heart was pounding.

"What's the matter with me?" she said to Caro in the crook of her arm. "I can't do anything right with that girl." Silent, Caro watched with large eyes as light from one window after another was let into the room.

"Baby," said Nathalie more calmly, holding her close and swaying in front of the window. "What shall I do?" she whispered, her cheek resting on the baby's head. "What shall I do?" she began to sing softly to a tune that seemed to come from nowhere.

She was still humming as she emerged from the house a few minutes later, the baby strapped to her chest in a canvas pouch, and as she glanced back from the curving walk to the ice-hung eaves and drooping pine tree, she knew it was Liza's tune that had come to her, the song from the shower. "Well, she's getting to me, all right," she said aloud to the dense air.

Shifting the weight of the baby slightly, she set off with her usual rhythmic, long-legged stride and deep, measured breaths to the market. It wasn't really so cold; isolated drippings could even be heard here and there, as if the crust of winter were prickling open. The damp air felt good on her cheeks.

On the bridge at the foot of the hill she paused and searched the thicketed banks for signs of change. There were yesterday's snow and ice-clotted bushes, today's mist, and this new percolating hint of thaw. It would have done Liza good to come along on the walk, but then it was probably doing her good to be at home performing those lengthy water rites. Nathalie stared down on a darkish opening in the snow that looked as if a small animal had been creeping in and out.

Caro was already making restless snufflings inside the pouch. "Yes, yes," said Nathalie, "It won't be long now," and as she walked on humming to the baby, she began mentally to put together a menu. Usually she was a marvel at planning anything. She saw ahead; she selected; she arranged. Things almost always turned out well under her hands. The feast — fish, new potatoes, small carrots, salad, some sort of fruit dessert — in its accomplished state already had begun to gleam in her mind. Now all she had to do was breeze along through the stores.

"Hush, hush," she said to Caro, "it's not nearly time for you to be hungry." The hooded face was now red with distress and the body pushed against her own.

In the fish store Nathalie drummed her fingers against the glass case and could not make a decision. The fish woman with the cloudy eye suggested sole and lifted limp pieces to the scale. "Fine," said Nathalie, "perfect," and she hurried on with her package to the fruit and vegetable market. Caro was crying loudly.

"Time for his feed," commented the proprietress.

"Not exactly," said Nathalie.

"Must be colic then."

"Colic?" said Nathalie.

"Three of mine were like that. I'll tell you, I wouldn't want them days again." With her thick hands the woman packed carrots and greens, lemons and grapefruit into the net bag.

"Well, good luck," she said to Nathalie. "Can you carry this? You've got yourself a load now."

"I'll be all right," said Nathalie as she hung the groceries from her shoulder.

"Pretty soon he'll be too big for that pack."

"She," corrected Nathalie, rather loudly, "the baby is a girl."

"She's big for her size. Oh, listen to that, mother, she's getting mad."

"Yes," said Nathalie, "I'll hurry along now."

Outside she stopped to adjust the weights that hung from her. "Hush," she said, "hush." By the time she was climbing the hill to home, she felt numbed from the baby's almost incessant crying and her own tiredness.

The blinds in the living room had been closed again and what appeared to be the humped form of Liza lay beneath a disorderly mound of blankets. In the kitchen peanut butter and jelly jars sat open on the counter beside an opened magazine. The water faucet dripped. Nathalie, still dressed in her winter jacket, the baby strapped to her chest, stooped in front of the refrigerator to put away the groceries. She stood, dizzy. Across the room the breakfast table seemed remote. She felt taken aback by this strange, hourless midday.

At first Caro seemed eager to nurse, but then she twisted away and began again to cry. "Hush-a-baby," said Nathalie "now stop, now stop. That's enough," but the crying did not stop. Nathalie paced the braided nursery rug. Exactly below Liza was asleep or perhaps now pretending to sleep. Pine tree and oak outside the nursery window were motionless in the somber light.

"Hush, hush my little baby," she sang. The monotonous crying had no direction. Little mallet blows of sound beat into Nathalie's mind, holding her in place. She didn't know what to do.

"Stop it now," she said, no longer singing. She lifted the baby in the air, and shook her gently and then not so gently. "Stop, stop, stop," she said, "this is ridiculous."

Caro now weighed eleven and one-half pounds. Her eyes, squeezed together, did not seem to see anything, even Nathalie. The veins in the small neck and forehead protruded. Her delicate fingers were splayed out rigidly in the air, as if she were an amphibian in the midst of a leap.

Nathalie caught her down tightly to her chest. If she could, she would have swallowed her, to keep her quiet, to keep her safe.

She laid the baby down and undressed her and put on a clean diaper and then she carried her down the hallway and plopped the screaming, nearly naked form in the middle of the big bed. Then she took off all her own clothes, leaving them where they fell, and opened the covers and drew the baby in against her skin. Nathalie pulled the covers high up over their heads until they were in a soft cave. Caro's angry feet beat against her belly.

"Do you want milk?" whispered Nathalie. "Here." But this time as the baby twisted away from the suction of nursing, she kept the tip of the nipple between her gums.

The pain was intense; it went straight to Nathalie's navel. She leapt out of bed. "That's it! That's enough!" she shouted down at the baby in the covers. For an instant only, Caro was startled into silence, then the crying resumed with fury. Naked, shaken, surprised at herself, Nathalie walked back and forth at the foot of the bed. "You're wasting a lot of time," she said. "Do you hear me? This is ridiculous." She crossed her arms across her chest and hunched her shoulders. "I've got a lot of other things I should be doing. Do you hear me?"

The chill of the room finally drove her back under the covers. "All right, this is it, baby." She rolled Caro over, curved her own body around and began to rub the small bare back. The shoulder blades, like unfinished wings, were scarcely the distance apart of Nathalie's forefinger. The baby made the tremendous effort again and again of rearing her head; finally the exhausted crying became muffled by the mattress.

Up the bumpy runnel of the back the mother's fingers travelled, up behind the ears, over the skull to the throbbing fontanel, back down the complicated topography of the spine, up and down. Nathalie closed her eyes. The crying continued, gradually at a distance. She herself was being drawn back into an earthly crevice, down past different realms of light, down to a deep glowing quarry, opened for her — was it possible? — by the birth of the baby. She thought she had been shown how to go to the heart, once and for all, if she could just remember the inward way, but now she began to ride higher up on a sea of sleep, salty, noisy, agitated, which suddenly gave way to a new phase, smooth, like the calmest water, easy to navigate, quiet.

When she woke, the room was nearly dark and Caro was stirring. "Here," she whispered and adjusted their bodies until the baby could nurse. For a while there was no other sound. Nathalie lay still, because of the baby, and because she felt there was something she might remember if she could be still enough.

The front door slammed; voices were in the downstairs hallway, Edward's voice, the voice of the guest, Liza's voice. Nathalie began to smile. Now in what dishevelled state, exactly, had Liza been found?

Nathalie stretched, yawned comfortably, propped the baby up beside her to be burped, and felt no desire to move an inch from this fullness. The evening could go ahead quite well without her or, if it chose, come and circle around her in this place.

The voices, however, continued on through the downstairs hallway to the kitchen. There was laughter, even Liza's. The sound carried energy, shape, rising and falling, sometimes merging. Water was turned on; ice trays rattled. In her childhood she had often listened like this, from one room into another, in anticipation. Now she was on the verge of getting up.

The voice of Edward separated itself; his footsteps rose; entered; the bedside light was turned on; he was present. "Here you are!" he said.

"Here I am."

He lifted the covers. "What's this I see — flesh?"

"Flesh."

He slid in beside them. "It is a pleasure to find you like this."

"We slept."

He pressed himself close and drew a shirted arm over both her and the baby. "I feel over-dressed."

"I like you any way. What's going on downstairs?"

"I've put them to work."

"What about Liza — is she presentable?"

"She has her outfit on, yes. She looks better tonight. What did you do for her today?"

"Nothing. I've done nothing all day long."

"True?"

"No, untrue. Plenty of nothing, I don't know. What time is it?"

He kissed her. "I wish it were ten o'clock and everyone else were in bed."

"But it's not."

"We could pretend."

"All right. The cows have been milked, the ship is moored, the town is quiet."

"And here we are, kissing and keeping the world safe."

"Is that true?"

"Absolutely."

"How do you know?"

"My research for the day," he said. "I know, I know." He lifted the baby over to his own chest. "Now then, kid, what do you have to tell us tonight?"

Caro arched her back and threshed with arms and legs as if she were swimming in place, fastened to her father at her navel. She made sounds; she smiled; she drooled. "Wonderful," said Edward. "Now what else?"

The baby squealed, then growled.

"Listen, will you?" he said proudly. "Has she ever done that before?"

"Not exactly. Actually, today she has been crying quite a bit."

"Crying? Why crying?" demanded Edward of the baby, rocking her on his chest. "Why crying?" He burrowed his face into her.

Nathalie lay on her side. With one eye she saw two close head shapes in the lamplight, an almost abstract eyeful of loving, and she, too, must be held within the pale of light, she thought. Downstairs dinner was being cooked by strangers, or near strangers. A year ago she and Edward had only just met, at the arboretum, on cross-country skis, one bright Sunday of new snow. . .

"Edward, we should go downstairs and be with our guests."

"That's right," he answered, without moving.

"What about poor Liza?"

"Poor Liza seemed to be having a fine time making a salad. John is scraping carrots."

"But then what?"

He sighed contentedly. "Then I suppose we must appear." He flourished the baby at arm's length above him. "And the wine will be opened and we will eat and drink to happiness."

Instantly, with a surge of good feeling, Nathalie stretched her body in a long, flat-bellied twist. "Ah!" she exclaimed, "I've had a good nap."

Edward put the baby to bed, but as it turned out, the baby did not want to be put to bed. Nathalie had no sooner dressed and made her kitchen entrance and begun laying out fish fillets than the message from upstairs became acute. Nathalie paused, her fingers wet.

"This must be a new stage," she said. "Where has my good little girl gone?"

"I'll go get her, shall I?" offered Liza. The blue bathrobe had been replaced by a long cotton skirt and a blouse, now clean but unironed, and the same quilted vest. She had brushed back her hair. Her cheeks were flushed.

"Wonderful," said Nathalie. "Would you please?"

Edward stood beside Nathalie slicing lemons; their shoulders brushed; close together, their hands skimmed and touched down over the variously colored food.

In front of them John paced before the island counter, talking, gesticulating, lifting and eating on the spot shreds of lettuce from the salad. He was indeed as tall as Edward had described, lean, bearded, younger than she had imagined, energetically jolly. "We were flown and then it was downstream all the way," he continued. "Man alive, the fishing was incredible."

"Much whitewater?" asked Edward.

"Enough to give us something to brag about. What a trip."

"Here," said Nathalie, handing him a knife, "why don't you slice the bread."

"I've been eyeing that loaf," said John. "If you think I haven't eaten all day, you're right. Too busy." He sliced off the heel of the loaf and stuffed it into his mouth. "You've got a great place here. I like old houses. How is it having a kid? One of these days I might get married and have a kid."

"So far having a kid is different around every bend, and you never know when the whitewater is coming," said Edward.

Nathalie laughed. Glancing up, she saw the bright nucleus of the room reflected in the new windows opposite; in motion were herself, Edward, the tall guest, and now here came Liza, carrying a surprising length of baby on her shoulder; it looked as if the little one had grown even in the last hour. The house, for a time, held them all.

"Shall I take her?" asked Nathalie, wiping her hands.

"Oh, that's all right, Nathalie. I haven't had her much."

Nathalie's eyes grew larger; she turned and slid the fish into the oven; she straightened up, a woman of forty, cooking food in a warmly-lit room of younger people. She no longer knew how to begin to measure herself, she thought, or anyone.

When the baby had been newly born, she had been placed for a few moments on Nathalie's abdomen and, feeling the new weight, Nathalie had raised her head and marvelled with some shock that this complete and thrusting creature, still umbilically connected but now with a once-vital layer of nature's protection withdrawn, had actually been carried inside her body; there couldn't have been space for all of that, she had felt, and what had been set in motion seemed then, as now, larger than she had known she had room for.

Edward had begun, with ceremonial flourishes, to open the wine.

"This bread," said John, "is absolutely fabulous. I could eat the loaf."

"Are your parents still living out West?" she asked.

"Nope," he answered, his mouth still full. "They died ten years ago. One day they were there" — he waved his hands — "and the next day they weren't. A small plane went down."

"Oh, I'm so sorry," said Nathalie.

Liza came closer with the baby. "What did you do then?" she asked.

"Then I lived with my uncle's family."

"Were they nice to you?" Liza pressed on.

"Oh, they were all right," he answered, "but what really made the difference was a biology teacher I had. He got me started."

"Like what do you mean?" asked Liza. She shifted the baby casually, expertly to the crook of her arm.

"Nathalie?" said Edward, nudging her hand. "Wine?"

She accepted the glass and found him smiling at her, one smile at the forefront of countless others; a smile it had been a year ago that had looped her in and stayed her heart where it could freely grow.

"I mean," said John, "that he knew where he was and he could open the door for others. It didn't take much, just a few words here and there."

"You were lucky," said Liza.

"Something just clicked and off I went."

By now the baking fish had begun to yield up its fragrances of deep seas and melting butter. Nathalie tested the carrots and potatoes that steamed on top of the stove, earth scents. From behind her came the unfretful baby sounds, gurglings, blowings, then testings in a higher register. Each of the other voices had its own compass, within which it ranged experimentally. Sounds lifted off into thin air.

She turned. it was delicious how light she felt, how spacious.

"Liza," she said, "listen to how happy the baby is with you."

Philip Damon

Davidson Among the Chosen

Hannah was her usual reticent self on the subject. "I don't trust them," was all she'd say. Reticent and cryptic. "What the hell you mean you don't trust them?" Brian kept asking her. "Nothing. I just don't trust them. That's all."

Brian was trying to find his sneakers. Hannah was no help on that score either. "Last time I saw them," she said, "was when you painted the kitchen." That was three weeks ago. And now she was too busy getting his son dressed and fed to help him find the damn things.

The one they called Izzie had brought up Brian's son last night, at the party. "I saw you playing football with your kid the other day," he had said. "You a football player?" Joel was barely three and he and Brian had been doing little more than rolling the ball back and forth to each other. "I played a little in high school," Brian had said. "Nothing spectacular."

Izzie had then nodded, and as soon as his drink was empty had disappeared into some other corner of the party.

Brian was the only gentile at the party. When asked about himself he would explain that he was from Pennsylvania, had lived there all his life, had done his doctorate at Penn where he had met Hannah, and was now happily married and the father of a three year old son, and teaching literature at Fairleigh-Dickenson University. There really wasn't much else to say about himself, he would say about himself, knowing that what he really wanted to say was that, except for his wedding which had been more a ritual than a social gathering, never before in his life had he been confronted by so many Jews and that it made him slightly uneasy.

Not that he hadn't known a good number of Jews. Graduate school was loaded with them. But that had hardly prepared him for this party. A short while after Izzie had vanished, another appeared, a good forty pounds heavier than Izzie, calling himself Mort. "First time you've ever been in a ghetto?" he asked. Mort was a stockbroker.

"Pardon me?" was the best Brian could muster in reply.

"Ghetto, man," repeated the burly Jew. "Like in Harlem. Or Warsaw. You dig ghetto, don't you?"

"I know what you mean," Brian said, "but, well, I guess it's difficult for me to see this little section of Fair Lawn, New Jersey as a ghetto."

"And why is that?"

"Well, I guess I associate ghettos more with things like poverty and oppression, segregation. And this is a very nice row of garden apartments."

"You never guessed that maybe ghettos might be the result of voluntary segregation?"

Brian thought for a moment. "No, I guess I never did."

And it was true, he never had. A ghetto was a place you escaped from, not one you retreated to. Most of the Jews he had known in graduate school were escapees from the ghetto, or at least from a constricting, homogeneous world. But it dawned on him then, as he stood alone in a corner of the large room, with the party going on all around him, that the Jews he had known before he had known as individuals, as isolated, tormented, intellectual individuals not unlike himself, and despite the fact that he had been married to one for four years this was the stereotype he still carried around in his mind.

Before Mort moved on he had said, "We see our community as a kind of Israel. And everything around us as a desert, populated by Arabs."

Brian would have liked to follow Mort and pursue the subject but soon after Hannah caught his eye and motioned with her head toward the front door. And at that moment Izzie returned with the invitation. "Hey, Brian," he had said. "Every Sunday at around eleven we have a game of touch football in the big field out behind Nabisco. How'd you like to play with us tomorrow?"

Brian of course knew all about their touch football games. The entire apartment complex knew. It was pretty tough to ignore ten or twelve shouting and laughing young men on a Sunday morning, playfully shouldering each other in the gut and firing bullet passes back and forth across the lawns and over the hoods of cars on the way to a game of touch football. Brian had watched them go off to the field each of the four Sundays he and Hannah had lived in the apartment, and even though touch football was far from his favorite form of recreation he had wished himself with them. He readily agreed to play.

"Okay," Izzie said with a smile. "Tomorrow at eleven." And then he said, "Oh, by the way. You teach literature, right?"

Brian nodded. "Are you interested in literature?" Izzie had said he was in dry cleaning.

"Well I'm no literary critic or anything," Izzie said with a shrug. "But there are some books I like. You ever read *The Enemy Camp*?"

"No, I don't think so. Who's it by?"

"Jerome Weidman."

Brian shook his head. The name rang no bells.

"*I Can Get It For You Wholesale.*"

Brian shook his head again. He couldn't tell if that was a title or a proposition.

"Right. Well you've read *The Merchant of Venice* I'm sure. That's an interesting story."

Brian was trying to decide upon an appropriate and diplomatic response when he saw Hannah standing impatiently at the door. He mumbled something about having to leave and leaned in that direction, afraid of offending Izzie but wanting to get away just the same, and then he heard Izzie say, "Do you think Shakespeare was an anti-Semite?" and he turned to answer, his mind in a state of confusion, no answer readily available to him, but Izzie had disappeared once again, into the party somewhere, and after standing there for a moment alone, he turned once again to the door and followed Hannah out into the night.

Just before they said their goodnights, he had told Hannah of the invitation to play this morning and she had simply said, "I don't trust them."

He found his sneakers, an aged and broken pair of Keds with yellow paint stains spattered about them, and after he put them on, careful not to break the rotting laces, he pulled on his hooded sweatshirt with the letters PENN across the chest. He debated whether to bring his gloves along, finally deciding — despite the reading of 40° on the thermometer outside the kitchen window — that it would be very unmanly of him to do so. Checking himself out in the dresser mirror he wished for a moment that he was not quite so blond, so that the stubble of beard on his chin and cheek might have been a bit more prominent.

Finally he went into Joel's room and took the football from the closet shelf. It said "The Duke" on it and was the official ball of the National Football League. Brian had payed seventeen-fifty for it at Two Guys. At the door Hannah asked him what he wanted for lunch.

"I'm not sure I'll be coming home," he said. "Those guys usually watch the Giants play afterward and maybe I'll just go up and watch with them."

Hannah nodded. "Well just in case you don't what do you want," she said.

He turned and looked at his wife. There were times when her eyes had the distance of thousands of years behind them. "In that case I'll decide when the time comes," he said, and slamming the ball into the palm of his left hand he left the house.

Izzie and a few other guys were already out in the court-yard, tossing a ball back and forth and generally cutting up. They were all wearing football jerseys with various numbers on the chest and stripes on the sleeves. Most of them wore sweatpants and striped shoes with rubber cleats. Brian felt very underdressed.

Izzie spotted Brian and shouted, "Hey, Brian Davidson," and broke into a flamboyant zig-out pattern between two of the courtyard shrubs. Brian faded back towards his own apartment steps and lauched a pass that wobbled and died yards short and bounced into one of the shrubs. "Sorry," he shouted to Izzie.

"No sweat," returned the diminutive Jew, bending into the bush to retrieve the ball, then exclaiming, "Hey, this is a great ball."

Brian smiled and broke into a little pattern of his own, nothing extravagant, and when he looked over his shoulder for the pass, saw Izzie throw it to someone else in the opposite direction. Brian watched his ball make the rounds of the jovial Jews, each one stopping to read the label and remark on the superior quality of the ball, and then, quite suddenly, everyone stopped and shouted his greetings as Mort descended the steps of his apartment. Brian noticed immediately that he was not wearing a numbered football jersey. Instead he was clad in a grey sweatshirt, the sleeves cut at mid-biceps to reveal a pair of super muscular arms, and with the legend "Super Jew" stenciled across the chest.

Mort didn't even bother to break into a pattern. He merely raised his hands and Brian's ball came floating into them. With a nonchalant flick of his heavy, hairy wrists he glanced at the wording on the ball. "Nice ball," he said and casually tossed a perfect spiral to one of the guys who had negotiated a pattern halfway down the street.

They were ready to leave for the field now. It was clear that they had been waiting for Mort, and anyone who was yet to come would have to catch up. Some of them ran patterns the entire way, making the trip in a series of tangential circles that reminded Brian of old penmanship exercises. Mort just walked.

About halfway there Izzie came up beside Brian, partly out of breath from running pass patterns, and said, "You ever read *The Sun Also Rises?*"

"Sure. A couple of times," Brian said.

"How'd you like it?"

"Well . . ." Brian fumbled for an answer.

"You think Hemingway was an anti-Semite?" But before Brian could say a word Izzie was off on a down and out pattern.

Just before they got to the field behind Nabisco, another of the guys, a lanky sandy-haired fellow with a row of freckles across his cheeks and nose the size of corn flakes, came up beside him. His name was Sammy Moss and he was a partner in his father's delicatessen. "You teach at Fairleigh?" he asked.

"This is just my first year there," Brian apologized.

"You know what we used call it back when I was a kid?"

"No, what?"

"Fairly Ridiculous." And Sammy Moss laughed and said, "I don't know if I could ever think of it as anything else."

There were two teams of five and Mort said, "Davidson, you're on my team." Brian noticed that Mort pronounced his name in a strange way, more as though he were saying *David's son* than Davidson. He nodded and joined Mort's team at their end of the field. Izzie and Sammy Moss were on the other team.

One of Brian's teammates kicked off and Brian went charging down the right sideline. Izzie took the kick and faked toward Brian's side, then went the other way, leaving Brian alone and out of the play. Izzie was touched after a return of about ten yards.

"You rush," Mort said to him as they lined up on defense for the first play and Brian dug-in, his heart pounding, his palms wet despite the cold.

Izzie was the quarterback, with one blocking back and three linemen, Sammy Moss among them at end. At the snap of the ball Brian charged. Izzie was backpeddling, looking for a receiver, and Brian almost laughed he was so certain he was going to get to him before the pass was thrown, and suddenly something hit him alongside of the head and he was out of the play. It was the forearm of Izzie's blocking back, a giant named Joab who lived across the court. The pass was complete for a good ten yards.

Izzie proved to be a very elusive quarterback and even when Brian was able to shake the hulking Joab, the diminutive Izzie would still manage to scamper free and get the pass off. And more often than not Sammy Moss would pull it in for a short gain. Brian was amazed at just how slippery Izzie was, and what made it double amazing was the fact that he also managed to keep up an unceasing line of chatter. Izzie was actually announcing the play-by-play of the game as he was playing it, his high voice shrilly piping the words, "Izzie back for a pass, looking for Moss in the flat, there's the pass . . . *complete* for a nice gain!"

On fourth down Mort intercepted Izzie's pass in the end zone and Brian's team took over possession of the ball.

"Another great interception by Super Jew, sports fans," piped Izzie, "thwarts the Izzie to Sammy aerial attack."

On offense Brian was the center. And once again it was the huge Joab confronting him. Joab was a rusher now and he lined up right over Brian. Each time Brian snapped the ball the hulking Jew would give him both forearms and knock him off his feet, then charge over Brian's supine form into the backfield. Mort was the quarterback. "Hey, David' son," he'd say after each play, "Try a little blocking next time, huh?"

This was the way it went, rushing at Joab on defense, being trampled by Joab on offense, with Izzie indefatigably announcing each play as well as finding his way into the thick of it, and Mort shaking his head and looking at Brian as if to say, "You are a hopeless case, man."

On the next defensive series Brian got through to Izzie. "Izzie back for a pass with David's son charging hard," Izzie announced, and just as Brian was bringing his hands down for the touch the shifty quarterback held the ball behind his head and suddenly it was gone. Sammy had come around from his end position and taken the ball on a Statue of Liberty play, and damn near scored a touchdown. It was clearly Brian's responsibility and he had not seen it coming.

"Hath not a goy eyes?" he heard Izzie say as he walked to the new line of scrimmage.

Joab had become his nemesis. He was covered with bruises from the big lineman's forearms and his head was beginning to ache. So far he had not been allowed to go out for one pass, nor to play in a position where he might intercept one. He was stuck in the line across from a man who outweighed him by fifty pounds and who was giving him a beating that was bordering on the sadistic. At one point he looked into the big man's eyes and almost thought he saw a flash of sympathy, and suddenly, irrelevantly, remembered someone telling him that Joab was a pediatrician but then the ball was snapped and he received a shot that sent him staggering for five yards. It was almost as though the giant was out to get him.

When they got the ball back he suggested to Mort that once Joab had charged past him he was wide open. All he had to do was pick himself up from the ground and Mort could toss it to him over Joab's head and he could take it for a sizeable gain. Mort shrugged and said they'd try it. Brian was almost desperate. He had to do something right. And it worked, except for the part where he had to catch the ball. Joab knocked him down and barrelled by, Brian jumped back up and sure enough the ball came floating right to him. He must have tried to run with it before he caught it because by the time he was in full stride he did not have the ball.

"Hath not a goy hands?" came Izzie's shrill voice from the defensive backfield.

He began spending more and more time on the ground. The pain in his arms and chest was something awful. He thought of Hannah and her cryptic "I don't trust them" and knew that she had known what lay in store for him. She knew but hadn't said a word to him other than those crumby four words. *Them*, she had said. It wasn't just Joab. These goddamn Jews were working him over, and for no other reason than the fact that he was a gentile. He looked at Izzie's mocking face and words went through his mind, words he had never permitted to pass his lips, words he had never really even thought. *Kike*, he thought. Izzie, you goddamn kike. *Sheeny*, he thought. You sheeny bastards, all of you.

He looked around him at these eleven Jews. Who only a short while ago had emerged from apartments in the same complex where he lived with his own Jewish wife. Whose front doors all had little mezuzahs nailed on the frame. Whose mothers and wives played mahjong every Wednesday night. I've been on your side all along, he wanted to shout. I've sympathized with you. I married one of you! I accept you why can't you accept me?

The thought flashed through his mind that perhaps this was some kind of intellectual ritual. Like a fraternity. Or some secret order, where the neophyte had to prove his manhood by withstanding great tests of pain and courage. Like an Indian movie he'd seen with Richard Harris. Of course. When it was all over they would come up to him and shake his hand and pat him on the back and tell him they were sorry but they really had to know just what kind of metal he was cast from. And he had borne up well. Then they would all go up to Mort's place, or Izzie's, or Joab's, and watch the Giants play on television and Brian would be the honored guest. The newly initiated.

This thought kept him on his feet through the rest of the game, or at least kept him from staying on the ground where Joab was still sending him. He had no idea what the score of the game was. No idea if Izzie and Sammy had combined for as many touchdowns as Mort had provided his team with. The whole game for him took place in that short distance of grass between himself and Joab.

And then his nose started to bleed. He wasn't even sure

whether it happened as a result of one blow from Joab or a whole series of blows. But it was all over his sweatshirt and along with the grass stains had made the letters PENN almost impossible to see. Now they'll feel sorry, he thought. Now they'll be forced to admit that I can take it. He looked around but nobody was looking at him. Nobody, that is, except Izzie. Izzie's voice was not so shrill this time. It was lower, more modulated. "If you prick him, does he not bleed?" he said.

In Brian's mind the end sweep took place almost immediately after Izzie's words. But time had become so confused for him now that it might actually have been an hour later for all he was willing to swear to. But it did happen. Mort was in the huddle, actually diagramming a play for Brian to run. He wanted to break out laughing. It seemed so beautifully appropriate that he wanted to sing. It *was* like some kind of sacrament. His blood had been drawn and now he was going to be permitted to enter into the game, to enter into the community of these men who were so strange to him. As Mort talked he remembered the horrible names he had thought and wished he could retract them. He looked around the huddle and across the defensive team, and loved these men with all his heart. He loved the kinky wavy hair. He loved their bent noses. He loved their swarthy skin. And he loved Hannah who was one of them.

He loved them for the pain he now felt throughout his entire body.

The play was an end around, not unlike the one that Izzie and Sammy had pulled on Brian earlier. Brian would be at end this time and he would count to three then circle around behind Mort, take the ball, and take off up the left sideline. The blockers would push everyone to the right. As Brian lined up at the right end he felt his heart beating under the blood-spattered N of PENN, and he hunkered down into his three-pointed stance with visions of Crazy Legs Hirsch in his mind. Was Crazy Legs Hirsch a Jew, he wondered, but before he had time to think on it the ball was on its way back to Mort and he was counting one two three and he was whirling on his battered sneaker and heading back into the backfield. Mort's arm came back as if to pass and *yes* there it was in his hands and he was cutting to the left sideline and out of the corner of his eye he could see the flow going to the right and he was clear, free, and then he could hear Izzie's voice floating across the field toward him *and it looks like a fake, sports fans, it look like David's son has the ball and not Super Jew and he's skirting left end, he's gonna go all the way, he's heading for the promised land* and then Brian felt something wrong and glanced back and saw that no one was chasing him, saw only the backs of the others, saw that they were walking away.

And he slowed down for a few steps and then stopped and then turned and finally saw that they were already off the field and on their way back toward the apartments. Izzie had stopped his play-by-play, there was no sound except for the rasping of his breath through the blood-caked nostrils, and he was standing there alone, with his football still clutched preciously to his chest.

Jay Neugeboren

Uncle Nathan

When I was a kid growing up in Brooklyn, and during the years when I was first falling in love with books and girls, I used to imagine that my Uncle Nathan was twins. Even back then, I guess, his life was a great sadness to me. What I couldn't figure out was how a man who worked eight hours a day, forty hours a week, fifty weeks a year, year after year after year, in the booth of a parking lot my Uncle Felix owned, could, at the same time, have once been the author of a real novel.

It didn't make any sense to me, and what I used to imagine was that the family was keeping the secret from me, but that someday before my Uncle Nathan died, he and his twin brother would show up at one of our family get-togethers and we'd find out that the other Nathan had really accomplished all kinds of incredible things in his life, since the time, when he'd been a boy of about my age, that he'd run off and forsaken the family. Sometimes when I was reading a book I loved and there was no picture of the author on the back, I'd imagine that he was my uncle.

I think the idea first came into my head when I was in the seventh grade and I used his novel for a book report. I was so proud to be able to tell the class that my uncle had written it that I found myself promising I would get him to visit our class and talk about it. But when I came to his parking lot that afternoon after school and asked him about coming, he got furious with me and told me he didn't know what had gotten into my mother to even let me know the book existed, much less read it. "She wants revenge," was all he said, and at the time I couldn't understand what he meant.

I think I told my class he couldn't come because he was getting ready to make a trip back to Russia or Poland, to research his next book, but I was pretty hurt, and I never mentioned his book to him again until years later, when just about everybody knew about it, it had become so well known.

Where he worked in those years was in a parking lot booth a few blocks from Ebbets Field, and on days when my father would take me to ballgames, we'd always stop by. Sometimes after school I'd walk down Flatbush Avenue to visit him, by myself, or with my cousin David, or with friends, and I could tell that it always made him light up inside just to see me coming down the street towards him. Most of the time he'd be sitting inside the booth, doing nothing — even in August, when it was broiling outside — but when he'd spot me, he'd step outside his booth and set up two wooden folding chairs that were shaped like walking canes, with little round seats — they were from the 1939 World's Fair — and we'd sit there on the sidewalk together, swapping jokes and stories. A lot of the Dodger players parked their cars in his lot, and it made me feel pretty special to get signed baseballs and programs from guys like Pee Wee Reese and Andy Pafko and Roy Campanella and Johnny Podres and Jackie Robinson and the others. The Dodgers had their really great teams back then in the early fifties while I was in high school, and when my friends and I would go on about how terrific they were, my Uncle Nathan would always say that the key to their success was their great third baseman, Billy Cox. "After all," he'd say to us, "think of it this way: where would the Dodgers be without Cox?" And when we'd all get the joke and start laughing, he'd just close his eyes and smile.

The other thing that surprised me about him was not that he wasn't married, which always seemed such a waste — he was the kind of man you wished could be your own father — but that, for such a little guy, who spent his life holed up in that booth like a dead man, he knew so much about

women, and — as I'd point out to my friends — that he
practiced what he preached. Sometimes at night, if the guys
and I were on Flatbush Avenue after a basketball game or a
movie, we'd see him going into Garfield's or Elman's with a
good-looking woman. In all the years I knew him I never saw
him with the same one twice, and I don't think there was one
of them who wasn't taller than he was. I tried a lot to get him
to tell me about them — I'd tell him which one I thought
was prettiest, hoping that would encourage him to see her
again — but no matter what I said, he'd never say much
back.

He was always interested in us and our girlfriends,
though, and he liked to collect our sayings. When I had a
good new one, I would give it to him right away, and then
I'd imagine that he would be using it with one of his women
that same night. He lived alone, in the house on Winthrop
Street in which he and my mother and their two sisters and
brothers and parents had all lived, and I used to imagine him
in different rooms with different women, putting the make
on them as they settled onto one of his beds together, by
whispering in their ears like a regular Charles Boyer, the lines
I'd given him — "If I said you had a nice body, my dear,
would you hold it against me?" — or, settling down onto the
oriental rug in the living room, and running his hands across
some woman's clothing while moving up towards her breasts,
I'd hear him asking, "Could this be silk? . . . Could this be
cotton? . . . Could this be linen? . . . Could this be felt?"

Whenever I had a new girlfriend I'd take her to visit my
Uncle Nathan as soon as I could, and his way of getting them
to laugh right away by teasing them ("Is my young nephew
treating you the right way?" he'd ask) and by telling them
his little jokes always made them more affectionate with me
afterwards. Still, no matter how good a time we'd have
together at his booth, when I was at home alone and I'd be
thinking about him, I'd always become very sad suddenly,
from as far back as when I was eleven or twelve years old — as
if he was a burden I was carrying around inside of me, and as

if he somehow knew, without saying so, that I understood things about him nobody else did.

During those years I was supposed to be some kind of cockeyed wonder. I was good in most things I tried, sports and music and school and acting and art and scouts, and everybody — my teachers and friends and relatives — kept praising me to the skies. Yet my very success turned out to be the link between me and my Uncle Nathan that made me so sad about him, and, at the same time, made me doubt myself so much. Because what made me feel that Nathan and I had a special understanding between us, even when I couldn't put it into words, was that he'd supposedly been a very precocious child too, and the fact of his book — which he wrote before he was twenty-three years old, and which I loved — proved it most of all.

We used to have this little game we played with each other, where I'd say, "My mother tells me I can be anything at all when I grow up," and he'd say, "Of course you do: you want to be *anything at all* — that way you can never be any one thing, yes?"

His book was called *The Stolen Jew*, and when I would read it — and I read it at least once a year all through junior high and high school and college — I used to feel that it was about me somehow — that he knew what my life was going to be like before it took place, and I used to imagine that I was all the main characters in it: the stolen Jew, and the man who has him stolen, and the boy for whom he is stolen, and the stolen Jew's father, and the stolen Jew's mother, and the wife of the boy for whom the stolen Jew is stolen, and the other woman he comes to love. In the book a young Jewish boy in Russia, in the middle of the nineteenth century, is stolen by the Kehilla — the Jewish council of elders of his town — to take the place of another Jew in the Tsar's Army for the dreaded twenty-five years service, and later he comes to America to kill the Jew whose place he took when he was a boy. That Jew has now become a great concert violinist with a fine family, and the stolen Jew has kept himself alive only by the dreams of revenge he nurtures in his heart, year after year, for almost half a century. The book is filled with scenes of violence and evil and hate, and the ending, when the stolen Jew slits the violinist's throat and disfigures his hands and then takes his own life, used to make me almost physically ill every time I read it.

The crazy thing, though, was that even though the book was supposed to be so grim — a picture of Jews preying endlessly on other Jews in a world which preys on them — for me, when I read it, it always seemed to be a life-*giving* book. There was some kind of energy in it — that seemed to go beyond the awfulness and sadness of the story itself, and it sometimes made me think that, in writing the book and in putting on all those different voices to do it, he had, like me, been somehow living up to the dream our family had had for him — of being able to be anything at all.

"You're the kind of person everyone else would like to be," he said to me once, and I never forgot it. We were standing next to his booth and I was admiring my fielder's glove, which he'd gotten Duke Snider to inscribe to me, and even though I should have been pleased, it made me uncomfortable to hear him say such a thing. I guess I sensed, for a brief glimmering instant, that it was hard — how hard I still don't even know most of the time — to be the guy everyone else always wants to be. It made me feel as if *I* didn't exist somehow. It was such a strange feeling that I felt there wasn't a thing I could say back to him about it that afternoon. His words stayed with me, though, and through the years I came to think that maybe he'd had the same kind of feeling when he'd been young and successful before he'd ever expected to be — before his dreams had a chance to grow enough inside him in the way they should have, in the way he'd wanted them to.

He seemed to be a man who went through life as if he'd already lived it once and was just biding his time now on the second time around. But such a thought didn't make sense to me all the time, because whenever I read his book, what I felt above all was that the man who wrote it was a man who was just *beginning* to live his life. Reading novels had always affected me that way, from the first — I could never get over how one person could understand so much about what was in the hearts of so many different kinds of people, even if, as in Nathan's book, the people had lived in a different time and place. To me it was almost as if he was God — creating and understanding and watching over and judging and deciding on matters of life and death. But if he'd understood so much — about Jewish history and Russian history and the violin and immigrant life in America and all the other things his book was made of — why then, I kept asking myself, was his life itself so small?

"My life is, I think, a mistake," he said one day, when I was visiting him with David and a group of guys, and I had the feeling he wouldn't have said the same thing if we'd been alone, just the two of us. He had just told us a shaggy dog Jewish joke, about a man who spends his life trying to find out the secret of life, and after all kinds of journeys and adventures he discovers that the secret of life is that "Life is a flowing fountain," only to return to his little village in eastern Europe, to tell his old friend the rabbi of his discovery, to have the rabbi think for a few seconds and reply, "But my friend, life is *not* a flowing fountain," whereupon the man thinks for a second, nods knowingly and says, "You know what? — You're right." It was while some of us were still laughing that I saw this terrible black look come across his face, and he nodded again, like the man in the story, and then he said what he did about his own life, but very softly.

There was one other time that I remember seeing that kind of look come over him, and it had to do with a Valentine's card I'd bought for my mother. I was in the eighth grade then, and I'd saved up money from my allowance so that I could get my girlfriend and my mother expensive cards from a store on Church Avenue, instead of making them, as I'd always done, from doilies and ribbons and tinfoil. My allowance then, without counting money for haircuts and things I had to buy for school, was only fifty cents a week, and it had taken me over three months to save the dollar and thirty-five cents that each of the cards cost, but they were worth it. They each had a heart made out of a piece of pink silk-like material that was raised up by some kind of cushion and had a beautiful scent to it — and inside the card the lettering for the poem was embossed in genuine gold engraving. The man in the store made me proud of myself when I bought the cards, and when I showed them to Nathan he'd made me feel the same way.

But when I handed my mother her card at supper-time and she looked at it, instead of being delighted, she actually flung the card back in my face. "Anyone can buy a card!" she declared. "But not every son can make beautiful cards like the ones you used to make for me!"

Then she stalked out of the kitchen, angrily. I was devastated. My father sat across from me at the kitchen table, and I looked at him — for help, for some explanation — but all he could do was to shrug and say something to me about trying to be more considerate of my mother's feelings. What I'd done wasn't such a terrible thing, he added, but he urged me to go to my mother and apologize to her — to go to my room and to make her the kind of card she expected from me.

I went to her first and apologized and tried to explain to her how long I'd been saving up to give her the kind of card the richer kinds in my class gave to their mothers, but she only replied by asking me if I thought she wanted me to be like everybody else. She glared at me with such anger and coldness (I was damned if I was going to do what my father had urged me to do, and humiliate myself by sitting in my room and trying to come up with something she'd love) that suddenly I found myself letting my own anger come right back at her. I told her that I'd bought the exact same card for my girlfriend and that she had *loved* it and shown it to everybody in our class and that I guessed that meant I was batting .500 for the day with the women in my life, and that I figured that wasn't such a bad average.

Then she really let me have it. I didn't listen to whatever it was she started spewing, though, because I was out the door pretty fast, slamming it as hard as I could, and then stopping for a second — cringing as I waited for the sound of broken glass (which never came), and I went straight to my Uncle Nathan's house and told him the story. I can remember the scene as vividly as any in my life. I sat cross-legged in his living room, in front of the big wine-red easy chair he loved to sit in — it had been his father's — and the more I told him about her reaction, and the more I kept pleading with him to tell me what I could do, the darker his face seemed to become.

But he didn't say anything at all when I was done, which wasn't like him. He just kept sitting there. He took my hand, though, and after a short while he bent over and kissed my fingertips and then he leaned back again into a corner of the chair so that he seemed, in the darkness, especially small to me, and he started humming to himself. I kept having the feeling that he was remembering everything their life had been like together when they'd been a brother and sister growing up in the same house, and I suddenly had the strangest feeling of all — that what made my Uncle Nathan and me so much like on another, even though he'd had three sisters and a brother, was that when he was a boy he must really have felt, in his deepest feelings, that he was just like me — an only child forever wishing that it wasn't so.

I had this crazy feeling that we were both somehow orphans, living in an abandoned orphanage together, and when that idea settled into my head I let it stay there, and I just let my mind wander where it wanted to, the way I imagined his was doing. I let myself feel just how much I hated being an only child, and just how much I was still wishing for a brother, or even a sister — how often I'd wished for one and then had tried to deny the wish — and how deeply I resented my parents for never having given me one.

It just never seemed fair to me — not that I had my parents all to myself (though that must have been part of it), but that nobody had ever joined me, as it were, to inherit my crib and my clothes and my baseball gloves and my toys and my books and my games and the rest. It was as if, without a brother or sister, I was incomplete somehow — as if my parents had never finished making me.

When I got home late that night, my parents were already asleep and the first thing I did when I got into my room was to open *The Stolen Jew* and read the opening page, which is told in the voice of Tsvi Toporofsky, the father of the violinist, who, when the book opens, has already seen his only son die at the hands of Mendel, the man who was kidnapped to take the son's place. "I understand loss," Tsvi says in the first line of the book, and I guess what I understood that night — the thing that was passing between me and Nathan in the silence of his living room — was that sometimes you can understand loss not just by losing something you love, the way Tsvi did, but by feeling that you'll never have the thing you love, to lose . . .

Whenever my mother would get angry with me later on, especially when I got to college and began going with Ruth, she would always try to use my uncle as an example and threat against me: When was I going to settle down and decide on one thing, one career? When was I going to stop wasting my life and my gifts and my precious energies on women who were unworthy of me? Did I want to wind up being like her brilliant brother — ?

The only thing wrong with her tactic, of course, was that the answer to her question was 'Yes, I did want to wind up like her brother,' and I suppose one of the reasons for wanting to, and for loving him, was his very ability to enrage her by the way his life had, in fact, turned out.

It was during this later period of my life that we each went through experiences that bound my Uncle Nathan and me even more closely to one another, only neither of us ever told the other the full story at the time, or since, and it seems to me now that it was the very fact that we'd kept so much of our stories secret, even while we kept sharing other things, and that neither of us tried to pry the secret from the other, that came to make us respect each other more, and, finally, to love each other in a new way.

My experience had to do with meeting a girl — Ruth — and falling in love with her in a way I never had before with any girl. I was a sophomore at Columbia then and she was a junior at Barnard, a year and a half older than me. We had the leads together in a Columbia Players production of *Our Town,* and at first, because of the differences in our ages and religions we were very "platonic" with each other. We'd spend hours together, walking up and down Broadway, and going into different places for cups of coffee and toasted English muffins, and telling each other all about our lives and our dreams and our hopes, and especially about the boyfriends and girlfriends we were going with, and had gone with.

She was seeing a much older man then, a young English professor at the College who'd already published two books (one of his poems, and one about T. S. Eliot), and he was putting the pressure on Ruth to marry him. She told me that she figured she probably would, but it was clear to me that she wasn't very enthused about it, and she kept thanking me for listening to her talk about it. The trouble was, she said, that she seemed to admire him more than she really liked being with him. The idea of marrying him seemed right, but being with him didn't. He didn't *excite* her, she kept telling me, and she wondered if I thought this meant there was something wrong with *her* somehow. She didn't understand why she could tell him she loved him, but could never feel very much when she did.

"I just keep feeling that I don't have the *right* to say no to him," was the way she put it. When she thought about it, she confessed, what bothered her most was that she couldn't imagine what they would ever talk about, for fifty years or so, over the breakfast table every morning.

I laughed with her, and then made my voice old and

quoted to her from what Doc Gibbs says in *Our Town:* "'Do you know one of the things I was scared of when I married you?'"

"'Oh, go along with you!'" she replied, imitating Mrs. Gibbs.

"'I was afraid we wouldn't have material for conversation mor'n'd last us a few weeks. I was afraid we'd run out and eat our meals in silence, that's a fact . . .'"

At the time I was living at home in Brooklyn and going out with different girls — "playing the field," as my father liked to put it — and still waiting for the one girl to come along who would change my life. I tried to explain this to Ruth — that I agreed with her, that I wanted a woman who would excite me too, but who would also be someone I'd never get tired of talking to, or afraid of being tired of talking to — someone I could share my every thought and wish with, and who wouldn't ever think they were silly. I didn't want to "settle" for anything less, and I told her that she shouldn't either.

Just talking to her about that kind of thing, I confided to her one day, had become one of the most important things in my life — it was as if I were talking to the sister I'd always wanted and had never had, I said, and when I'd said this, and then had gone on to remember what happened with the Valentine's card that time, and about my Uncle Nathan's reaction, she cringed. "But at least your mother always told you what she was feeling," she said. "That must have helped."

A day or two later I confided something else to her, something I'd never told anybody before. It happened after I'd brought a pretty Barnard freshman I was dating named Donna Schwartz, who'd been Homecoming Queen earlier that year, to a rehearsal one day. Ruth started in teasing me the next afternoon about all my "cute liitle Jewish girl-friends," and about how much advantage I took of them — what with my looks and talent and the rest — and finally I got angry with her, and then when the anger passed I told her that it might come as a shock and surprise but that, for her information, I was still a virgin.

I had expected her to laugh at me, but she only furrowed her brow in a way that made her seem years and years older. At first I imagined that she might say something I wanted to hear — I saw at once that maybe I'd been secretly scheming, and had really confessed to her so that she'd come back to me with a line like, "Well, we'll have to do something to correct that, won't we?" — but she didn't say anything at all. We were sitting in the luncheonette on the corner of Broadway and 115th Street, a few doors down from *Prexy's,* where in those years they used to sell something called "the hamburger with a college education," and she wouldn't look at me while she was considering what I'd revealed. Finally, to fill the silence, I found myself talking more to her — about love, and about acting in plays where I played lovers, and about love poetry (I was fascinated then with Donne, and Ruth and I had talked a lot about the idea that the climactic moment of love is also the moment in which the love, being fulfilled finally, begins to die) — and telling her that even though it felt crazy sometimes, it was also something that I guessed I still believed in: I was — like a good Jewish boy? I asked — somehow "saving myself" for the right girl.

"Well," she said then, in her dry Hoosier tone, "my mother would certainly approve."

We both laughed, but I knew that she took me seriously, and this meant everything. It was the thing about her that had been different from the start. She heard what I said, and she believed me when I spoke, and when we talked to each other I never felt that she was dissembling. She just didn't seem to have the ability to do things for ulterior motives, or indirect reasons, or out of cunning or malice or anything resembling deviousness. She couldn't stand people who went all around Robin Hood's barn, as she put it, to tell you what they meant, and she seemed — like no other person I'd ever known — to be in touch with her feelings, to know what it was she thought and felt, though she couldn't always find words for those thoughts and feelings.

During breaks at rehearsals she used to crack us all up with hilarious imitations of what we termed Hoosier dead-pan: "Yes, that's what it's like in our town. Hear tell the Methodists are fixin' to let their young people wear lipstick. Why, last year they even went out and brought a jukebox into their church basement . . ."

Ruth's father, who'd been a traveling salesman for Masonite, had died during her first year at Barnard. Her mother sold Avon products door to door in Greenwood, and the thing Ruth dreaded most was going home on vacations and having to accompany her mother on her rounds — to sit in living rooms and listen to everybody, especially her old high school friends, most of whom had not gone on to college, remark on how "different" Ruth had always been. The prouder they were of her, the worse she felt.

Yet as much as she would mock the narrowness of her small town and its values, and amuse us by reading sections from the Bible pamphlets her mother was still sending her (my own favorite was one called "Petting and the Scarlet Sin") — the same pamphlets that her mother would give out to friends and neighbors along with her Avon products — when Ruth would go to center stage to stand stiffly and sing one of her hymns for us — "Amazing Grace" or "Deep and Wide" (with motions) or "Just As I Am" — even while she would be wearing her best dumb Hoosier farmgirl look (arms at side, head jutted forward slightly, jaw slack) — I was always entranced by the songs themselves, and the beauty of her voice when she sang them — and I think there was something in their simple and pure lines that she loved too, despite herself.

It didn't take long for things to change between us, of course. The thing that did it was when I was out walking with some of my friends from the JV basketball team one afternoon in Riverside Park, down below Barnard, and I spotted her on a blanket with her young professor. Her head was on his lap and her skirt was wrinkled up above her knees and she was laughing in a way that made me ache all over with anger. She didn't spot me, and I didn't say anything to the guys, but I nearly went crazy afterwards, on the subway ride back to Brooklyn, imagining the two of them doing things together in his apartment, while he fed her wine and French food and his lousy poetry.

"Don't you know you'll just be throwing your life away if you marry him?" I screamed at her the next day. "Don't you see it? Don't you see that you're just letting your God-damned Baptist guilt destroy your life?"

She cocked her head to the side and smiled at me then. "Well," she said. "If what you say is so, I think it would make mother right proud, don't you?" I wanted to hit her, she had me so angry, but I just glared and she started in quoting some line about this world being only an impure state we were passing through on our way to live with God once again. I found my voice then and I kept at her about all she would be losing, until I had her crying pretty hard. We were down in Riverside Park, near where I'd spotted her the day before, and it was late, with not too many people around, but I guess neither of us would have cared anyway.

"You're not a selfish person," I kept telling her. "Do you hear me? You're not a selfish person and you've got to see that. You're a good person with lots of love inside you to give. There's a big difference between self-interest and selfishness, don't you see? Only mothers like ours do their best to train the difference out of us —" I even started in quoting Hebrew to her that I remembered from *Pirkay Avos* — from what my Uncle Nathan had once taught me — about "If I am not for myself, who then —?" — and telling her that if she kept living according to what she felt she *should* do her whole life long, then she'd wind up hating her husband, and hating her mother, and, worst of all, hating herself.

Then I launched into this terrific lecture about how she would probably turn out to be just like what she hated her

mother for being — a frigid old repressed conservative unhappy lonesome Baptist woman, whose heart and life had
turned to stone — and that what I believed and wanted her
to believe was that it just wouldn't be fair for that to happen — for her to deprive the world and herself and the
family and children she could have someday of the life and
love she had been saving up to give.

I told her I'd go through with the play with her, but
that when it was over she'd never see me again, and I prophe-
sied that one day, years from now, she would think of me
and what I was saying, and if she thought she was in pain
now while I was talking to her, the pain would be infinitely
worse when she would be remembering my words across a
lifetime of dullness and unfulfillment. She was crying so
much by this time that I thought she was gagging, but I
didn't do anything to comfort her. And when she leaned forward, while sort of gurgling, between sobs, "Please . . .
Please . . ." — and she tried to touch me, all I saw was a picture of her with her head in her poet's lap, and of him bending down to kiss her lips, and then I shoved her back hard,
against the tree trunk, and told her to get away from me, that
I didn't want any of her guilt rubbing off on me, that I still
had a lot of living to do — more than she did, I guessed —
since I was younger than she was.

That was when she started swinging with her fists. She
really let me have it — a solid punch on the neck, right near
my Adam's apple — and she was so wild I couldn't even get
hold of her wrists. "What do you *want* from me? . . . What is
it you *want*, for Christ's sake . . .?" she kept screaming. I
covered up and I didn't hit back. (Later I'd joke to her about
that — about how we had my mother to thank for having
trained me so well for just that kind of situation.) But when
she kept coming at me, I suddenly found that I was screaming back at her, "What the fuck do you want from *me* — you
tell me that, okay? What the fuck do you want from me?"

I had a strong urge to haul off and whack her, right
across the face, but just when the urge rose in me, she sagged

and collapsed. She leaned back against the tree trunk, out of
breath, and looked up at me. "I'm sorry," she said.

"Don't be sorry — it's what you really feel toward me."

"You feel the same," she said, softly, but with bitter-
ness. "Only you're too polite." Her voice reeked of sarcasm.
"My poor little Jewish virgin . . ."

Then I did slap her, as hard as I could, and the welts
seemed to rise on her cheeks at once. "Don't you see what's
happening?" she said, as if I hadn't even touched her.
"Don't you see why we're trying so hard to hurt one
another?"

"I was trying, if you'll forgive the phrase, to save you,"
I said. "That's all."

"Bullshit."

"Have it your own way. Backslide all the way back to —
to —" I tried, but I couldn't find a destination.

"I'm just so in love with you I don't know what I'm
doing sometimes," she said then. "Don't you see that?"

"You're *what?*"

"I love you, Michael. I've been in love with you from
the first time we met, from the first time I even saw you. It's
been awful."

"You're crazy," I said.

"I know. So just leave me alone, all right? Let's play it
your way — let's finish the play, let's give the folks their
money's worth, and then not see each other again. I'll wish
you a good life, you can do the same for me, and that'll be
that."

"I don't understand," I said, and I reached toward her
to touch her cheek, where I'd smacked it. "I'm sorry. I was so
damned jealous, I guess . . ."

She leaned forward again and put her head on my
shoulder, and this time I let her. "We could be so happy together, Michael," she said, very gently. "I shouldn't say it,
but I know it's so. What else matters? We could be so happy
together if we'd let ourselves."

Then I kissed her, and her lips were softer than I'd believed possible — and they were sweaty and a little salty too. We didn't press hard against each other and we touched tongues lightly and she ran hers over my lips softly, and the most wonderful thing of all for me was while we were kissing, when I could feel her body actually shudder.

She stepped back and took my hands and used one of my lines, from the play, from after George and Emily have been talking at the soda fountain. "'So I guess this is an important talk we've been having.'"

"'Yes,'" I said. "'Yes . . .'"

I had my parents and my Uncle Nathan come to performances of *Our Town* on different nights, and it was clear to all of them just how much in love Ruth and I were with each other. My mother and father reacted pretty much as I'd expected them to. "I like her," my father said to me, when my mother wasn't nearby. "If she was Jewish — I'll tell you the truth — I could love her too." My mother gave me the cold shoulder, and talked to my father about how I was being lured away from the traditions which had given me everything I had, and about how she hoped I would come to my senses after the stars were out of my eyes. In the meantime, she preferred to see me as little as possible, and Ruth not at all. I said that that was fine with me, and I moved out of their apartment in Brooklyn and in with my cousin David in his place near school, on 107th Street and Broadway. Living in David's place also solved the other major problem Ruth and I had — which was where to go to be alone.

My Uncle Nathan took to Ruth right away — and this was, of course, what was most important to me. Even when I was alone with her, and we were being very tender with each other and my eyes would be closed, I'd see his face smiling at me — approving — and then I'd let myself relax even more and I'd be happiest of all. He came backstage after the performance that first time and when he smiled at Ruth and told her he'd been hearing a lot about her, she smiled back at him in the shyest most beautiful way I'd ever seen. He took us out afterwards, downtown to the Stage Delicatessen, and what thrilled me most was how they had no trouble at all in talking to each other. He knew just the right way to tease her, and when she made some passing remark — after we'd been talking about the hard time my mother was starting to give me — about her own mother, Nathan seemed to understand what she was going through at once, and a lot of stuff just poured out of her then about how her mother would never understand what was happening, and how, even though this wouldn't stop Ruth from leading the life she wanted to live (she took my hand then, so Nathan could see), she didn't see why she had to leave her mother out of things, why she had to choose one or the other of us . . .

Then Nathan asked her to tell him more about her mother — he said, laughingly, that he might have some special insight into the lives of old people living alone, and Ruth smiled and kept talking, and I found out for the first time just how much she'd already written to her mother about me and my being Jewish, and about what her mother had written back to her about Ruth abandoning *her* heritage and denying her faith, and I found that I was getting angry — not only because she was, really, confiding such things to Nathan before she'd confided them in me, but more because she seemed to want him to find some way for her to please her mother too, when I guess what I really wanted was for her to be rejecting her mother (the way I had cut myself off from mine) and to be thinking only of me. It also bothered me to be aware suddenly of how much she loved her mother, of how deeply she desired, still, to be close to her mother, and of how dimly she seemed to me to be aware of this part of her. I'd never fully bought the version of her mother she claimed to believe — it always seemed to be exaggerated — but it had never occurred to me until then that maybe I'd needed to believe in it as much as she did.

The strangest thing that happened between her and Nathan, though, was at the end of the evening, when we were saying goodbye in front of the 50th Street subway station. Nathan gave her a kiss on the check and she gave him one back, and then he smiled and warned her to beware of her mother. "Remember," he said, "that without you she'll be Ruth-less."

I laughed, but Ruth didn't. "How did you know that?" she asked him. "And that it's true not just for her, but for me too. You knew that, didn't you?"

He shrugged. "Not to worry," he said.

Ruth turned to me, as if she were going to explain something she and Nathan had been discussing together for years and years. "It's the joke I make with myself whenever I'm feeling really low — the oldest pun in my collection — whenever I'm feeling that I don't have any right at all to my own life, to the things I desire, to the kind of life that will put me forever beyond the reach of my mother and all the others who knew me when I was growing up."

"Don't get yourself all worked up," I said, putting my arm around her. "Please. Don't get started —"

"Oh sure," she said, sarcastically, and pulled away from me. "You don't want to hear it again, do you? You just want me to keep on being your nice sweet little docile midwest cheerleader, don't you? Emily comes to the big city! Oh Michael — why can't you see *my* loss too?"

Her eyes were wild with despair, and I had nothing to say. "If I lose touch with all that — with my childhood and my mother and my friends — I lose myself too, don't you see?" She was pleading with me. "That's the source of that crazy self-destructive anger you've seen erupt in me before. Without myself, you see — when I try to obliterate what I see in me, in my past, and when I see what it is I despise in me — I'm Ruth-less too."

"Take it easy," I said. "I'm not against you. I'm —"

"Forget it," she said then, her voice suddenly normal. "Just forget the whole thing. I'm sorry, all right? I'll try to behave —"

She looked at Nathan, and his eyes were all kindness. "You should be careful of her," he said. "But don't be afraid. There's no need. Listen to me — you're her only child, yes? If it's a choice between accepting you or losing you, in the end she'll always accept and you'll always win.''

Nathan was right, of course. By the time of our wedding, a year and a half later — and even after Ruth decided, on her own, to become Jewish (I'd been in favor of a justice-of-the-peace) — her mother came to the wedding and walked Ruth down the aisle of our synagogue, and at the reception afterwards she even wound up dancing the Hora with Nathan and my parents and my other aunts and uncles.

By this time, Nathan's life had changed also. About three months before our wedding, and without ever having told any of us in advance, we discovered that his novel was being published again, and that it was being hailed by newspapers and magazines as a forgotten classic of the twentieth century. Ruth and I were thrilled, of course, and my mother and the rest of the family went a little nuts because of the publicity. It didn't seem to affect Nathan much, though. He'd lived too long, he said. He didn't put much stock in other people's opinions of him.

He let himself be photographed (for *Time* and *Newsweek* and *Look* and *Life*), but aside from a few brief factual answers — about having no plans ever to write again, about living alone in the house in which he'd grown up, about being pleased to have the money so he could give up his job in the parking lot, and about wishing he could have known more history when he was young so that the errors in the novel might not have been so blatant — he gave away almost nothing, either to me or to Ruth or to his sisters or to his interviewers.

On the outside, he seemed happier than ever — but what I sensed, and what he confirmed, was that his happiness wasn't coming from his book's second life, but from something else, and this was what he wouldn't ever tell me about.

''I'm in love,'' he said to me one day, when I stopped by his house and found him sitting in the dark in the upstairs room in which he'd originally written his book. "I'm in love and the love is stranger than anything I could ever have imagined. So unlikely, Michael. I was right to give up writing fiction — that's what my life is teaching me. My life is stranger than my imagination, and a real writer needs an imagination which is stranger than his life, yes?"

It was as if, Ruth and I said to each other, even if he couldn't see it or admit it, it was his book's coming alive again that had allowed him to come alive again — had allowed desire to reawaken in him. We'd spend lots of time with him during the year before our marriage, and Ruth had come to love him as much as I did. It even turned out that they shared the same favorite author — Willa Cather — and they could spend hour after hour together, not talking about her, but just retelling her stories to one another, and reciting sections from her books aloud. For them, Willa Cather knew about the important things in life: the passage of time, the fact of loss, the importance of friendship, the significance of early life and of family and of continuity, the hard life of the artist and the price he pays, all the different kinds of sadness and happiness. I loved to hear Ruth read sections of *My Antonia* or *The Professor's House* or *Lucy Gayheart* aloud, and when she did Nathan would lean back in his easy chair, his head just to the side of the dark grease-stain his father's hair had made, and, more often than not, tears would form in his eyes.

I remember most of all the time she read to him from what the narrator of *My Antonia* says about happiness. Ruth and I had just come back from Indiana — after having told her mother we were going to be married — and we went straight from the Port Authority Bus Terminal to Nathan's house. We told him the whole story and Ruth kept going back to the moment when, after turning her cheek away when Ruth had gone to her mother for a kiss, her mother had snapped at her: "Is all you care about in life *your* happiness?"

Then Ruth described how she had gone down on her

knees at her mother's side, and had lain her cheek on her
mother's lap, and had tried to explain to her how good she
and I were for each other, how much we loved each other,
how much we wanted her to share in our lives, and how hard
Ruth knew accepting us was — and how she had, suddenly,
wanting her mother to *know* just what it was we had experienced together, begun reciting the passage from *My Antonia*
(which had been her mother's favorite book too — the book
her mother gave to her for a present on her fourteenth birthday), in order to try to get her mother's heart to soften.

   She recited it again for Nathan, in his living room. "I
was entirely happy," she whispered. "Perhaps we feel like
that when we die and become a part of something entire,
whether it is sun and air, or goodness and knowledge. At any
rate, that is happiness; to be dissolved into something complete and great. When it comes to one, it comes as naturally
as sleep."

   Nathan didn't say anything for a while, and then, as if
she had heard his thoughts, Ruth said to him, "I'll try to
give her time. I'll try to imagine what I would feel like if I
were her . . ." And then I found myself trying to imagine
something else — what *my* mother would have done if things
were reversed and I were marrying on Ruth's territory, and I
thought I did feel something of what Ruth believed her
mother might contain — that largeness of spirit it would take
to overcome, not just the immediate fact of our marriage,
but the entire narrow view of the world Ruth had so often
described, and mocked, and yet which was, for her mother,
as real and natural as the sun and air themselves.

   During the next year and a half, as Ruth's mother
began, slowly, to come over to us, Ruth and Nathan's feeling
for one another seemed to grow with it — as if, sometimes,
they were the parents and Ruth's mother was now the child,
and as if they were proud of her for the progress she was
making, and proud of themselves for having understood how
to bring about that process, through the gentle patience and
loving kindness Ruth showed her mother. The process

speeded up after our wedding, and I sometimes think that, before Ruth's mother had her stroke several years later and had to be put in a nursing home, she really did come to understand how much we loved each other, and — especially after our first child, Jennifer, was born — just how good our life together was.

But during this period — from the time of Nathan's literary success and of our wedding, until sometime after Jennifer was born, a year later — though Ruth and I accepted the fact that Nathan was, in his words, "in love," we never knew anything more about it, except to suspect sometimes that he was either inventing the whole thing, or that it was only his way of referring to a new book he was secretly trying to write. The crazy thing, though, was that just when his love seemed to die ("Well," he stated one day, "it's over. I've been rejected."), the desire in him to write again was — openly — reborn, and I couldn't really tell whether his mystery love and his mystery woman had inspired the desire in him again, and if she knew that she had (in my own fantasies I would imagine that if he could finish some new work and send it to her and let her see the real changes her love for him had wrought in his life, she would be his again, and Ruth and I would then have been able to visit Nathan and his wife with our children and be a part of a kind of family we'd both always dreamt of and never quite had) — or if it was the loss itself, and the pain and disillusionment that came with it, that was the thing that had made him, after a parenthesis of almost fifty years, start in again.

But when he did begin writing again now, he didn't do it in any ordinary way. Nobody, he claimed, would be interested in new stories by an old man. Nobody, he claimed, would want to believe that a writer who had not written for almost fifty years could write again, could simply open a door inside himself and let what had been locked away for such a long time come forth, as bright and wild and original as it had ever been. Who would ever believe, he asked, that the stories he'd kept inside him would have improved from their long rest, would really have matured with age? So what he decided to do — and his idea about what to do with his writing seemed to delight him as much as his writing did — was to cash in on his small measure of fame. Libraries and collectors — especially those with special interests in early twentieth century American literature, and in Jewish literature — would pay more, he believed, for old manuscripts by writers such as himself then magazines and publishers would ever pay him for new stories and new books.

So what he began to do was to invent his one book, *The Stolen Jew*, all over again, making up new versions of the book, which he then offered to the world as if they were early drafts for the book that had appeared when he'd been a young man. He made small changes and large changes, he invented preliminary notes and lists, he deleted chapters and he forged variant endings and he added new material and new characters — all of which, he told his buyers, had never wound up in the original version. He went to old stationery stores and rummaged around backrooms to find the oldest paper he could, and he used old ink, and he baked his manuscripts in his oven and he wet them down with tea bags, and he kept them in his refrigerator, and he slept with them under his pillow, to make them look as if they'd aged the right number of years.

It killed me to think of him not getting the recognition or the readers he really deserved (since the new stories wound up, he said, in humidified rooms used by scholars only, or in the private vaults of wealthy Jews), and Ruth and I tried to talk him into submitting the stories the right way, but he wouldn't even bother arguing with us, and after a while what I began to see was that for him, at his age, it didn't really matter. To my mind, it was as if his new writing was being shut away in a box, the way his life had been shut away in the parking lot booth, but that was in my mind, not his. He was very happy simply to be writing again, and this seemed to be all that was important to him — except for the pleasure he took in putting one over on the experts, and for the pleasure he took in letting Ruth and me read what he was writing, and in having us tell him again and again how terrible it was that we were the only ones who could read the new stories.

And he was also, I thought, happy, once some time had passed, that he had loved again, even if he'd lost. What was most important to me, though, in the end, was that I could never know exactly what had happened inside him to make him love somebody and to make him write again, and it was my very lack of knowledge that seemed to make us — across the silence, as it were — understand each other better than we ever had.

I found, to my surprise, that I liked the idea that he would never know, even to his grave, exactly what had passed between me and Ruth when we first realized we were in love — and I think he liked the idea that, like a mischievous little boy, he now had his secrets from me too.

I remember giving my theory on all this to Ruth one day, on the way home from the hospital where Nathan was just before he died, and she nodded, and, caressing the back of my neck lightly, she said this to me: "My mother was the same, I think — about me. She even made a point of repeating it to me the last time she was with us, after Jennifer was born. When I was younger and she said it, I used to think, not only that she didn't really believe it herself, but that it was just another of the folksy things she'd picked up from Ann Landers or our minister — but it stuck with me. 'People who are overly dependent on each other,' she said, 'are never truly free. They can become truly close only by separating.' "

A great sadness washed across Ruth's face then, black like the sea under a storm cloud, I thought — and black like the look I'd seen on my Uncle Nathan's face that first time. "Tell me, Michael," Ruth asked me, "because I don't think Nathan will be here soon to answer my questions — but tell me what you think please: in this world, does happiness ever coincide with the desire that yearned for it?"

John McGahern

All Sorts of Impossible Things

They were out coursing on Sunday a last time together but they did not know it, the two friends, James Sharkey and Tom Lennon, a teacher and an agricultural instructor. The weak winter sun had thawed the fields soft enough to course the hare on, and though it still hung blood-orange above the hawthorns on the hill the rims of the hoof tracks were already hardening fast against their tread.

The hounds walked beside them on slip leashes: a pure-bred fawn bitch that had raced under the name of Coolcarra Queen, reaching the Final of the Rockingham Stakes the season before; and a wire-haired mongrel, no more than half-hound, that the schoolmaster, James Sharkey, borrowed from Charlie's bar for these Sundays. They'd been beating up the bottoms for some hours, and odd snipe, exploding out of the rushes before zigzagging away, was all that had risen.

'If we don't rise something before long we'll soon have to throw our hats at it,' Tom Lennon said, and it was a careless phrase. No one had seen the teacher without his eternal brown hat for the past twenty years. 'I've been noticing the ground harden all right,' the dry answer came.

'Anyhow, I'm beginning to feel a bit humped,' Tom Lennon looked small and frail in the tightly belted white raincoat.

'There's no use rimming it, then. There'll be other Sundays.'

Suddenly a large hare rose ahead, bounded to the edge

of the rushes, and then looped high to watch and listen. With a 'Hulla, hulla,' they slipped the hounds, the hare racing for the side of the hill. The fawn bitch led, moving in one beautiful killing line as she closed with the hare, the head eel-like as it struck; but the hare twisted away from the teeth, and her speed carried the fawn past. The hare had to turn again a second time as the mongrel coming up from behind tried to pick it in the turn. The two men below in the rushes watched in silence as the old dance played itself out on the bare side of the hill: race, turn, race again; the hounds hunting well together, the mongrel making up with cunning what he lacked in grace, pacing himself to strike when the hare was most vulnerable — turning back from the fawn. But with every fresh turn the hare gained, the hounds slithering past on the hard ground. They were utterly beaten by the time the hare left them, going away through the hedge of whitethorns.

'They picked a warrior there.'

'That's for sure,' Tom Lennon answered as quietly.

The beaten hounds came disconsolately down, pausing at the foot of the hill to lap water from a wheelmark and to lick their paws. They came on towards the men. The paws were bleeding and some of the bitch's nails were broken.

'Maybe we shouldn't have raced her on such hard ground,' the teacher said by way of apology.

'That's no difference. She'll never run in the Stakes again. They say there's only two kinds to have — a proper dud or a champion. Her kind, the in-between, are the very worst. They'll always run well enough to tempt you into having another go. Anyhow, there's not money for that any more,' he said with a sad smile of reflection.

Coolcarra Queen was a relic of his bachelor days that he hadn't been able to bear parting with on getting married and first coming to the place as temporary agricultural instructor.

They'd raced her in the Stakes. She'd almost won. They'd trained her together, turn and turn about. And that cold wet evening, the light failing as they ran off the Finals, they'd stood together in the mud beside the net of torn hares and watched this hare escape into the laurels that camouflaged the pen, and the judge gallop towards the rope on the old fat horse, and stop, and lift the white kerchief instead of the red. Coolcarra Queen had lost the Rockingham Silver Cup and twenty-five pounds after winning the four races that had taken her to the Final.

'Still, she gave us a run for our money,' the teacher said as they put the limping hounds on the leashes and turned home.

'Well, it's over now,' Tom Lennan said. 'Especially with the price of steak.'

'Your exams can't be far off now?' the teacher said as they walked. The exams he alluded to were to determine whether the instructor should be made permanent or let go.

'In less than five weeks. The week after Easter.'

'Are you anxious about it all?'

'Of course,' he said sadly. 'If they make me permanent I get paid whether I'm sick or well. They can't get rid of me then. Temporary is only all right while you're single.'

'Do you foresee any snags?'

'Not in the exams. I know as much as they'll know. It's the medical I'm afraid of.'

'Still,' the teacher began lamely and couldn't go on. He knew that the instructor had been born with his heart on the wrong side and it was weak.

'Not that they'll pay much heed to instruction round here. Last week I came on a pair of gentlemen during my rounds. They'd roped a horse-mower to a brand new Ferguson. One was driving the Ferguson, the other sitting up behind on the horse machine, lifting and letting down the blade with a piece of wire. They were cutting thistles.'

'That's the form all right,' the teacher smiled.

They'd left the fields and had come to the stone bridge into the village. Only one goalpost stood upright in the football field. Below them the sluggish Shannon flowed between its wheaten reeds.

'Still, we must have walked a good twelve miles today from one field to the next. While if we'd to walk that distance along a straight line of road it'd seem a terrible journey.'

'A bit of life itself,' the teacher laughed sarcastically, adjusting the brown hat firmly on his head. 'We might never manage it if we had to take it all in the one gasp. We mightn't even manage to finish it.'

'Well, it'd be finished for us then,' the instructor countered weakly.

'Do you feel like coming to Charlie's for a glass?' he asked as they stood.

'I told her I'd be back for the dinner. If I'm in time for the dinner she might have something even better for me afterwards,' Tom Lennon joked defensively.

'She might indeed. Well, I have to take this towser back to Charlie anyhow. Thanks for the day.'

'Thanks yourself,' Tom Lennon said.

Above the arms of the stone wall the teacher watched the frail little instructor turn up the avenue towards the Bawn, a straggling rectangular building partly visible through the bare trees, where he had rooms in the tower, all that was left of the old Hall.

Charlie was on his stool behind the bar with the Sunday paper when the teacher came with the mongrel through the partition. Otherwise the bar and shop were empty.

'Did yous catch anything?' he yawned as he put aside the paper, drawing the back of his hands over his eyes like a child. There was a dark stain of hair oil behind him on the whitewash where sometimes he leaned his head and slept when the bar was empty.

'We roused only one and he slipped them.'

'I'm thinking there's only the warriors left by this time

of year,' he laughed, and when he laughed the tip of his red nose curled up in a way that caused the teacher to smile with affection.

'I suppose I'll let the old towser out the back?'

Charlie nodded. 'I'll get one of the children to throw him some food later.' When the door was closed again he said in a hushed, solicitous voice, 'I suppose, Master, it'll be whiskey?'

'A large one, Charlie,' the teacher said.

In a delicious glow of tiredness from the walking, and the sensuous burning of the whiskey as it went down, he was almost mindless in the shuttle back and forth of talk until he saw Charlie go utterly still. He was following each move his wife made at the other end of the house. The face was beautiful in its concentration, reflecting each move or noise she made as clearly as water will the drifting clouds. When he was satisfied that there was no sudden danger of her coming up to the bar he turned to the shelves. Though the teacher could not see past the broad back, he had witnessed the little subterfuge so often that he could follow it in exact detail: the silent unscrewing of the bottle cap, the quick tip of the whiskey into the glass, the silent putting back of the cap, and the downing of the whiskey in one gulp, the movements so practised that it took but seconds. Coughing violently, he turned and ran the water and drank the glass of water into the coughing. While he waited for the coughing to die, he rearranged bottles on the shelves. The teacher was so intimate with the subterfuge that he might as well have taken part in the act of murder or of love. 'If I'm home in time for the dinner she might have something even better for me afterwards,' he remembered with resentment.

'Tom didn't come with you?' Charlie asked as soon as he brought the fit of coughing under control.

'No. He was done in with the walking and the wife was expecting him.'

'They say he's coming up for permanent soon. Do you

think he will have any trouble?'

'The most thing he's afraid of is the medical.'

Charlie was silent for a while, and then he said, 'It's a quare caper that, isn't it, the heart on the wrong side?'

'There's many a quare caper, Charlie,' the teacher replied. 'Life itself is a quare caper if you ask me.'

'But what'll he do if he doesn't get permanent?'

'What'll we all do, Charlie?' the teacher said inwardly, and as always when driven in to reflect on his own life, instinctively fixed the brown hat more firmly on his head.

Once he did not bother to wear a hat or a cap over his thick curly fair hair even when it was raining. And he was in love then with Cathleen O'Neill. They'd thought time would wait for them forever as they went to the sea in his baby Austin or to dances after spending Sundays on the river. And then, suddenly, his hair began to fall out. Anxiety exasperated desire to a passion, the passion to secure his life as he felt it all slip away, to moor it to the woman he loved. Now it was her turn to linger. She would not marry him and she would not let him go.

'Will you marry me or not? I want an answer one way or the other this evening.' He felt his whole life like a stone on the edge of a boat out on water.

'What if I don't want to answer?' They were both proud and iron-willed.

'Then I'll take it as No.'

'You'll have to take it whatever way you want, then.' Her face was flushed with resentment.

'Goodbye, then.' He steeled himself to turn away.

Twice he almost paused but no voice calling him back came. At the open iron gate above the stream he did pause. 'If I cross it here it is the end. Anything is better than the anguish of uncertainty. If I cross here I cannot turn back even if she should want.' He counted till ten, and looked back, but her back was turned, walking slowly uphill to the house.

As she passed through the gate he felt a tearing that broke as an inaudible cry.

No one ever saw him afterwards without his brown hat, and there was great scandal the first Sunday he wore it in the body of the church. The man kneeling next to him nudged him, gestured with his thumb at the hat, but the teacher did not even move. Whispers and titters and one hysterical whinny of laughter that set off a general sneeze ran through the congregation as he unflinchingly wore it through the service.

The priest was up to the school just before hometime the very next day. They let the children home early.

'Have you seen Miss O'Neill recently, Jim?' the priest opened cautiously, for he liked the young teacher, the most intelligent and competent he had.

'No, Father. That business is finished.'

'There'd be no point in me putting in a word?'

'There'd be no point, Father.'

'I'm sorry to hear that. It's no surprise. Everything gets round these parts in a shape.'

'In a shape, certainly, Father.' There was dry mockery in the voice.

'When it gets wild it is different, when you hear talk of nothing else — and that's what has brought me up. What's going the rounds now is that you wore your hat all through Mass yesterday.'

'They were right for once, Father.'

'I'm amazed.'

'Why, Father?'

'You're an intelligent man. You know you can't do that, Jim.'

'Why not, Father?'

'You don't need me to tell you that it'd appear as an extreme form of disrespect.'

'If the church can't include my own old brown hat, it can't include very much, can it, Father?'

'You know that and I know that, but we both know that the outward shows may least belie themselves. It'd not be tolerated.'

'It'll have to be tolerated, Father, or . . .'

'You can't be that mad. I know you're the most intelligent man round here.'

'Thanks, Father. All votes in that direction count round here. ''They said I was mad and I said they were mad, and confound them they outvoted me,'' ' he quoted. 'That's about it, isn't it, Father?'

'Ah, stop it, Jim. Tell me why. Seriously, tell me why.'

'You may have noticed recently, Father,' he began slowly, in rueful mockery, 'a certain manifestation that my youth is ended. Namely, that I'm almost bald. It had the effect of *timor mortis*. So I decided to cover it up.'

'Many lose their hair. Bald or grey, what does it matter? We all go that way.'

'So?'

'When I look down from the altar on Sunday half the heads on the men's side are bald.'

'The women must cover their crowning glory and the men must expose their lack of a crown. So that's the old church in her wisdom bringing us all to heel?'

'I can't understand all this fooling, Jim.'

'I'm deadly serious. I'll wear my hat in the same way as you wear your collar, Father.'

'But that's nonsense. It's completely different.'

'Your collar is the sublimation of *timor mortis*, what else is it, in Jesus Christ. All I'm asking is to cover it up.'

'But you can't wear it all the time?'

'Maybe not in bed but that's different.'

'Listen. This joking has gone far enough. I don't care where you wear your hat. That's your problem. But if you wear it in church you make it my problem.'

'Well, you'll have to do something about it then, Father.'

The priest was very silent but when he spoke all he said was: 'Why don't we lock up the school? We can walk down the road together.'

What faced the priest was alarmingly simple: he couldn't have James Sharkey at Mass with his hat on and he couldn't have one of his teachers not at Sunday Mass. Only late that night did a glimmer of what might be done come to him. Every second Sunday the teacher collected coins from the people entering the church at a table just inside the door. If the collection table was moved out to the porch and Sharkey agreed to collect the coins every Sunday, perhaps he could still make his observances while keeping his infernal hat on. The next morning he went to the administrator.

'By luck we seem to have hit on a solution,' he was able to explain to the teacher that evening.

'That's fine with me. I never wanted to be awkward,' the teacher said.

'You never wanted to be awkward,' the priest exploded. 'You should have heard me trying to convince the administrator this morning that it was better to move the table out into the porch than to move you out of the school. I've never seen a man so angry in his life. You'd have got short shrift, I'm telling you, if you were in his end of the parish. Tell me, tell me what would you have done if the administrator had got his way and fired you?'

'I'd have got by somehow. Others do,' he answered.

And soon people had got so used to the gaunt face under the brown hat behind the collection table every Sunday that they'd be as shocked now to see him without it after all the years as they had been on the first Sunday he wore it.

'That's right, Charlie. What'll we all do?' he repeated as he finished the whiskey beside the oil heater. 'Here. Give us another drop before the crowd start to come in and I get caught.'

'My brown hat and his heart on the wrong side, and you tippling away secretly when the whole parish including your wife knows it. It's a quare caper indeed, Charlie,' he thought as he quickly finished his whiskey to avoid getting caught by the crowd due to come in.

There was no more coursing together again after that Sunday. The doctor's car was parked a long time outside the white gate that led to the Bawn the next day, and when Tom Lennon's old Ford wasn't seen around the roads that day or the next or the next the teacher went to visit him, taking a half-bottle of whiskey. Lennon's young wife, a warm soft country girl of few words, let him in.

'How is he?' he asked.

'The doctor'll be out again tomorrow,' she answered timidly and led him up the creaky narrow stairs. 'He'll be delighted to see you. He gets depressed not being able to be up and about.'

From the circular room of the tower that they used as a living room he could hear happy gurgles of the baby as they climbed the stairs, and as soon as she showed him into the bedroom she left. In the pile of bedclothes Tom Lennon looked smaller and more frail than he usually did.

'How is the patient?'

'Fed up,' he said. 'It's great to see a face after staring all day at the ceiling.'

'What is it?'

'The old ticker. As soon as I'd eaten after getting home on Sunday it started playing me up. Maybe I overdid the walking. Still, it could be worse. It'd be a damned sight worse if it had happened in five weeks' time. Then we'd be properly in the soup.'

'You have oodles of time to be fit for the exam,' the teacher said, hiding his dismay by putting the whiskey down on the dressing table. 'I brought this little something.' There was, he felt, a bloom of death in the room.

'You never know,' the instructor said some hours later as the teacher took his leave. 'I'm hoping the doctor'll have me up tomorrow.' He'd drunk only a little of the whiskey in a punch his wife had made, while the hatted man on the chair slowly finished his own half-bottle neat.

The doctor did not allow him up that week or the next, and the teacher began to come every evening to the house, and two Sundays later he asked to take the hounds out on his own. He did not cross the bridge to the Plains as they'd done the Sunday together but went along the river to Doireen. The sedge of the long lowlands rested wheaten and dull between two hills of hazel and briar in the warm day. All winter it had been flooded but the pale dead grass now crackled under his feet like tinder. He beat along the edges of the hills, feeling that the hares might have come out of the scrub to sleep in the sun, and as he beat he began to feel Tom Lennon's absence like his own lengthening shadow on the pale sedge.

The first hare didn't get more than halfway from where it was lying to the cover of the scrub before the fawn's speed caught it, a flash of white belly fur as it rolled over, not being able to turn away from the teeth in the long sedge, and the terror of its crying as both hounds tore it began. He wrested the hare loose and stilled the weird child-like crying with one blow. Soon afterwards a second hare fell in the same way. From several parts of the river lowland he saw hares looping slowly out of the warm sun into the safety of the scrub. He knew they'd all have gone in then, and he turned back for Charlie's. He gave one of the hares to Charlie; the other he skinned and took with him to Tom Lennon's.

'Do you know what I'm thinking?' he said that night. 'I'm thinking that I should take the bitch.'

He saw sudden fear in the sick man's eyes.

'You know you're always welcome to borrow her any time you want.'

'It's not that,' he said quickly. 'I thought just to take her until you're better. I could feed her. It'd be no trouble. It'd take some of the weight off the wife.' And that evening when he left he took the bitch who was excited, thinking that she was going hunting again, though it was dark, and she rose to put paws on his shoulders and to lick his face.

She settled in easily with the teacher. He made a house for her out of a scrapped Ford in the garden but he still let her sleep in the house, and there was a lighter spring in his walk each evening he left school, knowing the excitement with which he would be met as soon as he got home. At night he listened to Tom Lennon's increasingly feverish grumblings as the exam drew close. And he looked so angry and ill the night after the doctor had told him he could put all thought of the exam out of his mind that the suspicion grew stronger in the teacher's mind that his friend might not after all be just ill.

'What are you going to do?' he asked fearfully.

'Do the exam, of course.' There was determination as well as fear in the sunken eyes.

'But you can't do it if the doctor said you weren't fit.'

'Let's put it this way,' the sick man laughed in harsh triumph, 'I can't *not* do it.'

The night before the exam he asked the teacher to bring up the clippers. He wanted a haircut. And that night as the teacher wrapped the towel round the instructor's neck and took the bright clippers out of their pale green cardboard box, adjusting the combs, and started to clip, the black hair dribbling down on the towel, he felt for the first time ever a mad desire to remove his hat and stand bareheaded in the room, as if for the first time in years he felt himself in the presence of something sacred.

'That's a great job,' Tom Lennon said afterwards. 'You know while we're at it, I might as well go the whole hog, and shave as well.'

'Do you want me to get you some hot water?'

'That wouldn't be too much trouble?'

'No trouble at all.'

Downstairs as they waited for the water to boil, the wife in her quiet voice asked him, 'What do you think?'

'He seems determined on it. I tried to talk him out of it but it was no use.'

'No. It doesn't seem any use,' she said. A starched white shirt and blue suit and tie were draped across a chair one side of the fire.

The teacher sat on the bed's edge and held the bowl of water steady while the instructor shaved. When he finished, he examined himself carefully in the little hand-mirror, and joked, 'It's as good as for a wedding.'

'Maybe it's too risky. Maybe you should send in a certificate. There'll be another chance.'

'No. That's finished. I'm going through with it. It's my last chance. There'll be no other chance. If I manage to get made permanent there'd be a weight off my mind and it'd be better than a hundred doctors and tonics.'

'Maybe I should give the old car a swing in readiness for the morning, so?'

'That'd be great.' The instructor fumbled for his car keys in his trouser pockets on the bed rail.

The engine was cold but started on the sixth or seventh swing. In the cold starlit night he stood and listened to the engine run.

'Good luck, old Tom,' he said quietly as he switched it off and took the car keys in.

'Well, good luck tomorrow. I hope all goes well. I'll be up as soon as I see the car back to find out how it went,' he said in a singsong voice he used with the children at school in order not to betray his emotion after telling him that the Ford was running like a bird.

Tom Lennon rose the next morning as he said he would, dressed in his best clothes, had tea, told his wife not to worry and that he'd be back about six, somehow got as far as the car, and fell dead over the starting handle the teacher had left in the engine from the previous night.

When word was brought to the school, all the hatted man did was bow his head and murmur, 'Thanks.' He knew he had been expecting the death for some days. And when he went to the Bawn a last time he felt no terror of the stillness of the brown habit, the folded hands, but only a certain amazement that it was the agricultural instructor who was lying there not he. Two days later his hat stood calmly among the scarved women and bareheaded men about the open grave, and when it was over he went back to Charlie's. The bar was filled with mourners from the funeral-making holiday. A silence seemed to fall as the brown hat came through the partition, but only for a moment. They were arguing about a method of sowing winter wheat that the dead man used to advocate. Some thought it made sense. Others said it would turn out to be a disaster.

'Your old friend won't hunt again,' Charlie said as he handed him the whiskey. The voice was hushed. The eyes stared inquiringly but respectfully into the gaunt face beneath the hat. The small red curl of the nose was still.

'No. He'll not hunt again.'

'They say herself and the child is going home with her own people this evening. They'll send a van up late for the furniture.' His voice was low as a whisper at the corner of the bar.

'That makes sense,' the teacher said.

'You have the bitch still?' Charlie asked.

'That's right. I'll be glad to keep her, but the wife may want to take her with her.'

'That'll be the least of her troubles. She'll not want.'

'Will you have something yourself?' the teacher invited.

'All right then, Master,' he paused suddenly. 'A quick one then. We all need a little something in the open today,' and he smiled an apologetic, rueful smile in his small eyes;

but he downed the whiskey, as quickly running a glass of water and drinking it into the coughing, as if it hadn't been in the open at all.

The fawn jumped in her excitement on her new master when he finally came home from the funeral. As he petted her down, gripping her neck, bringing his own face down to hers, thinking how he had come by her, he felt the same rush of feeling as he had felt when he watched the locks of hair fall on to the towel round the neck in the room; but instead of prayer he now felt a wild longing to throw his hat away and walk round the world bareheaded, find some girl, not necessarily Cathleen O'Neill, but any young girl, and go to the sea with her as he used to, leave the car at the harbour wall and take the boat for the island, the engine beating like a good heart under the deck boards as the waves rocked it on turning out of the harbour, hold her in one long embrace all night long between the hotel sheets; or train the fawn again, feed her the best steak from town, walk her four miles every day for months, stand in the mud and rain again and see her as Coolcarra Queen race through the field in the Rockingham Stakes, see the judge gallop over to the rope on the old fat horse, and this time lift high the red kerchief to give the Silver Cup to Coolcarra Queen.

And until he calmed, and went into the house, his mind raced with desire for all sorts of such impossible things.

Gina Berriault

Works of the Imagination

The silent train ascended through forest and alongside a torrent so cold and so swift the water was white, and small white birds flew up like spray. On a bridge undergoing repairs the train came to a halt. Just outside Thomas Lang's window, a workman in a black knit cap was hammering at a railing, and the silence all around isolated each ring of the hammer.

Lang arrived in Grindelwald in the evening, coming from Bern where, contrary to his intention to call on a friend from the States and tell him about the insoluble task his memoirs had become, he had stayed only half-a-day and called on no one. In the early night he wandered along a path on the outskirts of the town. The day was a national holiday, and fireworks opened in languid sprays all around in the dusk, and the boom of fireworks echoed against the mountains. Someone approached him on the path, a figure twice as tall as himself. Closer, he saw it was a little girl, half as tall as himself, carrying a long stick covered with tallow, the torch at its tip casting around her a high, black figure of shadows. Up on the dark mountains small lights burned here and there, far, far apart — fires perched on the night itself. In the morning a snowy mountain stood just outside his hotel window, brought closer by the sun almost to within reach of his hand.

On a small, quiet train he went higher, up to Kleine Scheidegg, up to an old hotel where twelve years ago he had stayed a few days in winter, and not alone. The mountains had impressed him then as a phenomenon on display, but now he was shocked by their immensity, hypnotized by their beauty and crystal silence. Cowbells and voices rang in the silence with an entrancingly pure pitch, and the density of the stone was silence in another guise.

The elderly, elegant manager registered him at the desk in the small lobby. A very tall, strong man, also elderly, in a dark green apron, whom Lang had observed carrying up four suitcases at a time, carried up his two, while another assistant, also in a green apron, a slight, dark man, surely Spanish, graciously shy, stepped in a lively way to the foot of the wide, curving staircase and gestured for him to go up. Lang climbed the stairs with his hand on the rail. He had not often assisted himself that way and had no need to now. He was an erect, lean and healthy sixty, and why, then, was his hand on the banister?

The silence in the room was like an invasion, a possession by the great silent mountains. The cloth on the walls, a print of pastoral scenes with amorous couples, flute players, and lambs, roused a memory of another room, somewhere else in this hotel, where he had lain in an embrace with a woman who, at the time, was very dear. All that he remembered of the previous visit were the three persons he had been traveling with — the woman, a close friend, and the friend's wife — all now no longer in touch with him and perhaps not with one another. They had come to watch a movie being made of a novel of his. In the novel there had been only a brief mention of the Alps, but the movie director and the script writer had worked out a counterfeit scene from that remark, and he had watched, amused and apart.

Once in the night he was wakened by his heart's terror. His heart always wakened him in time for him to witness his own dying, and he waited now with his hand over his heart. When the terror subsided he took his notebook from the bedside table and fumbled to uncap his pen. Through the translucent curtains the sky and the white mountains gave him enough light to write by, but his hand was given no reason to write. Was this another place he would leave, his notebook empty? Traveling all spring and into the summer, he had found no place where he could begin his memoirs. If one place had been so full of the sound of the ocean — not just the waves, whose monotonous beat often went unheard, but the threat in the depths — another place was too full of the sounds of the city — insane noises. And in quiet places he heard, in memory, the voices of his healers back in the States, men who had never truly known just what it was he had lost, and gave the loss such facile names — confidence, faith, whatever — and the names of several persons who had been dear to him and were lost to him. These healers had promised him his completed memoirs, and other novels in the future, if only he would begin, because, they said, work itself wrought miracles and brought the spirit back from the grave. But there was a loss beyond their probing, a loss they were unwilling to accept as the finality he knew it was, a loss, a failing, that might even be commonplace and yet was a terrible sacrilege. It was indifference, like a deep, drugged sleep, to everyone else on earth. Ah, how could that change have come about in himself when his very reason for being had been the belief that each human life was sacred?

He got up and drew aside the mist-like curtains. The train station was dimly lit, the awning rippling a little in the night wind. Out on the dark hills a few hazy lights burned through the night, miles apart. And beyond and all around, the luminous mountains. When he was inside the hotel their unseen presence warned him of his breath's impending abeyance, but now, gazing out at them, he felt his chest deepen to take in their cold breath across the distance, a vast breath as necessary to him as his own.

The day brought hikers up from the cities, way below. They came up in the small, silent trains, and wore big boots, thick socks, and knapsacks, as if bound for a climb of several days. But they roamed over the grassy hills for an hour or so and converged at the tables below the hotel's lower windows. They sat under colored umbrellas and under the windows' reflections of the mountains, and ate what appeared to be savory food. He kept a distance from them. There was room enough.

The only guests in the spacious parlor were far off, a family group playing cards at a table covered with green felt. On the parquetry floors lay rich, red Persian rugs, and the many couches and chairs of antique beauty took up only small space in the large room. A long and narrow glassed-in sunporch with an abundance of wicker chairs adjoined the parlor, and he paced along its length, remembering the hotel in winter, the parlor's black-and-white marble fireplace ablaze, the pleasurable jostling and agitation of the many guests, and the hieroglyphs of distant, dark figures against the snow. He settled himself at a large table in a corner of the parlor, but all he could do was trace the glow and grain of the wood around his empty notebook.

On his way down the hall, restless, wondering if he would move on the next day, he paused before the first of several framed photographs along the wall, an early one of four climbers assembled in the photographer's studio against a backdrop of a painted mountain, all in hats and ties and heavy boots, with pots, picks, a goat. Few attempted the scaling of mountains in these years; now climbers were swarming up every mountain on earth. Farther along, he stopped before a photograph of *Der Eiger*, the mountain looming up over this hotel and over the town, miles below, a sheer, vertical face of stone. White lines were painted on the photograph, marking the ascents to the top, and at the base were the names of the fallen, preceded by white crosses. He passed along before the faces of the triumphant ones, a row of them, all young, and spent a longer time before a couple from Germany, a man and a woman, she a strongly smiling blond and he a curly-haired handsome fellow, the kind who would take a woman along.

Then he went out, keeping apart from the many hikers who walked in a line toward Eiger as if on a pilgrimage. He strode over the lush grass, over the rise and fall of the hills, and on the crest of a hill he halted to take a look at the great stone's face. Two figures were slowly, slowly climbing. His vision lost them in an instant and it took him some time to locate them again, so small were they and at the mercy of the atmosphere, appearing and disappearing. He sat down on the grass to watch them, his hand above his eyes to prevent the sun from playing tricks on him. The roar of an avalanche shocked him, convincing him that a mountain was collapsing, and then he saw the source of the thunder — a small fall of snow, far, far away. Somewhere he had read that the Alps had moved one hundred miles from their original location in Italy, and he wondered if the move had been centuries long, or cataclysmic, in a time when there were no human beings around to be terrified and obliterated. When his eyes began to ache from the searching, from the finding and losing of the specks that were his climbers, he returned to his room and lay down, his hand over his stone-struck eyes.

Toward twilight, when no one sat under the mountains' reflections, when they had all gone down on the trains, he went out again, strolling to higher ground over patches of tiny wildflowers that were like luminous rugs on the grass. Up near the entrance to the train tunnel that cut through stone to the top of the Jungfrau, he came to a large, heavy-wire pen where several restless dogs roved. The dogs resembled wolves, tawny with black markings, and their wild intelligent Mongol faces reminded him of the faces of nineteenth century Russian writers. It was a comparison against his will, yet he was amused by it and felt lightheaded over it. They paused to look into his face and into his eyes, slipped by along the fence, then returned, curious about him as he was about them. Soon in the darkening air he felt he was gazing at Gogol, at Tolstoy, at Chekhov, their faces intent on each human soul.

Stumbling a time or two, he made his way back down to the hotel that stood in a nimbus of its own lights. Before he went in he took a last look at the great stone. No fire burned anywhere on its enormous expanse. The climbers had made a bivouac for the night on a ledge and were already asleep.

Once in the night he was wakened by a deep wondering about the couple on the ledge. The fact of their lying on a ledge somewhere on that great stone stirred in him a concern for all persons he had ever loved. Then he slept again, and the couple was lying somewhere on the cold vastness of the night, on no ledge.

In the morning he went out under an overcast sky, before any hikers appeared. The stone was monstrous. Each sight of it failed to diminish, by repetition, the shock of it. So steep was the north side, the mountain must have been split down the very center, and the other half was a hundred miles away. The climbers were not yet halfway up the wall. Often, as before, he lost sight of them, found one again and not the other, and then found the other after losing the first. After a time he covered his eyes to rest them. If they fell, would the silence and the distance deny to him their terror? He lowered his hand, searched again, and found one dark figure on a snowy ledge. The figure fell the instant he found it. It fell so fast he was unable to trace its fall and unable to find it on a lower ledge or at the base. Nowhere, now, was the other climber. Then both had fallen, and their terror entered into his heart without his expecting it. It was the same terror that wakened him in the night at the last moment so that he might witness his own dying. It was the same kind of moment now, under the sun. With his hand over his heart he went back over the hills to the hotel.

No one was at the desk in the lobby, neither the manager nor one or the other of his assistants in their green aprons. One of them would confirm the tragedy. Somewhere, back in an office, there must be a radio voice informing everyone of the climbers' fate. Outside, the murmur of the crowd under the umbrellas and the fitful, labored music of an accordion were like the sounds the deaf make, that are unheard by them. In the parlor he found the shy assistant passing through, the one he was convinced had been a child refugee from the Spanish Civil War.

"El hombre y la mujer en la montana, ellos se cayeron?"

The man smiled sadly, graciously, implying with his smile that if he did not understand Spanish at least he understood the importance of the question for the one who asked it.

With faltering German he tried to repeat the question, but a strong resistance, following disappointment, whisked away his small vocabulary. He went back to the lobby.

The manager, wearing a fine suit the same gray as his hair, was now standing at the desk, glancing through some papers. A fire wavered in the small fireplace.

"The couple on Eiger, they fell?"

The manager's brow, high, smooth for a man his age, underwent a brief overcast. "May I ask who?"

"The couple on Eiger."

"Ah yes, the photographs in the corridor? Only those who succeeded. Only those."

"The couple up there now," he said.

"There is no one climbing now."

"Then they fell?"

"No one is climbing and no one is falling."

Lang went up the stairs, hand on the rail, a weakness in his legs from the terror of the lives lost, no matter if they were specks, motes, undulations of the atmosphere. Up in his room he sat down at the desk, opened his notebook, and wrote the first word on the first of the faint lines that he likened now to infinitely fine, blue veins.

Andre Dubus

At St. Croix

Peter Jackman and Jo Morrison were both divorced, and had been lovers since winter. She knew much about his marriage, as he did about hers, and at times it seemed to Peter that their love had grown only from shared pain. His ex-wife Norma, had married and moved to Colorado last summer, and he had not seen David and Kathi since then. They were eleven and nine, and in June they were coming to Massachusetts to spend the summer with him. In May, Peter and Jo went to St. Croix to recover, as they said, from the winter. They did not mean simply the cold, but their nights tangled with the sorrow of divorce, with euphoric leaps away from it, with Peter's creeping out of the house while Jo's two girls slept, with his grieving for his children, and with both of them drinking too much, talking too much, needing too much.

The hotel at St. Croix was a crescent of separate buildings facing the sea. The beach was short and narrow, bounded by rocks that hid the rest of the coastline. About thirty yards out, a reef broke the surf, and the water came gently and foamless, and lapped at the beach. Peter could have walked to the reef without wetting his shoulders, but he stayed close to shore, swimming in water so shallow that sometimes his hands touched rocks and pebbles and sand. Jo was curious about him in that warmly possessive way that occurs when people become lovers before they are friends, and on the first day she asked him about the water. They were in lounge chairs near a palm tree on the beach, and she was watching his face. He looked beyond the reef at the blue sea and sky.

"I don't know. I've always been afraid of it."

"What about the beach at home. You said you liked it."

"I do. But I don't go out over my chest."

"Maybe you just went for your children."

"No. I love it. And this." He waved a hand seaward. "And body-surfing. The worst about that is when I turn my back. I don't like turning my back on the sea."

"Let's leave Buck Island to the fish."

She was smiling at him, and there was no disappointment in her face or voice.

"You'd enjoy it," he said.

"It's not important."

Each morning after breakfast he went alone to the hotel lobby and chose a postcard for David and Kathi from the racked pictures of the sea, beaches, a black fisherman squatting beside a dead shark on the wharf, scarlet-flowered trees, coconut palms, steep green hills, tall trees of the rain forest. He had not told them he was going to St. Croix with a woman, nor had he told them he was going alone, and on the postcards he wrote crowded notes about the island. On one he wrote that mongooses lived here but there were no snakes, so they ate lizards and frogs, and some of the young men killed them and soaked their tails in rum for two weeks, then wore them stiff like feathers in their hatbands. Then he realized that David would want a tail, so he tore the card and threw it away, and began watching from taxi windows for a dead mongoose on the road. He also wrote that he wished they were with him, and next year he would wait until June, when they were out of school, and he would bring them here. He did not send them a picture of the hotel. The wound he had opened in himself when he left them had not healed, and it never would; now going to St. Croix was like leaving them again. Jo was glad to be away from her daughters for a week, so Peter did not talk to her about his children.

Always the trade winds were blowing across the island, and Peter only felt the heat when he walked on the lee side of a building. The breeze cooled the town of Christianstead too, where they went by taxi in late afternoons, and walked the narrow streets of tourist shops and restaurants, and looked at the boats in the harbor and, on the third day, paid ten dollars to go sailing at sunset on a boat owned by Don Jensen, a young blond man with a deep tan, who kept their paper cups filled with rum punch from the ice chest in the cabin, told them he and his wife had come from California six years ago, that she taught painting at a private school on the island and, when the sun was low, he told them if they were lucky they'd see the green ball when it sank under the horizon, though he had rarely seen it. But he had seen dust in the sky, blown from Africa, hanging red in the sunset. And he asked if they were going to Buck Island. Peter and Jo were sitting on benches on opposite sides of the boat. Peter looked at the glittering water near the sun and said: "I'm afraid of it."

"Can you swim?"

"Yes."

"It's something you ought to see."

"I know."

"Nobody's ever drowned there. With the snorkel and fins, you just can't. I even take nonswimmers: kids who just hold onto a float and kick."

"I want to see it. I don't want to get home, and then wish I had."

"Are you sure?" Jo said.

"I think I'd like it when it's over."

They watched the sun go down, did not see the green ball, then sailed back to Christiansted in the twilight. That night Peter and Jo got drinks from the hotel bar and took them to the beach and sat in upright chairs. He watched the gentle white breakers at the reef, and looked out at the dark sea, listened to it, smelled it. Next morning at breakfast he told the waitress where they were going, and she said: I never go in the water. We have a saying: The sea has no back door. At eight-thirty he was on it, Don standing at the wheel next to the cabin door and working the sail, the long boat heeling so that when it rocked his way, to starboard, he could have touched the water with his hand, and the spray smacked his face and bare shoulders and chest, and when he looked up at Jo sitting on the port bench he could see only the sky behind her; when the boat heeled her way, he held onto his bench, and the sky was gone, and he was looking past her face, down at the sea. She bowed her head and cupped her hands to light a cigarette. When she straightened, Peter shaped his lips in a kiss. She returned it. He tried to care whether she was getting seasick or sunburned or was uncomfortable in the sea-spray, but he could not: his effort seemed physical, as though he were trying to push an interior part of his body out of him and across the boat to Jo. With a slapping of sail Don turned the boat and it steadied and now when it rocked Peter could see both sky and water behind Jo. The spray was not hitting them. He half-turned and watched the shore of St. Croix and the hills rising up from it, dirt roads climbing them and disappearing into green swells of trees. A tern hovered near the boat. Beyond Jo, toward the open sea, two black fishermen sat in a small pink sailboat. Peter crossed the boat, his feet spread and body swaying, and took one of Jo's cigarettes, his first since leaving home. She smiled and pressed his hand. He went back to the bench and watched the horizon and thought of shopping this afternoon for David and Kathi, then drinking at the roofed veranda of the Paris Cafe, where the breeze came with scents of cooking and sweet flowers.

He looked ahead of the boat at Buck Island, and sailboats anchored around a boatless surface that he knew covered the reef. The island was a mile long and steep and narrow, and stood now between them and the open sea. On this side of it the water and wind were calm. Beyond the uneven curve of anchored boats, people were swimming the trail, a waving line of them with snorkels sticking out of the water; most wore shirts to protect their backs from the sun. While Don dropped the anchor, Peter found children swimming in the line. He looked into the water beside the boat and saw the sand bottom. Don came up from the cabin, carrying masks and snorkels and fins.

"It's about a hundred yards, there and back. Maybe a little more. How are you?"

"All right, I think."

"Keep letting me know."

Don gave them fins and, when they had put them on, he showed them how to use the mask and snorkel. Peter took a snorkel from him and put it in his mouth and breathed through it, then took the mask and looked at the green island and up at the sky then pulled the mask over the snorkel tube and his face, and went to the ladder, feeling nothing that he could recognize of himself, feeling only the fins on his feet, and the mask over his nose and eyes, and the mouthpiece against his gums and teeth.

Don told them to swim near the boat until they were used to the snorkel, then he went down the ladder. Jo went next, and Peter looked at Don treading water then watched her climbing down; when she pushed away from the ladder he turned and backed onto it, and down: legs into the water, then his waist, and when his feet were beneath the last rung he still worked down the ladder with his hands until his arms were in the water, then he turned, swimming a breast stroke, his face in it now, his breathing loud in the tube, and he looked through the mask at the sand bottom and the anchor resting on it. When he saw to his left the keel and white hull of the boat, he jerked his head from the water and swam overhand to the ladder and grasped it with one hand while he took the snorkel from his mouth. Then Don and Jo were on either side of him, snorkels twisted away from their lips. He shook his head at Don.

"It's worse than I thought," he said.

"I was watching you. You looked all right."

"No. I can't do it."

Jo moved to Don's side, treading.

"I panicked a little at first," she said. "You just have to get used to breathing."

"No. You two go on, and I'll wait on the boat. I'll drink beer in the sun."

Their faces were tender, encouraging.

"I've got some floats aboard," Don said. "What about trying that?"

"Me and the kids who can't swim. All right."

He moved one hand from the ladder until Don climbed past him, then he held on with both again.

"I wish you'd go without me," he said to Jo.

"I wouldn't want to think of you alone on the boat."

"If you knew how I felt in the water you'd rather think of me alone on the boat."

"We could just go back."

He shook his head, and moved a hand from the ladder as Don came down with a small white float. Peter blew into the snorkel, placed it in his mouth, and took the float. Kicking, he stretched out behind it, and lowered his face into the water, into the sound of his breath moving through the tube past his ear; he looked once at the sand bottom then raised his head and took out the mouthpiece. Don was beside him. He knew Jo was behind him, but he felt only water there.

"That's it. I drink beer."

"How about this: you just hold onto the float and I'll pull you."

Now Jo was with them.

"That's a lot of trouble, just so I can see some fish and a reef."

"It's easy. I just hold the strap."

"Everybody's so kind around here, I don't have much choice. You won't let go?"

"No. Just relax and look. You'll be glad you saw it."

Peter held the corners of the float and watched Don's kicking legs that were his only hold on air, on earth, on returning to the day itself; and he concentrated on the act of breathing: in the tube it sounded as though it would stop and he would not be able to start it again; he emptied and filled his lungs with a sense that he was breathing life into the Peter Jackman who had vanished somewhere in the water behind him. He had no picture of himself in the water. He floated without thoughts or dreams, and when he entered the trail he saw the coral reef and growing things waving like tall grass in the wind; he saw fish pause and dart; fish that were black, golden, scarlet, silver; fish in schools, fish alone, and he could not remember anything he saw. He recognized one fish as it swam into a tiny cave and three breaths later he could not remember its name and shape and color. Scattered along the trail were signs, driven into the bottom. They welcomed him to Buck Island National Park, quizzed him on the shapes of fish drawn on a signboard, told him what was growing near a sign. . . . He found that he could remember the words longer than he could a fish or plant or part of the reef. He read each sign, and as he moved away from one he tried to hold its words in his mind; then the words were gone, and all he knew was the fluid snore of his breath, and the water: as though he were fathoms deep, he could not imagine the sky, nor the sun on his back; his mind was the sea-bottom, and was covered too with that blue-green dispersal of his soul.

Then he saw only water and sand. He watched Don's legs, and waited for the reef again; he looked for fish, for signs, but the water now was empty and boundless and he wanted to look up but he did not, for he knew he would see miles of water to the horizon, and his breathing would stop. Then he saw a white hull. He was moving toward it, and the legs were gone; he looked up at the boat and sky, took the snorkel from his mouth, let go of the float, and grabbed the

ladder. He did not look behind him. He climbed and
stepped over the side and pulled off the mask and sat on the
bench and took off the fins before Jo's hands then masked
face appeared on the ladder. She was smiling. He looked at
the deck. He watched the black fins on her feet as she
crossed it, then she stood over him, smelling of the sea, and
placed her hands on his cheeks. Don came over the side,
carrying the float.

"You seemed all right," he said. "How was it?"

"Bad."

Jo lifted his face.

"You didn't like any of it.?"

"I didn't see any of it." He looked at Don. "You know
something? I didn't even know you had turned and headed
back. Not till you let me go at the boat."

"You'd better have that beer now. Jo?"

"Please."

He went down into the cabin.

"I want you to tell me about the fish," Peter said.

"But you saw them."

"No I didn't."

"Maybe you'd better tell me about that."

"I want you to tell me about the fish," he said.

On the ride back he drank beer and smoked her
cigarettes and listened to her talking about the fish and the
reef. For a while her voice sounded as it did on those nights
when they fought and, the fight ended, they talked about
other things, past their wounds and over the space between
them. He did not watch her face. St. Croix was beyond her,
and he looked at the sky touching the hills, and listened to Jo
and Don talking about the reef. But he could not remember
it. Sometimes he looked over his shoulder at the horizon and
the dark blue swelling sea.

That night, after Jo was asleep, he dressed and crept out
of the room and went to the beach. Lying sunburned in a
chair he shuddered as it came at him over the reef, and he

looked beyond the breakers at the endless dark surface of it, and watched the lights and silhouette of a passing ship, fixed on it as though on a piece of solid and arid earth, and remembered the summer evening four years ago when he and Ryan, both drunk, had left their wives and children in the last of the charcoal smoke on Ryan's sundeck and had rowed an aluminum boat in a twilight fog out to the middle of the lake where they could drink beer and complain about marriage, and Ryan had stood in the bow to piss, and the boat had turned over; Peter hit the water swimming to the shore he could not see. He heard Ryan calling him back to the boat but he swam on into the fog, and when he tired he four times lowered his legs to nothing but water, and finally the evergreens appeared above the fog; he swam until he was in reeds and touching mud, then he crawled out of the water and lay on mud until Ryan came in, kicking alongside the overturned boat. When he and Norma and David and Kathi got home and he stepped into the shower and was enclosed by water he started to scream.

Yet in the summer of 1960 he was a Marine lieutenant at Camp Pendleton, California. One July afternoon his company boarded landing crafts and went a mile out to sea and then, wearing life jackets, floated to shore. Peter and his platoon were in one boat. He waited while his men, barefoot and free of helmets, cartridge belts, and weapons, climbed over the side and dropped into the sea. Then Peter went over and, floating on his back, he paddled and kicked into the cluster of his troops. Slowly, bantering, they formed a line parallel to the coast. With their heads toward shore, they started floating in on their backs. Peter kept watching them, counting them, twenty to his right, twenty-one to his left. He looked past their faces and green wet uniforms and orange jackets at the bobbing lines of the other platoons on his flanks. Sometimes he looked at his feet trailing white as soap in the water, then out beyond the landing crafts at the horizon. Always he saw himself as his troops did: calm, smiling, talking to them; their eyes drew him out of the narrow space where he floated, as though he were spread over the breadth of forty-one men.

Wind blew the palm leaves behind his chair. The ship's lights were fading; its silhouette started to blend with the sea and sky; then it was gone, and he saw Kathi one night two years ago, perhaps a month after he had left them. She was seven, and it was Wednesday night, the night he was with them during the week; they ate at a restaurant and planned their week-end and when he drove them home she said, as she always did that first year, Do you want to come in? And he did, and drank one cup of coffee with Norma, and they both talked to Kathi and David. But when he got his coat from the hall and went back to the kitchen Kathi was gone. He went from room to room, not calling her name, unable to call her name, until he found her in the den lying face down on the couch. She was not crying. He went to her, and leaning forward petted her long red hair; then he lifted her to his chest, held her while her arms went suddenly and tightly around his neck. Then she kissed him. Her lips on his were soft, cool, parted like a woman's.

Now, for the first time since going into the water that morning, he felt the scattered parts of his soul returning, as though in the salt air he breathed, filling his lungs, coursing with his blood. Behind his eyes the dark sea and sky were transformed: the sky blue and cloudless with a low hot sun, the sea the cold blue Atlantic off the coast at home, waves coming high and breaking with a crack and roar, and he was between Kathi and David, holding their hands; they walked out against the surf and beyond it and let go of each other and waited for a wave, watched it coming, then dived in front of it as it broke, rode it in until their bodies scraped sand. Then they walked out again, but now sand shifted under their feet, water rushed seaward against their legs, then she was gone, her hand slipping out of his quick squeeze, she was tumbling and rolling out to sea, and he dived through a breaking wave and swam toward her face, her hair, her hands clutching air and water; swam out and held her against him, spoke to her as he kicked and stroked back through the waves, into the rush of surf, then he stood and walked toward David waiting in foam, and he spoke to her again, pressing her flesh against his. Lying in the chair on the beach at St. Croix, he received that vision with a certainty as incarnate as his sunburned flesh. He looked up at the stars. He was waiting for June: their faces at the airport, their voices in the car, their bodies with his in the sea.

Jayne Anne Phillips

El Paso

DUDE

See I'd met this old dirt farmer in a bar the night
before. Said he was selling his truck cheap and I could come
down to La Rosa and pick it up. Said $300 and it didn't run
too bad but I'd better buy it now. So I hitched down Sunday
morning, mud churches on all three dirt streets ringing their
black bells. I found him wringing a chicken's neck in the
yard, did it quick and finished before he looked at me. Dark
seamed face under a broad hat and the chicken head a little
dangling thing hanging out his fist. I told him, said I'd come
about the truck, did he still want — thinking we were both
pretty drunk and he might have dreamed he had a truck,
since it didn't look like he had anything but a shanty house
that leaned right into the dirt. He spat and turned for me to
follow him, holding the chicken now by a splayed leg that
bright orange in the rising heat. The nails on his hands were
colored that same dull shine as hen's claws.

Us walking in the dust yard past old tires and a rotten
bedspring, mule tied to a pump by the chicken shed, and he
stands finally by this thing that's a red 50's Chevy with a
built-on bed shelved with chicken cages. Crosses and a
blackened corn husk doll hanging from the mirror, keys
strung on a hair ribbon. I got in and drove around the yard
fast, chickens squawking and the old cur dogs snapping at
the wheels. The old man squatted where he was, plucked the
hen. Feathers flew and dropped as I pulled up. I said the
truck ran good and if he had the title I'd pay him now and
take it.

He motioned me inside a house somehow dark even in

all that light. Smell of wool shawls and vinegar. Me blind stumbling into a table and voices, Spanish curses, stop and start. I look up and Rita, she's standing there not three feet away, having ripped the curtains off one window; she's screaming in her voice that goes throaty and harsh, and the light pours in all over her. Hot yellow gravy of light, her black eyes, and the red skirt tight, blouse loose old lace ripped at the shoulder. I wanted to roll my hand in her; I could feel her wet against my legs. The old woman stands by the stove, side of her face shining, and when she turns I see she's not crying but one eye weeps. Rita walks past me steaming from her hands, the cheap plastic curtains clutched and dragging.

I watch the old man rummage in a drawer but feel her at the end of the long room. Rita moving, bending over a small chair. Old man counts the money and I turn to watch her. The light rolling now, leaked into the dark, ripples the skin of the dark and flies fly up in loose knots. Low slow buzz in corners yellowed and pulled out by the light that rolls across the surfaces of things in yellow blocks. Dust in the light, and her body moving down the long room pulls a white path like an animal leaving water. She bends from the waist. Under the cloth her thighs are muscles, long curves, and she is bending over a chair. In the chair sits a baby whose head is too big. He makes a soft sound, like the low wheeze of baby sheep. His legs don't reach the floor; his skin is stretched tight and pale like the light is under it. His hair is white and fine, swirled on his man-sized head, and I know he is a child only by the way he cradles a shoe to his face. Rocks the shoe slow in short arms. Rita has her hands in his hair, her shoulders tensed and curved. A sound catches in her throat and comes out low, folding into the yellow room. Thick juice of light circling, curling us in. Child wheezing and rocking, rocking the shoe slow, his mouth on it. It is her shoe and Rita croons, rocking with him, pulling the shoe away.

RITA

I bought my mother those glasses so she wouldn't have
to live in the dark, spent $100 on an El Paso doctor so she
could see in the light without the eye burning. And she
wouldn't wear them. Would hide them and move like a bat
in the dark, the windows covered. The child in his chair with
his sounds, she singing her songs low in the dark, he weaving
in his chair. Me youngest of six, and at near fifty she gave
birth to him, his white skin and his head hanging like a
heavy bloom on the neck that couldn't move it. His eyes rolling back to see in that head that must have been a field of
snow inside. No father, she said, He is what was in me. And
the eye in her too, still pouring from her slow. Bringing grain
from the store on the mule, she crossed against the light and
a truck knocked her down, the mule kicking her face. And so
the eye weeps and hurts in the daylight. Pounding meal on
the wood table she sings in the dark like she sang then, my
five brothers building cars in the yard, and me they called
bruhita, little witch.

At dusk the townspeople came to be healed. Paid her in
corn and cloth. Then the corn stacked by the door and
tomatoes hung to dry and sides of bacon, their white fat thick
as my waist. She in her white shawls and her almost black
skin put her hands in powders ground from roots. The villagers knelt, her sound wheeling over them. Their eyes fluttered
and their hands unclinched, jerking as sounds came, Muertes
dios muerte muerte. They got up and bowed to the witch
their children wouldn't touch. Castanets slow dull clack followed them, their feet going away in the dark yard. From
the time I was a baby she gave me a sharp stick and told me
to draw them in the dirt to keep their spirits from coming
back. She made her witching dolls from husks; when I was
older she gave me paints to draw their faces. I made them:
farmer's heads and goitered women already old.

In the morning by the pump her hands were shadow in
the water and the buckets were full, stained and cold. She

straightened under them, her black hair loose in the desert winter. Her sons already men who wanted women and I by the door saw her touch herself, smoothing her old dress so it hung floating. She lifted the buckets and wet the dirt. Water darkened her feet, the toes yellowed and hard, soles calloused white. The way her feet arched: the castanets her long fingers; their fast loud clack in the house over the villagers' sounds. My father gone long weeks to Las Vegas, Reno. Sometimes when he came back we moved to hotels in El Paso and bought clothes in stores. Remember, she'd say, cracked voice clacking on her teeth, You ain't no Spanish brats — You got gypsy blood and your Daddy's Apache cheeks. I remember her long fingers on my face. He didn't come back. The house was her power and she wouldn't leave. The town still creeps to her at dusk, women with shawls low over faces. The priest says it's sacrilege, they heaping ashes by the door.

Already I was with men and she was big, her belly strained, and the labor went two days. Women from the town wouldn't help. She cut herself to let the child's head pass and the women, hearing she had a devil, burned candles by their beds. Later the old man came with his shriveled dolls, his silence, and no name I ever heard her say. He built a chair on rollers when the child could sit and kept lanterns lit all night to make the sounds soft.

Now the child's sounds are muffled and low except when I dance. He knows me, holds out his hands for my shoes. Presses his fingers blue against the buckles. The old man rolls up the rug, desert crusted in its folds, and sits cross-legged, palms open on the drum. Bones under his hooded eyes arch wide from beneath, seem to rise out of the skin. My mother takes dried cactus from a wood box and grinds it, sprinkles a powder on his hair that smells of flesh. Her castanets are rolled in cloth. I make the signs and the silvered wood warms in my hands; the child's chair in the center of the room and my feet on brushed boards start slow thud. The drum, her low voice quavering, my arms high, the clack silver clack and the child's eyes focus, hold me fast, faster, me spinning round him. He holds up his head, and under his skin I see the pale blue veins. Faster, my feet pound floor, her voice louder, and he whines a high clean whine that holds me spinning. Ceiling twists, floor circles smaller, small. My hands over him stop. Suddenly he sleeps, he sleeps and we lie, all of us, in the hot dark house. Listen to him breathe.

Now the old man sells his truck, won't take my money. He sees girls grind in city bars, knows how the money comes: my rooms, hotels, the avenue. The child's sounds are whispers now. When I dance he sleeps too long. At the white hospital, us black against walls, they say the shunt in his head won't drain. He won't eat anymore, drinks from bottles, watches me; why do I come here. She hacks at the naked chicken on a board. Her face, the eye drawn; I moving away through the yard. This dust on my legs yellow as meal is burning, burning.

DUDE

The child makes his sounds and she walks out through dirt yard to the road. I run, touch her arm. Her skin bare, dark walnut skin stained milky, and I stand, my hand drenched in her skin, ask her, is she going back to El Paso. In the truck the land goes by us glaring as a lidless eye, sun a high glittering ring. Seeming to whirl in itself like hornets, it throws its heat on land laid out flat to the burning. We glide horizontal on a strip of road. In the tiny room of the truck I feel heavy in the rivery heat. Between us on the cracked seat a space gets small. Her satin skirt is faded in circles I could crush to my thumb. I could feel the shape of her skull under her heavy hair, damp at the temples. My hands are deaf. Eyes stony with light, she watches me try to see the road; her opaled eyes seeming to come out at me yet falling back in their deep oil that scalds the side of my face.

I pull over, stop the truck, get out, lean against it. Up

the road a cafe, all night lights still on, runs a lit band of letters around its roof: hamburgers, thick shakes, onion rings fried gold. I walk up there and a woman with her hair dyed brass swabs the counter with a rag. Her wide grin red, her front tooth gold, she lets me talk and fingers my palm counting change.

Ice cream packed hard melts slow on my hands as I'm walking back. I see Rita hitching by the side of the road. I hand her a cone, get in the truck and start it. She climbs in. Motor idling, sweet cold in our mouths, I pull her across the seat and press my fingers hard at the base of her neck. My breath comes out a ragged curve against her eyes.

WATCHING

He so in love with her it was something to see. Dude so caught up and dedicated like a single eye to his own loving. How she touched it off. I suppose he was about to pack it in before he saw her and thought there was still something to do. Walking up the hill, touching him with her hip and walking, she moved; her hip was delicate and blue beside his thigh.

This was El Paso, 1965. She danced in topless bars, said really she was a painter but she needed supplies. Supplies she said are always hard to get, sometimes you just have to put out and get them and go off with them. It was plain he wanted to go off with her but in the summer in El Paso it's hard to move anywhere except down the street to the bars. I remember there was always dog puke on the sidewalks in El Paso. All those strays get the sweats around noon and bring up the garbage they ate in the back alleys of beanerys at dawn. Think about Texas and there's those skinny fanned ribs heaving.

Dude used to go down to Bimpy's nights and watch her dance. Bimpy was a greasy-kneed old faggot who liked him plenty and gave us free bourbon. She'd come over between

songs and do a number with us, wringing with sweat so she'd
wet the paper and we'd have to keep lighting it. She danced
on this three-foot-square red stage, under two old ceiling
fans that looked like little airplane propellers. She moved
under their sleepy drone; always there was something about
to break out. From our table in the corner I could smell the
old roses smell of her. She was dark-haired and black-eyed
though she swore she wasn't Spanish, medium-sized but
small-boned with green apple breasts; then suddenly her
twisted child-bearing hips that were somehow off-center and
rolled gentle to the left when she walked, rolling slow up the
hill past the plate glass liquor stores. Dancing, she'd throw
her dusty scent past the two old spots Bimpy had and the
cowboys threw bills on stage. Dude hated the dancing; said
she was frigid as hell afterward, like loving a wind-up doll
except for her mouth and the curves it took on in the dark.
She wouldn't even move with the lights on, he said.

After the show she'd stay and help Bimp sweep up and
then we'd walk out the door into the oily night. Everything
wide awake and the fat yam-skinned women talking
Spanish to their boyfriends, walking with their stemmed
words and twined fingers past the blank-eyed 5 & 10's. We'd
walk up the hill, they in front and me trailing behind. She
talked in her Texas voice about nothing usually, it just being
important there in the lit-up black to have her voice with its
honeyed drawl and bitter edge; she walking slope slide up
the hill, whisper of her nylons brushing and the Mexican
boys shooting craps on the sidewalk. They ain't but thirteen,
she'd say when they looked up at her heels clicking, Old
enough. My daddy made a small fortune at craps. He used to
call it dealin with the demon. She'd say that and slap Dude
on the ass.

She'd boil those stark black Columbian beans on a stove
in their flat and it'd heat up the kitchen so we'd have to sit
out the window on the roof. By this time the town was near
silent and steaming slow like a wet iron. Always drink hot
coffee on hot nights, she'd say, Brings the sweat to the

outside and lets you sleep. Dude dozed with his head in her lap and she'd turn to me, ask me, oils are on sale and could she borrow a few bucks till next week. You know, she'd say, twisting his hair in her fingers, Them stars are just holes in the sky after all. And while I'm sleeping in that hot bed everything I ever thought of having falls into em.

Finally I'd go to bed and hear them in the hall going back and forth to the bathroom, him usually drunk by then and tripping at the door. People up and down the hall behind doors yelled at him to shut up. Her arms reaching in the yellow blouse to grab the light string, her hips moving in their funny bumbling slow walk past my door, not quite touching his legs, and the mosquitos louder than her quiet laughter: this was 4 a.m. in El Paso.

I saw him a couple of years later in Toledo, said he was into racing junk cars, said it was some kick. Said you're tearing around and around under the light in these things that are all going to fly apart and pile up. Said he heard she was living down in Austin with some dyke. Said cracking up those cars was great, said he was making money and cracking them up was some kick, it was really something.

BIMP

When I opened the place in '46 I didn't think no one could pull nothin over on me again. I was in the war just like anyone else, ain't no one gonna tell me I got any debt. I had enough tin food and muddy boots and hair lice to last me. One goddamn big lie is what it was, I figured that out. There ain't no losing or winning anywhere is what I figured out, ain't nobody gonna pitch me into no fake contest again. I sailed into San Fran with a knee like a corkscrew and the salt air made it ache like a bitch. I came back home and opened the place and I figured I was standing ground. Back then the Mexicans used to skunk around at the alley door till I told em to beat it. I can see em now, slinking off in their red shirts under that one street lamp between the trash cans. My own grandmother was a Mex. She smelled like a rotten canteloupe and raved in Spanish about the goddamn Church that did nothin but bury her endless brats and the man that beat her. There ain't no losing or winning. These black-eyed thieves and yellow Mex boys think I got something they want, let em swagger in the front door so what. I could tell em if they ask — no matter what they got they got more to get and the thing don't end. Gaining like a squirrel on a wheel, sure. When I saw them three kids I knew what the game was. Her saying what I needed was a dancer, the dude pretty as a rodeo star, and his sidekick one of them hunched-up watchers. I said Listen, I got me a dancer, and she said Try me out. The dude stood there grinding a butt into the floor in his high-heeled boots. I said Well, I don't allow no dancers in here without escorts, gets plenty rough in here ya know, this ain't Philadelphia. She said she was from La Rosa, one of them dirt eating border towns, and I laughed, said You didn't get far didja. She smiled, her mouth dark pink and those flashy Spanish teeth strong as an animal's. The cowboy finally looked at me, said, rolling the filter of his cigarette, We'll be here at nine. The watcher stood there looking from face to face like he was judge of the whole damn game and I said Suit yourselves.

DUDE

Back then I was a carpenter like everyone. I quit school and went down to Texas, air so thick and slow it's like swimming. I was with her in small rooms, El Paso summer seeping at the walls. That flat-out heat comes after you and drinks you up. She'd been there all her life. I lost what I was thinking in rooms thick, full of us; her black hair in the sheets a wound thread, thick black lines of drawings she kept hid, her charcoaled fingertips. She worked on the avenue, turned tricks in a hotel room with a blue ceiling and one light bulb in a fringed shade. I told her, I said You got to stop this and she said Well, she'd dance but she wasn't carrying no slop to farmers in a beanery. The difference is, she said, I say how I'm used.

Walking at dusk through the alleys, bottle of cold wine in a bag, she held to my waist. Cats yowled, caught at our feet. Her skin was always hot, me pulling her to my chest late at night, my hands cut and sore from tarring feed store roofs. By noon those days I was a walking fever and since I first saw her, I come into the heat the place the heat like a bitch dog and lived with it.

See when I come home it is hot, late noon, and she's lying naked on the roof. Below the streets are crooked and past them the tracks run off white, cutting their light and crossing. Trains jerking sluggish change cars in the hard-baked yard. Beside her on the shingled heat, I smell her salt skin and she laughing pulls my face to her throat, hard soles of her feet on my legs. We roll, hot shingles pressed to our backs and later the shower is cold; her breasts so dark the nipples are a cherry black. We drink iced whiskey in jelly glasses and she dances up the hall dripping, throwing water off her hair.

In the stifled space, window at the end painted over and light through the cracked paint patterned on the slanted floor, her back is beaded and swaying. In the close heat she moves up the blue shadowed hall. Water backed up past the drain spills cold past my feet onto the floor and in our rooms we twist and wet the sheets, sleep in their damp. Her hair looped in my hands dries slow; past us the trains clack and whistle their low open howls.

It was too hot to cook and we ate avocados, jalapenos, white cheese. In bed, cold beer frothed in our mouths and past the window the factories changed shifts. City lights came on, blue and pink neon stood out cool and she leaning into the mirror painted her face for the bar. I forget all of it but her lacquered eyes. And she stepping off the curb in those high-heeled shoes, kids in Chevies grinning. The light changed and cars revved up; she caught my eye and fumbled between the buttons on my shirt, pressing her fingers hard into my chest.

Sometimes she came back from Bimp's so late the light was coming up. Been with a john: she only did it she said when the money was too good to pass up. She'd come home with a bottle of brandy, get into bed with a pack of cards and we'd play poker to win till the sun was flat on the floor. Cards buckled finally and thrown against the wall, shades drawn, we lay there see, until we could talk. Her face in the white bed, her face by the window, her hand on the shade drawing down the dark; light behind the shade as she stood there colored her face blurred and fading like a photograph. It's all right just come here.

BIMP

Like I said, I had another dancer. She was blond, from the east, up north I think. She had the look of someone didn't sweat much, just burned a coal inside. Ran off finally with some slick Mex to Panama. Could tell easy she was one to leave home over and over till her feet wore down to a root that just planted where she ran out of steam. The men liked that white hair and light eyes and those rhinestone shoes she wore. She had that hard crumpled look of a dame that's been around but don't know why. I knew she was thirty-five but I hired her anyway. Them white blonds is scarce down here.

I put em onstage together the first night and they set up a wheel the whole place was turning on, what with the smaller one and her seventeen-year-old's tits and them hips moving so you knew she'd been used since she was old enough to wiggle. Them border girls start with big brother in the alley, them towns full of female things dropping litters in the street. She moved with that clinched dark face, all of it a fist in her hips, and beside her the tall blond looked like a movie magazine none of em could touch. There was some kind of confusion, smelled like burning rubber. Spilt drinks and a goddamn brawl in the back at the card table. I got em offstage and turned up the lights and ordered everyone out of the place. Was just me picking up broken glass and the girls leaning by the bar and the two men dealing a hand at the corner table like nothin happened. The girls were dressed, the blond fooling with her necklace, talking low. Her blue eyes drinking that Spanish mouth, she say soft, Hey Honey, how long you figure on dancing with that sway back of yours and that funny hip — damn, can you get this thing fastened — no, here — Lemme put it on and you can maybe pinch it with your teeth — She leans over the Spanish, her red lips apart like she's still talking, beer tipped in her hand and dripping all over their stockings. And the smaller one, black hair to her waist, hands midway in the air, stands there like a stone, saying over and over, I can't fix it, I can't fix it.

After that I had em alternate nights and a week later the blond split. The cowboy and his sidekick was in here nights with the Spanish, the two of em diddling with cards and race forms in the corner. Figure it's been ten years ago. Gave me a few good tips and then same as now — when I hit at the track I blow it all same night, ain't nobody gonna tell me I won nothin.

THE BLOND

Rita. She left the avenue, the hotel, smell of urine and spent sex in the halls. We traded johns and other things; me by her door in blue light, cognac in my hand and my robe open. I asked her low, A toast to the hungry jokers? mouth on my raised glass and she let me in . . .

She let on like we never knew each other, but them hot nights I told her stories. Like how it was when I was seventeen like her. Ginette Hatcher was my name then, in Maine all the grey years. Ginette Hatcher born and died in Maine, she dying there still I guess. I took the name the first truck driver gave me, called me Babe and I answered to it ever since. I left my husband that I only saw in the dark after the boats come in or before they went out, that man always cold and fish slime on his hands. I left soon as the baby was born, thinking the best anyone could tell the kid was that Mama took off. There something out there besides that grey wet, that heavy roll. My cousins and uncles was all lobstermen. My dad too, but he died when I was so young all he is to me is a furred chest and smell of oiled rope. He died of lobster is what Mom said, and she killed hundreds of them. Scratch-clink of those claws against the boiling pots was a woman sound, a metallic scratch round as rings.

Wind and rock and weeds on the beach a grey stink, no color cold; I kept fish eyes in bottles and sold them all summer to the tourists, to the queers and dandies and the painted old things with poodles. Once an old woman with money asked me to come to her hotel and read the Bible to her. She opened it to the book of Job and I started in. After awhile I looked up and she was staring out the window like a sleepwalker, her old hat in her lap. She said what a blessed child I was to come to womanhood here by the sea so far from heat and corruption. I said Yes Ma'am. The fire comes from the feet, she said, From the walkers and the black hair. She didn't see me anymore. I grabbed my sweater and ran home across the hotel beach, the big umbrellas blind and rolling on their sides. I found twenty dollars in my pocket and I bought me some red patent leather spike heels. I hid them in my room and only put them on at night and I was the walker walking and the dancer in my firey feet, and holes in the floor where I burned through.

Tires on the big trucks burn. You smell them in the cab, smell the motor boiling; my suitcase wedged between my knees and the trucker laughing Well Babe, looks like you mean to keep going. I lived everywhere and been to Mexico. I danced mostly, waited tables, worked in a library once and couldn't feel my feet for the shiny floor. By the time I got to Bimp's those nights I was already loaded. Blur, dark oiled skins past the lights, ice in glasses. Cold melts in a circle, hot whiskey, hot Texas. And Rita showed up, black eyes smooth, sunk in, burned young. Onstage she scared me, made that cold ocean roll in my head . . .

They say the world ends in fire and ice; I say it's already over. That hot pavement burns you straight through; that's why I did it, kept moving — No slow cooking and my claws raking walls. These streets, raunchy brass, my feet on fire burns up that dead ice.

I split way south with a rich dude. Red birds and black-eyed men. Been some since then. I'm doing OK, I got it made, and the cold don't come so much now.

RITA

I lived with Dude those months in two rooms, rickety bed on blocks and past the windows the roof steamed be-tween shingles. Long noons I cut the thin tar bubbles with my nails, oils warm on the paper and the tubes heated till their lettering came off in my hands. I drew the trains: red gashes and the tracks black rips under them. His hands felt furred with dust. When he was roofing, the lines and crosses in his palms came out. Tar smudged them, left the whorls of his fingers and their black smell on my hips.

Some days in bed we kept the fans turning, buzzing; we had cold wine and coarse brown bread. At night the bars were crowded with drunks, some of them sick in the heat. Dancing, I saw the flat brushed land outside the house in La Rosa, looking tawny-colored from the shaded rooms, but out there, walking, you felt hard hot sand and the color spread into a wasted brown.

I think of what happened and it happens each time the same way. When I go back they are padding the cart with skins. Inside in his bed the child's face is drawn and blue. He breathes faint strangled bleats and my mother waits, sewing pelts to wrap him. At dark she feels his throat and says there's no breath; we leave with the cart. In the skins his face is white and his light hair long as a girl's. The hitched mule swings its head, flares nostrils at the fresh smell and moves skittish toward the hills. The old man bends in brimmed hat, shuffles to low chant, and she walks behind, scatters fine powder on the ground. Cart rocking slow and the child's face in my lap is sunken, lids on rolled eyes tight closed. All night we keep moving on the sloped land. Sand rolls its barren striped bars; sky is inked and slashed in the foothills where we stop, take bundled wood from the cart, tie it with cords. She knots leather in the dark and her moccasined feet walk slow around us. The old man's voice is hoarse. At dawn she piles brush and the corded wood; in the quiet we lift the child, straining, jangle the bracelets on his arms. She lights dried skins wrapped round a stick, touches him and he is burning. Through the fire I think I see his face move. It moves again and I throw her back, digging, clawing at the hot wood under him. They watch me pull flames, try to reach him; now he is all fire. Running round the stench I fall and their old faces over me say I have only dreamed. I smell the skins and his flesh, the incense burning under him.

Mule leading then down the ravine to where the light stretches out on land like a smooth film of egg. I stumble and touch the animal's hide, feel ribs under stiff mousey hair. The old man walking ahead is straight, his back a leathered board under cloth. She stays there by the smoking smell. Quiet, she waits to take the bones.

Hours walking, sun high now and the road a sudden empty strip. The old man waits for me, then turns in the glare and says, You dreamed. I see his knife and serape banded on his waist, know he's not going back for her. I won't go back to her either. Smoke still in my mouth, I smell the wheeling birds and the tight white face behind the bristled fire. Old man walking away on the road with his mule and there are trucks, horns, voices, Baby wanna ride?

DUDE

I remember the rains had started, blown in off the Gulf. She'd been to La Rosa. Always when she came back she was this hunted dog, stringy and gutted and ready to gnaw its own foot. I came in and she was walking circles in the room, rubbing her hands. I saw her fingers were torn, bruised purple under the nails. Smell of burning paint and there on the floor the rolled drawings were torn and smoldering. I moved to stomp it out and heard her low moan, turned, saw matches in her hands; she striking and tossing them in the air where they'd flare and fall smoking. I grabbed her arms and everything was breaking, chairs cracking on the floor and the light bulb splintering. I saw her hair on fire under my hand and I rolled her onto the bed. All the time she moaned long and low like I wasn't there except that this thing was on top of her. Her eyes were calm and her burned hair broke in my hand. I pulled her down and heard my breath coming high and watered like a woman's. I hit her hard and she fell and lay there; words now in the moaning, and her lips moving. She drooled and the spit flecked red where her teeth had cut. I stood over her and yelled for her to see me. Her eyes rolling past me pulled my hands to her clothes and the cloth ripped. I slapped her, kept slapping her and my hands were fists. I looked up and he's watching us, always goddamn watching us — then he is talking quietly and pulling her from under me.

I remember rains blown in and coming slow that night, me in the corner by the open window, rain on thin curtains whipping my face, The coffee boiled till it was thick and muddy, the whiskey in it burning, and my cut knuckles made it hard to hold the cup. He wrapped her in blankets, held her on the couch, watched her sleep; her hands twitching and her eyes moving under the lids.

WATCHING

He was ramming his fists into the floor beside her head but he thought he was hitting her and asked me later had he killed her. The floor was splintered, fine wood in his hands, and she under him stared glazed at the ceiling. Her mumbled Spanish mixed in the room with the sick sulphur smell of something burned. When I pulled her from under him I saw her hair was burned ragged and her shirt seared in the back. I took it off and wrapped her in blankets; she was shivering. There was broken glass and her fingers were bloodied somehow. She kept talking to nothing, tossing her head from side to side, hands clinched in my hair so tight that when I lay her down I can't move from her. Have to bend over her, my face close though she doesn't see me; I touch her lips, the cuts scabbing and her teeth flecked with the dull dried blood. I smell her breath coming shallow and fast, say her name over and over until she hears me. Almost focusing she slides her hands slow from my hair down my face to her breasts, holding them.

Late that night, Dude sits by the window. Rain spills in; he watches the smokey trains jerk in the yard, moisture on warm soot a fine dust in the air. Not watching her sleep, he blinks like he's slapped when he hears her clutch her throat and turn. I talk, Dude smells her on his split knuckles, and the streaked curtains move all night.

Toward morning he walked the room, circling from door to window, thighs tensed in his jeans. Hands held delicate, he looked at me. His eyes I think were grey and heavy-lashed; the lid of the right one drooped and softened that side of his face. Seeing me, his eyes paled in the slanted light. He didn't say anything and turned. His pointed boots tapped a faint click on the stairs each step down.

She woke up in twisted blankets and raised her fingers to her face. We ate the bread slow, her mouth bleeding a little. I'm seeing her in summer by the stove in their room, sweat clouding her hair and her lips pursed with cheap wine; she smoothing her cotton skirt and throwing back her hair to bend over the burner with a cigarette, frowning as the blue flame jets up fast. On the street under my window she is walking early in the day, tight black skirt ripped in the slit that moves on her leg. Looking back she sees me watching and buys carnations from the blind man on the corner, walks back, tosses them up to me. She laughs and the flowers falling all around her are pale, their long stems tangling. The

street is shaded in buildings and her face turned up to me is
lost in black hair. She is small and she is washed in grilled
shadow.

Fingers too swollen to button her shirt, she asked me
would I get her somthing to soak them in. At the drugstore
buying antiseptic and gauze I felt her standing shakily by the
couch, touching her mouth with her purple fingers. Walking
back fast I knew she was gone, took almost nothing. The
ashed drawings were swept up and thrown probably from the
window. He left for good soon after, thirty pounds of Mexican grass stashed in the truck for a connection in Detroit. I
went far north as I could get, snow that winter in Ottawa a
constant slow sift that cooled and cleaned a dirt heat I kept
feeling for months; having nothing of her but a sketch I'd
taken from where she hid them: a picture of trains dark
slashed on tracks, and behind them the sky opens up like a
hole.

Carolyn Chute

"Ollie, Oh . . ."

1

Erroll, the deputy who was known to litter, did not toss any Fresca cans or Old King Cole bags out this night. Erroll brought his Jeep to a stop in the yard right behind Lenny Cobb's brand new Dodge pickup. The brakes of Erroll, the deputy's, Jeep made a spiritless dusky squeak. Erroll was kind of humble this night. The greenish light of his police radio shone on his face and yes, the froggishly round eyes, mostly pupil because it was dark, were humble. His lips were shut down over his teeth that were usually laughing and clicking. Humbleness had gone so far as to make that mouth look almost HEALED over like the holes in women's ears when they stop putting earrings through. He took off his knit cap and lay it on the seat beside the empty Fresca can, potato chip bag, and cigar cellophanes. He put his gloved hand on the door opener to get out. But he paused. He was scared of Ollie Cobb. He wasn't sure how she would take the news. But she wasn't going to take it like other women did. Erroll tried to swallow but there was no saliva there to work around in his throat.

He looked at Lenny Cobb's brand new Dodge in the lights of his Jeep. It was so cold out there that night that the rootbeer color paint was sealed over every inch in a delicate film like an apple still attached, still ripening, never been handled. Wasn't Lenny Cobb's truck the prince of trucks? Even the windshield and little vent windows looked heavy duty . . . as though congealed inside their rubber strips thick and deep as the frozen Sebago. And the chrome was heavy as pots. And the plow! It was constricted into travel gear, not yet homely from running into stonewalls and frost heaves. And on the cab roof an amber light, the swivel kind, big as a man's head. Of course it had four-wheel drive. It had shoulders! Thighs. Spine. It might be still growing.

The Jeep door opened. The minute he stood up out in the crunchy driveway he wished he had left his cap on. The air was like paper, could have been thirty below. His breath leaving his nose turned to paper. It was all so still and silent. With no lights on in Lenny Cobb's place, a feeling came over Erroll of being alone at the North Pole. Come to his ears a lettuce-like crispness, a keen-ness . . . so that to the top arch of each ear his spinal cord plugged in. A cow murred in the barn. One murr. A single note. And yet the yard was so thirsty for sound . . . all planes gave off the echo: a stake to mark a rosebush under snow . . . an apple basket full of snow on the top step. He gave the door ten or twelve thonks with his gloved knuckles. It HURT.

Ollie Cobb did not turn on a light inside or out. She just spread open the door and stood looking down at him through the small round frames of her glasses. She wore a long rust-colored robe with pockets. The doorway was outside the apron of light the Jeep headlights made. Erroll had to squint to make her out, the thin hair. It was black, parted in the middle of her scalp, yanked back with such efficiency that the small fruit-shape of her head was clear: a lemon or a lime. And just as taut and business-like, pencil-hard, pencil-sized, a braid was drawn nearly to her heels . . . the toes, long as thumbs, clasped the sill. "Deputy Anderson," she said. She had many teeth. Like shingles. They seemed to start out of her mouth when she opened it.

He said: "Ah . . ."

Erroll couldn't know when the Cobb house had rotted past saving, yet more certain than the applewood banked in the stove, the smell of dying timbers came to him warmly . . . almost rooty, like carrots . . .

"What IS it?" she said.

He thought of the great sills of that old house being soft as carrots. "Lenny has passed away," he said.

She stepped back. He was hugged up close to the openness of the door, trying to get warm, so when the door whapped shut, his foot was in it. "ARRRRR!" So he got his foot out. She slammed the door again. When he got back in his Jeep, his coffee fell off the dash and burned his leg.

2

The kitchen light came on. All Ollie's white-haired children came into the living-room when she started to growl and rub her shoulder on the refrigerator. This was how Ollie grieved. She rolled her shoulders over the refrigerator door so some of the magnetic fruits fell on the floor. A math paper with a 98 on top see-sawed downward and landed on the linoleum. The kids were happy for a chance to be up. "Oh, boy!" they said. All but Aspen who was twelve and could understand. She remained at the bottom of the stairs afraid to ask Ollie what the trouble was. Aspen was in a lilac-color flannel gown and gray wool socks. She sucked the thumb of her right hand and hugged the post of the banister with her left. It was three fifteen in the morning. Applewood coals never die. All 'round the woodstove was an aura of summer. The socks and undershirts and mittens pinned in scores to a rope across the room had a summer stillness. They heard Ollie growl and pant. They giggled. Sometimes they stopped and looked up when she got loud. They figured she was not getting her way about something. They had seen the deputy, Erroll, leave from the upstairs windows. They associated Erroll with crime. Crime was that vague business of speeding tickets and expired inspection stickers. This was not a new thing. Erroll had come up in his Jeep behind Ollie a time or two in the village. He said: "Red light" And she bore her teeth at him like a dog. She was baring her teeth now.

There was an almost Christmas spirit among the children to be wakened in the night like that. There was wrestling. There was wriggling. Tim rode the dog: Dick Lab. He, Dick Lab, would try to get away, but hands on his hocks would keep him back. Judy turned on the t.v. Nothing was on the screen but bright fuzz. The hair of them all flying through the night was the torches of afterdark skiers: crackling white from chair to couch to chair to stairway, rolling Dick Lab on his side, carouseling twelve-year-old Aspen who sucked her thumb. Eddie and Arnie, Tim and Judy.

The herdsman's name was Jarrell Bean. He was like all Beans, silent and touchy, and had across his broad coffee-color face a look which made you suspect he was related somehow, perhaps on his mother's side, to some cows. The eyes were slate color and were of themselves lukewarm-looking, almost steamy, very huge, browless, while like hands they reached out and patted things that interested him. He inherited from his father, Bingo Bean, a short hair-cut . . . a voluntary baldness: Father's real name was also Jarrell, killed chickens for work and had the kind of red finely lined fingers you'd expect from so much murder. But Bingo's eyes everybody knows were yellow and utility. It was from Mother's side that Jarrell the herdsman managed to know what tact was. He came to the Cobb's door from his apartment over the barn. He had seen the deputy Erroll's Jeep and figured Lenny's time had come. He was wearing a black and red checked coat and the spikes of a three-day beard, auburn. It was the kind of beard men adrift in lifeboats have. Unkind weather had spread each of the hairs its own way.

He had travelled several yards through that frigid night with NO HAT. This was nudity for a man so bald.

In his mouth was quite a charge of gum. He didn't knock. The kitchen started to smell of spearmint as soon as he closed the door behind him. Ollie was rolled into a ball on the floor, grunting, one bare foot, bare calf and knee extended. He stepped over the leg. He made Ollie's children go up the stairs. He dragged one by the arm. It howled. Its flare of pale hair spurted here and there at the herdsman's elbow. The entire length of the child was twisting. It was Randy who was eight and strong. Dick Lab sat down on the twelve-year-old Aspen's ankles and feet, against the good wool. Jarrell came down the stairs hard. His boots made a booming through the whole big house. He took Dane and Linda and Hannah all at once. Aspen kept sucking her thumb. She looked up at him as he came down toward her, seeing him over her fingers. She was big as a woman. Her thumb in her mouth was longer and lighter than the others from twelve years of sucking. He fetched her by the blousey part of her lilac gown. She came away from the banister with a snap: like a Band-Aid from a hairy arm..."Cut it out!" she cried. His hands were used only to cattle. He thought of himself as GOOD with cattle, not at all cruel. And yet with cattle what is to be done is always the will of the herdsman.

3

When Jarrell came downstairs, Ollie was gone. She had been thinking of Lenny's face, how it had been evaporating for months into the air, how the lip had gotten short, how the cheeks fell into the bone. While Jarrell stood in the kitchen, he picked up the magnetic fruits and stuck them in a row on the top door of the refrigerator. He figured Ollie had slipped into her room to be alone.

He walked out into the yard past Lenny's new rootbeer color truck. He remembered how it roared when Leo at the Mobil had fiddled with the accelerator and everyone: Merritt and Poochie and Poochie's brother and Kenny, even Quinlan stood around looking in at the big 440 and Lenny was resting on the running board. Lenny's neck was getting much too small for his collar even then.

Jarrell went up to his apartment over the barn, his head stinging from the deep-freeze night, then his lamp went out and the yard was noiseless.

Under the rootbeer truck Ollie was curled with her braid in the snow. She had big bare feet. Under the rust color robe the goosebumps crowned up. Her eyes were squeeeezed shut like children do when they pretend to be sleeping. Her lip was drawn back from the elegantly twisted teeth twisted like the stiff feathers of a goose are overlaid. And filling one eye-glass lens a dainty ice fern.

4

It was Ollie whose scheduled days and evenings were on a tablet taped to the bathroom door. Every day Ollie got up at 4:30 a.m. Every evening supper was at 5:45. If visitors showed up late by fifteen minutes, she would whine at them and punish them with remarks about their character. If she were on her way to the feedstore in the pickup and there was a two-car accident blocking the road up ahead, Ollie would roll down the window and yell: "MOVE!!"

Once Aspen's poor body nearly smoked, 102 temperature, and blew a yellow mass from her little nose holes . . . a morning when Ollie had plans for the lake . . . Lenny was standing in the yard with his railroad cap on and his ringless hands in the pockets of his cardigan, leaning on the new rootbeer truck . . . Ollie came out on the porch where many wasps were circling between her face and his eyes looking up: "She's going to spoil our time," Ollie said. "We've got to go down to the store and call for an appointment now. She couldn't have screwed up the day any better." Then she went back inside and made her hand like a clamp on the girl's bicep, bore down on it with the might of a punch or a kick, only more slow, more deep. Tears came to Aspen's eyes. Outside Lenny heard nothing. Only the sirens of wasps. And stared into the very middle of their churning.

Oh, that Ollie. Indeed, Lenny months before must have planned his cancer to ruin her birthday. That was the day of the doctor's report. All the day Lenny cried. Right in the lobby of the hospital . . . a scene . . . Lenny holding his eyes

with the palms of his hands: "Help me! Help me!" he wailed
. . . she steered him to a plastic chair. She hurried down the
hall to be alone with the snack machine . . . HEALTHY
SNACKS: apples and pears, peanuts. She despised HIM this
way. THIS was her birthday.

5

In the thirty below ZERO morning jays' voices cracked
from the roof. Figures in orange nylon jackets hustled over
the snow. They covered Ollie with a white wool blanket. The
children were steady with their eyes and statuesque as they
arranged themselves around the herdsman. Aspen held the
elbow of his black and red coat. Everyone's breath flattened
out like paper, like those clouds cartoon personalities' words
are printed on. It may have warmed up some. Twenty below
or fifteen below. The cattle had not been milked, shuffling
and ramming and murring, cramped near the open door of
the barn . . . in pain . . . their udders as vulgar and hard as
the herdsman's velvet head.

6

At the hospital surgeons removed the ends of Ollie's
fingers, most of her toes and her ears. She drank Carnation
Instant Breakfast, grew sturdy again, and learned to keep her
balance. She came home with her thin hair combed to cover
her ear holes. In the back her hair veiled her ruby coat.

She got up every morning at 4:30 and hurtled herself
out to the barn to set up for milking. Jarrell feared every
minute that her hair might fall away from her missing ears.
He would squint at her. Together they sold some of the milk
to the neighborhood, those who came in cars and pulling
sleds, unloading plastic jugs and glass jars to be filled at the
sink, and the children of these neighbors would stare at
Ollie's short fingers, the parents would look all around every-
place BUT the short fingers. Jarrell: "Whatcha got today,
only two . . . is ya company gone?" or "How's Ralph's team

doin now? . . . that's good ta hear." or "Fishin any good now? I ain't heard." He talked a lot these days. When they came around he brightened up. He opened doors for them and listened to gossip and passed it on. They teased him a lot about his lengthening beard. Sometimes Tim would stand between Jarrell and Ollie and somehow managed to have his hand on the backs of Jarrell's knees most the time. As Ollie hosed out the stainless steel sink there in the wood and glass white white room, Tim's eyes came over the sink edge and watched the water whirl.

At night Jarrell would open Mason jars and slice carrots or cut the tops off beets. Ollie would lift things slowly with her purply stubs. She set the table. She would look at Jarrell to see if he saw how slick she did this. But he was not looking. The children, all those towheads, would be throwing things and running in the hall. There had come puppies of Dick Lab. Tim and a buff puppy pulled on a sock. Tim dragged the puppy by the sock across the rug. Ollie would stand by the sink and look straight ahead. She had a spidery control over her short fingers. She once hooked small Marsha up by the hair and pressed her to the woodbox with her knee. But Ollie was wordless. Things would usually go well. By 5:45 forks of beets and squash were lifted to mouths and glasses of milk were draining.

After supper Jarrell would go back to his apartment and watch Real People and That's Incredible or Sixty Minutes and fall asleep with his clothes on. He had a pile of rootbeer cans by the bed. Sometimes mice would knock them over and the cans would roll out of the room, but it never woke him.

Jarrell could not go to the barn in the morning without thinking of Lenny. He would go along and pull the rows of chains to all the glaring gray lights. He and Lenny used to stand by the open door together. That black and white pokadot SEA of cows would clatter between them. And over and between the blowing mouths and oily eyes, Lenny's dollar ninety-eight cent gloves waved them on, and he'd say:

"Oh, girl . . ., oh, girl . . ." Their thundering never ever flicked Lenny's watered down auburn hair that was thin on top. And there was the hairless temples where the chemotherapy had seared from the inside out.

Jarrell could recall Lenny's posture, a peculiar tired slouch in his pea coat. Lenny wore a watch cap in mid-winter and a railroad cap in sweaty weather and the oils of his forehead was on the brims of both.

Jarrell remembered summer when there was a big corn on the cob feast and afterward Lenny layed on the couch with just his dungarees on and his veiny bare feet kicking. His hairless chest was stamped with three black tatooes; two sailing ships and a lizard. Tim was jumping on his stomach. A naked baby lay on its back, covering the two ships. Lenny put his arm around the baby and it seemed to melt into him. Lenny's long face had that sleepy look of someone whose world is interior, immediate to the skin, never reaching outside his 120 acres. That very night that Lenny played on the couch with his children, Jarrell left early and stayed awake late in his apartment watching Tim Conway dictating in a German accent to his nitwit secretary.

Jarrel heard Ollie yelling. He leaned out his window and heard more clearly Ollie rasping out her husband's name. Once she leaped across the gold square of light of their bedroom window. Jarrell knew that Lenny was sitting on the edge of the bed, perhaps with his pipe in his mouth, untying his gray peeling workboots. Lenny would not argue, nor cry, nor turn red, but say: " . . . oh, girl . . . oh, Ollie, oh . . ." And he would look up at her with his narrow face, his eyes turning here and there on his favorite places of her face. She would be enraged the more. She picked up the workboot he had just pulled off his foot and turned it in her hand . . . then spun it through the air . . . the lamp went out and crashed.

Lenny began to lose weight in the fall. In his veins white blood cells roared. The cancer was starting to make Lenny irritable. He stopped eating supper. Ollie called it fussy. Soon Ollie and Jarrell were doing the milking alone. Sometimes Aspen would help. Lenny lay on the couch and slept. He slept all day.

7

One yellowy morning Ollie made some marks on the list on the bathroom door and put a barrett on the end of her braid. She took the truck to Leo's and had the tank filled. She drove all day with Lenny's face against her belly. Then with her hard spine and convexed shoulders she balanced Lenny against herself and steered him up the stairs of the Veteran's hospital. She came out alone and her eyes were wide behind the round glasses.

8

Jarrell had driven Lenny's rootbeer Utiline Dodge for the first time when he drove to the funeral alone. Lenny had a closed casket. The casket was in an alcove with pink lights and stoop shouldered mumbley Cobbs. They all smelled like old Christmas cologne. There must have been a hundred Cobbs. Most of the flowers around the coffin were white. Jarrell stood. The rest were sitting. The herdsman's head was pink in the funny light and he tilted his head as he considered how Lenny looked inside the coffin, under the lid. Cotton was in Lenny's eyes. He probably had skin like those plaster of Paris ducks that hike over people's lawns single file. He was most likely in there in some kind of suit, no pea coat, no watch cap, no pipe, no babies, no grit of Flash in his nails. Someone had undoubtedly scrubbed all the cow smell off him and he probably smelled like a new doll now. Jarrell drove to the interment at about 80 to 85 miles per hour and was waiting when the headlighted caravan dribbled into the cemetery and the stooped Cobbs ambled out of about 50 old cars.

9

Much later, after Lenny was dead awhile and Ollie's fingers were healed, Ollie came into the barn about 6:10. They were running late. The dairy truck from Portland was due to arrive in the yard. Ollie was wearing Lenny's old pea coat and khaki shirt with her new knit pants. Tim was with her. Tim had a brief little mouth and freakish coarse hair, like white weeds. His coat was fastened with safety pins. Ollie started hooking up the machines with her quick half-fingers. They rolled like sausages over the stainless steel surfaces. Jarrell, hurrying to catch up, was impatient with the cows when they wanted to shift around. Ollie was soundless but Jarrell could locate her even if he didn't see her, even as she progressed down the length of the barn. He had radar in his chest (the heart, the lungs, even the bladder) for her position when things were running late. God! It was like trying to walk through a wall of sand. Tim came over and stood behind him. Tim was digging in his nose. He was dragging out long strings of discolored matter and wiping it on his coat that was fastened with pins. One cow pulled far to the right in the stanchion, almost buckling to her knees as a hind foot slipped off the edge of the concrete platform. The milking machine thunked to the floor out of Jarrell's hands. Ollie heard. Her face came as if from out of the loft, sort of downward. HER HAIR WAS PULLED BACK caught up by her glasses when she had hurriedly shoved them on. SHE DID NOT HAVE EARS. HE SAW FOR THE FIRST TIME THEY HAD TAKEN HER EARS. His whole shape under his winter clothes went hot as though common pins were inserted over every square inch. He squinted, turned away . . . ran out of the milking room into the snow. The dairy truck from the city was purring up the hill. The fellow inside flopped his arm out for his routine wave. Jarrell didn't wave back, but used both hands to pull himself up into the rootbeer truck, slid across the cold seat, made the engine roar. He remembered Lenny saying once while they broke up bales of hay: "I just ordered a Dodge last week, me and my wife . . . be a few weeks, they said. Probly for the President they'd have it to him the next day. Don't it HURT to wait for somethin like that. Last night I dreamed I was in it, and was revvin it up out here in the yard when all of a sudden it took off . . . right up in the sky . . . and all the cows down in the yard looked like dominoes."

10

That afternoon Jarrell Bean returned. He came up the old Nathan Lord Road slow. Had his arm out the window. When he got near the Cobb place he ascended the hill in a second gear roar. As he turned in the drive he saw Ollie in Lenny's pea coat standing by the doorless Buick sedan in which the hens slept at night. She lined the sights of Lenny's rifle with the right lens of her glasses. One of her sausage fingers was on the trigger. She put out two shots. They turned the right front tire to rags. The Dodge screamed and plowed sideways into the culvert. Jarrell felt it about to tip over. But it only listed. He lay flat on the seat for a quarter of an hour even after he was certain Ollie had gone into the house.

Aspen and Judy came out for him. He was crying, lying on his stomach. When they saw him crying, their faces went white. Aspen put her hard gray fingers on his back, between his shoulders. She turned to Judy . . . Judy, fat and clear skinned with the whitest hair of all . . . and said: "I think he's sorry."

11

Ollie lie under the mint green bedspread. The window was open. All the yard, the field, the irrigation ditches, the dead birds were thawing and under the window she heard a cat digging in the jonquils and dried leaves. She raised her hand of partial fingers to her mouth to wipe the corners. She had slept late again and now her bloodpressure pushed at the walls of her head. She flipped out of the bed and thunked across the floor to the window. She was in a yellow print gown. The sunrise striking off the vanity mirror gave Ollie's face and arms a yellowness, too. She seized her glasses under the lamp. She peered through them, downward . . . STAR-TLED. Jarrell was a few yards from his apartment doorway, taking a pair of dungarees from the clothesline. There were sheets hanging there, too, so it was hard to be sure at first . . . then as he strode back toward his doorway, she realised he had nothing on. He was corded and pale and straight-backed and down front of his chest dripped wet his now full auburn beard. The rounded walls of his genitals gave little flaccid jogglings at each stride and on all of him his flesh like unbroken yellow water paused satisfyingly and seldomly at a few auburn hairs. On top, the balded head, a seamless hood, trussed up with temples all the way in that same seamless fashion to his eyes which were merry in the most irritating way. Ollie mashed her mouth and shingled teeth to the screen and moaned full and cowlike. And when he stopped and looked up, she screeched: "I HATE YOU! GET OUT OF HERE! GET OUT OF HERE!"

She scuttled to the bed and plunked to the edge. Underneath the shoes which Lenny wore to bean suppers and town council meetings were still criss-crossed against the wall.

12

That summer Jarrell and the kids played "catch" in the middle of the Nathan Lord Road. Jarrell waded among them at the green bridge in knee deep water, slapped Tim a time or two for persisting near the drop-off. They laughed at the herdsman in his second-hand tangerine trunks and rubber sandals. He took them to the drive-in movies in that rootbeer truck. They saw Benji and Last Tango in Paris. They got pop-corn and Good n Plenty's all over the seat and floor and empty paper cups were mashed in the truck bed, blew out one by one onto different people's lawns. He splurged on them at Old Orchard Beach, rides and games, and coordinated Aspen won stuff with darts: a psychedelic poster, a stretched out Pepsi bottle and four paper leis. Then under the pier they were running with huge ribbons of seaweed and he cut his foot on a busted Miller High Life bottle . . . slumped in the sand to fuss over himself. It didn't bleed. You could see into his arch, the meat, but no blood. Aspen's white hair waved 'round her head as she stooped in her sun-suit of cotton dots, blue like babies' clothes are blue. She cradled his poor foot in her fingers and looked him in the eye.

Ollie NEVER went with them. No one knew what she did alone at home.

One afternoon Ollie stared through the heat to find Jarrell on the front porch, there in a rocking chair with the sleeping baby's open mouth spread on his bare arm. Nearly grown puppies were at his feet. He was almost asleep himself and mosquitoes were industriously draining his throat and shirtless chest. On the couch after supper the little girls nestled in his auburn beard and rolled in their fingers wads of the course stuff. The coon cat with the abcesses all over his head swallowed whole the red tuna Jarrell bought for him and set out at night on an aluminum pie plate. Jarrell whenever he was close smelled like cows.

13

Ollie drove to the drugstore for pills that were for blood pressure. Aspen went along. The rootbeer truck rattled because Jarrell had left a yarding sled and chains in the back. Ollie turned her slow rust-color eyes onto Aspen's face and Aspen felt suddenly panicked. It seemed as though there was something changing about her mother's eyes: one studied your skin, one bored dead center in your soul. Aspen was wearing her EXTINCT IS FOREVER t-shirt. It was apricot colored and there was a leopard's face in the middle of her chest.

"Do you want one of those?" Ollie asked Aspen who was

poking at the flavored Chapsticks by the cash register.

"Could I?"

"Sure." Ollie pointed somewhere. "And I was thinking you might like some colored pencils or a . . . you know . . . movie magazine."

Aspen squinted. "I would, yes, I would."

A trio of high-school-aged Crocker boys in stretched-out t-shirts trudged through the open door in a bow-legged way that made them seem to be carrying much more weight than just their smooth long bones and little gummy muscles. One wore a baseball hat and had sweat in his hair and carried his sneakers. He turned his flawless neck, and his pink hair cropped there in a straight line was fuzzy and friendly like ruffles on a puppy's shoulders where you pat. He looked right at Aspen's leopard . . . right in the middle and read: "Extinct is forever."

His teeth lifted in a perfect cream-color line over the words and his voice was low and rolled, one octave above adulthood. Both the other boys laughed. One made noises like he was dying. Then all of them pointed their fingers at her and said: "Bang! Bang! Bang!" There are the insightful ones who realize a teenager's way of flirting and then there was Aspen who could not. To seel all the boys' faces from her plastic desk in school was to Aspen like having a small easily destructable boat with sharks in all directions. Suddenly self conscious, suddenly stoop-shouldered as it was for all Cobb's in moments of hell, Aspen stood one shoe on top of the other and stuck her thumb in her mouth. There is something about drugstore light with its smells of sample colognes passing up like moths through a brightness bigger and pinker than sun which made Aspen Cobb look large and old and the long thumb there was nasty looking. The pink-haired Crockers had never seen a big girl do this. They looked at each other gravely.

She walked over to where her mother was holding a jar of vitamin C. Her mother was arched over it, the veils of her thin black hair covering her earholes, falling foreward, and her stance was gathering, coordinated like a spider, the bath-tub spider, the horriblest kind. She lifted her eyes. Aspen pulled her thumb out of her mouth and wiped it on her shirt. Ollie put her arm around Aspen. She never did this as a rule. Aspen looked at her mother's face disbelievingly. Ollie pointed with one stub to the vitamin C bottle. It said: "200% of the adult minimum daily requirement." Aspen pulled away. The Crocker boys at the counter looked from Ollie's fingers to Aspen's thumb. But not til they were out-side did they shriek and hoot.

On the way home in the truck Aspen wished her mother would hug her again now that they were alone. But Ollie's fingers were sealed to the wheel and her eyes blurred by the glasses were looking out from a place where no hugging ever happened. There was a real slow Volkswagen up ahead driven by a white-haired man. Ollie gave him the horn.

14

The list of activities on the bathroom door became more rigidly ordered . . . with even trips to the flush, snacks and rests, and conversations with the kids pre-scheduled . . . peanutbutter and Saltines: 3:15 . . . clear table: 6:30 brush hair: 9:00 . . . and Ollie moved faster and faster and her cement-color hands and face were always across the yard somewhere or in the other room . . . singular of other people. And Jarrell looked in at her open bedroom door as he scooted Dane toward the bathroom for a wash . . . Ollie was CLEANING OUT THE BUREAU AGAIN, THE THIRD TIME THAT WEEK . . . and she was doing it very fast.

In September there was a purple night and the children all loaded into the back of the truck. Randy strapped the baby into her seat in the cab. The air had a dry grasshopper smell and the truckbed was still hot from the day. Jarrell turned the key to the rootbeer color truck. "I'm getting a Needham!" he heard Timmy blat from the truck bed. He pulled on the headlights knob. He shifted into reverse. The truck creaked into motion. The rear wheel went up, then down. Then the front went up and down. Sliding into the truck lights was the yellow gown, the mashed gray arm, the black hair unbraided, the face unshowing but with a purple liquid going everywhere from out of that hair, the half-fingers wriggling just a little. She had been under the truck again.

From the deepest part of Jarrell Bean the scream would not stop even as he hobbled out of the truck. Oh, he feared to touch her, just rocked and rocked and hugged himself and howled. The children's high whines began. They covered Ollie like flies. As with blueberry jam their fingers were dipped a sticky purple. The herdsman reached for the twelve year old Aspen. He pulled at her. Her lids slid over icy eyes. Her breath was like carrots into his breath. He reached. And her frame folded into his hip.

Marilyn Jean Conner

Bunco

Mrs. Endsley was paid to keep everyone happy. Her latest project involved composing a Conwoody Convalescent song, something on the order of a school song, but with some of the parts left out. And it was in her line of duty that, on a Wednesday in early May, just before supper, she smacked her little silver wand around inside the triangle hanging at one end of the dining room. Thurlow looked on the floor to see if he'd dropped his fork; Delmar patted his pockets for his hearing aid; Lulu admired a basket of biscuits. But the other forty-four Conwoody Convalescents looked toward Mrs. Endsley and the new girl who stood beside her propped in an aluminum walker. This new girl made forty-eight, optimum occupancy by Mrs. Endsley's reckoning.

Mrs. Endsley waited for the chatter to subside, then stretched on her smile. When she had everyone's attention, she said, "May I have your attention please? May I have your attention please? We have a new guest with us this evening. I'd like you all to meet Lizzie Taylor. She's been at Riverside Manor — What was it, a little more than a year, Lizzie? — but now she's moving up in the world to join the Conwoody Family. I know you'll all help to make Lizzie happy with us."

The women stared at Lizzie without shame. They wondered whether she was crazy or not. She looked pretty much crazy, what with the drooling and that limp eyelid, but they'd know for sure as soon as she sat down. Mrs. Endsley had the crazies sit at a table by themselves. She thought it made everyone happier. Sure enough, she led Lizzie down to the end of table four and sat her down by John, who had recently been demoted from table two for what Mrs. Endsley called unsociability. Lizzie was crazy. The other ladies didn't need to keep an eye on her and dismissed her as someone who did not need to be dealt with.

Post-introduction chatter rose, and Mrs. Endsley had to whack the triangle again to get everyone's attention so Delmar could shout grace. As the kitchen staff brought around plates of food, Lizzie sat with her head fallen to the side. She didn't seem to be aware of the plate of meatloaf and carrot circles that sat in front of her. Next to her, John held his fork like a toothbrush and ate carrots one at a time. One of his legs was gone above the knee, and he sat in a fancy wheelchair his son had sent him from Rhode Island. Lizzie scraped some of the carrots off her plate into her hand and put them in one of the deep leather pockets of John's wheelchair, right next to *The Sporting News*. John stabbed some more carrots, and Lizzie looked under her meatloaf. While he took a drink of ice water, she slipped three more carrot slices into his wheelchair pocket. He put down his water and said very clearly but so quietly that no one but Lizzie could hear him, "You do that again, lady; I break your arm off at the shoulder."

An attendant led Lizzie to her room after the meal, and Lizzie step-pushed, step-pushed listlessly along after her. While the attendant introduced Lulu as Lizzie's roommate and unpacked her things, Lizzie rested in a green sitting chair. A glistening drop of clear mucous hung suspended above her lip. When Lulu asked if her slippers were comfortable, she didn't answer.

After the aide dropped Lizzie's good shoes in the wooden closet with a clunk and left, closing the door behind her for nap hour, Lulu climbed up her little two-step stool and flopped her three hundred pounds in the middle of her bed. Her floral mumu got caught under her butt, and was pulling at her neck. She grunted around until she could lift her weight off the mumu. "Damn high beds," she said,

"Why don't they put them down where a person can get in them?"

Just as she got settled, Drexel banged the door open and wobbled in with his cane. Holding the back of his white gown shut with one hand, he shouted "Have you seen that goddam John with my goddam doughnuts? My grand-daughter brought me them doughnuts. They was in a white doughnut sack."

Lulu was startled when the door came open. "No. We haven't seen your stupid doughnuts. Keep track of your own stuff. And don't you ever come in here without knocking again."

Drexel looked glinty-eyed at Lizzie and Lulu. "Goddam John," he said, and wandered off.

Lulu wormed around and sat with her legs hanging off the bed looking at Lizzie like she was a broken vacuum cleaner. "What's your last name, Lizzie? I'm afraid I didn't catch what Mrs. Endsley said out in the dining room. Weren't those good biscuits? Mrs. Endsley says I'm only to have one, but I sneak a little extra now and again. That little bit of a dinner I got just whet my appetite." Lulu took a bakery snack out from behind her pillow and, holding her hand cupped beneath her chin to catch the crumbs, ate the rest of Drexel's doughnuts. She lifted her feet out in front of her and wiggled her bare toes. "You'll like it here, I think. You know I'm the youngest person here. I'm hardly past sixty, but I have a problem with my weight. I'm diabetic, you know. And a heart condition, too. I've had three heart attacks in the last two years, and I have to be very careful of my sugar." Lizzie rewarded her with a deep, phlegmy sigh.

Soon, a hugh belch erupted and rolled from Lulu's depths, hanging on until it faded into a thin, throaty gurgle. "Oh. My. Now that's what I was waiting for. Those cucumber salads do it. You know they have burpless cucumbers now? What won't they do next?" Lulu lay back, folded her hands across her stomach, and waited a little bit. "Do you think she's done unpacking your things?'' Lulu waited a few minutes longer, and then she reached over to the drawer of her bedside table, lifted out two crossword puzzle books, and got a box of chocolate candy out from under a copy of *The Dieting Gourmet*. Without getting up, she held the box out toward Lizzie, but not close enough for her to reach it. "Like some Whitman's chocolate? You're welcome to it, but don't tell anybody I have it. One of the janitors brings it in for me. He understands me.'' Lulu belched again and began to work a crossword puzzle with a fountain pen.

After her first night at Conwoody, Lizzie was put out on a patio to get some air for her morning activity. She sat downwind of a row of clay-potted geraniums whose nauseous odor wafted fresh across the patio at every breath. John sat nearby, and several yards away, a small group of the more socially oriented guests sat clustered around a small fountain which featured two naked children spitting at each other in long streams of recycled water. Near mid-morning, the breeze across the patio began to pick up. As it swelled in force, it blew the stone boy's water back in his face; gave Alfretta a thrill when it filled her skirt with cooling air; knocked a largish ash from John's cigar; and lifted a long stream of spittle from the corner of Lizzie's mouth. The breeze drew the spittle out to a fine, white thread, and let it fall gently across John's hand. John pulled hard on his cigar; there was an almost inaudible crackling, and he let the smoke ease out of his mouth of its own accord. After a clean, measured breath, he said to Lizzie, "Lady, you slobber on me again, I bust your mouth.'' He pulled a grey and brown handkerchief out of his pants pocket and dabbed at the back of his hand.

A spry old couple wearing matching sky-blue jackets strolled down the sidewalk past Conwoody. The wife smiled serenely, and the man still had all his hair. As they passed John and Lizzie, the man folded his newsaper and tucked it under one arm so he could take the net bag of grapefruit his wife carried. As they turned the corner at the end of the block, she linked her arm through his and patted his hand.

Lizzie inquired clearly, "Do you like it here?"

John stuffed a corner of the handkerchief back in his pocket, drew another lungful of cigar smoke, and said, "*Hell*, no." After this brief exchange they sat on as before until someone came out to haul them in for lunch.

In the afternoon, Lizzie was taken to her room for her nap, and Lulu got to stay out in the playroom to play euchre. After the door eased shut behind the aide, Lizzie rolled over on her side and looked wistfully at Lulu's bedside table, just out of her reach. She stretched one frail arm out toward the table, then scooted over so that she just barely hung balanced on the edge of the bed. She fell back with a sigh and looked at the ceiling for some fifteen minutes. Then she sat bolt up-right, swung around, and hopped down off the bed. She opened Lulu's drawer, lifted out the magazines, studied the candy map inside the lid of the Whitman's box, and took three toffee crunches and four chocolate-covered cherries from the still-untouched bottom layer. Before restoring *The Dieting Gourmet* to its concealing position, Lizzie lifted two sheets of pale blue writing paper and Lulu's fountain pen. She sat cross-legged and used a high, portable table that extended across her bed to write a note to John. After she composed her note, she hid Lulu's pen in the back of her own drawer, pushed her table back where it was, gobbled down the candy, and fell fast asleep.

At dinner, Lizzie slipped the note in John's wheelchair pocket. He raised his arm and looked mean, but Lizzie quickly touched her little dish of succotash so he could see that all the vegetables were still there. After television hour in the playroom, an aide helped Lizzie back to her room, where Lulu was in a state: "Someone took something from my drawer. I'm sure of it."

The aide was used to imagined thievery. "Calm yourself, Lulu. What is it that you've misplaced?"

"It is not misplaced. It could not be misplaced. It's my favorite pen. I cannot misplace things like that. I may be overweight, but I'm not stupid. I just saw it this morning." The aide looked half-heartedly under the bed and opened Lulu's drawer to search through it. Lulu sat up and started to have a pain. "That's all right. Don't bother. I never kept it in that drawer. Oh, my side. Oh it hurts. I think I have a cramp."

The aide's hand rested on *The Dieting Gourmet*: "Lulu, if you'll just let me look for it, I'm sure we'll find it, and you'll feel much better."

Lulu grabbed up one of her great gazebos and grimaced in pain. "Oh, oh, oh, I think I'm having another heart attack. Water, I need water. Thirteen swallows. I can't breathe. My chest feels so heavy." Often warned about Lulu's heart condition, the aide scurried to get some water and then loped down the hall to tell the nurse. Lulu gave Lizzie a long look. "If I weren't so tired out, I'd give you a good search-over, dribble lips." But Lizzie just sat leaned to one side in her green vinyl chair, and finally Lulu lay back in her bed, much calmer. "That was close. Oh my, I still can't catch my breath. It's not the pen so much, though I did win it as a prize one February for losing the most weight in the Fat Ladies' Club." Lulu poked around in her drawer and found a disposable ballpoint. "But what really fans my fire is that some sneaking asp, some low-down adder, took seven of my chocolates from the bottom layer. Every last one of my chocolate-covered cherries is gone."

The aide and the nurse came back armed for crisis, but found Lulu smiling sheepishly, panting only a little, and clutching the disposable pen. "Silly me. Silly me. Here it is. Here it is. It was in my pocket all the time. I don't know what's the matter with me. I must be getting old." The aide was relieved and the nurse irritated. They left as soon as they were sure Lulu had recovered. When they were out of ear-shot, Lulu said, "Believe you me, I'm going to find the snake that stole my lower layer.''

Back in his room, John sat in the bathroom with Drexel safely locked out and the water from the faucet just dribbling into the sink. He held Lizzie's note in both hands:

John,
I am not crazy. I have all my marbles. Fix it so I can talk to you. Do not let anyone see.

L.

P.S. Destroy this.

John looked at the note while Drexel whined at the door; he had to pee. When Drexel began hitting the door with his cane, John flushed the note down the toilet and let him in.

The next morning, it was too damp for an airing on the patio, and John and Lizzie were stationed so they could look out the big picture window at the visitors' parking lot. John waited until an aide had tucked his lap robe in around his thighs. He held up his *Sporting News* as if intent on last week's box scores and said, ''Well, what is it?'' Lizzie just left her head tilted forward as if she had no more sense than a loaf of white bread.

She kept her eyes focused on nothing and just moved her lips. ''They think I'm *non compos mentis*. I want to keep it that way.''

''You're nutty as a fruitcake. I'm only doing this because I'm a nice guy. Follow me in a little bit.'' John rolled over to a corner where a dusty rubber plant stood in a styrofoam pot. Lizzie struggled to her feet and aimlessly step-pushed the walker the other way around the room. In fifteen minutes, she got to John's corner and sat in a chair beside him. They sat with their backs to the rest of the room and appeared to be looking out, but their view of the parking lot was blocked by a scraggly yew growing in front of the window.

John held up *The Sporting News*, and Lizzie assumed her loaf-of-bread posture. ''You see, it's like this — what's your last name, John?''

"John Boston."

"You see, Boston, I found out real quick, when I signed into my first home, that the easiest thing to do in a place like this is play crazy. You can do anything you please, and they think, well, what can you expect from a fruitcake like that? And they leave you alone."

"Right. Leave alone. So what are you pesterin' *me* for?"

"Well, at Riverview, for the longest time I roomed with a real nice old lady — had cancer of the throat and couldn't make a sound. We got along fine. Then she died, bless her, and they put me in with a nasty old magpie with gall bladder trouble. I couldn't get things switched around, so I had my daughter get me in here. Now what do I get but Lulu? Most people, they figure you crazy, then there's no point in talking to you, but not her. Boy, when she's got me alone in that room, she never shuts up. I'm just looking for somebody with half a brain so I can talk back a little."

John turned a page. "Okay. *You* need someone to talk to. I don't. My wife talked to me for forty-four years."

Lulu dribbled a good bit, then asked, "How long's she been gone?"

"Two years, three months. Died hicuppin'. Hiccuped a day and a half, then konked out."

"Too bad, too bad. How long you been here, then?"

"About a year. I was having a high old time. Could get around in my wheelchair and watch TV, whatever I wanted, all the time. Then I spilled a pan of beets in my lap when I was taking them off the stove. Couldn't get 'em off my lap fast enough. Burned pretty bad. Then when I got out of the hospital, my son put me in here. Said he was afraid I'd hurt myself. Truth is, he just didn't want to worry himself about me, and *he* didn't have to pay for it. Damn Bastard."

"How bad did you hurt yourself?"

"Mostly just the skin, but I was burned pretty bad."

Lizzie sneezed without covering her mouth, checked to make sure no one saw them talking, and then asked, "Did you lose your leg in the war?''

"No. Hell, no. Wish I had. I fell on the ice going around the Pontiac to open the car door for Esther when we was going to Christmas Eve Services. Messed up my knee; it got infected, and they whacked it off two and a half weeks after Christmas. Damn. I didn't even want to go to church, didn't want to open the door, didn't want to piddle around with Christmas at all. But there we was. That woman could play hell. If she'd a caught the hiccups two months earlier, I'd be walking around today.''

Just then, a church tower chimed out a phrase from a hymn to tell the hour, and Alfretta was reminded of her Christian suffering. "OH LORD. OH LORD GOD. I GOT THE MISERY. I GOT THE MISERY IN MY BACK." A few people glanced up and looked at each other in shared disgust. Delmar said, quite loudly, that if he ran the place he'd put those idiots in a padded cell.

After Lizzie had been at Conwoody about three weeks, she and John got so they'd sit out on the patio and look like they weren't talking three, maybe four mornings a week. On the last morning in May, Lizzie and John sat silent for a minute while Drexel lurched by behind them. Before speaking, Lizzie had an ugly coughing fit so she could turn her head to see if anyone were close by. "Listen, Boston, how is it you get out of all them games they make them play?''

"Oh, it wasn't easy. When I first came here, those goof-offs kept trying to make me play those kid games. Finally I tripped Endsley with that damn dumb Drexel's cane — it's nice and stout with a rubber tip — and goosed her a good one while she was down. That taught her. She decided I was dangerous, put me at the ga-ga's table, and left me alone. And the others got enough sense to leave me alone anyways.''

As a conscientious objector, John was exempt from bunco, but Mrs. Endsley still had hopes of getting Lizzie socially oriented. So at the Friday night bunco game, she propped Lizzie at Lulu's table. Lulu took three cards, looked them over carefully, and put one in front of Lizzie, tilted so Lulu could keep an eye on it. Lizzie eyeballed the card and slitted her eyes so she looked as if she were falling asleep. Everyone was set. Lulu sat hunched over her cards.

Delmar assumed a noble stance, tumbled the wooden cubes in a cage, and began calling out the numbers with great style, repeating each one three times. He felt honored to be the caller and was used to shouting anyway. As he called more and more numbers, Lulu eagerly closed off four spaces on Lizzie's card. Along with the other players, she became more tense as Delmar called more numbers.

When he called out "0-71, 0-71, that is *000-71*," Lizzie already had four corners, but she didn't know if this was a four-corners game; the nincompoops hadn't reviewed the rules before they started. She couldn't decide whether to say "bunco" or stay dumb. She thought maybe she could be a crazy person who knew only one word. But she was afraid some of these clucks might wise up. Then Lulu's eyes brightened when she checked Lizzie's card and slid the little window shut on 0-71. She started to slide the card back in front of her and slip one of her losers in front of Lizzie. Lizzie decided to be a crazy person who knew only one word. Just missing the tips of Lulu's pudgy fingers, she whammed her fist down on her card with a frightful bang that made everyone jump. With a rhythmic idiocy, she said, "bunco, bunco, bunco."

Making a quick recovery as she checked the welfare of her nearly-missed index finger, Lulu chirped in her fat lady's talk, "Oh, Lizzie has four corners, doesn't she?" Mrs. Endsley came and read the numbers back to Delmar. It was a winner. When she gave Lizzie the girls' prize, a utility apron that wouldn't fit around Lulu anyway, Lizzie said, "bunco, bunco, bunco."

At the next morning's airing, Lizzie and John sat at the

edge of the patio peering over the top of the spirea hedge to watch the cars go by. Lizzie ranted about Lulu through closed teeth. "Do you know that tub of blubber tried to cheat me out of my bunco? And then when I catch her, she says, 'OOH, LIZZIE'S GOT FOUR CORNERS.' I'd like to fry some of the grease out of that lard head. Her eternal yapping is god-awful enough, but cheating — cheating is the absolute limit. Two things I never could stand was cheats and liars."

"Hell, woman, I thought you didn't want to play the damn game, anyway."

"Yes, but what's mine by rights is mine by rights." John cleared his throat, and with an expert's finesse, spat a glob of green phlegm straight across the hedge.

Early the next morning, Lulu put on her dress-up mumu and waddled off to chapel; chapel-goers got an early breakfast. Stepping up her campaign, Lizzie took Lulu's books of crossword puzzles and worked several of them while Lulu was at chapel. She continued during the week, and as she grew bolder, she started taking them into the bathroom and working them during nap hour. Lulu would find the puzzles filled in with wobbley letters which looked like they came from her fountain pen, and she would cock her head at them as if she were trying to remember when she did them.

Lizzie kept taking Lulu's candy regularly. Trying to catch the thief, Lulu kept an eagle's eye on Lizzie and searched through her drawers, her closet, and even her bag of dirty clothes whenever something was missing. When she found nothing, she was determined it was Drexel, and she'd sit in the playroom for hours watching the door of her room down the hall waiting for Drexel to sneak in her room so she could catch him.

Late one night in the middle of the summer, Lizzie was awakened by Lulu as she insulted the opened centerfold of a girlie magazine. Lulu looked at the magazine's pictures long and carefully and then got out of bed and hid it in the bottom drawer of her dresser under the box she kept her good corset in.

As soon as Lizzie was left alone long enough, she got into Lulu's drawer. Underneath the corset box she found a treasure of magazines containing pictures of shameless, fresh-skinned young tarts, all of them naked as jaybirds. At the bottom of the stack, she found a *Playgirl* which she hid behind the heater and sometimes studied while she munched on chocolates. When she could catch a chance, she took the other magazines into the bathroom one copy at a time and snipped out the best pictures with Lulu's toenail scissors. She rolled the pictures up carefully and smuggled them out to John, and for the last two weeks in July, she took him a new picture every afternoon. He especially liked a red-haired youngster with freckles. Lizzie said she thought freckles ruined the skin.

They didn't have full-length mirrors in the rooms at Conwoody, so Lizzie could only look at herself in halves. She locked the door to her bathroom and stood and looked at her top half in the mirror for a while. She slapped her garbanzas around trying to get them to sit up and take notice, but they still hung long and limp, like two soggy pink zucchinis. Then, wanting to get a good look at her bottom half, she stepped up on the seat of the toilet and then onto the vanity where she stood straddling the sink. She held onto the light fixtures and evaluated. Her grey bird's nest was going a bit baldy, but everything else, though a bit rundown, was in good working order.

The next time Lulu dug into her supply of girlie magazines it was around two o'clock in the middle of a still August night. She got out the three latest issues and got back in bed to look at them. When she found the best pictures gone, she started to swear quietly. Then she wiggled down out of bed and checked to see if the *Playgirl* was still there.

She took all the magazines out and scattered them across the floor looking for it. She searched through Lizzie's dresser, and even looked inside the cover of the chair cushion and under the shelf paper in the closet. Finding nothing, she got back in bed and cried in little gasps until Lizzie thought she was asleep, and then she got up again suddenly and looked all through the magazines one more time. Then she put them all away under the corset box and sat up in bed holding the open box of Whitman's and polishing off a whole layer before finally falling asleep. Lizzie told John about Lulu's antics the next afternoon, and he said what a pitiful business.

Lizzie let up on Lulu for a long while after that until a Sunday in October when Lizzie's daughter came to visit and brought along some cherry turnovers. Lizzie ate one while her daughter read her letters from the family. When she'd kissed her on the cheek and left, there were three turnovers left. Lizzie folded the top of the turnover sack down, fastened it shut with a bobby pin, and hid it on the windowsill behind the drapes. Lulu came in directly.

"Lizzie's little girl was just here, wasn't she?" Lulu came over to Lizzie's side of the room and looked in Lizzie's cabinet, then in her drawer. "Did she bring Lizzie any goodies?" She opened the wooden closet and shoved aside Lizzie's bag and shoes to make room to step up on the raised floor so she could see what was on the top shelf. Lizzie sat in her chair, and Lulu looked until she found the turnovers behind the drapes: "What's this? What's this? Turnovers? And if I didn't know you were my best friend, I'd think you'd hidden them from *me*." Lulu heaved up into her bed and ate them right down. As she brushed flakes of glaze off her bosom, she said, "You don't mind sharing with Lulu, just to tide her over, *do* you?"

Lizzie found a minute with John after supper, and that night they put a plan they'd been working on into effect. He shared some Spanish peanuts with Drexel, fetched him three glasses of water when he got thirsty, and then helped him out when he felt the call of nature in the middle of the night. In the morning, he rolled down to Lizzie's room with a shiny silver container carefully tucked inside his robe. Lizzie dumped it in Lulu's bed while she was taking a bubble bath. Lulu noticed the dampness as she sat on the bed to pull up her support hose. She looked at once surprised and guilty. She went over and jerked the covers off Lizzie's bed and felt it. Then she made Lizzie stand up so she could feel her nightgown. She looked in the closet and down the hall.

"I have not done this. Someone has wet my bed. I would not do this." Lulu felt her own nightgown to make sure. "You saw who it was. You saw. Who was it, you nincompoop?" She ripped the sheets off her bed and threw them in the hall. When an aide came in to see what the commotion was, Lulu was shaking Lizzie by the shoulders. Lizzie sat and let her head flop back and forth just right.

"Lulu, Lulu, Lulu," the aide said in her command voice, "Stop that this instant. What are you doing to that poor woman?"

"Poor woman? Poor woman? She wet my bed, or else she saw who did it. They've been after me for months."

"Wet your bed? You wet your bed? That's nothing to worry about; it happens to everybody. That's why we use the rubber sheets. Now you just relax, and I'll get you some protective underwear just till we make sure you're okay. You won't have to be embarrassed about it again."

"Now you're trying to put a diaper on me. I did not wet the bed. I'm a grown woman. My husband worked at the bank. You'll have to knock me down to get a diaper on me." Lulu worked herself into such a frenzy that she had to sit down and take a heart pill. She wouldn't relax until Mrs. Endsley, who said she only wanted Lulu to be happy, promised to call Dr. Findly that afternoon. When he came, he told Lulu he believed her and left a little bottle of pills.

An Indian summer breeze blew out John's third match as Lizzie slumped next to him waiting for Drexel to stop looking her way. When Drexel found a stick along the hedge and began seeing if he could plug up the fountain boy's mouth with it, Lizzie cleared her throat. "You know Lu heads for chapel every Sunday morning like clockwork. She hasn't missed a one since I been here."

"It's them religious breakfasts they have."

"She's gone maybe an hour and fifteen minutes, an hour for sure, every time she goes. And nobody comes in to wake me up until chapel's all over with."

"I reckon when it comes to eatin', Lu's a mighty regular woman."

"Now that you mention eating, you know them beets?"

"Them whats?"

"Beets, the ones you spilled in your lap."

"Oh. Sure. Damn things. Never have liked beets." John hunted up another match and then tried to light it with a flick of his thumbnail.

"You know, it doesn't seem like you could get burned too bad by a bunch of piddly beets."

"It was bad enough for me." As John fished for his matchbox, the breeze shivered a sparse shower of leaves from the hedge. He located the matchbox and lit the match along its side.

"Well, John, your whim-wham still works all right, doesn't it?" John dropped the match, and it made a small brown-edged hole in the green fabric of his empty pantleg before he could slap out the flame.

Before dawn the next Sunday morning, Lizzie made sure Lulu's snoring was regular to the count of fifty, then slipped quietly out of bed and into the bathroom. She laid Lulu's towel along the bottom of the door so she could turn on the light to put her dentures in some fizz water. After she brushed her teeth up good and put them in, she flapped some dusting powder around under her arms and put on a new green nightgown that had a big red apple right smack on the front. She turned off the light, threw the towel over toward the bathtub, and tiptoed back to bed.

She fell asleep and didn't wake up again until Lulu was gargling mouthwash for chapel. After Lulu scurried off to breakfast, Lizzie stretched herself out on the bed, hiked her nightgown up around her waist, and waited for John. Soon, his wheelchair scraped against the door as he maneuvered it through the doorway. He pushed the door to and wheeled to the side of Lizzie's bed. "I hope you got something sensible in mind because I haven't been able to think up an idea of how we're going to work this."

As Lizzie hopped out of bed, she said, "You just get your whim-wham to cooperate, and I'll take care of the rest of it. Can you get up in the bed?"

"Not without somebody to help hold me up on the one side, I can't. Are you sure you're strong enough?"

Lizzie was already tugging John up out of the chair. "I lived on a farm and did a man's work every day of my life." In proof of her claim, Lizzie picked John up by both thighs and tilted him face forward on the bed.

"Jesus Christ, woman, you're going to wear me out before we get started."

"You don't get enough exercise. That's what I keep telling you." While Lizzie started pulling at the legs of John's pajamas, he fumbled madly to untie the drawstrings before she tore something. They finally slipped off. Lizzie tossed them on her chair and brusquely rolled John over on his back.

"Now listen here, stop tossing me around like I was a bale of hay."

"You've got no passion in you — no imagination. Now just relax." Lizzie attended to John's whim-wham with the firm-fingered dexterity she'd used to milk cows. It soon perked up, and she was pleased with herself. "Now what do you think of that?"

"Hell's bells, I could have done that much myself."

Lizzie scrambled out of her nightgown, pulling it half over her head, but a button at the neck caught in her hair. She struggled for a moment with her arms crossed above her head inside the nightgown. After she yanked off the gown, a thin, stiff strand of hair stood straight up from her head. Lizzie kneeled naked on the bed beside John, and he lay wondering what she would do next. Just as she put her hands on his chest and threw one of her stringy thighs over his waist, they heard someone hurrying down the hall.

"Oh, Jesus, let me up."

"No. No, now shut up and hold still." Lizzie pushed John back down on the bed, pulled the blanket over their heads, and lay stretched out on top of him peeking out through the loose weave of her blanket. Lulu slammed through the door and straight into the bathroom without giving a glance into the room.

John began trying to get up. "Let me up. I'm getting out of here." He half-sat up suddenly and smacked his head squarely into Lizzie's nose. She lost her balance and caught at John's short hair for something to hold onto. As they rolled off the bed, John grabbed at the blue thermal blanket. After the blanket slithered off the bed to rest on top of them, the bathroom door crashed open, and Lulu came out struggling to pull a huge pair of underpants up from around her knees. Lizzie rolled John off of her legs and grabbed up her gown.

She stood up and cowered in the corner, gown clutched to her chest, strand of hair still pointing upward, and said, "Bunco, Bunco, Bunco."

Lulu, wide-eyed, still tugged at her underwear, and John began pulling himself into his wheelchair. "Forget that," John squeaked, "and give me a goddam hand here."

"What's going on here? What's going *on* here, Mr. Boston?" Lulu gave up on her pants and let the skirt of her mumu fall to cover all but the huge dangling rubberized crotch. When Lizzie heaved John into his chair, Lulu's face turned a deeper red with each of her quick, hoarse breaths. "You. You fake. You *have* been tricking me. You ripped up my magazines, you preevert." John wadded up his pajama bottoms into his lap, pulled Lizzie's blanket up to his waist, and maneuvered his chair around the foot of her bed. Lizzie scrambled over the bed and began tugging at the drawer of Lulu's cabinet. Lulu began sucking in air in huge, wheezing gasps. "My bed. You peed in my bed. You did that to me. They think I'm crazy. I'll snatch you bald."

Lulu blocked John's way, and he said, "Excuse me, ma'am, excuse me. I've got to be going."

Lizzie got Lulu's drawer open, threw *The Dieting Gourmet* on the floor, and held the box of Whitman's up in front of her. "You lay a fat finger on me, and I'll show 'em what you're feeding your face with every day."

"You can talk. You can talk. I'll murder you," Lulu hissed as she began to tilt forward. As John scraped out the door, Lizzie raised the box of candy in case she needed to bash Lulu on the head with it. But just as she reached Lizzie, Lulu finished falling. She hit the easy-care carpeting with a grunt and lay with one hand around Lizzie's ankle, the underpants still tangled around her huge knees. Lizzie put the candy back in Lulu's drawer, wiggled her ankle free, and felt the pulse on Lulu's neck like she'd seen those cute firemen do on TV. Lulu's neck was too fat to feel anything anyway, but Lizzie could tell by the way Lulu lay smack flat on her face with both feet looking off under the bed that she was stone dead. Lizzie was sitting wide-eyed with the sheet pulled up to her chin when an aide found Lulu. Lizzie looked at Lulu and said, "Bunco. Bunco. Bunco."

It took three of them to get Lulu on a stretcher. When they shook their heads at each other and covered Lulu over with the top sheet of her bed, Lizzie thought it was the best bit of luck she'd had since she'd found the ten dollar bill in the hymnal in 1949. When they found Lulu's candy, they said no wonder.

At the Sunday afternoon airing, the other guests were looking at Lizzie a lot because they knew she'd seen Lulu keel over. In the playroom the four ladies of the Conwoody Chorus were rehearsing Mrs. Endsley's Conwoody song. And John and Lizzie were content just to sit together, quiet in the autumn sun. Then John reached over and nudged Lizzie's arm. "Look who's coming." The couple who fancied they were enjoying their retirement came down the sidewalk toward the nursing home. John and Lizzie had watched them as they passed that way each afternoon, usually carrying a small sack of groceries or something from the dimestore. They always wore their identical jackets and lived in a new senior citizens' condominium a block and a half from Conwoody.

Lizzie sat up expectantly, "Wait until they get to the fire hydrant." As they approached, the lady looked at the pair peering over the hedge and said something quietly to her husband. He nodded agreeably.

"Ready." As the couple reached the fire hydrant, Lizzie and John stuck their tongues out in unison. John's stuck out rigidly until the couple passed by, but Lizzie, aggravated by the lady's permanent, wiggled hers wildly and squinted up her eyes in the ugliest face she could manage. After the two had increased their pace and hurried past, Lizzie felt much better. "That'll serve them creeps right. I bet they won't walk this way anymore. They think they're so damn superior."

Pamela Painter

The Intruders of Sleepless Nights

They own no dogs; the maid sleeps out. The catches on the windows are those old-fashioned brass ones, butterfly locks. No alarm system or fancy security. He memorized everything Nick had to tell about this job. He pulls on black cotton gloves, soft and close like ladies' gloves. He is no longer just a man out for a late-night walk as he enters this strange driveway wearing black gloves. If the cops come they would be hard to explain away. The porch is just like Nick described it, screened in, running the entire back length of the house. He mounts the brick steps slowly, slits the screen and opens the door. Listens. These small pauses set him apart from other second-story guys he knows, take time away from the seven minute in-and-out rule. But he ain't never been caught either. He pulls a roll of masking tape and a straight-edged knife from his jacket pocket. Nick said the easiest window opens into a bathroom off the front hall. Two over from the back door. Quickly the taped asterisk takes shape — corner to corner, up and down. He always varies the pattern, uses different width tape. As he hits the window sharply, once, in the center, it splinters and holds. He folds the sagging shreds of glass outward toward him, loosens more from the caulking, and puts them on a wicker table. Once more he listens — not taking Nick's word for everything. He hopes the sound wasn't loud enough to wake the sleeping couple eleven rooms and two floors away.

•

Her husband is asleep — finally. His back is to her, his

right shoulder high, and now his breathing has slowed to a steady pace like some temporarily regulated clock. She has been lying on her back, staring at the ceiling, her silence a lullaby for him. Now she lifts her arms lightly from the bed, readjusting the blankets, placing more folds between them. She thinks of her husband as the mountain range to her lower plain in their nightly landscape. She flexes her fingers, her toes, stretches her legs until her tightness leaves, absorbed by the bed. She feels an energy at night that she cannot use by day moving around this house with too many rooms. If she were alone — always in some other smaller place — she would live at night. Who else is up at this time while her husband dreams of secretaries and waitresses. Should she buy twin beds, electric blankets, or a divorce attorney? Or new garbage cans to foil those damn raccoons!

•

His wife thinks he is sleeping. He knows this by the way she begins to move, adjusting the sheets, almost gaily like a puppet released to life. He dislikes being able to fool her so easily, and sometimes he varies his breathing just to feel her freeze — he hopes into an awkward unnatural position that hurts. But usually the game bores him, he'd rather sleep. He sleeps better with his girlfriend, Nan, when they finally go to sleep after making love. A last night-cap. 'What an old fashioned word' she said. Nan will be listening to PBS, propped up in bed with three or four books, cigarettes, ashtray, crackers, nail polish, cotton balls, a miniature magnetic chess set, a hair brush. Nan lives on crackers — wheat thins, water bisquits, matzo, alvah. She likes to brush her hair as she watches television though it makes him nervous. He is ahead of her in games won at chess. Barely. He hears a noise somewhere near the library or patio. Raccoons again. They have both heard it, he can tell.

•

Carefully he removes the remaining shards of glass from the edge. Then he twists, first to put his head and arms through, then his shoulders. He can't see a thing. The room smells too sweet. His stomach heaves as he dives slow motion toward the sink. His belt pings softly against something, his hands find the sink's edge, the curve of the toilet seat. He balances unevenly for five seconds while he drags his legs across the windowsill. Finally he lowers himself to the floor which he has taken for granted. He sits on the soft carpet, breathing hard, and lets his eyes adjust to the light. Then he pulls a nylon stocking over his head, stretching it out near his eyes, pushing back his hair, raising and lowering his eyebrows. He stands to squint into the mirror at a face even his mother couldn't finger. Next he locates the back door, leaving it open and ready for his exit.

•

What will Cola think if she buys twin beds, or say to her friends, trains of cleaning women going home to Chicago's South Side. Friends who pass the talk on to "their women" as they call them. She herself hears a lot of gossip this way, making Cola a sandwich for lunch in their particular reversal of roles. Cola has five children to her own two, and a husband she gives a weekly allowance of $10.00 to keep him coming round to see the kids. They both know, but don't say, what else for. She thinks of getting up to read, write letters to the children, an old roommate from college, or Betty Ford — 'was the face lift really necessary' — but she never does. She is more aware of herself at these times than any other. It might have something to do with the thin nightgown she wears, her breasts loose and softly flat. Sometimes she lies perfectly still and tries to feel the silk against her stomach, her thighs. She regrets that her mind's eye has no picture of herself naked as a young woman. She sees herself dusting, running the vacuum cleaner, shopping for a china pattern. She would like to do her own cleaning again.

•

For the hundredth time he wonders where he will go if he leaves. What will he take from this house as perfectly arranged as a stage set. He has not yet said 'when' even to himself. Nan has given him a deadline but he knows he'll let it pass. He has stopped counting deadlines — they and the bright cheerful women who make them after an elegant dinner or as the bedside light is about to be turned off are all gone. But the children are gone too, and that was the deadline he made for himself when they were still in high school and he slept in spite of The Rolling Stones, or maybe because of. Then, the woman was Francine, he thinks. He doesn't know this woman next to him any more. She reminds him of the sad aging ladies who sell the perfume and lingerie he buys for Nan. She could be the owner of a smart mauve boutique, or an efficient travel agent, glasses dangling on a gold chain — should he suggest this to her? Sometimes he is surprised to see her across the breakfast table, as if the maitre d' has doubled up on tables. He is having more and more trouble sleeping next to her. What *does* she want? As in "What do *those* women want?"

•

He locates the silver in the diningroom to retrieve on his way out. He pulls the usual shallow drawer out and the silver gleams dully like rows of fresh dead trout. Then he returns to the pantry where the maid's stairway opens onto an upper landing which leads to the second floor, to the master bedroom where the woman keeps her jewelry. He has memorized the floorplan sketched by a nervous Nick over a couple of beers at Tandy's. The other guys left them alone when they moved to a booth, carrying their beers, and Nick's first sketch on a napkin. You can always tell when someone is planning a job, the way they lean together, taking the beer slower than usual, and you know to leave them alone. No one says this, it just happens. But he and Nick can't go on much longer, been four years already — Nick, the inside man giving inspections on insurance riders, sitting in livingrooms of the rich, taking notes about rings and things while he's drawing the floorplan in his head. Shit — forgetting to mark the uncarpeted stairs. He'll have to take it slow up the sides.

•

What will she do? She feels divorce coming like unreported bad weather, even though her husband has been giving her cheery predictions each of the past eight years she brought it up. Divorces have left two friends with large empty malevolent houses, looking for work in a young woman's world of Olay. Could she get thin again — she isn't fat but curves seem to have gone to the wrong places like misdirected traffic. She has stopped hoping for airline crashes, car accidents, a coronary as her husband straddles his most recent girlfriend who, she knows, wears Chloe. It was the dream that did it — when they were selling the grand piano a year ago. Even now, she shivers sending ripples across the cover of the bed as she recalls that early morning dream before dawn. A man's voice, rough like some milkman or mailman, said "I have just killed your husband. You owe me ten thousand dollars." Finally she woke sweating and wet to the shrill sound of the phone across her husband's empty side of the bed. She answered the seventh ring, terrified, but hoping; it was some early riser who wanted to make sure the piano was his. Her disappointment turned petulant, she told him "you're too late." She was shaking as she hung up the phone — alone, still married to a man probably very much alive. That squeak — like Cola on the stairs.

•

He resents her relaxed movements when she thinks he's asleep. He himself lies there tense, missing Nan, finally drifting into a dense exhausted sleep where he dreams of moving from his college room into his first apartment, an orange U-haul and four drinking friends to help. His wife — and Nan — are both waiting for him. The apartment has one bedroom but two kitchens although neither woman cooks. He wakes with stomach cramps before he has to choose whose dinner he will eat. He practices saying 'I want a divorce.' But he would have to turn to her. Even now, even thinking it, his back feels vulnerable. When he sleeps with Nan she curves around him, her knees behind his, her stomach breathing him to sleep. He pictures her large bed where she does everything, reads, eats, polishes her nails, studies chess books, talks to him on the telephone. For the first month he insisted on the formality of the couch for at least cocktails, but she sat there so stiffly as if she were still at her drafting board, that they were soon back to her bed, pillows propped against the quilted headboard although he is never entirely comfortable. It is the only detail of their affair, this cave-bed, that he has kept from his shrink. Cracker crumbs everywhere like a sandbox. Crunching — the springs like the squeak on the stairs.

•

Next the landing and then another short set of stairs. Big houses amaze him, like living in a hotel — everything so far away from the kitchen, a room for this and a room for that. At last he stands at the entrance of the bedroom, adjusting to this new light, letting his face cool beneath his nylon mask, turning his head from side to side. He listens for sounds of breathing in sleep. Two figures on the bed — one turned toward the far wall, the man; one flat on its back, the wife. The dresser is long and low just inside the doorway wall, the jewelry box on the far side. Maybe some things in her first drawer. 'Put your purse away' he is always telling his own wife. He can hold his breath for one minute 35 seconds last time Nick clocked him. He checks for shoes, junk in his path and starts across counting as he moves past the threshold of his fear. He never uses a light.

•

She knows what she heard even before she sees a man appear in the doorway. She lowers her eyelids to slits, pulls air in and out of her lungs to mimic sleep. Her hand is within inches of her husband's buttocks but she can't move, or else she can't bring herself to touch him there. Slowly the shadow slides across the wall, its back to the bed, searching for her diamond ring. What else — her emerald brooch, the long rope of pearls from her mother's graduation. 'No not the pearls' she wants to cry out. 'I was mother's little girl.'

•

It was a slight change in the tone of light. He knows there is someone else in the room. Sighting down the rifle of his legs he brings the man into view. His breathing practice of countless nights keeps his body under control. He wishes he had a gun. Should he call out, reach for a lamp or phone, alert his wife by groping for her hand? But she is awake, surely she sees the figure. If she knew he lies awake beside her, it would be one more evidence of his cowardliness. Her jewelry is only so much furniture anyway — just smaller.

•

They are both sleeping, he checked that, but there is something different about the way they sleep that nags him. As if they have been forcibly tucked in, both coiled side by side, head to toe. He moves down the dresser searching for the box. Going after just three pieces listed in the rider Nick copied from the office files. A big diamond — maybe three, four carats — an emerald pin, and pearls. The pearls are lying out as if they'd just been worn. He slips them into his pocket to the waiting folds of cotton gauze he uses to muffle sound. Next the wooden box, wooden inlaid with three drawers. He bends slightly to see more clearly. Still counting — at ninety-five seconds he will have to leave to breathe. The pin. Into his pocket. The ring — should be there cause she don't wear it, Nick said. And there it is, must be four gorgeous carats. Ba--by. Into his glove and he turns to go. "Kill him," a voice whispers. Slowly he turns to the bed, not believing his bad luck.

•

"It's O.K.," she whispers again, trying to keep her voice calm, persuasive. "Kill my husband. I'll pay tomorrow." The words come out as if they have been planned last week, last year, rehearsed for months. She can barely see the man turn toward her voice. Her body no longer feels attached to anything, sheets, bed. She cannot live through this moment, and then the next as he takes a step toward the bed. She breathes in, to rasp out again, "ten thousand." He comes another step closer. His features are molded by a stocking into a grotesque vegetable shape. She is going to faint. His face is a dream she wants to flee. And now no sound can come. "Jesus," he says, his flat lips moving like dark red worms. Eyes like the sockets of dead men. He makes no sound as he turns and goes, out the door, down the steps not quiet now, and she supposes wildly, keeps on going into the night. Tears leak from her eyes, slide down to her ears, to the pillow. How would she have lived with that? She has to leave him. Why has she waited for her husband's move as a deserted warehouse begs for arson in the night. It really is the end. She has been saved.

•

He is disbelieving. *She said it twice.* She spoke to that dark shape as if her life depended on this one chance. He almost sees her real again, feels his heart warm to the heat of her desperation. It is the first time he has respected hate. Yet he is frozen into a target so still and ready that even now, that the man is gone — although he could come back —, he can't move. There could have been that stocking around his neck, his tongue as thick as now and dry, but hanging out. Or blood so deep it would have floated both of them to freedom. Would she have lain and watched? How could he have taken so much for granted — like her resignation to his lies, her days, her life. He will lie here till morning, stark awake, lie here for the last time; he knows that for certain until some morning sound sets him free. Then he will surely leave; his staying he sees now unfair to both of them. They will call the police so their last day together will be a public one. Questions from some officer with a dull pencil and yellow pad. Did either of them see him? They will both answer 'no' with averted eyes. Hear anything? Only the valuables are gone.

•

He is out the door in ten seconds flat not stopping for the silver. He is getting too old for this. Thought he was a goner sure as hell, but she wasn't talking to her old man lying there beside her. *She was talking to him.* He peels stocking, gloves, the cotton fingers are sticky wet, but he ditches them finally before he reaches the street. Je--sus. He ought to go back and give it to *her* — except it ain't his thing. He doesn't carry a gun — professionals don't need them. The car parked two blocks away seems the next country. No sirens, or flashing lights yet. Did she call the police, wake her husband? Or Christ, kill her old man, laying blame. Nick'll have to fence these way out of state — it's a losing proposition. And he'll have to keep an eye to the newspapers — he don't need a murder rap. The deserted streets tempt him to speed, but he drives bumper to bumper with what might have been, still might be. He drives careful. He is too old for this. Monday he'll call his uncle, get into the hardware business for once and all. Stay home nights. Be nicer to his wife.

Stuart Dybek

Bijou

The film which rumor has made the *dernier cri* of this year's festival is finally screened.

It begins without credits, challenging the audience from its opening frame. Not only has it been shot in black and white, but the black and white do not occur in usual relationships to one another. There is little grey. Ordinary light has become exotic as zebras.

Perhaps in the film's native country they are not familiar with abstract reductions such as black and white. There even vanilla ice cream is robin's egg blue, and licorice almost amethyst when held to the sun. No matter what oppressive regime, each day vibrates with the anima of primitive paintings — continual fiesta! Ambulances flash through color changes with the rapidity of chameleons as they siren. In the modern hospital, set like a glass mural against the sea, ceiling fans oscillate like impaled wings of flamingoes above the rhythm of nurses.

Black and white are not native to these latitudes. And grey requires the opaque atmosphere of Antwerp or Newcastle, Pittsburgh or Vladivostok, requires the Industrial Revolution, *laissez faire,* Imperialism, Seven Year Plan, Great Leap Forward, pollution, cold war, fallout, PCB, alienation . . .

Nor does the film appear to be alluding to the classic black and white films of Fritz Lang, King Vidor, Orson Welles. Nor to the social realism of the 40's or neo-realism of the 50's. In fact, the only acknowledged influence is an indirect one, that of an obscure poem by Victor Guzman, the late surrealist dentist of Chilpanzingo.

Trees, for example, are blinding white, rather than the darknesses so often etched against a dying sky.

Shade is white.

Fruit is white.

Asphalt roads are white.

It is the windowpanes through which one sees them that are black. Smoked with kerosene or smeared with shoe polish for secrecy or air-raid blackouts, who can determine?

It is true that at times the film closely resembles a negative — the moon a sooty zero in a silver nitrate night. But the gimmick of shooting in negative is used with restraint. It's obvious that the film-makers are after something beyond the simple reversal of the values of light.

Take the clouds — plumed, milky black in an albino, noon sky. But are they clouds? Or the smoke from a burning village, bombs, an erupting volcano?

In another sequence, an execution, there is a close-up of bullets being x'd to make the heads dum-dum. The lead is white. And later, when the flower sacks are removed from the prisoners, the wounds are white. The camera pans along the riddled convent wall. In the distance are mountains tipped with anthracite. To put it another way, black is not meant to define white, nor vice-versa.

The first color goes almost unnoticed.

The pink washrag of a cat's tongue as it grooms in the bleached shadow of the jail.

Almost unnoticed — but a subconscious shock registers through the theater.

Gradually, it becomes apparent that tongues, only tongues, are assuming color: dogs panting in the dust of traffic, snakes and geckos flicking from drainpipes, color licking and poking from a thousand tiny caves.

Even tongues ordinarily colorless take on brilliance: the black lash of the butterfly uncoils azure at the flower: the cow masticating its cud lolls a tongue suddenly crimson as black jeeps siren past down the alabaster highway to the interior.

There, the guerillas have been ambushed, surrounded, betrayed. A chopper flattens palms as it drops in CIA advisors. The camera pans the faces of the rebels in macro lens close-ups as if a boil or a louse swelling among beads of sweat might reveal a man's character; or as if white hairs sprouting from a mole, a childhood scar beneath a stubble beard might tell his past.

And it is here that the tongues begin to obsess the camera, that the realistic soundtrack of birdcaws, gunshots, shouting, machinery is intercut with the whispered litany of Guzman's lines from *Laughing Gas: gold-dust tongues, ochre tongues eating earth, walking tongue, candy tongue, milky tongue, sleeper's tongue, passion tongues, cankered tongues, tongues tinctured yellow, flaming tongue, epiphany tongue* . . .

The screen is nearly technicolor with tongues.

Canisters of nerve gas explode.

Then, in a sequence more excruciating than any since *The Battle of Algiers,* the guerrillas are captured. Scene follows scene documenting torture in the modern military state. Cattle prods probing for confessions, electrodes taped to eyelids, tongues, genitals.

At night, out by the black fire, the guards have begun to drink. Soon they cannot tolerate the refined torments of electricity. Fists, truncheons, empty bottles, boots pummel bone.

The prisoners refuse to talk.

Near dawn, in a drunken rage, the guards take them one by one and mock their silence by tearing out their tongues with wire snips. They are forced to kneel, mouths wedged open with a wooden stake, and tongues forceped out in a scream and dark gush of blood — blue, green, yellow, orange, violet, red tongues. The tongues are collected in a coffee can the way ears are sometimes collected, and stored on the colonel's desk. Each new victim stares at the can as he is questioned for the final time. The tongues brim over and flop to the floor and the guards pass out from drunkenness, their own tongues gaping from snoring jaws.

"Raspberry tongues," Guzman wrote, "the entrails of a clown."

The audience stares in silence. Some have turned away; there have been gasps. But, on the whole, they have been conditioned to accept, almost to expect, this violence on screen; have watched blood spurt and limbs dismembered in Peckinpah's choreographed slow-motion, brains sprayed across a wall, bodies explode, monks topple in flaming gasoline, eyes gouged, chain saws buzzing through bone, decapitations in 3-D. They are not at the festival to censor, but to discern: where is violence statement and where merely further exploitation? When does Art become carnography? Is this perhaps the Cinema of Cruelty?

They watch as the next morning a young private is assigned to clean up the night's excesses. He takes the coffee can to bury in the old graveyard behind the cathedral while bells chime through an intermittent hiss of wind and mewing of gulls. His shovel bites dirt and he breathes louder with every scoopful he flings over his shoulder into the blurred eye of climbing sun. He sweats, his breath becomes panting, then gagging, and suddenly he's doubled over retching into the hole, mumbling the Lord's Prayer in between spasms. Still heaving, he rises, kicks the can in, frantically raking over loose dirt, smacking it down with the flat of the shovel, raining down blows as if he were killing a snake.

The soundtrack cuts off.

The whump of the shovel the last sound, though on screen the soldier continues to beat the earth.

Now the screen seems even more unrelievedly black and white — no more background strumming of guitars, mountain flutes, birdcalls, wind, distant thunder of gunfire. Not even the unavoidable drone of a jet overhead on its way to another country. A world of action suddenly mute as Griffith's galloping Klan, as Melies blasting off for the moon, as

Chaplin twirling a cane. Only the racket of sprockets 16 times a second.

Subtitles begin to appear. Too fast to read. Partially telegraphed messages. Single words or parts of words flashed on screen: AWE   DIS   KER

Static as the words, a progression of freeze frames the bled tones of tabloid photos dissolve one into another: peasants on their way to market, slum children, childen with rickets, a beggar with yaws, fruit loaders sweating among flies, miners underground with only eye white showing, an outdoor market of gutted fish, piled monkey skulls, tourists.

In churches and universities, on corners beneath bug-clouded lights, people are opening their mouths to speak, but everywhere it appears the mouths are black, gaping holes. There is only continual silence, inter-cut dissolves, subtitles flashing on and off, sometimes like fading neon signs, sometimes like a collage, commenting on the action (WHERE THERE IS NO FREEDOM WORDS FILL THE MOUTH WITH BLOOD.)

The footage continues running faster, almost blurred, as if a documentary were being filmed from a speeding train — assassinations, bombed motorcades, bombed restaurants, bombed schools, strikes, soldiers firing into a crowd, smoldering bodies, mothers in mourning, black coffins, black flags, the revolt of students, the revolt of the army, newspaper offices ransacked by blackshirts, presses smashed, mobs, fires, men hauled out into the street and lynched from lampposts before the shattered windows of the capitol, streets littered with books from the gutted library and all the while a sound rising from underground like a subway roaring down a tunnel, its brake shoe scraping metal from track, metal on metal whining into a siren pitched screech (EVEN THE HANGED HAVE NO TONGUES TO PROTRUDE!)

The house lights flick on. The audience, many of them North Americans, is stunned. Some talk as if making sure

they still can. Some weep. Others leave the theater cursing —
what? The film? The oppressors? It isn't clear. Someone in
the balcony shouts BRAVO! And another in front, LONG
LIVE THE REVOLUTION! People are up from their seats
and applauding as if it were a live presentation.

"The ultimate praise for a film," one critic is heard to
remark on his way to the lobby, "to treat it as if it were a play
deserving curtain calls, to confuse celluloid images with flesh
and blood, to transcend the isolated private dream state of
the movie theater by merging with the mass in simple applause . . ."

Tomorrow the Arts sections will carry rave reviews: *a new
and daring fusion of avant garde technique with documentary sensibility* . . .

A journalist for the *Voice* will write: "Uncompromis-
ingly powerful, it demands to be seen, though a film like this
might be better kept secret, protected from the corrupting
influence of the Hollywood glamour and promotion machine, the invidious American penchant for reducing substance to marketable style . . ."

While another reviewer, writing for a more conservative
publication will comment: "This looks like the year for
Terrorist Cinema. Another fad pretending to usher in a
change of consciousness, but lacking the moral imperative of
the Civil Rights Movement and Peace Marches that launched
the 60's. . . ."

The audience files out through the mirrored lobby,
backs turned on the posters of stars, out under the winking
marquee squinting at the pink smolder of dusk. Behind
them, on the silver screen in the houselit theater, a final
frame hovers like the ghost image phenomena sometimes
haunting TV screens, a blown-up image that could only have
been shot by a camera implanted in a mouth, of an indigo
tongue working at a husk of popcorn stuck in a goldcapped
molar.

And across this image a delayed rolling of credits begins:

the names of actors, writers, cameramen, assistant director,
director, producer, editors, sound, music, make-up, gaffers,
soldiers, officers, generals, politicians — a cast of thousands
— workers, students, peasants, the audience, the victims, the
maimed, the maddened, the myriad names of the dead.

Maxine Kumin

West

It is morning. After Lena has stripped Marigold's udder and strained the goat's milk into the refrigerator jug; after she has fed the horses and the dogs; and after she has shooed Evvie's gander off the lawn to the edge of the fire pond and scattered a handful of grain there to keep him interested, she goes to the little one-room building where Evvie lives. The building housed a generator once, before the county brought power up the hill. This improvement took place after World War II, the war Lena's dead husband used to call The Biggun, as if it had been a hurricane or World Series game. Now the cabin holds a young woman — a sort of flower-child, Lena thinks, who takes her cats to bed. Sometimes her electric guitar-playing lover stops by. He is allergic to cat hair. If Lena looks out in the morning and sees the two cats mooning around stalking chipmunks, she knows Malcolm is visiting.

Evvie is supposed to help out around the place summers in return for room and board. In common with her generation she has a remarkable capacity for sleep. To sleep late, sleep through, fall asleep, stay asleep, sleep in the daytime — all these enviable talents Lena has lost.

Evvie goes barefoot. She bakes bread with no additives, she rinses alfalfa sprouts and keeps them in dark places in jars. Naked to the waist she mows the lawn. Barefoot she goes into the pasture to fetch the horses, her thick defiant hair bouncing on her shoulders. Sometimes Lena braids it for her in one wide plait down her back and Evvie complains with each tug.

"It's too tight. It's giving me a headache."

"Stand still," Lena says automatically. She is back

braiding the hairs of her daughters. "Your part is crooked. Did you comb this mop at all? Stand still."

On her days off Evvie hitchhikes into Portland as if the world were good and all cars were in the possession of kind, mannerly people. Still, no harm befalls her. Whereas Lena's younger daughter Nell, working for a UN agency that resettles refugees in Uganda, has not been heard from in six weeks. Top officials in Geneva say it is not safe to assume anything. Neither assume that she is alive and well in the bush, far from roads, postal services or phones, nor that she has been ambushed, raped, butchered.

"So what you're saying is, it is safe to assume it is not safe," Lena says, long-distance, into the telephone. She uses a dangerous, controlled tone that lies just this side of hysteria.

"Neither the one thing nor the other," the dry voice repeats in a British English. It says *neither* with a long i.

That conversation took place a week ago. Lena deals with it by keeping going. Like most grown women, she has had considerable practice.

She has to rap really hard to break through the curtain sleep has hung between Evvie and the day.

"You don't want roast goose, you better get out here and take charge of Jeeper." It is Lena's standard threat. "Spinach souffle, *caca d'oie* all over the lawn again, Evvie. *Toujours*, dammit."

Jeeper is the gander. Evvie is attached to the word; it was the first word she said, seventeen years before, when she and her mother had a working relationship.

"You mean you don't talk to each other?" Lena asked her once.

"Oh, we talk, all right. We just don't communicate."

"Tie him," Lena says, safe in the knowledge that birds cannot be tied. "Do something, then. Make him a pen."

Lena can put up with almost anything in the animal department except poultry. She does not trust the bird

around her grandson Joshua, who is six and wants to hug
Jeeper. Joshua, her older daughter's child, visits every
August. He likes living with Lena so much that he is staying
through September this year for the Fall Foliage Festival. He
is going to be in the parade!

Each autumn, with a parade and a fair, the town of
Ramawa celebrates the phenomenon of the leaves turning.
City people from as far away as Boston and Providence drive
up for the day. They all wear their cameras, they stand in
polite lines for the chicken barbecue, they buy up the local
crafts and the dregs of the previous summer's antiques. The
Farmers Market unloads bushels of apples and several
varieties of squash. Pyramids of pumpkins diminish rapidly.
The glint of money excites the community. The town fathers
talk about a new police cruiser, about getting the road grader
repaired.

Evvie's parents are prominent citizens of this town. Her
father owns both the piano and crutch factories; the latter
admittedly is a dying industry. Aluminum prostheses are
doing it in. Nevertheless, his workers still set ash, birch and
maple to soak, bending them to their supportive uses. Lena
has a cutting board made of tag ends from the crutch
materials. Warren G. Harding Morrison, an itinerant carpenter who rode across Kansas in the US Cavalry in 1934 and
rebuilt Lena's back porch in 1962, made if for her. It was a
Christmas present the last winter he spent in Maine.

Evvie's father also owns the town's sand and gravel pits.
It is his credo or boast that he takes care of His Men. When a
fire wipes out the dreadful shanty three generations of
Jenkses have inhabited, Evvie's father directs the building of
a new cottage. He installs the first indoor toilet in the history
of the Jenkses. Evvie's father routinely puts up bail money
for His Men when they get drunk during the last of hunting
season; frustrated from not having brought down their deer,
they tear up the town. He sends the truly sick to his own
doctor and fires the malingerers. Hot noon meals are served

to him. Women, he believes, are meant to prepare these.

Evvie, with her seeds and nuts and soymeal grains, is in retreat from his benevolent tyranny. Evvie's father is a good person; the town depends on him.

Evvie's mother always has the best float in the Fall Foliage Festival parade. She has won Best Float for ten years running. No one thinks seriously of competing against her. She borrows — seizes actually — something motorized and strong from the piano factory or gravel-pit garage two weeks before the parade. She incarcerates the fork-lift, dump truck, or backhoe in her driveway, while layering it with bunting or crepe paper, purple-dyed cheese-cloth, boughs of autumn leaves. She tends toward the simpler statements of patriotism: Pilgrim Fathers, Betsy Ross sewing the flag, the first Thanksgiving, complete with Indians.

"You know what would make her the happiest woman in the world?" Evvie says.

"What?"

"If she could be float-maker adviser to the Rose Bowl Parade. She'd die a happy woman."

Evvie wants to be Lady Godiva in the parade. Lady Godiva in a flesh-colored body stocking, her electric hair flowing loosely around the stocking. It's a protest against taxes, she has read somewhere. She wants to ride bareback on Doc, Lena's peaceful Palomino. Doc, who does as little as possible, is about to be pressed into service behind the high school brass band in the parade.

Fortunately, Lena thinks, animals are not able to anticipate. Doc is eating the late ladino clover, the last before September frosts turn it all to straw. Frost comes early along the midsection of the Maine coast, the growing season is woefully short. In summer the mosquitoes attain mythic proportions.

The reason Lena lives here at all, she will tell you, is inertia. Ten years ago, after her husband was killed swerving his station wagon to avoid a deer on the Maine Turnpike and striking instead a concrete abutment, she came back here to stay. This farmhouse had been their summer place, site of their best times. Nell and Joshua's mother, who is her older sister, had already left home by then. The sense of how it had been gives Lena the courage, yet again, to resist changing it. The four horses, including the now aged gelding her husband used to ride, stay put in pasture and barn. She takes them out in rotation or enlists neighbors' children to ride with her. There is the harvest, enough produce to fill the freezer, and after that, the bone-jolting frosts, and then the snows. A long time of shovelling out to the barn to feed. A long, slow time of protracted twilights, gray mornings. She does her grieving in solitary in the dark, mourning the absent daughters as much as the so-suddenly removed husband. What a strange procedure, to raise another woman! How different, how much the same her daughters' lives and hers!

It would fill a book, Lena thinks, trying to reconstruct how it is. Evvie takes up some of the empty space. Joshua is a brilliant migratory bird. The vacant side of Lena's bed overflows with mushroom handbooks, wildflower texts, small press collections of poems. She reads sociobiology, anthropology, natural foods cookbooks, African folk tales. There is time for the back issues of all the magazines the Ramawa Library subscribes to.

Little by little Lena has become an accepted Ramawan. In winter Evvie's father sends one of his men up to check on her wood supply, her state of mind and body, the battery in her Jeep. When the first green shoots arrive in spring her nearest neighbor, a lobsterman's widow, walks up to gather fiddleheads.

Now that Joshua has entered her life Lena gets to do some cosseting. She writes stories for him, she takes him to pick blueberries and catch butterflies. She gives him A-plus in spying out puffballs. Next year she will find him the perfect pony. This year he will be in the parade.

But this is not an idyll. Loneliness enters in, days pass

without exchange of human speech. Lena has some arthritis. She commences every day hurting. Cold weather makes it worse. Summers, unless the onshore breeze reaches into the hills, the deerflies bite cruelly. Joshua's parents have separated, his mother has had an abortion. With Nell first in New York, then in Geneva, training to go into the field — here Lena has a vision of vast, dry meadows — the phone bill equals that from the Ramawa General Store. During periods of crisis the sisters call each other, day and night. The mother calls the daughters, who tell her not quite what they tell each other. The daughters call the mother; then they must check back with each other. All the anguish and tenderness of these phone calls, all the complexity and caring of these relationships is lost forever in an age when nothing personal is written down. What a pity, Lena thinks, that no one is recording this oral history for a Ph.D. project.

The New York *Times* arrives in Lena's mailbox a day late. She follows events in the Third World, so far as they are reported. Before this assignment, Nell has worked in Haiti, in Recife, even in Sri Lanka. Mail has been spotty. Letters that are written come, scatter-shot, out of sequence. The pale-blue feathery envelopes accumulate three and four deep; some letters are never delivered. The quality of the six-week silence is only more ominous, Lena tells herself, because Idi Amin has been missing, reportedly sighted here and there in the countryside with his last-ditch followers. A week later he is said to be elsewhere, hiding perhaps in Libya.

Libya, Lena says to herself. Togo, Niger, Mali, Burundi. She says the words under her breath, but nothing takes shape in her head. It is not like whispering, Michigan, Minnesota, Florida, and seeing instant lakes, coastlines. Nevertheless, somewhere in Uganda at this moment a woman Lena's age is milking a goat. Into the cool, late September sky comes an African sun, fierce on the veldt, stinging the back of Lena's neck.

Evvie usually does the evening milking. Marigold jumps
onto the platform in the barn and puts her head through the
stocks so that she can reach her pail of sweet feed, a mix of
grains made sticky with molasses. Joshua is waiting with a
plastic saucer. He is going to feed the barn cats, two grown
toms who disdain milk and stalk Joshua from the ledges
around the tops of the horses' stalls.

" 'Michael, row your boat ashore, . . .' " Evvie sings,
pressing her head against Marigold's accomodating flank.

"Me too, Evvie," Joshua implores. She changes the
song to "Joshie, row your boat ashore," and the child chimes
in on the hallelu.

Tonight Lena and Evvie will finish the costumes for
tomorrow's parade. Joshua's will be laced together with raw-
hide shoelaces borrowed from Lena's winter work boots. He
will be a child of the Westward Movement. Parade watchers
will know this. Everything, except the dark hole of Nell's
absence, is explicable.

Memory gets things all wrong, Lena thinks, reviewing
whole patches of Nell's life, season by season. In one frame
Nell is in the kitchen skimming the great boiling froth of
strawberries for jam. She saves the scum in a soup bowl; both
she and Lena love it stirred into yogurt. She is climbing back
from the mailbox at the foot of the hill, vulnerable,
unseeing, yet dodging stones and little pyramids of horse
manure as she walks, reading a letter. One letter is an
occasion for tears. As Lena, traitorous, watches from the front
window, Nell stuffs the pages in her back pocket, blows her
nose, enters. "Anything for you?" Lena asks, taking her
packet of newspaper, throwaways, and a bill. " 'Fraid not,"
Nell replies with a lilt. How cheerful her guile. Did this
happen?

Home over Christmas, Nell is in the barn mucking out,
making the best of it as Lena does when sawdust and manure
freeze overnight. Everyone looks moth-eaten. Camels are
handsomer. And there she is grooming the horses in spring.

Handfuls of their shedding fur fly up into the breeze. The birds will take tufts of it for their nests. Lena begins to remember the two daughters at Richard's funeral, one on either side in the University chapel; then she stubbornly puts this frame away — not to be revisited until safe. Memory glosses over, invents, modifies. Surely there were quarrels, fits of depression. Pots spilled. Toilets backed up. The daughters are there; they glow.

It is morning of the second day. All over town backyard ponies are being curried and combed. Burdocks are picked out of their tails. Candy-box ribbons are braided in their manes and bacon fat is rubbed on their hooves to make them shine. Children, awake far too early, are putting on costumes that will fall into tatters before the day is over. At least fourteen local farmers are polishing their oxen for the pulling contest. A dozen others, preparing for the annual chopping exhibition, are honing their axes and splitting mauls. Simple Ben, who is said to have lost most of his wits in the last Great War and ever after has ridden his bicycle up and down route 27, rain or shine, is putting on the top half of an old Air Force uniform. He strokes the cap, especially the visor. Today he will cover the route of the parade a dozen times.

The banner bearing Health, Head, Heart, Hands, the 4-H insignia, is being freshly ironed in the Milzcuiski kitchen. In Portland, the Shriners Marching band, complete with purple fezzes, clambers aboard a rented bus for the trip to Ramawa. On the Ramawa green three workmen with wrenches tighten the pipe connections for the ferris wheel. Vendors' stands are being set up in a fairly orderly fashion. There will be some jockeying for better places later on.

On Lena's hill, Evvie is still sleeping. Even on her Lady Godiva day, sleep holds Evvie fast. She will drift in its grip until Lena raps her awake. Joshua, who has been up for hours, is trying to eat breakfast. Lena worries that nothing will stay down if she bullies him. He swallows some milk.

Two bites of toast. Later, Lena consoles herself, there will be quick energy from cotton candy.

After the parade begins, all too soon Lena reaches the point of restlessness. She foresees a picture of the Ramawa Fall Foliage Festival shining forth from the Portland Sunday rotogravure. Everyone quaint in town — Ben on his bicycle, Herman Haverness atop the antique fire pumper, Lila Baines gotten up as a belly dancer perched on her white Arabian stallion — is fixed in time by the glossy taint of too-bright colors bleeding into one another. The drum majorettes are a sickly pink. On the Betsy Ross float the basting seams of the costumes rip open to expose dungarees and tee shirts, a ragbag of red, white and blue.

Only Joshua is in harmony. Astride one of the matched oxen pulling Evvie's mother's prize-winning float, a covered wagon built onto a flatbed tagalong, Joshua frowns importantly into the sun. His bleached floursack tunic and his shock of blond hair intensify the rich brown of the animals' burnished coats. Joshua is going West in triumph.

Four of Nell's letters from Kampala also move West on this day. From Dakar they catch an Air France flight to New York. Tomorrow or the next day they will come by mail truck from Portland to the postmistress's cage in the general store downtown. Evvie's father, who inquires secretly every morning on his way to the piano factory, will personally bring the letters up the hill.

Lena goes out the door to deal with Marigold. Jeeper excretes on the front lawn. News of Nell, only eight days old, makes its bright way West.

Stephen Wolf

The Legacy of Beau Kremel

So far, I thought while snipping hairs from my nostril, the visit was going fine. I hadn't been expected, first of all, and so the initial surprise pleased my parents so much that any mention of our past difficulties dissolved in the affectionate air. Rather than asking — either pained or demandingly — why I haven't been home before this, they merely smiled, were grateful, and said, "It's been a long time."

"Too long," was the only complaint, but issued by my mother who threw her arms around me again. "It's good to have you home."

For nothing pleased my family — or so they believed — like a night spent together. And many nights were spent so. My brother still lived at home, for one thing, and though my sister was married and, allegedly, on her own, she could appear at my parents door in just fifteen minutes — and did quite regularly. But my continual absence at their continual gatherings was not unnoticed, and punctuated, I imagined, with genuinely heartfelt sighs and the words "Don't you wish Stephen could be here?" directed at anyone save my father who was — we all knew — as much responsible for that empty chair at the table as I was. But when the opportunity arose — and so unexpectedly — of having all of us together for awhile, then let by-gones be by-gones, what's past is past and it's out for dinner we all were to go.

"Where would you like to eat?" they asked me once we found ourselves hugged and kissed out with nothing jolly left to say.

"It doesn't matter," I replied complacently. "Anywhere is fine with me."

"How about the Ivanhoe?" my mother asked. "We

haven't been there for so long and you like it so much.''

''The Ivanhoe's fine.''

''But it's so far,'' my father complained. ''That's half way to the Loop. What about The Cork over here on Skokie Avenue,'' and his weighty arm gestured towards the closet.

''Fine.''

''I hear the food is terrible.'' my mother declared.

''No!''

''*Ter*rible. Eileen ate there three days ago and nearly got food poisoning,'' but then she turned to me and again and said eagerly,

''Unless you'd like to eat there, dear.''

''Doesn't matter. Anyplace is fine.''

''How about Fanny's?'' my father asked her.

''How *about* Fanny's'' she said to me.

''Fine.''

''Should I call for a reservation?'' inquired my father.

''Oh, we don't need one,'' she scoffed. ''Unless we go late.''

''Are you hungry?'' he asked me.

''Starved.''

''Why didn't you fix him something?'' he asked my mother angrily.

''Do you want me to fix you something.'' she asked.

''I can wait,'' I said to her.

''Wonderful,'' she exclaimed and scurried towards the telephone. ''I'll call Susie and we'll all get ready and —''

Good idea: let's keep busy, for we can never be sure what ghosts will rise once families turn silent. And so upstairs I went, scanned the bedroom where I once lived and that my brother had completely usurped, cracked open my suitcase, grabbed my dop-kit and headed for the Master Bath.

The bathroom had been redecorated into something vaguely resembling a science fiction movie. The wallpaper, that also spread across the ceiling, shined like paper mirrors. Little yellow butterflies, trapped and motionless, formed regular patterns throughout the paper, and the yellow

window curtains and the yellow shower stall and the yellow
toilet paper and the yellow kleenex box and — impossibly
— even the yellow rosebud soaps in a shiny soap dish all
matched the butterflies' color perfectly. On one entire wall
and just above two separate, round-bowled, shiny sinks set in
a black marble counter-top, a large, glissening mirror
reflected the sparkling and yellow room. So sparkling and
harmonious, in fact, that I had the distinct impression that I
was the first person ever to set foot in here, and as I stood
snipping those nostril hairs I hoped that my farts would be
hushed and odorless and that water would not bead in the
sink.

"Hi," I said, turning to my father as he entered.
"Quite a place you got here."

He frowned uncertainly at the room, then at me, and
after tugging several times at the elastic of his boxer shorts he
concentrated on the array of shaving utensils stored in a small
drawer beside the sink. I kept watching him as I wet and
lathered my face — he had gained more weight and his bulky
body seemed resigned to it — and though his moody
brooding often anticipated his erratic rage, he seemed pre-
occupied, as if something confusing and far away was eating
at him. Not until I had rinsed my razor and started shaving
did he finally speak.

"So how was the trip up here?" he asked tonelessly, his
fingers and eyes still buried in the drawer.

"Fine," I said lightly and turned to him. "It's spring."

"Any trouble with the car?"

"None at all."

He frowned slightly as if his fingers came upon something that displeased him.

"Why don't you take the car over to Frank's tomorrow.
Tell him to give you a grease and oil. Put it on my bill."

"Oh, I had a grease and oil change less than two weeks
ago. Thanks, though, dad."

He pulled a razor from the drawer and studied it
somberly: I knew he didn't believe me about the car and that

nothing short of producing a bill could convince him otherwise. For an instant I wanted to embrace him, to kiss his saggy face and assure him the car ran well.

But before I did, he asked,

"Do you need anything while you're home?"

"No," I replied seriously. "I don't think so."

"No underwear? No socks?"

"None."

"How about a few of those summer golf shirts I wear?" he asked, a wavering glimmer in his eyes.

"No, nothing, dad. In fact, I think I still have shirts like that from last summer I haven't worn yet."

"No underwear? Socks?"

"I think I've got plenty," I replied. "But thank you."

He returned his focus to the razor, but I could see his expression and distrust swell in his eyes. I knew, from our past, what was happening here — how my refusals of what he offered denoted some rejection of what he had to give. This would anger him, and though the anger was only the underside of deep pain and frustration, that made it no less dangerous: I can remember, for example, when he grabbed me once, slammed me into the refrigerator and screamed, "Don't let me *ever* hear you say no one loves you in this house!"

And so wanting to avoid a confrontation this early in the visit, I decided to finish shaving and do whatever else I had to do in here once my father was done. I hurried through the next few strokes with the razor as his ponderous silence filled the room more than the steam from my faucet, but once I rinsed my face and made to put my razor away my father exclaimed,

"Good Christ, look at yourself!"

A dozen tiny cuts were scattered across my face, and a deeper one below my chin dripped blood slowly down my neck.

"It's not as bad as it looks," I said bravely. "They're all surface cuts. I just put in a new blade."

With our eyes meeting in the mirror, he leaned forward suspiciously and asked,

"What type of blades do you use?"

"Personna 74 I think."

He turned quickly and reached into the small drawer, slapped something on the counter and shoved it towards me.

"Use these," he declared and revealed a packet of razor-blades still in their cardboard wrapping. "They work just as well and they're not as sharp. Your face is still too soft to use tungsten."

He turned back to the mirror and began lathering his face aggressively.

"Will they last as long?" I wondered, careful not to sound argumentative.

"Sure, why not?"

He ceased his lathering and turned to my reflection in the mirror.

"And if they don't, I'll buy you extras. I'd rather spend a few more pennies than have you walking around with your face sliced open."

Suddenly he grabbed the razors and held them an inch from my nose.

"They're better for you," he cried. "I'm telling you," then he slapped them down again.

I stared at the packet for a moment, conscious of him watching me in the mirror as he slashed away at the whiskers on his throat: whether I need them or not — and regardless if they cut my face less — these razors had better leave this room with me.

I reached over and dropped them into my toilet bag.

"Thanks, I'll take them."

And if this were a movie then faint, sweet music would begin, for with my words the tension dissolved in his face and he shaved calmly: long, graceful strokes that left pink highways through the snow. I thought I even detected a smirk emerge in the corner of his mouth.

"I'll tell you what I *could* use," I said, assisting my visit with a request I genuinely intended to make anyway. "Some hair tonic or something. My hair's been dry this winter."

"I've been telling you that for years," he announced triumphantly. Again he reached into the drawer beside the sink and this time set a little green jar on the counter.

"This is just what you need."

"I'm not using that stuff," I cried.

"It's not greasy!"

"No," I insisted, sorry I had ever raised the subject at all. "I don't want to plaster it down. It's just a little dry, that's all."

He glared at me impatiently for a moment — he knew I had just betrayed him — then he shouldered me aside and reached into the cabinet below the sink. He brought out a tall bottle that had some yellowish liquid splashing about the bottom.

"This stuff isn't greasy at all," he declared, a husky insistence in his voice. "Dave at the barber shop gave it to me," and he pointed proudly to an ornate label. 'For Professional Use Only' ran the inscription. "It's terrific stuff."

"Thanks, I'll use it," I said and took the bottle immediately, hoping to end this. "Sure you got enough?"

"Plenty. I've a whole 'nother bottle."

Suddenly his head snapped back and his eyes went blank. Then he hurried from the bathroom, leaned over the bannister and called downstairs.

"Ella!"

"What is it?" my mother responded.

"Where's that other bottle of Beau Kremel?" he asked, straining forward to hear.

"In the linen closet."

He straightened up, reentered the bathroom where he rinsed the lather from his partly shaven face, then said,

"I just realized you can take some back with you," and hurried from the room, over to the closet. He opened the door, pushed sheets and towels aside — a few spilling to the floor in broken folds. His large body squeezed further into the closet; bottles were unended and I heard the faint rumbling of obscenities. Finally he emerged, his face red and his hair all disarranged, with an unopened bottle of the hair tonic he had just offered me.

"Christ, I can't take all that."

He picked up the sheets and towels, stuffed them back into the closet and slammed the door. While walking excitedly back to the bathroom, he ripped at the plastic seal around the neck of the new bottle.

"I'll put some in there," he said anxiously, indicating the other bottle with a glance. "There's not enough in there to do you any good."

He tossed the plastic seal at the waste basket.

"I just want to give you a little more."

My father unscrewed the caps of both bottles, then carefully tipped the new one upside down so the spouts touched. But each spout had only a small hole and so just a solitary drop dangled from the spout and fell faintly to the liquid at the bottom. After a moment another drop appeared, hesitated, then slid reluctantly down the old bottle's side. He waited for a third drop, but one never appeared.

He turned the new bottle upright, glared at it reprimandingly, then, grabbing the old bottle, he squinted his eyes as if taking aim. Quickly, he tipped the new bottle and the spouts clinked together, hair tonic squirting into my father's wrist. He tried again, but again he missed. He continued jerking at the bottle, repeatedly harder and harder, no longer taking aim but believing that hair tonic would find its way to the other spout simply because of his intense commitment.

"Dad, this'll take you all night," I said as little yellow drops dripped from the hair on his forearm and fell steadily to the counter-top. "If the stuff works and I like it, I'll take more back with me the next time I'm home."

I reached over and took the proffered bottle, but he snatched it back and shoved it to the counter.

"You could be bald by then," he said darkly, then

turned to the bottles with steadily angrying eyes. While he frowned at the bottles, the anger in his eyes spread throughout his face: these bottles, it seemed, had done him a great wrong, and now that he had them at his mercy he planned what way to show none. Finally, with a precise and concentrated gesture, he put his thumb on the spout of the new bottle and clutched it by its neck. He tipped the bottle upside down, gripped the old bottle with his other hand, then placed the spouts together with his thumb in between. He eased his thumb out, the spouts came together, then he shook both bottles simultaneously. The spouts separated but he continued shaking them as hair tonic squirt all over the bottle, onto his fingers, squirting, even to the counter-top. That his plan wasn't working didn't stop him at all: it made him only angrier at the bottles and he shook them wildly until a spout banged his finger joint.

"Christ!" he cried and snapped the new bottle upright. He looked at them with unforgivable reproach, turned, ripped a towel from a rack, and wrapped half around the old bottle. He grabbed the new bottle and dumped it over so the spouts touched again, disregarding the hair tonic spurting out the hole. He wrapped the remaining towel around the neck of the new bottle, clutched both bottles by their thickened spouts and shook them until he resembled a man on a pneumatic drill. I could hear the muffled glass scratching together, and after several moments the towel around the spouts grew dark and wet. Hair tonic soon oozed from the towel between my father's fingers and began dripping to the counter-top. Drops gathered, and a little yellow lake spilled over the side in a steady stream and was sponged up by the rug on the floor.

It wasn't working and he knew it, for he finally slammed the bottle to the counter-top, tore off the towel which he used to mop the counter, and flung it in the tub. His hand reached down and sucked up the rug and he flung that, too, in the same general direction. We turned back to the bottles: the new one was nearly half empty now, and the amount in the bottle he had given me had not visibly changed.

"Dad," I cried weakly, "this is *fine* for God's sake, I've got *plenty* in this one," and I moved towards the bottles.

"Stay out of the mess!" he snapped. "We're going out for dinner you know."

He turned and looked me in the face.

"You want hair tonic," he whispered, "you'll get hair tonic," and he stormed out the door.

Helpless, I tried thinking what to do before the visit splashed to the floor along with the hair tonic and our reconciliation. Responsible for this and unable to prevent it from occurring, I felt that my car — even with the brakes on — was skidding unavoidably into the back of a truck. It was happening, I couldn't stop it, and — worse yet — I had time to watch it occur.

My father lunged into the bathroom carrying — of all things — a single sheet of paper. With his head bent down and taking large, heavy steps, he marched directly to the window and threw it open; his wet hands smudged the glass and left three dark stains of the curtain. He returned to the counter and rolled the sheet of paper into a tight funnel, an end of which he stuck into the spout of the bottle he had given me. He widened the lips at the top of the funnel, picked up the new bottle of hair tonic and frantically poured into the rolled paper. Streams of hair tonic jumped into the funnel with irregular spurts, making a damp 'smack' as it hit. My father jerked at the bottle with hard, rapid strokes. More and more hair tonic streamed into the paper. He stopped, readjusted the funnel, then poured even harder and more rapidly, up and down, again and again. Tiny drops of perspiration ran down his forehead, hid in his eyebrows, reappeared above his lip. He began breathing furiously.

"Anything happening?" he gasped.

"Yes," I replied miserably. "The paper's soaking up all the hair tonic."

"Damn!" he cried, banging the bottle to the counter-top, directly on the razor that spun and jumped to the floor. He turned, kicked at the razor and sent it flying across the room.

"Do something for a change," he yelled. "Here!" and he shoved the bottle into my chest. "You pour."

Exasperated and panting, he flicked thick fingers through his eyebrows, then across his lip, and, after taking one deep breath like he was diving under water, he crouched towards the wet and already shedding funnel and cupped both hands around it. He froze in this position for an instant before yelling,

"Today, today, let's go!"

I jumped towards him while muttering apologies, then began pouring.

"It's working," he cried, his eyes following each drop falling into the bottle. "Pour a little faster."

With his hysterical eyes and half shaven face, my father looked like the mad scientist whose creation lived.

"Good," he exclaimed, a hilarious smile in his eyes. "Harder!"

I pounded away, saved from disaster by my father's persistence and whoever invented the funnel. But then that funnel — having absorbed so much liquid — gave way entirely and melted over my father's hands just when hair tonic exploded from the spout, all over his belly, pressing hair wet and yellow against his pink skin.

"Shit!" he screamed and jumped back, his arm tipping the bottle that fell and skidded to a stop in the sink. He grabbed for another towel and furiously scrubbed his belly while groping for the overturned bottle.

"Seymour," cried my mother from downstairs as hair tonic gurgled down the drain. "Seymour!"

"What do you want?" he shouted back, his body in a twist of contrary motions while his face strained towards her voice.

"What's that awful smell I smell?"

"Not a God damn thing," he yelled, lurching from the

bathroom and still rubbing his belly with a towel. "I'm giving your son a little hair tonic."

"Well I can smell it down *here*."

He was about to scream a reply, hesitated, then dragged the towel across his perspiring face.

"We're just having a little trouble," he said faintly. He returned to the bathroom, avoided my eyes, leaned heavily on the counter-top and stared at the two bottles. Both were nearly empty, and when he reached for one the decorative label shed into his hands.

Just then my mother appeared in the doorway with a worried face that transformed into astonishment: the mess in the bathroom had gathered enough force to knock her back a step, what with hair tonic across the counter-top and streaming in puddles to her bare floor, the rug and towels limp in the tub, a razor in the corner, the windows smudged — and with her soaking husband, desperate and partly shaven, and my pathetic eyes.

"What's been going *on* in here?" she asked, amazed.

My father, not turning to her, waved a hand despairingly my way.

"His hair's dry."

His head swung back and forth and his mouth fidgeted like he was about to say more. But no words came and his confusion exhausted him: his excess weight sagged on him and he turned sad-eyed to my mother who yanked in a breath, blew it out, and began rolling up her sleeves.

"Alright, everybody out," she said nervously while moving through the room. "I'm cleaning this up *right now*."

She fussed with her sleeves a moment longer, picked up the razor, then pounced on the heap in the tub. She wrung and squeezed at something — I wasn't sure, for just then my father folded his towel neatly, placed it beside the bottles on the counter, and quietly left the room.

Robley Wilson, Jr.

Fathers

"Why don't we forget about the ball," the young woman said. "Why don't you just take a drop?"

The man, considerably older, was in the short rough just off the seventh fairway. He was walking carefully, looking down, swinging the head of a two-iron across the tops of wild flowers.

"It's a Titleist," he said.

"It's not as if you couldn't afford a new one."

"You just want to add to my score."

"You won't break forty anyway," she said. "Take a drop."

"I can maybe break eighty if we play a second nine." He rested the club on his shoulder and looked broodingly into the scrub pine that separated the seventh fairway from the sixth. "You suppose it's in there?"

"I haven't a clue. You hooked it so badly I couldn't follow it."

"I sliced it," he said. "After all this time I should think you'd know the difference."

"There isn't any difference," she said. "Either way, you can't find the ball."

"You should learn to tell a hook from a slice," he said.

"Maybe you ought to play one of those new orange balls," the young woman said. "It might be easier to find."

"I couldn't," he said. "It would be like knocking a tangerine around the course." He came back toward her, head down, still carrying the club on his shoulder. "Maybe I'd better take a drop," he said. "I don't suppose there's any point in hanging around here all day."

The seventh green was at the top of a broad hill, trapped on both sides and at the back. From the foot of the hill where the man's fourth shot had landed, the flag was hidden, and he stood for a long time pondering. His golf bag—plaid, its leather trim badly scuffed—lay on the fairway behind him.

"What do you think?" he said.

"I think it's to the left and toward the back of the green." She sat on the grass nearby, pulling her crossed ankles under her. "If I were the pin, that's where I'd be."

"I mean do you think a seven-iron or what?"

"Seven or eight."

He stooped to haul the iron out of the bag. "Seven," he said. "I don't think I can reach with an eight."

"Not unless you hit it squarely," she said.

He addressed the ball, which lay in a dark green patch of clover. After a few moments of settling his feet, dancing the club head behind the ball, assessing the long sweep of the hill, he straightened up and stepped back.

"I think I'll go take a look," he said.

He trudged up the slope, the club in his right hand. The grass was green to the eye, but down near the soil it had a brownish cast and felt brittle underfoot. He climbed until he could see the flagstick, the flag made of stiff red plastic with a white numeral; it was set in the back left corner of the green, about ten feet in from the froghair. He stood, leaning on the club, and looked back down the hill to his ball. The young woman waved; she wore bright yellow shorts and a white blouse, and her hair was held back from her face with a narrow yellow headband. The ball was a white dot not far from her bare legs. It looked like and eight-iron shot after all.

When the ball dropped over the rim of the hole, it rattled in the cup with a sound like crockery in a dishwasher. The woman fished it out and tossed it back to him. Then she reset the flag and followed him off the green.

"Double bogey," he said. "I'll be lucky to come in with a fifty."

"Think of the fresh air you're getting," she said. "Think of the dew on the greens and the nice exercise."

He hitched the bag to his shoulder. "You really don't like this game, do you?"

She shrugged.

"Next time why don't you rent some clubs and try it yourself? If you started to enjoy it, I could buy you a set of your own."

"Maybe," she said. She held out her hand to him. "Here, this is for you."

"What is it?"

"A four-leaf clover. I found it down the hill."

He took it, looked at it, put it carefully in the pocket of his shirt.

"Thank you," he said. He reached out to draw her against him and kissed her on the forehead. "Let's just do the nine holes and call it a day."

The eighth hole was a par three, a hundred-and-ten yards from the high tee to a green nested in a natural bowl. The hole was trapped all around. There was scarcely any fairway; instead the steep hill was sandy and rocky, as if in a permanent state of disrepair. Because the green was invisible from the tee, the young woman had been sent down the hill, and now she stood at a halfway point so that if the ball caromed, or buried itself, or went far off-line, she could keep it in view. She positioned herself beside a dead oak and waited. The man appeared above her, standing at the lip of the hill, shielding his eyes against the sun.

"You ready?" he called.

"Ready," she answered.

He stepped out of sight. After a short time she heard him call out "Fore," and heard the whack of the club head. In the same instant she saw the ball; it was hit short, and landed in the rough just above her, but it was moving at great speed and bounced past her toward the green. A little further downhill it struck something solid—a large rock, an old stump, she could not tell—and took renewed flight. It landed just at the edge of the green, danced toward the hole and struck the flagstick straight on. She watched the ball vanish into the cup.

"Did you see where it landed?" The man had found a path from the back of the tee, down through the trees to where she stood. "Am I in trouble?"

"It landed about there," she said, pointing at the hillside.

"In all those damn rocks," he said. "Wouldn't you know it. Did it ricochet?"

"Straight toward the green."

"Thank God for small favors," he said. He started downward, lugging the bag like a valise. "Tell me how far."

She followed after. "You'll be surprised," she said.

"I'll bet." He stood at the front of the green, looking down into the trap. "Where is it?"

"In the hole," she said.

"Don't tease me."

"No, really."

He laid the bag down and walked to the hole. He reached in alongside the pin and took out the ball.

"You put it there," he said.

"How could I?"

He studied the ball. "It actually went in? It's actually a hole-in-one?"

"Actually," she said. "It wasn't the most wonderful shot I ever saw—it must have hit every rock on the hill coming down—but it did the job."

"What do you know," he said. Abruptly, he turned away from the young woman and flung the ball with all his might at the tops of the trees behind the green. She took this to be an expression of joy.

"When I started playing golf, I had to use my father's clubs," he said.

They were sitting over drinks in the clubhouse. The decision to stop at nine holes was sound; he had gone over the last green with a clumsy pitch, then three-putted, and he took his failure at the ninth as an evil portent. With a decent pitch, he would certainly have made par.

"The clubs had funny names: mashie, niblick, brassie. You didn't call them by number. It was as if they had distinct personalities. And they were wooden shafted. The heads were held on the shafts with this heavy winding of gutta percha twine, and the whole club was varnished to a fare-thee-well."

"What kind of wood?"

"I don't know," he said. "Something resilient. Hickory? You could feel the wood sing when the club head made contact. And the shafts weren't really true; they all had a bow in them. You felt like W. C. Fields playing billiards."

The young woman smiled. "And did you wear knickers?" she said.

"No," he said. "But I went in for argyle socks and sweaters." He pondered the scorecard open beside his Collins glass. "Forty-six, even with the eagle on eight," he said. "Can you imagine it?"

"Did your father teach you the game?"

"After a fashion. He wasn't much of a golfer, I'm afraid—though it took me a while to realize just how bad he was. I think he learned his swing from watching sandlot baseball."

"You're quite a good golfer," the young woman said. "In spite of him."

"How one generation resists the faults of another," he said. "Anyway, it's an old man's game."

"Nonsense."

He took a last wistful look at his scorecard.

"Who'd believe this thing?" he said. He put his arm around the young woman and gently kissed her. "Would you?"

Eve Shelnutt

The Pilot-Messenger

"To dream with one eye open. . . ."
Santayana

Sometimes the three of them would awaken simultaneously and lie still under the pique coverlets, watching the light seep through the curtains until they were suffused. Or close their eyes against the light, remembering and reinventing. There was, of course, no way to prove the times of their bodies had caught them at once in this combustion of waking, the mother and the father in one bed set apart from the girl by a thin wall covered in roses and half-moons of ochre. Nor proof that they also imagined bodies unlike their own in repose against the white, white sheets — longer legs and toes uncurled, skin smooth as marble table-tops, pores tight, and breathing that would go on forever.

They were ordinary, so ordinary who would notice?, the question itself a bodiless heartbeat.

But, those rare times, they listened for the same sounds, which came in flat country across miles — wind in the grasses and the weeds such as Queen Ann's lace, dogs foraging in the wood's recesses, and the train bound for Atlanta. Then, their own impatience, rising. "Are you awake?" they would call to one another, as if the tiny house had numberless rooms where one of them might be lost.

In the interval between the asking and a slow lifting of "yes" in the three voices, so different, it seemed time had stopped and that there was a fourth person among them, lodged invisibly inside, and moving. Air, around the veins and the little coveys where the muscles bunched.

The curtains moved in the morning breeze — whitecaps on the bottomless day — and the light began to make the four rooms appear shabby, a mistake occurring before them. The birds set against one another, in cacophony. So the three would get up, begin, their bodies closing, as the roof of a child's doll house, the miniature brass hinges disappearing. And then this fourth person would take his own sleep, no longer alluded to in the hot desolation of three people waking at once.

The girl dressed herself, in pinafores on whose thin straps grew ruffles. And she wrapped the sashes tight so that, with time, her waist narrowed — the first of shapeliness. Her father watched her leave, dressed like this for the outer world, as if by her body's timing he judged his own. He wouldn't work — "Shit, no, unless I get a connection," which meant Florida, where, in his mind's eye, flamingoes stood always one-legged before a backdrop of sunset. Or New York: incalculable. And then — would he take them along? I expect not, his eyes said, surveying.

But maybe *she* would be wholly beautiful. Then he would move himself, her body a current, and his own death a lighthouse above them. So he fooled time, sat in the blue-covered chair, smoked, watched the yellow bus disappearing in the dust. *Annie.*

Who chewed her hair in sleep. If you came upon her dreaming, you might see her teeth loosen it, and the ends of the braids would lie flat on the pillow-slip, which would dampen. He had felt the spot. Then, slowly, the ends of the braids would curl. Sometimes she cried out; he would touch her, as if to enter the dream. He loved her; and she would not turn out entirely beautiful. Her face would move with every thought and, in time, only the thoughtful would watch her go by on a street. *If* she could be opened, then what?

He would sit by her, thinking. When it was hot, he would fan the air between them. *Pauline.*

What did the mother know of this formal setting, her daughter's youth the damask cloth whereon would one day sit the silver shakers, goblets, and the tiny swans of salt? Or, knowing, think? Really, there was nothing to think. And often the father would lean above his wife, head resting in the palm of one hand, his elbow making an eddy of darkness in the pillow. He would watch the curving cheek or the spread of her lashes, the beautiful parts. Sometimes *she* would cry out, and then listen to his breath hold. So what were words.

Yet, often, at the school where she taught, when the children were outside eating from lunchpails under the chinaberry trees, she stood looking out past these trees, still and with one hand held waist-high, as if she were just stepping forward. She would stand this way for minutes, and in the heat of the sky where she was looking was nothing at all. She seemed almost weightless, and the sun shone through the plaid dress so that the shape of her body was visible.

She doesn't eat, and when the children return, she looks up startled, recalling them. The children like her because they are not everything to her and what interests her is a mystery. Where did she come from and where is she going? To tease her from absorption, they ask her this. Her hands fan out, she smiles as if embarrassed, she is almost pretty, and she says, "Oh, lots of places," until they think London, Paris, the state capitol. It is a little secret, *place* the angle of his blue chair, in any house, and the girl moving between them and the times of waking together: Pauline, Annie, him (the sleeper), and the pilot-messenger wanting the broad daylight.

Miles from Pauline's desk, to the east, sits Annie's school made of concrete blocks, with long, low corridors jutting this way and that as if it had been the architect's dream to fill all pastureland. After months, still the building frightens Annie. Once in her desk, she presses her body to its chair and feels her smallness as reassuring. In the room, she is silent, but, to be polite, as Pauline has taught her, she keeps her eyes on the teacher's face, and all of her teachers have thought her studious, when, in fact, she is dreaming.

At recess, sometimes a girl will inch up to Annie and ask, "What does your daddy do?", as she pictures her own father in the work shirts of forest green, with wisps of cotton clinging to the collar, the white tee-shirt edging up on the adam's apple. "T.V.," says Annie. "Sometimes he's on T.V." And the girl will say, cocking her head, "I bet I saw him on the The Edge of Night when I was sick. *Was* he on The Edge of Night?" Annie will look away, lifting a wing of her pinafore as the girl says, "I bet he was."

When Annie runs home, always running!, and sees him in the afternoon, light coming over his left shoulder, one leg crossed and the Camel held near the left knee, the hand still and the smoke blue as the filament of dragonflies, she will think anything is possible.

So she read, everything they never asked at school, this knowledge wordless as the air between them in the house. "You," he would often declare at dinner, pointing a fork or a half-piece of the white bread, "are a bundle."

"*Am* I?" she would ask, seeing her mother's head tilt their way and her fork hold.

And he would say, solemnly, "Yes." Then, Pauline would giggle: "Crazy, I swear," getting up with the plates and shaking her head over them, her two wonders, while he would wink, try to slap her fanny as she passed. So anything could happen. *Echo, appendages, walking stick, the icy mountains of China.* Could I ask you anything I wanted, in the whole wide world? He would say, Why sure, Sweets, ask away.

A presumption, as the use of feet or a hollow at the collarbone: he moved them here and there, to acquire such knowledge, looking. "You two pack what you have to, the precious stuff, and don't dilly-dally around." As if suddenly starved. And Pauline watching him, Annie's eyes on her: What's all over you, Honey, (let me tell you) you don't have to understand. Music, down the spine.

"You drive." Pauline drove.

Annie would turn all the way around in the car seat to look at the house — growing smaller.

Traveling, those long days and nights longer still, there was no (proofless) waking together, the car air and the air in the two-bit motels stale. They would grow silent, he would have to remind them: "Perk up for Christ's sakes and pass the bag with the sardines." Annie worried, a debauche in the area of the stomach. Pauline would understand, but she was listening, elsewhere. And thus Pauline annointed each new house, tilting her head, stilling it anew, as though the house were a shell from a beach on which he had landed them. All schools, Annie learned, were the same. Sometimes they left the cows out in the back where the cheerleaders got to park their cars. Most houses had roses twining up the walls. They didn't own a T.V. set. *Who* was missing?

He didn't die; he began to corner Pauline in the kitchen by the opened refrigerator, and say to her, "I got an idea." Then there would be no sound at all from the kitchen, and was he, then, touching her?

Annie would run, letting the screen door slam and the bushes hit her face. Found, on her own, a boy — whose hair was yellow curls and on his forearms yellow curls; where she put her hand on his back nothing at all but the coolness of water, *her* secret, as he touched her nose and her shoulders under the pinafore.

He was nobody, he was Curtis Johnson Junior, and on weekdays delivered the *Belton Express* on a Schwinn painted silver; and none of her men, ever, would be anybody at all, the cool absence, anything possible if only they didn't talk.

Sometimes the father, still, would watch her in sleep, placing his own hand along the bridge of her nose, feeling with the other hand the boniness of a knee or where the leg muscles bunched, sore. He wanted off scott-free. Every god-damn house has a leaky faucet somewhere in it, you know that? he told Pauline, easing into her and holding one of her arms tight against the pillow. another under her as she thinned.

Finally he wanted luxury. It might be a vase he saw in a window in Charleston as they walked after eating the peck of raw oysters near the battery. Or the juice-squeezer he won as a door prize at the auctions in Hendersonville, where the fattest twins in the world rode their motorcycles on main street. A second-hand harp, for Annie, his watching her as she picked out a song almost oriental: a picture, Pauline hissing as she cooked, rolling her eyes heavenward, and waiting.

Sometimes when night came, it seemed they were the same as they had always been, Pauline sewing under the brass lamp and his head thrown back against the blue chair as his eyes shut and the Max Brand western dangles from a finger, and Annie not listening for cars. Light soft in the room, water, somewhere, dripping, and heat as a presence.

Pauline would hum, and when she held up against Annie the dress, with long, tight sleeves, on which she had been sewing, she would say, "Well!," standing back, looking with her eyes narrowed and the mouth a half-curve, a benediction. Annie could feel in that instant a mouth on the back of her neck or along the inside of an arm, the softest spot. Soon they would all. . . .

But she didn't know. And when he was watching her in sleep, when the light was diffuse in the grass and there was no sound in the house, not even, it seemed, Pauline's even breathing, nor wind coming from any place, and his tie loosened at the neck and dangling between his knees as he sat curved toward her — then, if she asked him anything at all, he wouldn't answer, no.

Before they moved, his closet bloomed with shirts of spring green, the palest blue, and yellow of dyed eggs, with the pins of the wrappings still stuck in the collars or holding one arm in a fold while the other dangled. The collars were

white, the french cuffs white, where, already, links of silver
or gold, with tiny red stones as eyes of fish or butterflies,
shone on the stiff whiteness — *alabaster, marble, sand of the
Boudini's, or clouds.*

And when they moved, *he* packed what was pretty,
writing on each box such things as ''Cloth, twelve napkins''
or ''Lalique glasses'' or ''Vase, brown and gold, fragile.'' As
Annie helped carry the boxes to the little four-wheel trailer,
he would turn to Curtis, straddling his Schwinn, watching,
and he would make a sign with his right hand, the thumb
and third finger forming an ''O,'' shake the hand. Or point
to Annie and wink, say, ''My little cosmopolite,'' by which
Annie thought they were headed for a city. It was the last
move.

If, in the new house, Pauline and Annie awoke at once,
listening and feeling themselves as tall beneath the covers or
feeling the blankets as a hot weight as sleet or rain pebbled
the windows, they did not call out to one another. And at
night while Pauline sewed, Annie took little cat-naps. It was
as if she was always sleepy, or always awake and needing
sleep, or afraid to sleep, or wake.

Sometimes Pauline would say to Annie in the evening,
''Give me your change, I've got to go call my sister,'' and
Annie would watch her winding down to the service station
and, after a time, watch a dog follow her home.

The first winter he did write to them — stationery from
The Pickwick Hotel on 49th Street, its facade etched on the
left-hand corner above the address — saying, ''. . . so I told
Jay, sure, I'd do it for him, if he got me the residuals.'' Or,
''If you can imagine (Pauline would look up, say, ''I
can't.''), he wanted a weather show without a talent fee. So I
said not on your life, baby.''

Pauline would add, ''How he talks,'' and look past
Annie out the window where the clothesline waivered, white
and fat with frost.

When he sent the suit, made, it said, by Evan Picone,

with pale blue and grey woven into herringbone, heavy on the tissue paper, Pauline's voice rose, wild and high: "Where am I supposed to *wear* it?" And she went to stand before the mirror, turning and turning until her plaid dress swirled.

Walking together now to the same school, always the dog — black, with matted fur — was behind them. All day he sat on the steps near Pauline's door, waiting. But still she wouldn't feed him, "Not *me*."

Annie wouldn't write to him. To write would be a transgression.

In the spring, he visited — the one real visit — and brought a T.V. set. At night, he watched, his face blue in the light. He took them one day to Rutherfordton, Pauline in her suit, and showed them film clips in a dark studio. He sat, in the films, in a brocade chair, one leg crossed and smoke rising from his cigarette. In the collar of the blue shirt was a stick pin; fleur de lis in a pattern on the tie. Behind them, on a white plastic chair, he smoked and said, "Not bad," and, "Just a little promo." Annie turned all the way around in her seat to look at him.

Now, just before the little roof closes, the brass hinges disappearing, Pauline and Annie can be seen, in the room with roses, half-moons of ochre, blue light like an aura, and the sound of even breathing, sitting forward on the sofa, straining, looking for him behind the girl with the long, gold hair, and the curling leaves of the potted plant on the studio table.

Then, he is there before them, seated in a Queen Ann's chair, smoking and uncrossing one leg. He turns; someone is opening a door, and outside is, apparently, the broad, clear light. And, from miles away, he smiles at them.

Jack Pulaski

Minnie the Moocher's Hair

Mother said, "You know? — your father was an only child." The insight was not so much given as discarded. She brushed the sleeve of her housecoat across her brow. "You see," she gasped — and I saw quite vividly, although I was eight years old and still partially invisible; my invisibility enhanced Mother's soliloquies. Mother paused to embrace me, confirming my presence and her own. My little brother Teddy, who was six, was also a presence, remote in another room of the apartment, and he too delivered soliloquies. Teddy's spiels were whispers, hoofbeats, Tarzan's jungle yodel, Captain Marvel's declaiming "Shazam," and giggles. If Teddy's fantasies failed to transport him elsewhere, he picked his nose until it bled.

"You see," Mother said, "he beat his own mother. After, he cried and bought her a new bathtub. Look, his parents were mockies, they couldn't talk English, they had your father late in life after they already gave up hope of having children — they thought he was a god. His mother advised me 'Give him his way, he can't help himself.' My mother advised me, 'After all he's a devoted provider.'" My brother hollered "Shazam". My mother said, "Really, Momma couldn't understand in this country I didn't need a dowry. Your grandmother figured at fifteen I was already an old maid. And so I turned sixteen years old and I'm going on my honeymoon. I never even traveled on the subway alone before. Your father was seventeen, a man of the world, he bought me a corsage." Mother sighed, "Anyway at that time the Broadway Central Hotel was a fancy place."

Teddy waddled into the doorway, naked, except for the

dishtowel he wore as a loincloth. He removed the bread knife
from his clenched teeth and howled Tarzan's jungle cry to the
elephant herds; it was a plaintive call, as if Tarzan really
didn't expect the beasts to respond; blood drooled from his
nose.

* * *

I was thirteen. Father and I were walking around the
block. It was the end of a summer day, people were sitting
out on their stoops. Father had had his supper. He walked
along not saying anything and smoked a cigar. I was
remembering the Broadway Central Hotel and Mother's
description of their honeymoon. The conflagration of twilight was reflected in the row upon row of tenement windows
above the street. I thought of that window some thirty stories
above the street in the Broadway Central Hotel. Father
walked along and said nothing. Mother had asked him to
talk to me about girls. We had walked halfway around the
block. Father paused, cleared his throat, and re-lit the stub of
his cigar. I waited for him to say something. He started to
walk again. When we were almost in front of our own
building, he stopped, tugged me towards the edge of the
curb, away from a couple of old women sitting on wooden
boxes and said, "Lissen, you lissening?" "Yeah." "Well, we
live inna neighborhood with a very low moral standin, an uh,
— I don't expect you to turn down nothing that comes your
way — only you should go first to the drug store and get
rubbers — ask the man for Trojans, o.k., say Trojans." "Tro-
gins." Back in the house Mother asked, "Well, did you talk to
him?" Father said, "Yeah, yeah, nothing to worry." That
night I lay in my bed in the darkened room and thought of
the window in the Broadway Central Hotel. I wondered if it
had happened the way Mother said. It must have because I
knew she never lied — it was an incapacity, she wasn't able
to. Without even closing my eyes I saw the window. Just like
on the walk with my father the window was lit with its
portion of the sun's glory. It was their honeymoon. Outside

the window, perched on the ledge, thirty stories above the street, my father, naked. Mother had said she wasn't ready. She was just a girl. She needed more time. She promised some other time. Only not now. Please. He had cried, screamed, climbed out on the window ledge, naked. When my mother told me about it she wondered what would have happened if she had said, "Jump."

*   *   *

But this happened after, and years before my father advised me about girls. It was winter. I was about eleven. Teddy was nine, the apartment was freezing. In every room including the kitchen, where the stove's four gas jets burned you could see your breath. The snow had turned to a dirty freezing rain. After school Teddy and I remained indoors bundled in our mackinaws, woolen hats and scarves. The milk stored on the sill outside the ice-glazed kitchen window had frozen in the bottles. Mother moved about the kitchen wearing two sweaters, and had wrapped herself in a quilt. She sipped endless glasses of steaming tea. An iciness misted from the kitchen walls. The damp cold rising from the floor slipped under the layers of clothing insinuating a chill deep in flesh and bone that seemed permanent and produced a stupefied melancholy. Except for Teddy. He was in the living room hollering "Mush" and cracking his invisible whip in the air, driving his sled and huskies across the frozen Yukon. Teddy used a wooden kitchen chair, its back rest laid down to the floor as his sled. He stood, his feet on the two legs of the chair and he was the six dogs barking, the wind howling, and the whip cracking in the air. The ice cold pipes and radiators banged with the protests of our freezing neighbors; the hammering on the pipes had commenced at dawn. From time to time Mother's eyes crossed. Teddy alternately pushed and dragged his screeching chair-sled across the living room floor. Mother endured the source of his contentment, (and in solidarity with the other freezing inhabitants of the building) the incessant banging of the pipes; although she herself would not join in the banging. The hammering was the only form of protest the tenants ventured.

It seemed unlikely that Christian Stevanovitch could be disturbed by noise. Stevanovitch (known among his own as Chriser the Mad Polack) was the landlord's new janitor. My mother, along with a number of the Jewish tenants, was haunted (quite aside from the cold) by the notion that Mr. Schiff, the landlord, would vindicate the views of anti-semites. After all, Stevanovitch was the landlord's economy measure, some said his golem. Stevanovitch and family lived in an apartment in the basement, adjacent to a locked door that led to the coal furnace. As instructed the janitor fired the furnace with just enough coal to keep the pipes from freezing. Stevanovitch himself seemed impervious to the cold, to weather of any kind. On those occasions when the police had come (never less than two squad cards and four police, anything less seemed to infuriate the janitor as some-how dishonorable) because Mr. Stevanovitch had been bouncing Mrs. Stevanovitch off the walls and Mrs. Stevanovitch continued to scream while airborne and long after she lost consciousness, Christian Stevanovitch would parade down the hallway, flanked by the four policemen, barefoot and in his undershirt he marched out into the snow and the waiting squad cars. Handcuffed and half-naked in the street, Stevanovitch basked in the freezing night as though lolling under a tropical sun. It was said that Chriser the Mad Polack's body fluids were about a hundred and thirty proof, he used vodka for blood, and his breath could blister the sidewalk. He was of an awesome size and my own stealthy study of the janitor had sent me back to my uncle Seymour's birthday present, H. G. Wells' "Outline of History." I turned to the illustrations in the chapter titled "The First Living Things," "The Appearance of Fur and Feathers," and "An Age of Hardship and Death." I found resemblances. It occurred to me that the missing link had probably walked upright and may have been blonde and blue-eyed.

All that day there had been endless visitations of shivering neighbors; they leaned toward Mother and whispered. Mother, as always, kept herself apart from the neighbors, her obvious distaste for their relish of conspiracy, along with the purged cleaner-than-clean cleanliness of our apartment left even the most meticulous of the women somewhat cowed and diffident. But time itself seemed frozen, the icy day eternal, the hammering on pipes and radiators endless as my brother traversed the frozen tundra forever; finally Mother blew on the tips of her blue fingers and said, "I don't know we could have here, God forbid, a tragedy." Then the neighbors insinuated that it was because of Father that they were plagued with the golem Stevanovitch. True enough, Father had leaned pretty hard on Stevanovitch's predecessor for more heat, and the man complied; also the landlord had given up collecting the rents personally after Father screamed in his face, "Capitalist bastard, you think you're gonna sew pockets into your shroud, huh. The workers are gonna make telephone wire out of your kishkes anyway." The landlord, who was no longer young and had barely escaped Poland with some portion of his family fortune, turned white, reached for his heart, which was under layers of fat, and staggered from our door.

The moon, a hunk of frozen debris, hung over the neighboring tenement roof, which was also Mr. Schiff's property. When Father had left for work at five that morning the moon had been a white glacial haze. From six until six he was foreman at Yussie Shinefeld's Textile Waste, then he ran over to Mercer and Canal Street to work the baling press at Moe Dershwitz's sweat shop for a couple of hours; his third job was on Saturdays and sometimes Sunday mornings, sorting rags at Louie the Cripple's place under the Williamsburg Bridge. After the injury to Father's back and the first of his hernias, Mother had advised that Father find work at the Navy Yard; the pay was good and a forty-hour week the rule.

He tried and didn't last the day; early in the afternoon he arrived home, disgusted. Mother had asked "So what's the matter?" He said, "I can't stand it, they send six guys to find a screwdriver. Same thing with the docks," he said, "they mostly hang around, they ain't workers they're playboys."

The gray slush in the street had turned into a churned leaden mass; the sidewalk and gutter had the appearance of a turbulent river that had frozen in a moment of ultimate seizure. Looking out the window I saw Father coming, hatless, in his unbuttoned pea coat, grasping his baling hook; he trod on the frozen rippled slush and he looked oddly to be walking on water. The fire escapes jutting out of the sides of buildings were whiskered with snow stalactites and extended skeletal iceladders and cages up into the pitch night air. In front of our building Father stopped, bewildered by all the people congregated there, as if it were a summer night. It was late in the week, after three or four sixteen hour long work days, and he stared dumbfounded at his neighbors who were all talking at him at once. He pressed on through the crowd and into the narrow corridor of hallway which was also jammed with people. My brother and I ran out into the hallway following my mother who carried a deep steaming bowl and a wooden spoon. Mother made her way through the crowd muttering in Yiddish and English "leave him be, leave him be —." The message was picked up and echoed up and down the corridor in Polish, Russian, Lithuanian, Yiddish and English. Finally Mother stood next to Father, my brother and I behind her. Father's face began to take on "The Look." Mother took away his baling hook and handed it to me. The neighbors shoved and pushed. Mother dipped the wooden spoon in the bowl and swiftly brought it up into Father's gaping mouth. He swallowed and lapsed into something like a sexual coma. His mouth opened. Mother ladled up more of the groats and noodles. The neighbors muttered, "Eat in good health." Mother fed him. In between spoonfuls she whispered, cooed, stroked his arm with the wooden spoon. Father's eyes opened. Mother ladled in more groats and noodles, whispered to him, stroked him. Someone belched in his behalf. Mother said thank you. Father swallowed, his face shone with a momentary bliss that mothered an expression of almost philosophical beatitude. Mother uttered a weighty "Nu?" which was a beseeching to all that was ultimately imponderable, and a claim to on high that she had done all she could. The hall reeked wonderfully of chicken fat, fried onion, kasha and noodles. Mother handed me the bowl which was still half full. A pair of hands reached out tentatively, withdrew, then reached out again and clasped the bowl. I let it go. Father stirred, and people made way, he walked through the hall and down the steps to the basement and the Stevanovitch apartment. Mother, Teddy, I, and the tenants, followed at a distance.

Father descended into the semi-dark of the basement. It was in this dark, during the fall, that I had played with Helene Applebaum. I was Nick Carter, private detective, and over and over again Helene practised fainting into my arms. I stood, legs rigid, arms outstretched, palms up, and Helene swooned stiff as a cadaver except for one limp fluttering hand — into my arms. My knees would buckle and I almost fainted. Over and over again in that dark all through September and October Helene Applebaum fainted into my arms. I sweated and shivered, the sweet weight of her nearly pulling me into oblivion. Remembering it, I trembled and felt as though I had to go to the bathroom. But when Father knocked on the Stevanovitch door and walked in closing the door behind him, I forgot that I had to pee. Someone tapped me on the shoulder, I turned, and the kasha varniska bowl was returned to me, empty. I stood, my head pressed against Mother's waist; in one hand I held the warm empty bowl against my chest, in the other Father's baling hook, which touched the floor.

Mrs. Stevanovitch's voice commenced a steady low pitched wail. Behind me several women commiserated with

Mrs. Stevanovitch, another said in Yiddish, that Mrs. Stevanovitch had earned her damnation. Christian Stevanovitch's voice growled in Polish. Father, sounding friendly and patient, as if he were warming to the pedagogical possibilities of the situation explained, "Lissen Stevanovitch, this is America, you gotta understand over here the only thing lower than a nigger is a Polack." There was for an indeterminate number of seconds a silence like choking. Something smashed against a wall. The sounds of breaking glass and furniture echoed in the dark basement along with Mrs. Stevanovitch's steady low-pitched wail.

Father appeared in the doorway carrying four wooden kitchen chairs and part of a table. He turned sideways in the doorway loaded with the chairs and the hunk of table, its one remaining leg scraped the wall as he squeezed through the door. Bent over and festooned with the Stevanovitch kitchen furniture, he turned right, lifted a leg and kicked in the locked wooden door that led to the coal furnace. The four chairs and piece of table he smashed into kindling on the stone floor. A neighbor stepped forward with a shovel and turned to the glistening mountain of coal.

All through the month of February Christian Stevanovitch wandered drunkenly about the building and streets as though he had misplaced himself somewhere and it required an enormous effort for him to remember to maintain the search. In March he disappeared.

April: the smell of spring leaked through the pavement. The nights were warm and the stoopfronts flooded with people. After three o'clock when school let out until dark my friends and I payed stick ball, punch ball, johnny-on-the-pony (also known as buck-buck), kick the can, and ring-a-levio. Ring-a-levio was a war-like variant of hide and seek, in which one was not merely found but captured. One evening Mutty Sperber, trying to elude capture, scrambled out of a cellar with Jo-Jo and Augie chasing after him. Mutty dashed across the street; the laundry truck which did not slow down,

missed him, Mutty oblivious to all but capture achieved the
other side of the street and leaped for the pavement, trying
to clear the large brass bed which blocked an alley-way
leading to further networks of ladders, firescapes, rooftops,
hallways, and cellars. From my hiding place in the back of a
parked seltzer truck, I pressed my body flat to the floor and
peeked between slats, venturing one eye beyond the perimeter of stacked cases of Fox Brothers chocolate syrup. Fat
Mutty's boneless body climbed the air, his arms furiously
breast stroking, legs pumping frog-leaps Mutty rose miracu-
lously, cherubic in the splendid twilight, above the brass
bed. Mutty hovered over the pavement where the brass bed,
up-ended bureau with its open drawers drooling socks and
underwear, a dilapidated couch, a smashed portable record
player, and broken records cluttered the street. Ties, socks, a
woman's slip, forks, spoons, dishes and cups, some already
reduced to debris, and an odd assortment of shoes were
strewn over the gutter.

Mutty, momentarily suspended on the golden light,
thrashed to fly over the brass bed and escape; but loaded
with the heft of his mother's love, angelic, ample-assed
Mutty sank. Augie and Jo-Jo, chasing an arm length behind,
leaped — Augie wearing a brassiere on his head: the two
sharp pointed cups stuck up like leprous rabbit ears. Jo-Jo,
mummy-faced under a nylon stocking, woof-woofed in
pursuit. Augie and Jo-Jo tackled Mutty in mid-flight: in the
immediate collision, rubicund Mutty, a domestic godlet
being brought to earth, yelled "Beahstids"; the six-legged
many-headed creature of boys thrashed, something terrible
being born on the air, they tossed and fell, exploded in the
brass bed. Separate boys geysered up out of the crippled bed,
hit, and rolled over the pavement.

Then I heard my mother's voice. From three stories up
she called from the window, "Jackie, Jackie, come home." I
was mortified. I climbed out of the truck. The sky was
turning gray, heavy.

I turned my face up to the rain-threatening sky and whined, "Aw, Ma." Ma repeated, "Upstairs." I squinted and yelled, "Later." She leaned out of the window her neck craning up and head turned sideways as though she did not want to see what was happening in the street. A curtain of dark hair obscured her face; the voice from under the hair called, "You want to discuss 'later', with your father? 'Later'?"

I trudged up the three flights of steps under the weight of my humiliated heart. My friends would think I was being saved from being rained on? Protected from the game? Hurt? When I walked through the door into the kitchen, Mother smiled benignly and waved toward the glass of milk and cookies on the table. She ruins my name in the street and offers me milk! My guts heaved poison, and my face was hatred. Mother's face looked at my face, registered shock, hurt; red hot thunder exploded on my cheek; my ears rang. My kid brother yelled, "Wow." The thunder on my cheek resounded and boomed in heaven above the rooftops and rain fell in sheets outside the window. Mother took me in her arms, said she was sorry, cried. She talked. I nodded, cried inside my chest. She explained all in a rush, lathering my cheek with kisses, while my brother tugged at my hand, pulling me toward the window, to look down, see the couch, bed, the household in the street being drowned. Mother's voice explained and I heard the isolated talismanic words that had wormed foreknowledge into my sleep — "Konahora" — the evil eye — misfortune is contagious. Lord knows what I would trail into the house after climbing over that bed in the street, a pity on them, the poor people. "Oy, poor Mrs. Stevanovitch," she said, "deserted, dispossessed and disowned by her own — with a ten-year-old to raise yet."

Evening arrived moonless; the rain declined into a steady drizzle. A wet fog drifted in from the East River shrouding the dim cataract eye of the lamp post. The street below was a steamy void, the gutter seen through the wafting fog glistened black. Within and under the wet steamy fog

the usable remnants of the Stevanovitch household disappeared.

Mother had washed and waxed the floors and cleaned
our four rooms. Before the rain had started, she washed the
windows until they achieved the illusion of non-being; the
long horizontal crack in the glass appeared to be a hair
floating in the air. The doorknobs shined. The faucet
gleamed. She prepared a supper of potato latkas and sour
cream, vegetable soup, and herring. Father came in from
work, walked to the kitchen sink, turned on the cold water
tap and stuck his head under the faucet. He stood over the
sink shaking his head like a dog shedding rain. Mother
frowned. Father opened a cabinet door, poured himself a
water tumbler full of schnapps, and sat down to supper.
Mother pressed a fist against her temple trying to push
something from her brain; she glanced at the table and
turned away as though nothing she could do would entitle
her to eat. Earlier she had paused in her work to climb down
the three flights to go into the street and save for Mrs.
Stevanovitch some pots and pans, dishes, as much as she
could carry. Several minutes later, while Mother was grating
potatoes, Mrs. Sperber had come to the door. Reluctantly
Mother asked her in and offered her a chair. Tillie Sperber
lowered her heavy body carefully onto the chair, and pressed
her soft voluminous hips, trying to limit the exploding
symmetry of her body to the shape of the wooden chair. Mrs.
Sperber said, "Nu?" and began to whisper in Yiddish.
Mother explained in English that she was sorry, she was really
very busy. Tillie Sperber said that Mrs. Stevanovitch wasn't
really a Stevanovitch, but a Bubbitz and the Bubbitz family
had mourned her as one dead. Mother said "Please." Tillie
Sperber said, "And to lay down with one of them, to make a
'momser' yet." Mother's voice rose and fell, confused
between entreaty and command. Tillie caught her breath,
her eyes reconnoitered, searched the room and encountered
the countertop where Mother had piled Mrs. Stevanovitch's

pots and pans. Tillie Sperber smiled knowingly at Mother, and whispered that she had gotten a perfectly good teapot. Mother recoiled, got to her feet, "Really, Mrs., I have to make supper!" Tillie Sperber rose slowly, her cheeks flushed; she winked at Mother and went out the door.

Father had all of Saturday off from work, and at about noon he left for the Turkish baths with a large brown paper bag of food and a bottle of schnapps. After he left, Mother sighed, her face loosened, and she moved easily through the luxuriant quiet of the apartment.

Upon opening his eyes Father had stumbled to the kitchen and had breakfast: coffee, cigar, and a shot of schnapps. In his jockey shorts he went to the living room, turned the phonograph on, twisting the volume knob high as it would go. He sat down and pressed his ear to the speaker. Fats Waller sang "Ain't Misbehavin'" at a pitch that made the window panes shiver. Father blew wreathes of cigar smoke and sang along with Fats, Father's bare feet beating rhythm on the floor.

A little while after Father left for the Turkish bath, Teddy and I went off to the Saturday matinee at "The Dump." The three feature films, two serials, six cartoons and coming attractions kept us in the theatre eight hours. Teddy and I staggered out of the dark movie house squinting, giddy, and blind, in the very last light of evening.

When we arrived home it was dark and Mother had the table set for supper. The Friday night chicken had been converted to soup. The white oilcloth on the table glistened, the gold-colored soup steamed pungently, and a large loaf of black pumpernickle sat on a white cloth napkin at the center of the table. At my elbow was a dish of left-over reheated and still-delicious potato latkes, and a bowl of sour cream. Mother said, "Don't wait, eat."

I had finished the soup and was watching my brother sculpt a sour cream moustache on his lip when our door, which opened from the vestibule into the kitchen, swung

open. Father ducked and entered, his face was radiant, eyes
booze merry, and on his shoulder sat a boy of about my age;
the boy perched on Father's shoulder sat very still and chewed
on his wrist. The mother, Father hauled behind him. Mrs.
Stevanovitch moved in lock step with doom, her silent face
appeared to be screaming. Father said "She can talk," and
gave her a little shove. Mrs. Stevanovitch's arm reached up
toward her son sitting on Father's shoulder, the boy's head
almost touched the ceiling. She said "Dispossessed" and she
said "Stop." I couldn't tell whether "Stop" was directed at her
son feasting on his wrist, Father who was shoving her toward
the center of the room, or the world at large; beyond the
open door, in the vestibule, a group of neighbors stared into
the kitchen. Father slammed the door in their faces, took the
boy from his shoulder and stood him on his feet. Father said
"Anna." Mother leaned back against the gas range, her chest
heaved. Father motioned toward Mrs. Stevanovitch and said,
"She's got a little history, but she's not a goy." Now Mother
had no choice, Mrs. Stevanovitch's misfortune was kosher.
"Mrs." said Mother to Mrs. Stevanovitch, breathless with the
effort the speech required, "Mrs., sit please, have a glass tea?
Soup?" Mrs. Stevanovitch remained standing and tottered
like a sleepwalker that had been halted in her wandering, her
silent face clenched around a scream only she could hear, but
threatened to arrive, any moment to deafen the deaf world.
Father stared at her face and blinked like a monkey — "What
the hell has turned this woman's head into a shroud?" he
asked in Yiddish. He pressed on her shoulder and lowered
her into a chair. "Abe! Be careful with her," said Mother.
"Yeah," he said. My brother wiped the sour cream moustache
around his mouth, enlarging it into a beard, and nudged me
with his elbow. Father shouted in Mrs. Stevanovitch's face as
if the woman's silence were a symptom of deafness. "I'm
going to the street to get what's left of your stuff." Mother
winced and set a bowl of soup in front of Mrs. Stevanovitch
and urged the boy gnawing on his wrist, to sit at the table.

The boy sat, looked up from his raw bloody wrist and threw furtive ferocious glances at me and my brother. Father went out the door. Teddy and I jumped up and ran to the front window, choking on spooky laughter. We could hear Mother saying, "Don't pay attention to them. Don't pay attention."

There was a bright full moon. Teddy and I, with arms around one another's shoulders swayed back and forth in front of the window. The brilliant moon rolled with our swaying across the rooftops. The lamppost and the moon doused the street in a stark theatrical light. Father picking through the dishes, pots and pans, strewn over the curb, was drenched chalk-white. The moon was too luminous to have a face but the brilliance of moonlight and lamplight shadowed a frown on the stubby fire-hydrant; a helmeted troll, it watched with an air of martial neutrality as Father lifted a broken record from the wreckage of the Stevanovitch household and read the label.

There was not much left. The couch was gone; the brass bed had been carried off, the mattress lay on the pavement, old Yutzie the rummy crapped out on it. The bureau was still there, all the drawers pulled out, most of the clothing gone. The broken phonograph had disappeared. Father read the record label, yelling the name of the song up at the window; "Minnie the Moocher" he called. And then, as an afterthought, as if to cheer up Mrs. Stevanovitch, Father, at the top of his voice sang: "Minnie the Moocher, she was a mighty hootchie-cootcher, she was the roughest and the toughest, but Minnie had a heart as big as a whale." From several surrounding windows came a ghostly applause. A small group of neighbors, sitting on the stoop enjoying the mild spring night, clapped uncertainly; there was a small sputtering of soft laughter and whispers. My brother and I speculated on who got what of the Stevanovitch household goods. Father's enthusiasm lived in its own right and the largesse of booze. He bowed vigorously to the timid applause, and sang another chorus, this time louder: "Minnie the Moocher, she was a mighty hootchie-cootcher," as the inhabitants of the stoop vanished, one by one. Father bowed to the empty stoop and darkened windows. With the exaggerated elegance of a stage magician he approached the mattress Yutsie the rummy lay on; he yanked the mattress as if he were whisking away a fine linen tablecloth, careful not to upset the china, silverware and long-stemmed goblets of wine. Yutsie's head bounced on the pavement. Father retrieved a battered work shoe from the gutter and placed it under the drunk's head for a pillow. Father lifted the mattress which was as deeply inhabited as the city and carried it into the building; climbing up the steps with the mattress on his back, he sang, "Minnie the Moocher," thus naming Minnie, Minnie. If this naming was a further desecration of Mrs. Stevanovitch's life, Minnie said nothing, living on the edge, inside the impending scream.

They stayed four weeks, a month of days, and every day seemed to defy the possibility of ever becoming the past. Mother cleansed and bandaged the boy's right wrist and he began chewing on his left. His name was Herman; and when Teddy, Herman and I left for school in the morning, Herman never got there.

When Herman was twenty, he reverted to his mother's maiden name and was known simply as "Bubbitz." Like Napoleon and Attila, for "Bubbitz," the one name was sufficient. Bubbitz rose to become the pre-eminent loan shark for the Williamsburg and Greenpoint sections of Brooklyn. It was said that if during a business negotiation Bubbitz's wrist began to twitch towards his mouth, all discussion ceased. But Bubbitz's rise to success is another story.

Mother would not let Father bring the mattress into the house. The mattress, which needed purging, was stored on the top floor, in an alcove, near the roof.

Minnie and Herman slept together in our living room, on a couch that opened into a bed. In the morning Mother stripped the sheets and blankets and folded the bed back

into the couch. Every day Mother laundered the bedding.
After waking, Minnie shuffled to the bathroom and stayed
there until Father pounded on the door. Standing nearby as
Mother cooked or cleaned, Minnie recoiled, warding off
invisible blows until she was settled in a chair. Sitting,
Minnie's body appeared in a state of collapse so profound it
was practically repose; her face remained fixed around the
silent scream. The days passed; life was suspended in a
monumental pause, during which, awaiting the scream, our
hearing became painfully acute; a knife tapping on a plate,
the ticking clock, the dripping faucet, all gained an ominous
volume. Father went and came from work as always, hungry
and oblivious. Teddy and I escaped to the street. Where
Herman wandered I don't know; he returned in the evening,
remembering a feeding place; he moved like a piece of livid
rope, but with his wrists freshly bandaged and bathed in all
of Mother's good intentions Herman slunk to the supper
table and tried to hide his feral looks.

The brunt of Minnie fell on Mother. On a Saturday
morning after Teddy and Herman took to the street, I
lingered behind dismantling an old umbrella. I was going to
trade the metal spokes for a bag of marbles. Eddie Pacheco
fashioned the spokes into arrows which he used to hunt alley
cats. Eddie P. was twelve years old and an accomplished
archer. I was flattered by the attention of this older fellow; in
that quaint age of zip-guns Pacheco had a future to look
forward to as a weapons manufacturer.

I had been sitting very quietly in a closet in the rear of
the apartment, pulling the thin metal spokes from the tat-
tered umbrella. I could hear Mother talking to Minnie in the
kitchen. Mother's voice, weighted with sad exhortation,
gathered strength as she worked her way towards conviction.
"After all," she said, "we finally got a Roosevelt and you go
out and marry a pogrom. All right, Roosevelt's dead a long
time already, finished, but the war is over, you don't see no
more Hoovervilles, either. The sweat shops are going fine,

there's plenty work — no one has to go hungry. These are good times. And if your parents hadn't come from the other side and you had been in Europe, you'd be a bar of soap, a lamp shade. Mrs.! You have a child to raise."

As I made my way to the front door clutching the umbrella spokes, Mother stood over Minnie, sitting in a chair; Mother, startled by my passing, brought her hand to her mouth and turned her face from me; embarrassed, as though she had been caught talking to herself. I went out the door and down the steps wanting to say something reassuring. My face burned and when I had gone down one flight of steps I decided that I was not being replaced as exclusive and totem repository of Mother's history. What Mother offered Minnie was not the human specifics, but gristle and afterbirth, mere wisdom.

A week later, on a Saturday or Sunday, as I went out the front door I saw Mother with a pair of scissors in her hand standing over Minnie who sat in the same kitchen chair. Mother waved the scissors in the air, still exhorting Minnie toward the life-giving possibilities of motherhood.

Minnie had what the Puerto Ricans in my neighborhood referred to as "bad hair," which is to say the texture gave a hint of dark origins and a fistful looked resilient enough to scour pots; it was red, wiry, and rose from her head in spontaneous combustion; it seemed that the scream that was a subliminal presence resided in that hair — as well as other living things. Mother rid Minnie's hair of what crawled, washed it, cut it short into a kind of Joan of Arc novitiate-for-the-fire style. The scream slunk low on Minnie's skull, went underground and reconnoitered in the bewildered trenches of Minnie's eyes. Walking in on Mother ministering to Minnie caused Mother's hands to fly to her face in odd stealthy movements. I took to leaving the apartment from my bedroom window. I climbed down the three flights of firescapes and ladders, let myself fall the last half story through the air and absorbed the shock of the pavement through my legs and back.

I returned home through the kitchen door whistling, heavy-footed, announcing my arrival before my hand reached the doorknob. The day I handed Mother the letter from school Minnie sat fondling her shorn head, her face fidgeted toward the promise of speech, mouth open, shaped around the impending scream. Mother stood behind Minnie and read the letter from the principal. She asked my brother why he didn't behave in school. Teddy whinnied, stamped his hoof, whopped a war cry and galloped off toward the great plains beyond the bedroom door. The letter said that it would be necessary for Mother to come to school and confer with the principal and Teddy's teacher.

The teacher and the principal said that they feared that Teddy's misbehavior was not a matter of recalcitrance; he seemed to enter fantasy at a depth where he could not be reached; Teddy transfigured to mythic beast and super hero; Batman, Red Ryder and Little Beaver, he galloped and flew about the class room and could not be recalled to being Teddy, hands clasped, seated quietly behind his desk.

Father said, "So he's nuts," ready to beat horsiness, cowpokes, Indians, and all flying ubermenchen from Teddy's hide; and he would have, but that day Herman had revenged himself on Teddy.

I had come upon Herman in the street playing with my model airplane; a World War II Flying Fortress made of balsa wood, paper, the four propellers strung with rubber bands, the craft did fly. When I demanded that Herman hand over the plane, he snapped off the wings. I threw the first punch and Herman was all over me, like a stink on shit. I took a couple of shots to the sides of my head and on my shoulders. Two of Herman's swings flew over my head and another punch was short. This happened twice, three times. I moved in a circle just beyond the range of Herman's fists, and the frustration was too much for him. Herman sunk his teeth into his right wrist, chewed ferociously, and flailed away with his one left arm. I tied up Herman's left arm with my right, and banged away, free with my left. The circle of kids surrounding us laughed, the whole street gaining a strategy for dealing with Herman.

Herman took off and returned around supper time to find Teddy standing on the stoop dreaming the panorama of passing sky into a herd of rogue elephants; Teddy a kindred spirit to the sky herd trumpeted a high-pitched call to the heavenly mammals floating between the rooftops. Herman gnawed at his raw bloody wrist, stuck in his mouth, wound up his left arm, punched Teddy in the face, and ran away.

My mother stuffed Teddy's nostrils with toilet tissue and cotton wadding. Teddy's nose drooled blood. My father pressed cold keys and a chunk of ice wrapped in cheesecloth on the back of Teddy's neck. Father said, "A lead pipe would be good, next time open up his head with whatever is handy." Teddy nodded in agreement, the bloody cotton wadding and pellets of toilet paper spilling out of his nose. This was happening in the kitchen, everything happened in the kitchen; procreation and sleep ostensibly in the bedroom. I'm sure our astral bodies dreamed and were joined on and around the kitchen table, each of us inhabiting sleep at our accustomed eating place. Teddy turned his head up toward the ceiling, the blood flowed sideways down his cheek soaking the towel on the kitchen table. My father said, "Yeah, a lead pipe would be good." Minnie, seated at the table, opened her mouth and exhaled breath. My mother told me to run to the grocery store and use their phone to call Dr. Schacter.

Dr. Schacter came and went as always, leaving us confused between his refusal to accept anything but the most minimal payment, and his sour misanthropic face. He wore a black battered homburg which he never removed and a dark striped double-breasted suit. The suit looked like it had been slept in for a hundred years and reeked of camphor. Before attempting any diagnosis, Dr. Schacter always muttered the same advice in a heavy German-Jewish accent: "Yah, Von must keep assets liquid, suitcases packed, lif close to the border, yah." The doctor attempted to speak English with precision and exploded all his "t's" and "d's" so that after he closed the door behind him, his tongue having laboriously detonated the two syllables — "Blee-der," bleeder reverberated in the kitchen, rocking Mother who had turned very white, holding in her hand a prescription for a tonic to thicken Teddy's blood. Doctor Schacter left on the run, as though the police were chasing him, his wire-framed glasses propped on his forehead, stethoscope dangling from his neck.

Teddy sat at the table, two long strips of gauze hanging out of his nostrils. The ends of the gauze strips that were in his nose were dipped in a chemical that cauterized the wound, burning tissue until the bleeding stopped. Teddy called the strips hanging out of his nose "spaghetties." He said, "I am a spaghetti tree," and swung his head back and forth, the hanging gauze strips fluttering from his nose. Tears rolled out of Teddy's eyes but he said he wasn't crying; "just water" he said, pushed out of his eyes by the hot medicine.

Mother had chased after Doctor Schacter in the hallway. She returned and announced, "Not hemophilia, but I should take him to the hospital next week for tests." She dispatched Father to the drugstore to get the prescription filled, grabbed at Father's sleeve as he reached the door and in a Yiddish whisper that wasn't a whisper instructed Father to find Minnie's relatives, a philanthropic organization, someone — something; it was time for Minnie and Herman to move on. Minnie sat crazy-eyed, her jaws chewing on the palpable silent scream. Herman did not return that night, the next day, or ever; he took up what would be his habitual residence — hallways, rooftops and cellars, until he emerged as the pre-eminent "Bubbitz".

In the morning Mother jammed a large tablespoon of

the tonic down my throat, as well as my brother's; might as well thicken my blood for the same money. The stuff had the consistency of molasses, the cherry flavoring did not entirely disguise the rank taste that slithered down the throat alive.

Mother was going food shopping and she insisted that Teddy and I accompany her. She worried about Herman returning and our fighting, and indeed, I did have plans for Herman. Mother left breakfast on the kitchen table for Minnie: freshly squeezed orange juice, two scrambled eggs, home fries, a toasted bagel and butter, and a glass of coffee.

In the street, my brother and I walked beside Mother, petulant, dragging our feet and giving off the airs of captives suffering profound injustice. Mother said that when we got to the city market she would buy the codfish "live" so that we could play with it in the bathtub for a while, before she prepared it for supper. This was happy news and we picked up the pace. Teddy ran on ahead, his arm beckoning us onward, he was a scout guiding us across the thoroughfare which was for him a dangerous mountain range, hostile Indians behind every rock. Mother called out for Teddy to stop at the curb, but he was already out cantering between a beer truck and a taxi. Teddy waited for us at the next corner, where we regrouped. Mother bent her head so that her eyes were level with his; she would have cuffed him, except that Teddy's being a bleeder granted him a certain immunity. She waved her finger under his nose and asked rhetorically whether he could distinguish between a green light and a red light — "Maybe it would be best to put him on a leash, like a little dog." Teddy neighed and whinnied as Tillie Sperber came upon us swinging a shopping bag, and announced that she had something urgent to say to Mother. Teddy and I took the opportunity and ran off a little ways and waited. Tillie spoke. Mother said, "What," as though she hadn't heard or hadn't understood. Tillie continued to talk, her shopping bag on the pavement, her hands cupped around her mouth. Mother turned whiter than she had been when Doctor

Schacter had said "Bleeder."

For the rest of our walk to the city market, which was only six blocks from home, Mother walked like one condemned, a zombie pace; staring straight ahead she would not answer when Teddy and I talked to her.

At the city market we guided Mother past the grocery concession, and the fruit and vegetable concession, past the pyramids of oranges and grapefruits that dwarfed the fruit and vegetable man who gave Teddy a free plum. The fruit and vegetable man smacked his lips, tugged at Mother's sleeve and challenged, "Take a bite, one bite, Mrs. — " We passed the Italian butcher with skinned rabbits and pig heads, hindquarters and hooves hanging on hooks — turned right, passed the haberdasher waving ties to arrive at the kosher section, and the fishman. The short, muscular fishman wore thick glasses and a green visor which gave his stubbled face a mossy under-sea pallor. He stood leaning on a butcher block, a huge sink behind him. On the block, next to a newspaper piled high with fish parts, lay a fish, its head and tail chopped off, its flesh filleted — the woman for whom the fish was intended paused momentarily in her negotiation. The fishman smiled at Mother. Mother never argued price with him; and he said in Yiddish, "Ah, Mrs., health to you and yours. May I help you?" The other lady put her hand to her cheek and said, "Oh my, the queen of England." Mother opened her mouth and no sound came from her white face. "What?" asked the fishman tenderly, "codfish, herring, flounder, speak." I pointed to what was swimming just under the surface of the water in the sink. The fishman took the cleaver that was up-ended in the butcher block, turned and yanked the large thrashing codfish from the sink. He held the wriggling fish up in the air by its tail and asked, "Fifty cents?" not so much to bargain as to offer something of a gift, the price of which Mother could determine. Mother opened her mouth. The scream came out. The fish vendor recoiled, dropped the fish and waved the cleaver

in the air. The other customer backed away, arms in front of
her face to ward off a fatal blow. The scream rose a
concussion of air. The fishman's one thick bloody hand
scattered fish heads and tails, pike, cod, and flounder eyes
rolling like grapes from the wooden chopping block; the
silvery scales that had covered the fishman's aproned stomach
in reptilian armor, loosed by my mother's scream, a radiant
silver blizzard. My brother talked to the fish which was
thrashing on the bloody floor.

When we got home Mother screamed Minnie out of the
house with the testimony Tillie Sperber had whispered,
common knowledge in the street: prior to her stay with us
Minnie had tried to make ends meet with the only end she
had, bartering with the landlord and the grocer. Mother
began to wash her hands with the condemned and assiduous
fervor of Pontius Pilate. Over and over she washed her hands,
the hands keeping a keening, cleansing, and beseeching
motion, that never stopped. Minnie's scream found its voice.
A door slammed, I tipped a glass of milk, my brother hic-
coughed — all precipitated the scream. The scream devoured
more and more of Mother's language; with what store of
words she had left she speculated that she should have worn
gloves, rubber gloves, then the scream would not have been
able to slip under her fingernails and travel her blood to the
throat.

Father lay sleeping in his underwear and torn socks.
Mother said, "See the animal — a man who brings whores
from the street for his wife to wash and manicure." Father
woke, had his breakfast: coffee, schnapps, and a cigar. He
put a record on the phonograph, turned the volume up and
pressed his ear to the speaker. The Andrew Sisters sang "You
Get No Bread with One-un Meatball". Mother washed and
cleaned the apartment. She scrubbed every inch of the place,
drenching the floor, walls, cabinets, tub and sink in reeking
disinfectant. When the paint dried, she began to wash and
scrub again. She screamed. Between screams she recounted

how during the Depression — "You were an infant — your Father took the rent money and went out and bought me lingerie and perfume to have me stink like a slut, and wear a nightgown you can see through." Teddy gave out a coyote howl; discovering some nascent erotic life, he humped the wall in his room. The paint dried. Mother repainted the place white, white. She did not cook and clean, she battled famine and disease. After two months the scream was very strong: Mother weighed eighty-seven pounds. Father said, "You have to eat more than toast and tea." Mother screamed from the ladder and went on painting the ceiling.

She had given up toast, and swayed languorously as she swung the paintbrush; the paint dripping on the floor made her cry. The scream was robust. Father called Dr. Schacter; Dr. Schacter called in a colleague, Dr. Reinburg, a psychiatrist.

Dr. Reinburg said Mother would have to go to the hospital and recommended electric shock therapy. Father said, "You're the doctor." Mother's side of the family came to the house and called Father "murderer." Dr. Reinburg said that Mother had to forget; this was the only way past pain, the only way to subdue the scream.

Mother was gone for a month. Relatives came. I imagined Dr. Reinburg's treatment as somehow analogous to Dr. Schacter's dictum, "Keep assets liquid, bags packed, live close to the border," the only cure for hurt, flight and amnesia; I remembered being very little and sticking a fork into an electric outlet. The shock had thrown me across the room. I remembered nothing else of that day.

My brother and I went to the movies, then I thought of Dr. Frankenstein sewing together the parts of dead bodies, stitching a lunatic's brain into a discarded skull; the creature raised on a platform into the thundering electric night, and lightning had made it live. The piteous monster, not knowing where he came from, did paw at the light. And Benjamin Franklin even — I had seen a picture in school, Benjamin dancing the birth of America, the discovery of electricity. Old Ben cavorted on the heath, hanging on to the cord of his flying kite, the kite bounced high up in thundering heaven, the key hanging from the cord shuddered with electric light, old Benny's eyes wide with epiphany.

Mother came home accompanied by her sister, Aunt Tessie. Father was at work. Mother wandered slowly through the apartment, the place seemed vaguely familiar to her. She studied my brother and I, turned to her sister and said, "Such nice-looking boys." We ran to her, hugged her, held her hand. Mother rocked on her heels from the impact of our running into her; bewildered, she accepted our marauding embraces. She said, "Jackie?" I said, "Yes Ma." She turned to her sister, "He looks like Moishy, no?" Moishy was my uncle, Mother's brother. Aunt Tessie said, "Yes, when Moishy was a boy." Mother repeated, "Yes, when he was a boy," her brow furrowed, she seemed to struggle with a stubborn juxtaposition of time, then and now asserting themselves by some odd whimsy. "He's still angry", Mother said, "cause Momma fed us his pigeons — it was Depression years" she yelled at me, "Nobody had what to eat, Momma had no choice." "It's O.K." I said. She flushed, "I know it's O.K." "Jackie?" she said.

Mother continued her survey of the apartment, Aunt Tessie, Teddy and I following after her. In her bedroom she paused at her dresser, picked up and fingered the comb and hairbrush. She opened the drawers, took out a box of pins, scissors, sewing utensils, a pair of stockings. She placed these things neatly back in the drawers, pushed the drawers shut and looked up, startled by the woman staring at her in the mirror. She smiled courteously, raised her hand to her hair, surprised that she could animate the woman in the mirror with so simple a gesture.

Aunt Tessie said that Teddy and I should go out and play. She gave me a dollar for Teddy and I to have lunch at the Greek's.

When we returned there was an hour of daylight left. As it grew dark Mother began to remember. Aunt Tessie prepared supper. A half hour before Father returned from work Mother began to scream. Aunt Tessie brought her back to the hospital.

Mother's sisters, my aunts, Tessie, Zelda and Esther, took turns preparing meals for us and maintaining the house. As Aunt Zelda cooked, she glanced at Father's chair and said, "Poison I should put in." When serving supper Aunt Zelda would put a pungent steaming plate of something in front of Father and say, "Choke." Teddy and I she patted on the head and bribed with quarters to eat second and third helpings; there was no need for bribery, she was an excellent cook. Finally, Father arranged to have his Aunt Dora come and help out so that he could take his meals without recrimination. My aunts on Mother's side said Aunt Dora was a lousy housekeeper. In the morning before school I fixed breakfast for Teddy and myself. Aunt Dora would arrive around four-thirty, pick up, sweep and prepare the evening meal.

One day, about a week after Aunt Dora began coming to our house, Teddy got into a fight after school with a kid named Marvin Winkler. I think it was about marbles. I was told that Teddy put up a pretty good fight, but Marvin's sister Maxine stepped in and belted Teddy in the face. My class had been dismissed from school from an exit around the corner from where my brother's class had been dismissed. A kid in Teddy's class came running up and told me what happened.

Blood was gushing all over Teddy's chin and shirt. I bunched my tie up and pressed it under his nose. We ran home like that, Teddy holding the crumpled tie to his nose, me squeezing his nostrils shut with my free hand, Teddy running open-mouthed. I called Dr. Schacter, he was out, so Teddy and I went to the emergency room of Greenpoint Hospital. In a little while Doctor Schacter arrived. He conferred with several other doctors and they decided to keep Teddy in the hospital for a couple of days "under observation." Dr. Schacter said there was nothing to worry about, I could go home.

Aunt Dora had prepared supper and left: mushroom and barley soup, salad, hard-boiled eggs, gefilte fish with horse radish and rye bread. Father and I sat at the table, alone in the house. He drank a glass of schnapps and cracked a hard-boiled egg against the table top. The sound of the white egg cracking in the white kitchen crept into my ear, a soft white persistent noise. My ears were ringing. I watched Father's jaws working, his eyes gone, deeper than sleep, past all meditation, he ate. In my chest I felt the weight of a weeping that hadn't happened, my achey flesh recovering from something I couldn't remember. Father looked up, saw me thinking about Teddy and Mother. He swallowed and paused, "Yeah" he said, "it's a pity on them, they're sick people, they ain't healthy." He reached for the horse radish. I thought of running away to sea, like in the movies.

David Low

Winterblossom Garden

I have no photographs of my father. One hot Saturday in June, my camera slung over my shoulder, I take the subway from Greenwich Village to Chinatown. I switch to the M local which becomes an elevated train after it crosses the Williamsburg Bridge. I am going to Ridgewood, Queens, where I spent my childhood. I sit in a car that is almost empty; I feel the loud rumble of the whole train through the hard seat. Someday, I think, wiping the sweat from my face, they'll tear this el down, as they've torn down the others.

I get off at Fresh Pond Road and walk the five blocks from the station to my parents' restaurant. At the back of the store in the kitchen, I find my father packing an order: white cartons of food fit neatly into a brown paper bag. As the workers chatter in Cantonese, I smell the food cooking: spare ribs, chicken lo mein, sweet and pungent pork, won ton soup. My father, who has just turned seventy-three, wears a wrinkled white short-sleeve shirt and a cheap maroon tie, even in this weather. He dabs his face with a handkerchief.

"Do you need money?" he asks in Chinese, as he takes the order to the front of the store. I notice that he walks slower than usual. Not that his walk is ever very fast; he usually walks with quiet assurance, a man who knows who he is and where he is going. Other people will just have to wait until he gets there.

"Not this time," I answer in English. I laugh. I haven't borrowed money from him in years but he still asks. My father and I have almost always spoken different languages.

"I want to take your picture, Dad."

"Not now, too busy." He hands the customer the order

and rings the cash register.

"It will only take a minute."

He stands reluctantly beneath the green awning in front of the store, next to the gold-painted letters on the window:
WINTERBLOSSOM GARDEN
CHINESE-AMERICAN RESTAURANT
WE SERVE THE FINEST FOOD
I look through the camera viewfinder.

"Smile," I say.

Instead my father holds his left hand with the crooked pinky on his stomach. I have often wondered about that pinky; is it a souvenir of some street fight in his youth? He wears a jade ring on his index finger. His hair, streaked with gray, is greased down as usual; his face looks a little pale. Most of the day, he remains at the restaurant. I snap the shutter.

"Go see your mother," he says slowly in English.

According to my mother, in 1929 my father entered this country illegally by jumping off the boat as it neared Ellis Island and swimming to Hoboken, New Jersey; there he managed to board a train to New York, even though he knew no English and had not one American cent in his pockets. Whether or not the story is true, I like to imagine my father hiding in the washroom on the train, dripping wet with fatigue and feeling triumphant. Now he was in America, where anything could happen. He found a job scooping ice cream at a dance hall in Chinatown. My mother claims that before he married her, he liked to gamble his nights away and drink with scandalous women. After two years in this country, he opened his restaurant with money he had borrowed from friends in Chinatown who already ran their own businesses. My father chose Ridgewood for the store's location because he mistook the community's name for "Richwood." In such a lucky place, he told my mother, his restaurant was sure to succeed.

When I was growing up, my parents spent most of their days in Winterblossom Garden. Before going home after school, I would stop at the restaurant. The walls then were a hideous pale green with red numbers painted in Chinese characters and Roman numerals above the side booths. In days of warm weather huge fans whirred from the ceiling. My mother would sit at a table in the back where she would make egg rolls. She began by placing generous handfuls of meat-and-cabbage filling on squares of thin white dough. Then she delicately folded up each piece of dough, checking to make sure the filling was totally sealed inside, like a mummy wrapped in bandages. Finally, with a small brush she spread beaten eggs on the outside of each white roll. As I watched her steadily produce a tray of these uncooked creations, she never asked me about school; she was more concerned that my shirt was sticking out of my pants or that my hair was disheveled.

"Are you hungry?" my mother would ask in English. Although my parents had agreed to speak only Chinese in my presence, she often broke this rule when my father wasn't in the same room. Whether I wanted to eat or not, I was sent into the kitchen where my father would repeat my mother's question. Then without waiting for an answer, he would prepare for me a bowl of beef with snow peas or a small portion of steamed fish. My parents assumed that as long as I ate well, everything in my life would be fine. If I said "Hello" or "Thank you" in Chinese, I was allowed to choose whatever dish I liked; often I ordered a hot turkey sandwich. I liked the taste of burnt rice soaked in tea.

I would wait an hour or so for my mother to walk home with me. During that time, I would go to the front of the store, put a dime in the jukebox and press the buttons for a currently popular song. It might be D3: "Bye Bye, Love." Then I would lean on the back of the bench where customers waited for take-outs; I would stare out the large window that faced the street. The world outside seemed vast, hostile and often sad.

Across the way, I could see Rosa's Italian Bakery, the Western Union office and Von Ronn's soda fountain. Why didn't we live in Chinatown? I wondered. Or San Francisco? In a neighborhood that was predominantly German, I had no Chinese friends. No matter how many bottles of Coca-Cola I drank, I would still be different from the others. They were fond of calling me "Skinny Chink" when I won games of stoop ball. I wanted to have blond curly hair and blue eyes; I didn't understand why my father didn't have a ranch like the rugged cowboys on television.

Now Winterblossom Garden has wood-paneling on the walls, formica tables and aluminum Roman numerals over the mock-leather booths. Several years ago, when the ceiling was lowered, the whirring fans were removed; a huge air-conditioning unit was installed. The jukebox has been replaced by Muzak. My mother no longer makes the egg rolls; my father hires enough help to do that.

Some things remain the same. My father has made few changes in the menu, except for the prices; the steady customers know they can always have the combination plates. In a glass case near the cash register, cardboard boxes overflow with bags of fortune cookies and almond candies that my father gives away free to children. The first dollar bill my parents ever made hangs framed on the wall above the register. Next to that dollar, a picture of my parents taken twenty years ago recalls a time when they were raising four children at once, paying mortgages and putting in the bank every cent that didn't go toward bills. Although it was a hard time for them, my mother's face is radiant, as if she has just won the top prize at a beauty pageant; she wears a flower-print dress with a large white collar. My father has on a suit with wide lapels that was tailored in Chinatown; he is smiling a rare smile.

My parents have a small brick house set apart from the

other buildings on the block. Most of their neighbors have lived in Ridgewood all their lives. As I ring the bell and wait for my mother to answer, I notice that the maple tree in front of the house has died. All that is left is a gray ghost; bare branches lie in the gutter. If I took a picture of this tree, I think, the printed image would resemble a negative.

"The gas man killed it when they tore up the street," my mother says. She watches television as she lies back on the gold sofa like a queen, her head resting against a pillow. A documentary about wildlife in Africa is on the screen; gazelles dance across a dusty plain. My mother likes soap operas but they aren't shown on weekends. In the evenings she will watch almost anything except news specials and police melodramas.

"Why don't you get a new tree planted?"

"We would have to get a permit," she answers. "The sidewalk belongs to the city. Then we would have to pay for the tree."

"It would be worth it," I say. "Doesn't it bother you, seeing a dead tree everyday? You should find someone to cut it down."

My mother does not answer. She has fallen asleep. These days she can doze off almost as soon as her head touches the pillow. Six years ago she had a nervous breakdown. When she came home from the hospital she needed to take naps in the afternoon. Soon the naps became a permanent refuge, a way to forget her loneliness for an hour or two. She no longer needed to work in the store. Three of her children were married. I was away at art school and planned to live on my own when I graduated.

"I have never felt at home in America," my mother once told me.

Now as she lies there, I wonder if she is dreaming. I would like her to tell me her darkest dream. Although we speak the same language, there has always been an ocean between us. She does not wish to know what I think alone at night, what I see of the world with my camera.

My mother pours two cups of tea from the porcelain
teapot that has always been in its wicker basket on the
kitchen table. On the sides of the teapot, a maiden dressed in
a jade-green gown visits a bearded emperor at his palace near
the sky. The maiden waves a vermillion fan.

"I bet you still don't know how to cook," my mother
says. She places a plate of steamed roast pork buns before
me.

"Mom, I'm not hungry."

"If you don't eat more, you will get sick."

I take a bun from the plate but it is too hot. My mother
hands me a napkin so I can put the bun down. Then she
peels a banana in front of me.

"I'm not obsessed with food like you," I say.

"What's wrong with eating?"

She looks at me as she takes a big bite of the banana.

"I'm going to have a photography show at the end of the
summer."

"Are you still taking pictures of old buildings falling
down? How ugly! Why don't you take happier pictures?"

"I thought you would want to come," I answer. "It's not
easy to get a gallery."

"If you were married," she says, her voice becoming unusually soft, "you would take better pictures. You would be
happy."

"I don't know what you mean. Why do you think
getting married will make me happy?"

My mother looks at me as if I have spoken in Serbo-
Croatian. She always gives me this look when I say something
she does not want to hear. She finishes the banana; then she
puts the plate of food away. Soon she stands at the sink,
turns on the hot water and washes dishes. My mother learned
long ago that silence has a power of its own.

She takes out a blue cookie tin from the dining room cabinet. Inside this tin, my mother keeps her favorite photographs. Whenever I am ready to leave, my mother brings it to the living room and opens it on the coffee table. She knows I cannot resist looking at these pictures again; I will sit down next to her on the sofa for at least another hour. Besides the portraits of the family, my mother has images of people I have never met: her father who owned a poultry store on Pell Street and didn't get a chance to return to China before he died; my father's younger sister who still runs a pharmacy in Rio de Janeiro (she sends the family an annual supply of cough drops); my mother's cousin Kay who died at thirty, a year after she came to New York from Hong Kong. Although my mother has a story to tell for each photograph, she refuses to speak about Kay, as if the mere mention of her name will bring back her ghost to haunt us all.

My mother always manages to find a picture I have not seen before; suddenly I discover I have a relative who is a mortician in Vancouver. I pick up a portrait of Uncle Lao-Hu, a silver-haired man with a goatee who owned a curio shop on Mott Street until he retired last year and moved to Hawaii. In a color print, he stands in the doorway of his store, holding a bamboo Moon Man in front of him, as if it were a bowling trophy. The statue, which is actually two feet tall, has a staff in its left hand, while its right palm balances a peach, a sign of long life. The top of the Moon Man's head protrudes in the shape of an eggplant; my mother believes that such a head contains an endless wealth of wisdom.

"Your Uncle Lao-Hu is a wise man, too," my mother says, "except when he's in love. When he still owned the store, he fell in love with his women customers all the time. He was always losing money because he gave away his merchandise to any woman who smiled at him."

I see my uncle's generous arms full of gifts: a silver Buddha, an ivory dragon, a pair of emerald chopsticks.

"These women confused him," she adds. "That's what

happens when a Chinese man doesn't get married."

My mother shakes her head and sighs.

"In his last letter, Lao-Hu invited me to visit him in Honolulu. Your father refuses to leave the store."

"Why don't you go anyway?"

"I can't leave your father alone." She stares at the pictures scattered on the coffee table.

"Mom, why don't you do something for yourself? I thought you were going to start taking English lessons."

"Your father thinks it would be a waste of time."

While my mother puts the cookie tin away, I stand up to stretch my legs. I gaze at a photograph that hangs on the wall above the sofa: my parents' wedding picture. My mother was matched to my father; she claims that if her own father had been able to repay the money that Dad spent to bring her to America, she might never have married him at all. In the wedding picture she wears a stunned expression. She is dressed in a luminous gown of ruffles and lace; the train spirals at her feet. As she clutches a bouquet tightly against her stomach, she might be asking, "What am I doing? Who is this man?" My father's face is thinner than it is now. His tuxedo is too small for him; the flower in his lapel droops. He hides his hand with the crooked pinky behind his back.

I have never been sure if my parents really love each other. I have only seen them kiss at their children's weddings. They never touch each other in public. When I was little, I often thought they went to sleep in the clothes they wore to work.

Before I leave, my mother asks me to take her picture. Unlike my father she likes to pose for photographs as much as possible. When her children still lived at home, she would leave snapshots of herself all around the house; we could not forget her, no matter how hard we tried.

She changes her blouse, combs her hair and redoes her eyebrows. Then I follow her out the back door into the garden where she kneels down next to the rose bush. She touches one of the yellow roses.

"Why don't you sit on the front steps?" I ask, as I peer through the viewfinder. "It will be more natural."

"No," she says firmly. "Take the picture now."

She smiles without opening her mouth. I see for the first time that she has put on a pair of dangling gold earrings. Her face has grown round as the moon with the years. She has developed wrinkles under the eyes, but like my father, she hardly shows her age. For the past ten years, she has been fifty-one. Everyone needs a fantasy to help them stay alive: my mother believes she is perpetually beautiful, even if my father has not complimented her in years.

After I snap the shutter, she plucks a rose.

As we enter the kitchen through the back door, I can hear my father's voice from the next room.

"Who's he talking to?" I ask.

"He's talking to the goldfish," she answers. "I have to live with this man."

My father walks in, carrying a tiny can of fish food.

"You want a girlfriend?" he asks, out of nowhere. "My friend has a nice daughter. She knows how to cook Chinese food."

"Dad, she sounds perfect for you."

"She likes to stay home," my mother adds. "She went to college and reads books like you."

"I'll see you next year," I say.

That evening in the darkroom at my apartment, I develop and print my parents' portraits. I hang the pictures side by side to dry on a clothesline in the bathroom. As I feel my parents' eyes staring at me, I turn away. Their faces look unfamiliar in the fluorescent light.

II

At the beginning of July my mother calls me at work.

"Do you think you can take off next Monday morning?" she asks.

"Why?"

"Your father has to go to the hospital for some tests. He looks awful."

We sit in the back of a taxi on the way to a hospital in Forest Hills. I am sandwiched between my mother and father. The skin of my father's face is pale yellow. During the past few weeks he has lost fifteen pounds; his wrinkled suit is baggy around the waist. My mother sleeps with her head tilted to one side until the taxi hits a bump on the road. She wakes up startled, as if afraid she has missed a stop on the train.

"Don't worry," my father says weakly. He squints as he turns his head toward the window. "The doctors will give me pills. Everything will be fine."

"Don't say anything," my mother says. "Too much talk will bring bad luck."

My father takes two crumpled dollar bills from his jacket and places them in my hand.

"For the movies," he says. I smile, without mentioning it costs more to go to a film these days.

My mother opens her handbag and takes out a compact. She has forgotten to put on her lipstick.

The hospital waiting room has beige walls. My mother and I follow my father as he makes his way slowly to a row of seats near an open window.

"Fresh air is important," he used to remind me on a sunny day when I would read a book in bed. Now after we sit down, he keeps quiet. I hear the sound of plates clattering from the coffee shop in the next room.

"Does anyone want some breakfast?" I ask.

"Your father can't eat anything before the tests," my

mother warns.

"What about you?"

"I'm not hungry," she says.

My father reaches over to take my hand in his. He considers my palm.

"Very, very lucky," he says. "You will have lots of money."

I laugh. "You've been saying that ever since I was born."

He puts on his glasses crookedly and touches a curved line near the top of my palm.

"Be patient," he says.

My mother rises suddenly.

"Why are they making us wait so long? Do you think they forgot us?"

While she walks over to speak to a nurse at the reception desk, my father leans toward me.

"Remember to take care of your mother."

The doctors discover that my father has stomach cancer. They decide to operate immediately. According to them, my father has already lost so much blood that it is a miracle he is still alive.

The week of my father's operation, I sleep at my parents' house. My mother has kept my bedroom on the second floor the way it was before I moved out. A square room, it gets the afternoon light. Dust covers the top of my old bookcase. The first night I stay over I find a pinhole camera on a shelf in the closet; I made it when I was twelve from a cylindrical Quaker Oats box. When I lie back on the yellow comforter that covers my bed, I see the crack in the ceiling that I once called the Yangtze River, the highway for tea merchants and vagabonds.

At night I help my mother close the restaurant. I do what she and my father have done together for the past forty-three years. At ten o'clock I turn off the illuminated white sign above the front entrance. After all the customers leave and the last waiter says goodbye, I lock the front door and flip over the sign that says "Closed." Then I shut off the radio and the back lights. While I refill the glass case with bottles of duck sauce and packs of cigarettes, my mother empties the cash register. She puts all the money in white cartons and packs them in brown paper bags. My father thought up that idea long ago.

In the past when they have walked the three blocks home, they have given the appearance of carrying bags of food. The one time my father was attacked by three teen-agers, my mother was sick in bed. My father scared the kids off by pretending he knew kung fu. When he got home, he showed me his swollen left hand and smiled.

"Don't tell your mother."

On the second night we walk home together, my mother says:

"I could never run the restaurant alone. I would have to sell it. I have four children and no one wants it."

I say nothing, unwilling to start an argument.

Later my mother and I eat jello in the kitchen. A cool breeze blows through the window.

"Maybe I will sleep tonight," my mother says. She walks out to the back porch to sit on one of the two folding chairs. My bedroom is right above the porch; as a child I used to hear my parents talking late into the night, their paper fans rustling.

After reading a while in the living room, I go upstairs to take a shower. When I am finished, I hear my mother calling my name from downstairs.

I find her dressed in her bathrobe, opening the dining room cabinet.

"Someone has stolen the money," she says. She walks nervously into the living room and looks under the lamp table.

"What are you talking about?" I ask.

"Maybe we should call the police," she suggests. "I can't find the money we brought home tonight."

She starts to pick up the phone.

"Wait. Have you checked everywhere? Where do you usually put it?"

"I thought I locked it in your father's closet but it isn't there."

"I'll look around," I say. "Why don't you go back to sleep?"

She lies back on the sofa.

"How can I sleep?" she asks. "I told your father a long time ago to sell the restaurant but he wouldn't listen."

I search the first floor. I look in the shoe closet, behind the television, underneath the dining room table, in the clothes hamper. Finally after examining all the kitchen cupboards without any luck, I open the refrigerator to take out something to drink. The three cartons of money are on the second shelf, next to the mayonnaise and the strawberry jam.

When I bring the cartons to the living room, my mother sits up on the sofa, amazed.

"Well," she says, "how did they ever get *there*?"

She opens one of them. The crisp dollar bills inside are cold as ice.

The next day I talk on the telephone to my father's physician. He informs me that the doctors have succeeded in removing the malignancy before it has spread. My father will remain in intensive care for at least a week.

In the kitchen my mother irons a tablecloth.

"The doctors are impressed by Dad's willpower, considering his age," I tell her.

"A fortune teller on East Broadway told him that he will live to be a hundred," she says.

That night I dream that I am standing at the entrance to Winterblossom Garden. A taxi stops in front of the store. My father jumps out, dressed in a bathrobe and slippers.

"I'm almost all better," he tells me. "I want to see how the business is doing without me."

In a month my father is ready to come home. My sister Elizabeth, the oldest child, picks him up at the hospital. At the house the whole family waits for him.

When Elizabeth's car arrives my mother and I are already standing on the front steps. My sister walks around the car to open my father's door. He cannot get out by himself. My sister offers him a hand but as he reaches out to grab it, he misses and falls back in his seat.

Finally my sister helps him stand up, his back a little stooped. While my mother remains on the steps, I run to give a hand.

My father does not fight our help. His skin is dry and pale but no longer yellow. As he walks forward, staring at his feet, I feel his whole body shaking against mine. Only now, as he leans his weight on my arm, do I begin to understand how easily my father might have died. He seems light as a sparrow.

When we reach the front steps, my father raises his head to look at my mother. She stares at him a minute, then turns away to open the door. Soon my sister and I are leading him to the living room sofa, where we help him lie back. My mother has a pillow and a blanket ready. She sits down on the coffee table in front of him. I watch them hold each other's hands.

III

At the beginning of September my photography exhibit opens at a cooperative gallery on West 13th Street. I have chosen to hang only a dozen pictures, not much to show for ten years of work. About sixty people come to the opening, more than I expected; I watch them from a corner of the room, now and then overhearing a conversation I would like to ignore.

After an hour I decide I have stayed too long. As I walk around the gallery, hunting for a telephone, I see my parents across the room. My father calls out my name in Chinese; he has gained back all his weight and appears to be in better shape than many of the people around him. As I make my way toward my parents, I hear him talking loudly in bad English to a short young woman who stares at one of my portraits.

"That's my wife," he says. "If you like it, you should buy it."

"Maybe I will," the young woman says. She points to another photograph. "Isn't that you?"

My father laughs. "No, that's my brother."

My mother hands me a brown paper bag.

"Leftover from dinner," she tells me. "You didn't tell me you were going to show my picture. It's the best one in the show."

I take my parents for a personal tour.

"Who is that?" my father asks. He stops at a photograph of a naked woman covered from the waist down by a pile of leaves as she sits in the middle of a forest.

"She's a professional model," I lie.

"She needs to gain some weight," my mother says.

A few weeks after my show has closed, I have lunch with my parents at the restaurant. After we finish our meal, my father walks into the kitchen to scoop ice cream for dessert. My mother opens her handbag. She takes out a worn manila envelope and hands it to me across the table.

"I found this in a box while I was cleaning the house," she says. "I want you to have it."

Inside the envelope, I find a portrait of my father, taken when he was still a young man. He does not smile but his eyes shine like wet black marbles. He wears a polka-dot tie; a plaid handkerchief hangs out of the front pocket of his suit jacket. My father has never cared about his clothes matching. Even when he was young, he liked to grease down his hair with brilliantine.

"Your father's cousin was a doctor in Hong Kong," my mother tells me. "After my eighteenth birthday, he came to my parents' house and showed them this picture. He said your father would make the perfect husband because he was handsome and very smart. Grandma gave me the picture before I got on the boat to America."

"I'll have it framed right away."

My father returns with three dishes of chocolate ice cream balanced on a silver tray.

"You want to work here?" he asks me.

"Your father wants to sell the business next year," my mother says. "He feels too old to run a restaurant."

"I'd just lose money," I say. "Besides, Dad, you're not old."

He does not join us for dessert. Instead, he dips his napkin in a glass of water and starts to wipe the table. I watch his dish of ice cream melt.

When I am ready to leave, my parents walk me to the door.

"Next time, I'll take you uptown to see a movie," I say as we step outside.

"Radio City?" my father asks.

"They don't show movies there now," my mother reminds him.

"I'll cook dinner for you at my apartment."

My father laughs.

"We'll eat out," my mother suggests.

My parents wait in front of Winterblossom Garden until I reach the end of the block. I turn and wave. With her heels on, my mother is the same height as my father. She waves back for both of them. I would like to take their picture, but I forgot to bring my camera.

Jocelyn Hausmann

Offices of Instruction

When my mother read to us, her voice wasn't like a woman's voice. She sat on the couch and read chapters from long books. It was night, and my father was at work. He took the violin wrapped in chamois in the leather case and played at the hotel in the city. He walked across the livingroom and the front porch. He had a dark moustache, and his hair was white and thick next to his ears. When he was home my mother was with him, and her voice was like a woman's. But when he was gone she changed. She read the long books that were always adventures, and her voice was different.

When my father was there her legs were long and smooth. She wore the red silk robe in the mornings and sat on the bed with the coffee cup. She laughed, and her hair was loose on her neck; and when she said my father's name her voice turned. But when she read to us I thought that Christ must have had a voice like that. She wore thick cotton socks, and her legs had lumps and veins on them. And I make the voice in my head like that voice, at first a boy's and then a young man's.

My father was always the same. Sometimes he was furious, and Allen and I were afraid. Still he was the same; when he chased us with his belt to stop our fighting, it was the same as when he would get us. We would run and jump under the covers. He would tickle us through the comforter, and his hands were just on the edge of being too strong.

Sometimes when he went to the avenue to buy something he would take me. I'd sit in the front seat of the car next to him. He always bought me something. Sometimes it was only ice-cream or candy, but once it was a dark blue skirt with embroidery on it. We saw it in the window on 86th Street, and he looked at it a long time. I didn't say anything. I just followed him inside, and he bought it. When we got home my mother laughed like a woman, and I didn't want the skirt.

In the summer my father worked in the mountains. He would go first, and then when school was out we'd ride the train out of the city. The trains were shiny and blue and elegant, and when we rode them my mother was beautiful. We'd sit in the club car, and men in gray suits would light her cigarettes. She wore full dresses made out of silk or fine cotton like a handerchief. Her hands were long, and she moved her shoulders slightly when she talked. She didn't wear make-up, but she had crystal bottles of French perfume. She put them on the tops of the dressers in the cottages we stayed at in the mountains, and she and my father took long naps in the afternoons. Allen and I would play under the pine trees, and sometimes I would look up at the shaded windows of their bedroom.

Claire was my mother's younger sister. She had long blond braids. She came to our house after school and sat in the kitchen. She and my mother talked, and Claire felt the silky ends of her braids. When we went to Grandmother's house, Claire would swing me on the sidewalk. "Allen is too big," she'd say. Then she'd put her hands under my arms and swing me around and around. My legs would go sailing out, and I felt that I was flying.

Then Claire got sick. It was cold, and we walked up the hill to 92nd Street. Allen and I got under my mother's big coat, and the shadow swayed on the sidewalk in front of us: a fat woman with six legs. Grandmother's house was at the top of the hill, and it had a round tower with a roof like a witch's hat. Claire had rheumatic fever, and Dr. Simone said she had to go to the sanitarium to protect her heart. Grandmother took her in the shiny black car, and they let us kiss her. "It isn't contagious," Grandmother said, and they drove away.

After what seemed a long time, we went to see Claire. It was raining, and we drove up through the city. The sanitarium was on the palisades above the river, and it was built of gray stone. It had gardens with white marble benches, but it was raining and Allen and I had to wait inside. We sat in a big room that my mother called the winter garden. The floor was red tile, and there was a fountain coming out of the wall. The water came out of the open mouth of a dull green face. It was a man's face, but it had horns half-hidden in its curling hair, and the water gushed out from between the curving lips into a marble basin. The marble was cool, and Allen and I put our faces against it. Then my mother and father came back with Claire. I saw that she'd cut off her braids, and I wanted to touch her hair.

The room was bright, even on the rainy day, and Claire's hair looked silvery. She had on a gray dress and sheer stockings. The skirt swung across her knees as she walked, and when I put my arms around her waist my cheek pressed against the place between her breasts and her hips.

She would come home next week, she said. When she bent to kiss Allen, her loose hair slid across itself and over the curve of her breasts. And for the first time she had on lipstick, the dark red of the nineteen-fifties, of the platinum-haired women in magazines, and in the movies we went to on Saturday afternoons. The women I always noticed after that. I would squirm on the prickly seat when they swung their hard satin-covered hips and lifted the curled hair at the backs of their necks.

When Claire came home she was different. At first she was quiet. She just sat, sometimes in the wicker chair around the curve of the porch and other times upstairs in the round room in the tower. And she didn't stop at our house after school any more, or swing me around the sidewalk. After a while she stopped sitting and began to be always moving, walking down to the water alone, or around the big house, climbing the stairs slowly, moving through the rooms in the cotton dresses and saddle shoes that seemed all wrong, now, with the loose, sliding hair and high-boned cheeks. And when I went to the house I wanted to be near her. I didn't want to play with her or talk. I wanted to be next to her without her knowing. So I climbed the stairs after she did, so quietly that I could hear my own breath and sat in the dark hallways outside the rooms she sat in, listening for the sounds she made when she moved on the other side of doors.

And she always wore the lipstick, dark like the movie women but different on her; and yet not like the princesses in Grandmother's thin green story book, princesses who suffered and wore long, high-waisted dresses and were always saved. Their lips were red and slightly thin like Claire's. But she wasn't like them because I never liked those stories. They were never real. I couldn't feel the night in them or hear water or men's voices at a distance the way I could in the books my mother read us. The princesses were like the queens on playing cards, and their feet were too small. Claire was real. She had fine hairs on the top of her legs and veins on her wrists, and the inside of her mouth was dark pink.

That summer we went away to the mountains for the last time, riding the train through the blue mountains to a high place where we could see for a long way. When we got there my mother was angry. Allen and I couldn't stay with them at the hotel. My father had arranged for us to board with some people who lived in the country. My mother sat against the door in the car and looked out the window. "If I'd known I wouldn't have come," she said. But Allen touched my leg with his in the back seat because we didn't like staying at the hotels where we had to dress for meals and break the dinner rolls into dainty pieces. If I slouched in my chair or took the wrong fork my father would give a disapproving look, and I'd feel ashamed. I wanted to grow up so I'd never feel ashamed again.

The people we were to stay with were named Grace and

Ronnie, and before we went to their house we went to my
parents' rooms at the hotel. The rooms were like all the
others my parents lived in, even their bedroom at home,
because my father had come into them and brought his wine-
colored robe and whiskey and put his cigarettes and money
on the dresser. There was also the violin and the spiral note-
books that he wrote the music into. The notes weren't separate and distinct like the ones in my piano book at home.
They were intricate and racing, and when I tried to read them
I got lost.

Allen and I knew about the violin. There were parts of it
that should never be touched: the strings above the bridge,
the white hairs of the bow, the resin-dusted wood over the
sound post. But neither of us had ever touched any of it. I'd
look at it carefully when no one was around, bending over
the case lying open on a chair. I could tell from looking that
it was old, but it wasn't old the way things in museums were.
The wood was worn and imperfect like the back of an antique
chair, but the resin dust under the strings was new, and my
father took it and played it.

The violin was there that day in the sittingroom,
unwrapped in the velvet-lined case. My parents had a drink,
and Allen and I sat on the sofa and drank our ginger ale
politely. I looked at Allen and at the leather case lying open,
showing its dark red lining. And when my parents took their
nap we touched the violin. First Allen touched it, then I did.
We held it by the neck and put it under our chins. We took
the bows with their loosened hair out of the top of the case
and touched the mother of pearl handles and the thickened
wood at the head that bent back and gave the bows their
spring. Then we opened the compartments in the case and
touched the spare strings, and bridges, and mutes, and
opened the velvet bags of resin. And before my mother
laughed in the next room, and we knew they were awake, we
had put it all back without touching any of the places that
should never be touched.

All summer Allen and I lived with the couple at the house in the country. The man had flat, oily hair, and the woman was always afraid. She bent her head to the side when she talked, and her hand shook when she poured the coffee. Once at breakfast she upset the cup, and the coffee burned her thigh. She jumped up, and the man left his plate on the table and went to work.

Sometimes she would stand at the sink with her hands in dish water and look out the window at the field behind the house. When the man came home he worked in the basement or read his paper in the brown chair in the parlour, and they never touched each other.

There was a field away from the house, down from the wide, treeless yard, a field with blackeyed susans, and chickory, and queen anne's lace. And sometimes there were cows that belonged to someone we never saw. I was afraid of the cows because they were thick and heavy and silent. Allen would shout at them and wave his arms, and they would stare at him, just stare, with the flies clustered around their eyes and their skinny tails flicking. When he ran at them they would run off a little way. Their hoofs made a heavy, danger-ous sound, and they would look back over their shoulders and stare stupidly.

Beyond the fields were woods. Allen and I found a secret place there, a room with trees for walls and a rock floor with steps broken out of the sides of it. The steps led to plat-forms covered with moss and pineneedles. And in the middle of the rock floor there was a crack and a small triangular hole. If you looked in the hole, it was dark and empty, but if you put your ear against it you could hear water running under the ground.

Sometimes we would go deep into the woods and be gone all morning. When we got back the woman would be hanging the wash by the side of the house or vacuuming the livingroom, and when we told her how far we'd gone she'd always say the same thing. She'd look up from whatever it was she was doing and tell us no, that we were being silly, that we couldn't have gone that far because she had heard our voices the whole time.

Once when my parents came to get us at the house, I could tell that my mother had been crying. They came in the Pontiac, and my father sat behind the wheel. My mother got out of the other side, and her eyes were swollen. We got in, and my father drove slowly, and they talked. I understood from what they said that Claire had run away. She had taken only the small blue suitcase, the one the doll had come in, the doll with long blond braids and gingham dress. Claire had kept the doll in the suitcase under her bed. She had never played with it, but when I came to visit she would take it out so that I could see. Now she had taken the doll out and filled the suitcase with other things and run away all by herself.

Two years later Claire came home. Grandmother called one night to tell us she was on the way. Claire had called from Baltimore, and she was coming home to stay. She was married now and she had a baby. She and her husband were driving up from Baltimore. I kept thinking of the car traveling the highway with Claire and the man and the baby inside it. I imagined the man having brown hair, but I couldn't see his face, only his loose shoulders and careful hands. But Claire's face was clear, and she was still beautiful.

Grandmother said the man's name was Jim. The baby's name was Sherry. I wished they'd chosen a different name because I thought Sherry sounded cheap. When we visited Great Grandmother in her apartment in Brooklyn Heights, Great Grandmother and my mother always drank sherry from crystal glasses. I took sips from my mother's glass, and the wine was thick and sweet. But it seemed cheap to name a baby after wine.

Sherry had curly hair, and I thought all babies should have hair like that. I sat in the rocking chair and held her.

Her arms and legs were fat. But Jim and Claire didn't bathe her, and Sherry had scabs behind her ears, and her skin looked gray. She reached her hand back on the stairs to grab at my mouth, and I saw the old dirt on the inside of her arm and the gray splotches where water had splashed.

Claire was pregnant, and when Jim moved to kiss her at the bedroom door, she turned away. She stood in the doorway in the fancy blue bathrobe, and her hair was curled too sharply behind. Jim turned without a kiss, and Sherry crawled quickly down the hall toward the open front door. Her fat hands slapped on the oily floor. She sat up and her bottom flattened out. Claire nudged Sherry with her foot, moving her so the door would close. It was raw outside, and the wind gusted suddenly into the hallway, fluttering against the walls and rattling the framed pictures and the sliding parlour doors.

I came on Saturday mornings to play with Sherry, to choose and iron one of the wrinkled dresses crammed into the bureau in the corner of the nursery. I would polish her shoes and search for socks and bathe her downstairs in the sink in the kitchen. And on Saturday mornings Grandmother would be gone. She would have gotten up early to hide her car from Jim, driving it miles away and taking the bus back from wherever she parked it and not coming back until late in the morning. She had put her car in Jim's name as well as her own, and now she had changed her mind, so she had to hide it from him.

That morning I ironed a plaid dress for Sherry. It had a white collar, and I found a plaid ribbon to put in her hair. We played in the upstairs hall, and the wind blew around the corners of the house, and the old house rattled and creaked. I took Sherry down to the nursery and closed the door. I could hear the television through the register in the floor, and I knew that Claire must be watching it in the livingroom. I got Sherry to call through the register. "Mama," she said, "Mama," and she slapped at the grate, and Claire came into the square of floor we could see and waved up at us and laughed. "Hello, Baby," she said. Then she walked away, and I looked down on the top of her head for a second and her big, pregnant belly sticking out in the blue robe.

Grandmother didn't come back from hiding the car that morning, and when I went home at noon Sherry crawled out of the livingroom and sat in the hall to watch me go. She started coughing, and Claire lifted her up by her arms to make her stop. I walked home, and the wind pressed into my coat and chilled the satin lining. The streets were empty, and the branches of the sycamores creaked and rattled against each other. I ran the last block with my bare hands over my ears, moaning as I jumped up the brick stoop and across the porch.

Allen had built a fire, and he was sitting in front of it in his underwear, poking at the coals and lifting the split pieces of wood so that the fire would roar up. His legs were covered with dark hair, and he had the knee of one leg up so I could see the dent inside at the top of his thigh. I looked up at his face because I didn't want to see the lumpy mound in his soft shorts.

I turned away from Allen and went to my bedroom to put my coat away. That's when my mother called out to me. She and my father were lying in bed. She had her head on my father's chest, and he was playing with the hair on the back of her neck, lifting it and curling it around his fingers. She had the sheet pulled up under her arms, but her back was naked, the sheet angling off over the curve of her hip. I stood in the doorway. It wasn't my mother's room. It was his, his desk and bureau, and his side of the bed with the pillow that smelled like him. And always when my mother was with him she was different. He would touch her the way he was now, twisting the hair around his fingers, and she would laugh in that woman's way of laughing

But when they fought she cried. She'd lay on the bed with her face turned; that was her woman's crying. It wasn't like her real crying. Her turned face made me feel ashamed, and I wanted her to stop. It was always the same when they fought. My father would yell, and his face would be horrible, and they would argue. Then she would go and lie on the bed like that, and my father would wait and apologize.

I stood in the doorway because it was his room. He had never told me not to come in; still I wouldn't have. All the things my mother owned were things I could use, and her body was comfortable. When I was small her arm had reached out and picked up the things I couldn't reach, but even my father's sweat was different. Like the undershirt I'd found in the livingroom one morning. If it had been something of my mother's I'd have thrown it in the hamper, but I'd just stood there holding it. Finally I'd left it on the chair and gone back to my bedroom. Because the undershirt was like the violin, and the whiskey, and the quick music, and the papers pigeon-holed in the desk. And my mother became that way, too, when he touched her, and she laughed in bed.

Marilyn was my friend then, and that afternoon I went to the movies with her. She was the prettiest girl in school, and her breasts were beginning to show. It was a Dracula movie. There was a blond woman in a white nightgown and a bed with curtains around it. The bat fluttered down and crawled across the bedspread while the woman slept. The bat was lumpy, and it jerked when it crawled over the soft bedspread. Marilyn yelled at the woman to wake up, and she did. Then it happened again, and the bat landed on the woman's neck. It lay there twitching, moving its wings against her hair, and I wished that I could joke about it the way mother would have. Marilyn gasped next to me in the dark. The woman's breasts lifted, and her hands moved and fell back against the sheet. I was angry with Marilyn because she was being stupid. She said, "Oh, God," in the darkness and gasped again, and it made me angry. The bat sucked blood from the woman's neck, and its wings moved slowly and rhythmically like a heartbeat. I could feel my own pulse beating in my throat, and I wanted the bat to finish and fly away.

After the movie was over I didn't go to Marilyn's house the way I usually did. I didn't want to go into her bedroom and talk about boys. I told her I had to go out with my parents, and I walked home with my coat open, hoping the wind would blow the stale movie theatre smell off my clothes.

On Monday night Grandmother came. She stood in the livingroom with her coat on. My father was getting ready for work, and he came down the stairs in his tuxedo. He looked at Grandmother standing there, and he said, "What's wrong?" "They didn't think," she said, and then she told us. Dr. Simone had gone out into the hall and called the other doctor and the nurse, and they stood in the room together, the two men and the woman, just there, looking at the baby, at Sherry, sealed in the tent. "Come look; she's so lovely," he'd said. They'd thought that she was all right. They hadn't been worried. He was leaving, but he'd wanted them to see her, and then the bubble came out of her mouth, and she died. I always wondered about the bubble and the room with the curtained screens around the bed.

There were white, louvered screens behind the coffin, and people looked and said she was pretty in the plaid dress. She was dead, and Claire lifted her out of the coffin. The arms fell back, and I grabbed the wooden chair, afraid something awful might happen because she wasn't real any more. Claire was crying. "I'll never," she said. The black dress was tight across her pregnant belly and Jim pulled on her shoulders. My mother's hand was white on the wooden chair, and her face was angry.

"Mother's trying to pretend it didn't happen." My mother had said that about Grandmother. My parents were in the kitchen. I heard the ice clink when my father moved his glass, and I drew a line to diagram the next sentence. There was a place for each word. "But Alexis told me," she said, "Claire beat her with the cord from the old iron." And I stopped with my hand on the book, the sentence half put away, the lines waiting like empty shelves. "She beat her until they had to put her to bed. That's what caused the pneumonia." Her voice had been angry and white like her hand on the back of the wooden chair.

The slatted chairs were neat, and the first row was empty. My father put his head down and pressed his hand across his eyes hard until his fingers were white. Jim pulled on Claire's shoulders, and her hold on the body loosened, and the body slipped back inside the soft coffin, but the arms were crooked.

"Pneumonia drowns you," my mother said. We were in Grandmother's bathroom. "Your lungs fill with water." I sat on the edge of the tub and blew a spit bubble between my tongue and teeth. My mother sat on the toilet with her black skirt gathered up around her hips. There was a noise from downstairs. Someone laughed, and I heard the toilet paper roll bump against the wall. My mother wiped herself, pulling the paper up between her thighs to look at it. And then she just sat there looking at the folded paper that was slightly bloody. "Look," she said, and she held it out to me. There was a small thing on the toilet paper, round and soft like a bubble of soft flesh.

"I was pregnant," she said. "That was the beginning of it. It would have been a person like you or Allen." I bent closer and looked at the small fleshy thing, and it amazed me.

Lew McCreary

Static Discharge

The things it never does any good to protest. With our only son, Billy Frank, Jr., in a Mexican jail for having been intercepted with something illegal strapped to his leg. With daughter Mary Jo making daily visits to the shot-doctor for "vitamins," leaving her probably autistic child in a playpen fitted with baubles and color television. There are far too many opportunities, if you know what I mean.

And last week I discovered Billy Frank, Sr. sitting alone, as quiet as you please, in his car in the dark garage. It was eleven o'clock at night. He claimed he'd been home for almost five hours, but I never heard the electric door slide up, never heard the car pull in, and never (I don't think I'd have missed *this*) heard the metal scream where the door binds in its track on the way back down. That's the thing: these days you can hardly come home without being noticed. There are too many adjectives that go along with common movements and separate them each from the other.

He said he'd been thinking. Well, that's perfectly okay. We all think, don't we? But to sit for five hours in an automobile and listen to a football game on a radio with rotten reception when there's a terrific color televison inside and a dinner to put in front of it, that's peculiar (if he's telling the truth; if not, I don't know what to call it). And in all that time the only thing I did that was out of the ordinary was take a wrong number from a party making an emergency call to the service department of a company that merchandises copying machines. I also listened to the symphony on the radio while dinner got clammy. And the paper-boy came to collect (perhaps, now that I think of it, Billy Frank came home while I was upstairs getting change).

Since when does a football game take five hours? There's a good answer for every stupid question: you listen to the pre-game show, then the first half, then halftime, then the second half, then the overtime period in case of a tie, then the post-game wrap-up. And then, after all of that (just to kind of unwind), you listen while some mean-spirited creep takes calls from lonesome strangers and gives you the opportunity to pretend you're thinking. So that when you beep the horn by accident and your wife finds you just sitting in your car, you have something to say by way of explanation. Well, I wish I had my own car. I wish there were a special place for me in the green glow of radio light. I'd go out for a ride every evening around rush-hour and try to find that fabled narrowing of the road where everything goes faster for a while. Bernoulli's Principle, which I remember from school and studying the properties of liquids. Can it possibly work?

The other night on television, I saw an actress selling the kind of camera where the picture develops in your hand. She aimed the thing right at me, and for just a second I hoped I could watch myself emerge from a blank. And then I realized it had to be the movie crew she was snapping. I thought how courageous it would be if they let us all see the technicians and equipment humming away in the ring of shade beyond all the lights it must take. Why courageous? I don't know, but I remember when Jerry Lewis used to run around the studio during his show years ago, trying to get one camera to take the picture of another camera. I used to laugh so hard at that. A better word is honest. I get fairly bored and upset thinking about things like this until I remember how much they amuse me. You could probably go on forever amusing yourself if it never occurred to you how stupid you were being. But you always seem to reach the point of becoming ashamed. Even when I'm alone I think there must be someone watching and evaluating, as if thoughts were audible. The temptation is to be always worthwhile, to impress the secret evaluators. Ha-ha! I keep thinking that if one camera took the other one's picture, they would both explode, beginning a long chain of explosions, the booms getting closer to our house block by block.

My daughter and her husband have produced a damaged infant. But he isn't a moron. He is only disturbed. Actually, we're not really sure about Mary Jo's kid, a boy named Nick. We have two medical opinions to choose from, one good, one bad. A third could ice the cake one way or the other, though it might just create more confusion. I don't see this nice young couple rushing off to a new specialist yet, so perhaps they prefer things to remain happily in balance. However, Cora, Mary Jo's domestic, is eager to join the lobbying. And she could upset the whole apple-cart. She swears the child's a "sleeping giant," a phrase I imagine she heard on television, probably the news, perhaps while looking over Nick's shoulder as she dusted him one day. I'm not sure what she means by it, but it sounds like a compliment.

He really does have his very own TV set. A little color console that his father made special brackets for. It attaches to the bars of the playpen. And mirrors. So that if he has trouble getting to a sitting position, he can still find an angle from which to watch. He can have his jolts of the world straight on or reversed. Nick. A little boy. I have spent many hours resting quietly in a chair by the window in his nursery, watching him watch. And I have no opinion at all. They show such crap on television. If it weren't for Nick's feelings, whatever they are, I would leave the room. Honestly. His father thinks it will help. But wouldn't it just be better to rig him up in a sling in front of the window? Wouldn't he be happier watching something real? Dangling like an asparagus fern in the sunlight, taking in the day. But of course Cora would probably water him to death the way she does the rest of the plants. And what about the ultra-violet? Carcinogenic, n'est-ce-pas? Can it possibly matter in the long run? We are all a little bit too precious about our health.

Once, just to see, I went with Mary Jo to the shot-doctor. I didn't feel right for days after. My sense of time went all to pieces and I tingled all over as if current were passing through me. I found myself constantly in a very big hurry. I burned things by accident: casseroles, my hair, the tips of my fingers, holes in the carpet. I became enchanted with little activities, furious in the grip of undirectable energies. I would stare angrily at the plump nails of flame coloring out of the gas jets on top of my stove, wanting to make something out of them. I wanted to turn everything to a different purpose, away from its intended function. Leaving the doctor's office was like spilling out of a machine that eradicates the many details we cherish without quite knowing that they keep the world from making nonsense. I enjoyed it for exactly five minutes, feeling like a primitive: ooga-booga. Then I got bored and scared. My daughter does this all the time. She says it helps her stay "peppy." It's a wonder she can even drive a car. She wanted to get me involved in this because she's afraid I blame her for Nick.

Well, I do. But, so what? Billy Frank, Sr. blames *me* for Nick, blames me for having a daughter who's a junkie. Billy Frank, Jr. blames me for the nasty conditions of his captivity in Mexico. He thinks I should make his father send more money. Money is comfort, he says. Even in jail, especially in foreign jail. He complains of piles from sleeping on the stone floor of the prison compound. I suspect him of lying (can it really be *that* bad?). He says the other Americans have more money. They sleep on tiers of wooden pallets (when he was a boy, he said all the other children had better baseball mitts). Still, I talk to his father. His father says he should have thought twice before trying to sneak a controlled substance across an international border. I send him boxes of suppositories. It's all I can think to do. The suppositories melt in transit, oiling the letters I wrap the boxes in. I don't want to think about things like this.

What I want is to wander around the house making faces at the light fixtures, tooled gargoyles drooping from stucco, sconces tilting out of floral prints, slippery looking cones flooding our future antiques, the bent-chrome chairs, the vacation cottage blueprints etched into a slab of glass that is a table-top. These are a few of the many items we have taken in and fit ourselves against. Our ship of a home, it shines across the lawn. The furnace works just fine. We are warm when it's cold outside and cool when it's meltingly hot. Everything has its place, a niche or a cupboard. We aren't overcome with clutter like some of our friends. Things hang or sit or are stacked out of sight. And the slot at the back of the medicine cabinet, that's where we put the used razor blades. Though I think sometimes it looks more like the opening into a suggestion box.

We have had an early snow, and the weather is quite cold. Below normal for the season leading up to the winter solstice. There is hardly anything normal anymore; it's all either above or below, a deviation. It seems nowadays the only thing we can expect is strangeness. We have to prepare for variances to which we may then respond with more sophisticated fears.

Shuffling across the deep carpets at home, I shock myself on almost everything I touch. It began with the clock on top of the television set and spread through the house. I'll never as long as I live get over the surprise, no matter how often it happens or how much anticipation I build up inside. I dislike becoming over-cautious, hesitating when I reach, jerking my hand away before making contact. But I hate even more the little crackling sound at the end of my finger where the static discharges. I'll bet there are people who love it, who enjoy filling up with a load of electrical fuzz. There must be ladies somewhere right now rushing through afternoon hallways just to shock themselves on doorknobs. Am I being unreasonable?

The children across the street are building other children out of snow, fat white figures to which they are donating items of clothing, lunch-boxes, book-bags. Their lawn is becoming a sloppy cross-hatch of green stripes where they've rolled up the snow. I've seen this game before, and I know how it's played: the children are making opponents, smaller

versions of themselves. Soon they will destroy them with
snowballs. Little white heads will lie shattered and melting
among six-foot scarves and knit caps and soggy gloves. It will
end up looking like wreckage, like an avalanche. Mother will
come to the door and call them inside for a hot drink, something made from lecithin and soybeans. It'll get dark even
earlier because the solstice is coming.

One weekend recently, we went for a ride in the country, Billy Frank, Sr. and I, out to where they still have farms.
Tall stalks of corn stood unharvested, sun-dried and bleached
the color of worn, tan khaki, cobs on the ground picked
clean, crisp and red, by the crows. Billy Frank sat at the wheel
and I stared out the window, feeling his comfort and his
discomfort. He likes to drive but dreads the possibility of
having to get out of the car. Except at a restaurant (unless he
can find the kind where they bring the food from inside and
clamp it to your door).

I wonder what it must be like for him, driving home
from work each night through the black part of town, the
doors locked and the radio tuned to the helicopter station
that gives away exact positions of police speed-traps. Or with
the deep baritone of a Vaughn Monroe descending through
the darkness among nervous violins into Billy Frank's car as it
clicks beneath green lights timed to help him get home
without having to stop. Does he think about the gauntlet,
the street numbers rising like terror, little black boys playing
tough at football in dirty lots, their daddys looking from
streaked windows or over distended Cyclone fences, faces
shining like we mud? Would you, a stranger, ever get out to
ask directions? My husband's car is his fortress, shooting
through the distance between two points. This fear of stopping, it's a habit.

In the country, we slip among pockets of atavism, ogling
Druids. Billy Frank works hard at steering the tires away from
potholes. A woman in a sack-cloth dress and black bonnet
buries potatoes in the earth so they'll keep through the
winter. She digs on her hands and knees with a trowel, pota-

toes piled beside her like a cairn. She wears her clothes until they tatter utterly; they look like turning leaves ready to fall. The woman is very old. Why does an old woman work? When she could have the county bring hot meals to her door for free, and the weight of buried potatoes would fly from her mind. She'd forget them like a dog forgets his bones.

Mangy dogs stalk at the ends of long chains. They bark at the car as we go past. Children with square, heavy foreheads walk along the side of the road, alone or in pairs. They stare at us with their bad teeth. Hill people, farm people, coming from another geologic time, somewhere down a yellowed, crinkled chart rolled up shade-like in an empty classroom. You almost expect them to howl just like their dogs.

We pass a group of men gathered at a gas pump that looks kind of like an ornate beer stein, something we might buy as an antique and rip from the ground to have in our recreation room. Just squeeze the handle and out comes . . . beer! I can hear the conversation crowding around it at our next party. With a thing like that . . . One of the men looks up, not at us exactly, but across the hood, as if we were a coincidence arriving at the precise moment of his animal twitch of alertness to something happening in the distance.

Woods stretch along beyond the fields. I imagine houses hiding behind course after course of timber, ancient people looking out from the houses at us, unseen by us, calling their children to the windows in a strange language, and pointing after our car with hard thrusts as we almost disappear around the next diving curve into the next peculiar precinct. They are so far away from us; they have no substance. They can't be genuine creatures, can they, with a life apart from my projections? Still, I feel some form of watching going on. Even without the evidence of their breath, rank from unusual foods, or the sight of their shabby garments flickering from behind slashes of bark.

There is a barely perceptible film of haze between the solid trees, and it stops my vision just short of hard focus. A cold blue haze. I rack my eyes in and out to find the point, but it doesn't help. It's as though deep in the woods something were burning frozenly. Some sacrifice against incursion. Some dirty vestigial magic medicine. Those people in there, they better watch out. One of these days, we'll get them.

Billy Frank climbs the stairs, home from work, bushed, unhappy. I can tell by his sound. Steady footfalls on the stair runner, never changing over the years, always a perfect signature like the dripping of certain faucets. His sound climbs the stair-well, cushioning against the walls of the upstairs hallway. Who could live in a house without levels? Who could stand not having the choice of going up or down? The air changes from riser to riser. Descending or climbing, it doesn't matter. There are differences you can feel.

He stops on the upstairs landing and hesitates before opening the door to the attic. Thinking, perhaps, how cold it will be in the big, unheated third floor room. Or hearing, perhaps, some movement I have made shifting in my chair. I hate this moment when he struggles to decide between coming in to peck my cheek hello and tell me about his day, or going directly to his strange avocation in the attic. I don't much care which decision he makes, but I do not like the uncertainty at all. It is the great suspense of my daily life, over which I make bets with myself, planning dinner according to my instincts, whether to prepare for eating late or early. The leather soles of his wing-tip oxfords tap on the attic steps.

He has a 400 millimeter lens for his 35 millimeter camera. Up in the attic he's cleared a perimeter around the junk we've collected and stored there. He spends his leisure dragging a tripod from window to window, framing shots of unsuspecting neighbors and running off long sequences of pictures, kachunk, kachunk, kachunk, with his rapid-advance motor gizmo speeding the film through the camera frame by frame. He devotes a single roll of film, 36 exposures, to each of his subjects. Never more, never less. He processes the negatives and prints them on contact sheets which he places in albums in chronological order. Each sheet bears careful notations of the date, time of day, description of subject, and camera position. The albums fill an entire closet which he has air-tighted and moisture-proofed. He secures the door with a combination lock and hasn't the slightest idea I've discovered those secret numbers.

Although he tantalizes me with descriptions of his hobby and its purposes. Billy Frank refuses to let me watch him work. But I've peeked through the transom window over the door at the top of the attic steps. So complete is his concentration that he would never notice himself being spied upon as he spies upon our neighbors (and, for all I know, as some of them spy on us).

We have gabled windows in the attic on all exposures of our mansard roof. Four sides. Twelve total windows which take in the better part of the neighborhood's expanse, houses and lawns winking in and out of sight on a circling of the room. I hear Billy Frank above me wheeling the tripod along the floor. In the past he has talked about laying down a track around the attic, with rails to which the wheels of the tripod can be fitted, so that each camera position remains a fixed distance from its respective window. He wants to limit the possibility of variation in the process; he uses only the one lens, only one kind of film, and follows strictly the readings of his light meter. No frills, no fancy effects. He says his goal is to take himself out of the picture completely.

He is dedicated to this effort without being what you'd call "passionate." He wants to turn his home into a camera, a machine for recording limited history. And he hasn't any creative pretentions. The camera never leaves the house; he shows absolutely no interest in taking a picture that is not from his home's point of view. When we go on vacation, for example, I'm the one who takes the snapshots (with my own camera, a fruity-looking black plastic item that hangs from my finger by a woven nylon strap). When they invent a lens long enough to focus in on the Andes, say, from our third floor windows, perhaps then he'll consider taking pictures of Peruvian Indians. Though, in that event, he'd force himself to think of them as nothing more than very distant neighbors. He wants only to be the eyes of our house, to see what the house sees and capture it for the archives.

He will take his pictures in any conditions of light or weather; at night or in the middle of a blizzard or a rain storm. He accepts without question every result. His attitude is thoroughly placid, thoroughly even-handed. There seems to be no place for either jubilation or disappointment in his efforts. On rare occasions, however, I have seen him take a kind of pride in the very steadiness of his approach. During such spells, he can be stunningly tedious. As far as I know, he never enlarges a single frame of which he is fond. In fact, as far as I know, there *are* no frames of which he is fond. Affection simply doesn't enter into it.

Sometimes when Billy Frank is in the attic, I will wander around the house, climbing up and down between the cellar and the second floor, looking out through every window trying to guess what image he is framing. He transmits certain clues from above as I hear him moving around. Sooner or later, though, I lose track of him for long periods of time, and finally it tires me to chase about the house straining my eyes and wondering. After all, it's Billy Frank's hobby, not mine. And I really do have better things to do, even if it doesn't sound like it.

Still, I'll admit there's a kind of fascination. Now and then, catching sight of some shift in light or movement behind diaphanous curtains in a window across the street, I will get this rush of excitement and think how there may exist, at just that instant, a triangular relationship between my vision and Billy Frank's. Is he twisting the focus collar at the end of that long lens? Is the shutter beginning to consume little pieces of private dusk? I never ask what he's photographed, but sometimes he mentions certain of his subjects in a way that helps me confirm occasional synchronous movements. More often than not, however, he is probably scanning precincts I haven't the power to see. The lens is quite strong, perfect for neighborhood astronomy. He has that technical edge over the naked eye. Perhaps he reads magazines left open on coffee tables in living-rooms many blocks away. If he doesn't come downstairs pretty soon, I'm going to eat dinner without him.

I am riding on a bus, a public conveyance, coming home from a shopping trip downtown, noticing on the window by my hand an oval configuration left on the glass by someone's oily hair. It erupts through the uniform skin of condensation and looks like the imprint matted grass leaves on my shins when I get up after pinching out stands of creeping veronica from the lawn in back of our house. In fact, the condensation spreads through parts of the pattern, presumably the places where there is no oily residue. Billy Frank, Sr. would not like the idea of my riding on a bus, unless it was a charter-party mounted with friends to a football weekend upstate for homecoming. If it comes to that, he would say, if you don't feel like waiting until you can have the car, then take a cab . . . or stay home.

I can't help thinking that the man in the seat in front of me is dead. He is an old white man in a poorly fitting over-coat that has either been his for so long that it outgrew his shrinking body, or that he has gotten from a trash barrel or from the Goodwill people (it might even be one of Billy Frank's old coats, discarded into that big yellow collection bin in the middle of our supermarket parking lot; the size looks to be about right, and the brown herringbone tweed under all that grime and wear . . .). He has silver-grey hair that comes off the back of his head like tinsel charged with static; he hasn't shaved this week, maybe not last week either.

He climbed aboard so slowly that the driver lost patience and started up abruptly sending him and his clutch of paper bags down the aisle like a spastic skittle and making him spend all his energy to throw himself sideways into an open seat slot, which didn't quite work, for he caught one seat-back with his hip and was spun around so that his lower spine banged into the molded plastic lip on the aisle half of the seat behind. He dropped his paper bags and grabbed at the handle bar on top of the seat in front of him. From one of the fumbled bags rolled a can of soup, picking up forward speed as the bus began braking for the next stop, and magically caromming from the base of the fare box out through the opening front doors. The passenger getting on recovered the can and held it aloft as he came down the aisle looking for its owner, but the old man was gasping with his head turned aside and his eyes closed, so I took the can and replaced it in the soggy-bottomed bag, which I also noticed contained some ratty looking bedroom slippers and a saucepan whose handle had fallen off (it looked like one of my old saucepans, the one with the loose handle, and I vaguely wondered whether we, our family, were in some way, and without our knowledge, assigned directly to this old man by downtown agencies whose job is to insinuate people like us into the machinery of social welfare operations).

I'm not sure why I think he's dead. He might only be resting, dreaming of ways to stretch yet another winter out of Billy Frank's coat, or a method of moving my old, bubbling, handleless pot from hot-plate to table without being burned. But he hasn't moved in probably thirty blocks, a stony still-ness. His head lolls against the window, making another unsightly splotch of scalp oils, rolling with the motion of the bus and not from any inner momentum of his own. I'm glad I won't be on board when the driver finds him dead. At one time I might have been interested. I might have speculated in projections, imaginations, filling his seedy room with my own ideas of its contents and the way he navigated among them, spilling clumsily from certain vessels adapted for uses not suited to their design, barking his fragile Dresden shins on appropriated wood-slat cartons, shaving with a clamshell or using a dirty finger to rub his teeth clean with a little cone of Ajax, or muttering in a foreign language at the edge of his hideous bed because his sister (I would once have been certain that he had one, but now I'm not so sure) was too tired to come across town for a simple goulash dinner.

When I was a young girl, maybe twelve or thirteen, with brown hair that fell all the way to just above my widening hips, in a room that closed around me like a warm hand, lying at night on a bed that drove up through me with its softness and melted me back down into it, I was curious for information about things to which access was routinely denied me. Streets, buildings, distances, words, conditions, a few chosen night sounds that came from outside and seemed both evil and sweet to my ears. I would have trouble falling asleep (perhaps, according to my mother, for the lack of a single hard pea beneath my mattress which, she said, would have been an easy problem to solve). And the large, white-faced clock on the wall, each hour celebrated with an illustration in the famous sequence of cow-jumping-over-moon, seemed, as it got later, to brighten the room with my own exhaustion and panic. I would lie there and listen, breathing calmly, trying not to be anxious at lingering awake in a house that was quiet except for its own creakings, to these sounds of the very late night. They seemed to come out of the walls without belonging to the walls. Screech, scream, whistle, siren, horn, scuff, shout: very dim sounding and indistinct, like the nervous respiration of a troubled someone in a downstairs room. Scary, but you wanted to go see . . .

Or I would note how the city's light-looming appeared to grow larger the longer I looked. Pinkish and vaguely appetizing out in the dark. I wanted to know where it came from, why it was there, what people did at night when every-one I knew was apparently safe, sleeping or trying to sleep. If there were people out doing things all night, where did they go in the morning? Were they sleeping while I was at school? What occupied them all day? Were they criminals? Or were they like the Druids, measuring the year in nights instead of days? Naturally, I had no idea then (as I later learned) that my restless curiosity was a gift from certain recently activated hormones. Or, as Mary Jo would say, "a sex problem, dear."

And now they are a terror to me. People like this old man, who seem to have grown up from the night like molds and mosses. It doesn't interest me to learn what we might have in common; the differences are too compelling by themselves. I want nothing directly to do with them. Their lifelessness give me a headache. It angers and hurts me to see how little they have, how shrunken their mean appetites must be. I'm just so far on the other side of them now, beyond that metastasis from which my fears have sprung. Mary Jo titters and calls me an agoraphobe, "one who shirks the public places." But I'm not, really. My memory often complains to me. It whines that I used to care and dares me to come out and ride the bus. I keep thinking there must be something to look at. And, from a distance, it is still so beautiful to me. Edgeless and featureless, melting lines like an Edward Hopper painting, a rich dream framed between the street and the railroad trestle, all shadows and then projected light spilling from windows. Sounds of things frying, tires through rainwater, brushes on steps, coughing, matches flaring . . .

As I am standing after buzzing for my stop, the dead man breaks wind like the rollicking of a motorcycle taking my son off to Mexico.

Janet Desaulniers

Age

Last night I was seduced. "Lord," you must think, "this I've heard before." But then I could be wrong. I constantly overestimate my powers of intuition. Some days I walk to my store, my small shoebox of a bookshop, and feel the women near the bus stop stare at my balding head, my cracked shoes wound with electrical tape. I turn to face them and say, "It's not so bad." They look confused and I wonder: Were they really looking at me. Were they interested at all, or were they looking past me, to a store window, perhaps at a new pocket-book or spring coat. What do you think? I think you may not be interested in the seduction of a sixty-three year old man, that you may view the seduction of a man past his prime, past ambition, past desire's tap on the shoulder, as a shade perverse, slightly off the scheme of things.

You may be nowhere near sixty-three. Perhaps you are young — your body and mind firm and uncreased. Perhaps you think of seduction in terms of young men and women who move in and out of doorways as if always following some distant strain of music. If so, some day I think you'll find, as I did, those people have only a small role in the final order of things. Not that I don't appreciate them. Not that I don't see their long legs, their faces turned up and open — almost pious in their ease. I see, God, I see. But they are a diversion —bestseller fiction before bedtime. At sixty-three, you will be able to think of at least five things more important. I can: good wine, quiet sleep, easy digestion, less pain, something *new*.

Or perhaps you are older than sixty-three. Perhaps you think of seduction as that one bright glint in a shadowy past

— the red scooter when you were nine, or the face of your wife the first morning she touched your arm as you rose from bed, the first time *she* took *you* — the trembling in your hands and knees. I take your hand in mine. To you, I offer comfort. To you, I say it can happen again.

I wonder if you believe me. I am balding, overweight, and alone. My body hangs from my shoulders like a coat that has lost its shape, its definition. From around my bald spot, my hair grows wild and unstyled. Often I don't comb it. I think, Why should I. I am poor — too poor for cars and clothes and casual drinks. My drinks, when I can afford them, are serious, meaningful. I wash my gray undershirts and socks in the bathtub and hang them to dry over my furniture. I read. That's all. I sit in my tiny, failing bookshop. I hear it sigh, give up and fail all around me, and I read. Otherwise, I do nothing. C.S. Lewis understood the dangers of nothing. He wrote: "Nothing is very strong: strong enough to steal away a man's best years not in sweet sin but in a dreary flickering of the mind over it knows not what and knows not why." C.S. Lewis is right more often than I am. Still, nothing is what I do most days. Like my shop, I gave up. I gave in. I sit quietly inside myself like a motionless pond. But this is important. This is what I'm trying to say: I am all these things, but last night I danced.

I suppose I should tell about the woman. I am impatient with the way this is going. The woman is not the most important thing. There are the places, the days, even the people who remind me of her — all scattered about in a shambles of significance. The woman is at the center, but alone, isolated, she'll look small, maybe ridiculous. Finally, though, she saved me — a save as clean and final and close to the heart of matters as any surgeon's stitch.

Lily is twenty-four. Perhaps I've been too abrupt. I can imagine the young people nodding and the old folks shaking their heads. But Lily is twenty-four, and though I'm hesitant to mention this now, she is also lovely though she's too thin like all the rest of the young ones. Women have lost respect for hips and breasts these days. I'm sure I'll suffer for saying that, but I don't understand. I have always envied women, praised them. Women are balanced, fluid, as if always something about them is in motion. Men are hard, clumsy, unyielding. Women can take men inside them. They can feel men grow inside them and feel themselves grow around the men.

A poet wrote those last two lines — a young poet with small chapped hands who rented the room above my bookshop for two years and left his poems as a final payment of sorts. The sound of his typewriter came down to me through the vent over my cash register in fits and starts, like an animal fretting over a wound. He wrote only about women. Afternoons, when the lunch hour browsers abandoned me and the sun came through the front window to draw harsh edges around the clutter and the quiet, I imagined him up there, barechested in the heat, crossing his ankles and rocking in his chair, transfixed by the implications of his own words. He knew women though. In his poems, he knew them as I think they might choose to be known — tender and complex, opening slowly, over time, the way a small bud unfolds and unfolds until finally, it overwhelms. That young poet knew women's power; he held it in his mind, examined it. The sad part, the tragic part, is that all this was only on paper. Standing next to a real woman, he unraveled. I wanted to reach out and quiet his shoulders. He blinked, stammered, and the fear moved up in lines around his eyes. But on paper he found solace. There he could study women closely, impose an order upon them he could believe in, and though none of that order was real, none of it workable, its beauty was relentless and blinding. Finally, even I believed. It was a quiet, personal deception — one that caused my first disagreement with Plato, who argued that poets and painters should be denied a place in the City of the Good. I would save that young poet a place if it were my city. But I digress. The poet and what his poems did are a seduction of another kind.

Lily. Lily is a woman — a young one, thin and long-legged, with great eyes and a full but serious mouth. Her hair is long and auburn. She thinks she might cut it when she turns twenty-five. I hope she doesn't; you would, too, if you saw it. Its shine is like a mahogany cabinet. Everything about Lily wants to believe it's tough, unaffected — sensible sandals, no jewelry, never a pocketbook or a hat or a handkerchief, not even an umbrella on drizzly days. She says things like, "Hey. Howya doin'." — but softly, hesitating, as though the gangly familiarity is a ruse she hasn't fully accepted, and in her face there is something distant, quizzical, even sweet. When she stands among the stacks in my shop, I sometimes think if I reached out to touch her, she'd suddenly be gone. Her mouth is always open just a bit, and her eyes are always wide, as if she is standing just outside herself, viewing herself and her small life as a very interested, perhaps awestruck, spectator. She likes books (how else would we have met), mainly fiction, mainly contemporary, and works evenings as a waitress on the Square.

The Square brought Lily and me together. We both hate it — though she works in it and my bookshop leans against it like a poorly dressed cousin. I don't know quite how to describe the Square with fairness. It is a thorn in my side, a raucous painful reminder of the way things are, but it is important — the backdrop against which I've lived out my silly life. When I bought my bookshop in 1950, before the collapse of city neighborhoods, the buildings on the Square housed an upholstery shop, a bakery, a beauty salon, a tobacconist, a market, a movie house and a drugstore that doubled as neighborhood meeting place for the idle and garrulous. Now those same buildings accommodate clothing stores for the very young and very chic and countless bars and restaurants all bursting with overgrown ferns, brass fixtures and tinted glass. Lily works in a restaurant called the Soup Kitchen decorated in (it embarrasses me to say this) a Depression motif with blown up photographs of bread lines and Apple Annies and cold, hungry looking children. A bowl of split pea soup costs $3.95 there.

Sometimes I think I should have left the Square when I had the chance. During the Sixties, a group of young people pooled their tuition money and bought a few of the storefronts that had been abandoned in the rush to the suburbs. They worked hard — refinishing the doors and wood around the windows, planting small gardens of herbs and flowers in the sooty dirt of the back alley. Sometimes, at dusk, when the cars and buses moved away from the city, when it seemed everyone was leaving, I would sit and have tea with the women who ran the sandwich shop. I liked those people. They were, for a time, fully young and fully earnest. One of them, a carpenter, helped me build new shelves for the north wall. Each morning, he'd arrive with his tools under one arm and his baby daughter under the other. Her name was Star, and she was a fat, good baby; her father used to say she was a baby of character. Mornings she'd sleep through the noise in a crate I'd used to store old magazines, and afternoons she'd sit up eating bananas and watching the door. It thrilled her to hear the bell over the door ring. Even then, my customers were few and far between, but Star was patient, and when one finally did come in, she'd laugh at him and laugh at us and then raise her banana in a kind of cheery salute. By the end of the first day of work, Star and her father and I were friends. When we finished the shelves, I gave them twenty dollars and they gave me a beret. I wore it every day. I let my hair grow. It had just reached the middle of my back when a developer decided he liked the site and offered to buy all of us out. I tried to convince the others to stay, but they had plans — a commune in Vermont, farmland in Arkansas. The carpenter asked me to join him, but I couldn't. This was the only place I knew. All right, I'll say it, I was afraid. I kissed

Star goodbye and stayed. For months, I watched the renovation, and sometimes, even with a customer in the shop, I wept at my window.

Now I sit with a picture window view of the way things are. Lily agrees that people have changed less than I thought. I have changed more. The old drugstore came down last week. Late-night bar trade requires more parking than you can believe.

I did not mean to strike so bleak a note. As I tell women I imagine to be watching me in the street: It's not so bad. Lily. Lily waits tables in a tight jersey floor-length dress. It is a silly dress — meant to be sexy and demure at the same time. Lily knows this, but she wears the dress constantly, marketing and running errands in it before and after work. When I mention it, she holds the dress away from her hips as if it were diseased. "I sold out," she says. "Why should I try to hide it." Lily means she makes more money waiting tables four nights a week than I have made in any one week of my thirty-one years of bookselling.

Lily always seems to be caught up in some emotion. This is the part about her that angers me, frustrates me, and yes, even summons up desire. Some of you may think desire after sixty must be something like an echo trapped in a deep cave, but I tell you, if it is an echo at all, it is one that knows no logic, one that has lost its trajectory, its mathematical predictability. I hear it reverberate crazily, bouncing out of nowhere off the wall over my shoulder as I walk home at night, throwing itself up in front of me, randomly, in the shape of a simple dress in the window of Three Sisters or in the color of ripe oranges. Lily knows a similar kind of desire, but one less random, more pervasive. Always Lily seems to be longing for something — better cheekbones, a new job, wisdom, spontaneity. In someone so young, such silliness is both maddening and charming. A young face touched with longing lights up; so does an old face, I suppose, but you must admit a lost look in young eyes is more appropriate, somehow prettier.

The problem is Lily tries to think about these emotions. Like the poet, she tries to order them, give one precedence over another. She is ill at ease with her longings. When she comes to me to talk about them, to think them out, I watch her grow heavy and careful right in front of me. I watch her pull her arms in, close secret doors, grow old. It angers me. She thinks about her longings so much that finally, before she has decided what to do about them, they pass. I can't help it — when this happens, I have to give her advice. I lean back in my chair until it squeaks, I put one hand on each knee, and then I tell her what to do. She never does it, but I think she believes I never notice that. I used to justify all this by telling myself she was saving all my advice, hoarding it in expectation of the one time she would really need it, and now I know she was.

A few weeks ago, Lily came into my shop with a decision that had to be made. Lily lightens my shop the way Star and her bananas used to. Without them, the shop is simply dark and quiet, and the only way I know to characterize it is to say that I lost control of the clutter years ago. The aisles are narrowing, and some have simply disappeared. I haven't been able to get through to the shelving against the back wall for at least two years. I've forgotten what's back there. But the shop just seems to recede and make room when Lily comes in. She sidles through the stacks and crawls over boxes and stands on crates, all the while crooking her neck so she can read titles. Every so often she'll call out an author she doesn't recognize and ask if she should read him. I pretend to think a moment but always say yes, and then she stands there, holding the book in her hand as if she's weighing it, before she puts it back and says, "I'll remember that."

The day of her decision she leaned against my counter and poked through a box of paperbacks I'd bought from a college kid that day. She said, "I waited on the director of that new dance company tonight. He said I should join. He said they have classes for beginners." I said, "Dance, Lily, you should," and thought of her in tights and leotard. I didn't tell her I thought that. Lily always catches me when I say things women don't like to hear anymore. I know she wouldn't like what I said about hips and breasts.

"I don't know though." She walked to the window and stared out into the street. "It's too late for me to be good. I'm already too old, and I never dance — not even socially. That sounds foolish, doesn't it. Social dancing. Maybe it's all foolish. Frivolous."

I had to interrupt her here. I mean, I thought of Martha Graham and Isadora Duncan.

"Lily, dance is movement," I said. "Movement is life. Everyone should move. Lord, Lily, Aquinas even defines God as the prime mover."

She turned from the window and looked at me.

"He does?"

"Yes."

"I don't know though — if I could do it."

"And you're not too old."

"Maybe. Not really, I guess. I don't know."

She walked around the shop, trailing her hand along the shelves and sometimes stopping to pat the spines of a row of books as if they were all lovely children. Lily punctuates all our conversation with wandering. Often she disappears behind the shelves for long periods. I can't see her. I can only hear her voice. That day she went behind the religion shelf. I think she was looking for Aquinas. Her voice floated out to me.

"But I was going to take that course in literature you told me about. I mean, I don't know a thing about books. I probably haven't read one-fifth of all the great ones."

"Maybe not even one-twentieth."

"See."

I think she was back in the corner when she said that. I began to get angry. I wanted her out in the open. I liked her to look at me when I gave her advice. I raised my voice and my chin, as if searching for her in a crowd.

"Then do it," I said. "Study literature. Go to the university and read the other four-fifths of all great books in the world."

Maybe I will." She raised her voice to match mine. "I just might."

"Do it," I said and stopped looking for her. "Go."

She was silent for a time, long enough to have read a few pages. The store was quiet without her voice, quiet the way it is in the afternoon — an oppressive quiet that seems to move in like heat and hover in the six inches of space between my tallest shelves and the ceiling. The quiet made me think of the poet and miss him. I even missed Lily. I knew she wasn't reading. I knew she was back behind a shelf imagining herself as someone else, as someone who had read all five-fifths of the great books in the world, perhaps as someone who said things like, "God is the prime mover."

"Lily."

"What."

"Why don't you just do both?"

"Oh — money."

"Money? You make lots of money. Enough for you and two more like you."

"I'm saving it."

I craned my neck and saw her peeking inside an old armoire I use to store books I want to read before I die.

"What are you saving for? What could you need?"

"I don't know. Something might come up."

"Lily, nothing is going to come up. Nothing ever comes up. You know what you should do with that money? I'm serious now. Are you listening?"

"Yes."

"Buy a little red sportscar, Lily. A convertible. Then find

a young good man. Lord, buy one of those, too. You can buy anything these days. Then drive around, Lily. Drive around fast until you feel like dancing. Then do that. Dance. That's what you should do, Lily. That's what you should do with your money."

She poked her head from behind a shelf directly in front of me. She surprised me. I could never keep track of her when she was in the shop.

"Are you making fun of me?"

I didn't answer because I wasn't sure. I looked down into a box of books I'd traded for that week — criticism from the twenties. They'd never sell. Lily was out from behind the shelf and in front of me before I could look up.

"What would you do?" she said. Her voice trembled a little. "Would you drive around town, whistle at people and let your hair blow behind you in some silly damn car?"

"Lily, I'd do some silly damn thing."

I was tired of both of us when I said that, and I know I shouldn't have said it. Lily and I had a pact of sorts. You don't accuse someone of doing nothing when you have a pact. So I can't blame Lily for whispering, "You would not. You would not," and walking out the door. I do wish I could blame someone for the way the door closed behind her — quietly, slowly, like the end of some sad story. Even with the melodrama, it frightened me.

For ten days, she was gone; it rained for seven of them. People walked by under newspapers, plastic head scarfs and low, heavy clouds. I missed her. Lord, I read with one eye always on the door. Late last night after closing, she came back. I was reading behind the counter, and though I knew from the knock who it was, I walked to the door slowly. I composed my face. She stood there in her silly dress, swaying. She was out of breath and looked cold. Her face and dress seemed drawn, pulled tight against her, as if she had been running from something that stood right outside the door.

"Are you all right?" I said.

"I've been drinking. I'm cold."

She came into the shop, and I moved behind my counter to my chair, settling in like a judge.

"So what's the problem?" I said.

She looked at me hard until I felt a touch of foolishness
at the way I sat, the way I crossed my arms on my chest. Then
she said, "I think we should take your advice tonight."

"What advice?"

"I think we should go dancing."

How can I say what I felt when she said that. I was sixty-
three years old, and hadn't danced, hadn't thought of it, in
over thirty years. I leaned back in my chair, and for once, the
squeak startled me. I was cold, and tense, as though some
intruder were standing over me, armed with a weapon
against which I had no chance. But I could feel the chair
against my back. I was in my own shop. I told myself I was
safe.

"No, Lily," I said, smiling and shaking my head. "I
don't think we should."

"I do. Really."

She was still swaying, but her eyes were firm. I said,
"Lily, sit down," but she didn't sit down. She put her hands
on the counter and leaned over until her face was just inches
from mine. For a moment, I thought she might kiss me. I
was confused. I wanted her to. Instead, she looked into my
eyes — a long unflinching look, a look that made me wonder
what she saw there.

"I don't want to sit down," she said. "I think we should
go dancing. Tonight. I think you should lock up this store
and walk down the street with me. And I think we should go
into that bar under the blinking purple sign. We should
dance."

She took my hand. Maybe that's why I followed her out
the door, or maybe I thought I could bolt down an alley,

outrun her, or maybe she just overwhelmed me, her face that close to mine. We walked slowly down the street in a fine rain. Lily was looking straight ahead, as if expecting to meet someone, and she looked different than she had in the shop, moments before. She looked frightened and young. I put my mouth next to her ear and said quietly, "Come on, Lily. I'll walk you home." She raised her head, and her face was like a child's face.

"When we go in, we'll walk straight to the dance floor, okay? We won't stop or look around. We'll just walk straight up there. And I'd like you to hold my hands when we dance."

What could I say? Lord, she was standing in the rain and shivering. So we went into the bar under the blinking purple sign. I felt the stares, but I looked only at Lily's dress, drenched and dragging behind her like a tiny wake. We walked straight to the dance floor. I took her cold hands and looked at her face. She looked shy. The music was very loud. People all around us were dancing. They looked like they were born to dance, bred to dance. I thought of running again, and then I thought of standing very still in hope that I might disappear the way a telephone pole or a street sign can disappear in a landscape that is otherwise alive and in motion. But Lily said, "We have to move." So we moved, clumsily, drawing close for protection. I looked at my feet, concentrating only on moving them back and forth with Lily's, trying to remember anything about dancing. Gradually, the back and forth shuffling became comfortable, or at least automatic. The crowd moved in so close they didn't matter. I looked up to see Lily watching me, her mouth open, in surprise, as if the moon had just sat down next to her.

"We're dancing," she said.

Inside, I felt a delicate tug, the way healing aches when a scar forms, when the body makes peace with its wounds, and then I remembered something. I remembered it the way the blind must remember color or the way the dead must remember life — a memory rising strangely, all at once, like something buoyant moving up through water and exploding onto the surface. I raised my arm and, with it, Lily's hand, and I said to her, "Spin." She looked at me for a moment, and then she smiled and did it. She spun. At that moment, our lives cracked open and held out a small, very important opportunity. In the end, I did not seduce her and she did not seduce me, but something that lived in the very center of her and even of me, that breathed and moved, seduced us both.

Ivy Goodman

White Boy

She had first seen him wearing sweat socks bunched down between the first and second toes of each foot to accommodate black rubber thongs. She associated this foot garb vaguely and incorrectly with an Eastern religion. She noticed he was prettier than she. He was nice to her because he was nice, and she imagined many beautiful women he'd been even nicer to.

They were next door neighbors on the second story of an oblong efficiency apartment house. Often from her sofa she watched him clomp along the outdoor catwalk that rimmed the second story and linked the twin outdoor staircases. When he passed her windows he looked straight ahead. When she passed his she pretended to survey the parking lot. In quest of a dime he once came to her door clutching ten pennies, and she asked him inside.

It turned out he had no telephone. He'd been on his way to the booth at the nearest gas station. "No telephone?" she said, suddenly embarrassed that she had one.

"I've heard yours ringing," he said.

"How annoying."

"Not at all. May I use it sometime?"

"Peter, of course."

"Now?"

"Yes, but . . ." She glanced down at his thongs, at his mittened feet, dapper tonight in thin black socks embossed with hexagons. "What should I do? Should I leave?" she asked.

"Oh, no, Robin. Stay, unless you mind."

"The phone's over there, beside the refrigerator." She

smiled. "I guess I'll go sit down."

On the sofa by the windows she pretended to read while he dialed endlessly. "Hi, this is Peter. . . . Hello, Richard? Peter. . . Peggy, it's Peter. I said I'd call. . . ." And he was a man of his word. How many people he knew whose numbers Robin would find on her next month's bill! She eavesdropped until she wearied of so much good nature. She peeked at him, seated now on her dining table for a long call. Legs crossed, he kept time to his talk by shaking his feet. Those stockinged feet gave him an air of being housebound. Where could he go in thongs and socks? Not far, certainly. Though this evening the invalid had dressed — in sporty trousers and a plaid shirt — his feet reminded that tomorrow he'd be back in bed. And yet how brave he was, as he struck his heels against his innersoles and made a sound like running to console himself because he could not run. How uncomplaining, pale, beautiful, and nearly dead. The languishing Prince! Hail!

She knew he had been hailed. She knew by the ease with which he guffawed now, pounded her table, and said, "He bit the dust, I don't believe it, who was the girl? Naw! Her?"

He was blessed, whatever he might do, and she had come to life as an immigrant, large-nosed, far-fetched, straight from the hold. If she'd been dealt her features fairly, she'd have thrown them back, forfeited a turn, and hoped for better luck next time. As it was, she remained one of the less fortunate, envious of him, and yet admiring.

He was quiet now. She watched him stand. The table shuddered. He stretched one arm toward the wall and hung up the phone. "Thanks, Robin, but it's getting late. I've got to go." Grinning, he headed toward the door and almost sneaked off.

"Wait." She lowered her book and stared at him unobstructed. "Are you sure you're done?"

"Yes, unless. . . ." With one funny foot he held the door

ajar. "Do you want something? It's not midnight yet. There's the corner store."

"Don't do me any favors. I'll send a bill."

"Oh, right." Nearly caught, he pretended to come forth voluntarily. "By the way — some of those were toll-calls . . ."

"By the way? Thanks for nothing. See you, Peter."

"What?"

"Just goodnight."

"Goodnight then."

She might as well have turned to him in profile and stuck out her tongue: look at how awful I am. Oh, let him think what he wanted, which probably was nothing, she realized. Days later, inside on a rainy afternoon, she watched him run through all the puddles in the parking lot. He wore galoshes. He carried a sodden grocery bag. He chose the farther set of stairs and bounded up. With his head in a hood, he hurried by. She heard his bolt click, his door whine open. She half-expected some sort of greeting next: "Look at you, you're soaking wet. Off with your clothes and into this bath." But no, her neighbor lived alone.

She neared their common wall as if it beckoned; she tilted her head. Dimishing creaks. The plaintive to and fro of metal cupboard doors. A pot lid dropped. Clatter in the kitchen. Silence in the pipes. His bathtub dry.

But would he need baths, really? She imagined his sweat would smell of pennies, damp, like the ones he'd held out. *Do you have a dime?* What would he smell on her? Onions? Fish? The back of a shop? Her shop. He'd open the door and rattle the tin bell dangling from the transom on a piece of string. At first he wouldn't see her, then he would, wiping her hands across her apron bib. "What do you want?" "May I use your. . ." "No. Ours is a business phone. The pay booth's up the street." On his way out, past the barrel in the aisle, she would falsely accuse him of theft. "Put that back." She'd grab him by the arm and pry his fist, finger by finger, until his pennies scattered on the worn linoleum. He would leave without bothering to stoop for them.

She turned and pressed her forehead to the wall. Not quite in the corner, she stood like that for a long while, as though she'd found a bearing for her head, which she rolled now and then in order to look out the window briefly.

The rain storm ended. She heard him, in his box, move closer to hers. Then, three creaks in place, hesitation, impatience, a stationary shuffle: altogether signalling departure soon. As a way of getting ready, he seemed to wait for someone. *Hurry up. What's keeping you?* His door opened. He stepped out. His door shut. She watched him trot past as purposeful as a dog. Could he really have somewhere to go? something to do? His footsteps stopped. He knocked. "Robin? May I use your phone?"

In the weeks that followed, he visited often, always bringing with him his small leather telephone book. Once, when Robin glimpsed a gray-lined page, she was shocked to see addresses noted too. Had he filled that blank as a matter of form, or did he actually write letters sometimes? He sent birthday cards, he said. He was a true friend. He still had friends from the second grade.

She imagined he'd been loyal all his life, and beneficient. At two years or three, he'd probably leaned forward in his stroller to offer strangers cookies, gnawed around the edges and damp with drool. "How darling. His name is Peter? No, thank you, Peter. You eat that. That's yours." He'd laugh and shake his head and take another nibble. What were cookies to him? He could always get more from his mother, or kindly bakery clerks. "Would the little boy like a cookie? Yes? Chocolate chip?" He risked nothing, while his reputation for being generous grew.

And so he said to Robin now, "I wish I could do you a favor." He had just finished dialing, and for a moment he held the receiver aloft. Then his call went through. A thin male voice cried out, "Hello? Hello? Who's there?" Peter placated it: "Doug? Peter. Hold on a second, would you?" He turned back to Robin, who was thrilled a friend of his had to wait for her. She felt contemptuous and special, until she remembered she was paying for the call. Why hadn't she gotten up the nerve to bill Peter yet? "Anything in my apartment," Peter went on, "borrow anything, Robin, long-term. Put a lien on it." He laughed. "Though I have to admit there's nothing much there."

She laughed back. "Your call," she reminded, "your friend." She walked away to her bookcase and selected another volume to hold.

She still could not read with him there. If at first she had chosen to eavesdrop, she had no choice now. She was enthralled. Each time he knocked, she felt as though she gobbled a bowl of sugar fast before answering the door. "Peter! It's you! Hello! Come in!"

She took an aspirin soon after he arrived, and between his calls she served tea. Over tea cups, they discovered they were the same age ("Twenty-six, too!") and had gone to college in neighboring states. She grew up in the East, he in the West, and neither cared about his or her current job very much. After graduation, he had lived in Europe for a year. "Peter! Is that true? You're a man of the world!"

But was Peter a man of the world? No. More likely he was a large version of the child a mother might drag anywhere. *Nope. No problems with Peter. He's so well-behaved.* Nothing affected him really, not even indulgence. All that money Robin had spent treating him to phone calls? Wasted. She should have saved it for her first European tour.

"Robin, is something the matter?"

"Hmm? No." She looked up. And she saw again that he was beautiful and she was all wrong. He was good: that was it. She was back at the sugar bowl again, between spoonfuls thinking how good he was. "Do you know I'm corrupt?" she said.

"You? You're the most corrupt woman I've met."

"I'm serious. You're too good to understand."

"What?"

"That's right." If he ever discovered her thoughts, her deceptions, her motives. Calculations were tricks with sums to him. "Peter, you might find this insulting, but I have a crush on you."

"Robin, I have a crush on you."

"Yes?"

"We'll have to do something, won't we?" Across her kitchen table, he stared out, not exactly at her. She felt as if she'd handed him a dollar, and he was dazzled by a vision of the candy he might buy. "It would be a shame not to, still I want to think about it," he said. Sugar babies, honey bits, peppermint sticks, malted milk balls. In suspense, permutations could be worked out. "Let's surprise each other some time." He meant, let me surprise you. He was a hoarder and might save his dollar for weeks, but she would have him run now to the store.

"Would you kiss me?" she said.

"Sure."

They pushed from the table, met near the sink, embraced, bent down, and scrambled all over the floor on their knees together, kissing, laughing. Then they got up to take off their clothes.

Peter stepped back to look at her. "Around, around." He stirred his finger through the air. "Whirl."

She turned. "Am I all right?"

"All right? You're lovely."

"Then both of us are."

Love-ly, love-ly. What a lovely lie. She would believe it. In truth, they were clumsy together, and the only lovely things were his sounds, let out at last, low and lovely.

Afterwards she hoped they might lie still for a minute. But no, immediately he lifted his head and asked, "Do you want to hear a joke?" She said, "Yes," and thought, he must ruin our closeness because it frightens him. But she also thought she brought them even closer because she understood. Then again, by now he might feel absolutely nothing. She heard his joke and laughed at the rapture she had found in that deluded moment before he reared his head. He was an oaf. On the chair she saw his yellow chamois chapparal shirt, reminiscent of a dust cloth; on the floor his scattered foot wear, thongs and socks. She wanted him to dress, be gone. But then he spoke to her. With his hands he turned her head. "Here, Robin, here, here."

He left before she fell asleep. Listening from her bed, following his progress, she pretended he was merely walking to another room, not to a separate apartment.

They always slept separately. Twice a week or three times, after finishing his calls, he undressed and stayed another hour. Or else he said, "Come to my place for a while." At best, Robin decided, he was simply pleasurable. And he was very polite to her. *Say, 'Pass the sugar, please.' and do not grab, Peter.*

Even she, the immigrant, knew a little etiquette. Requesting a whole night from him would be unmannerly. Besides she only pretended to want it. Without pretence, she had no pleasure. But Peter was easy to love. He would kiss and kiss, then not kiss and with force not let her, until not kissing was better than kissing some nights. She told him, "You're tough." He hid his face in a pillow and said, "You embarrass me." He used his imagination, put it away, and in a moment was himself again, while for weeks she half-believed she loved him, though she knew better.

She listened; she waited. She could not be at home without waiting for him. Was he out? Was he in? Would he knock soon? For him, their affair just made them better friends.

"It's not passionate, is it?" he asked.

"No." She was kneeling on the floor and gathering her clothes. She stared up. "Have you ever had a passionate one?''

"Last summer, and then I hated her. But you and I, we're friends. Yes?''

"Yes.''

As part of their secret, only he and she shared his slights. They had no company. though Robin imagined some: a party with Peter seated at its center, smiling, drinking, garrulous. Across the room, conscious of the air she displaced, Robin perched on a window sill. In her hand a nearly full beverage glass warmed and sweated. Even in daydreams she never outgrew herself; her time to acquire grace had passed. Peter's party-voice slid by. Though in the dark, after something arduous, he spoke just to her: "Water, water, quick, we're dying of thirst. Bring water!''

He was playful. He made up rules: they must undress each other. When she reached down her leg for her sock, he said, "No help allowed. Let me.'' What fun, she should have liked this, but she wanted them quickly to undress themselves and then go slowly. For him, sometimes being naked was enough. When he pushed too soon, she couldn't say, "Please wait.'' Instead, embarrassed, furious, she made room. Part of herself got up and watched a man and a woman on the bed.

But if pleasure was the point, she must come back; she must feel herself beneath him. His smile blew out breath across her face, and she wondered what technique of hers was laughable. In the dark his perfect, good features vanished on a plain with holes for eyes, mouth, nostrils. His brows were fine sketches of brows, and his hair, cut to look neatly ruffled, looked no more than neatly ruffled. Across his hairless chest he was so white. White boy, she named him secretly, though his skin was not whiter than that of any other man she'd known. White boy, whitest. When he became a man he would grow hair, but now he was still a boy, above her with a man's shoulders. Even a boy could make her lose herself. The hardship came in parting from him. "Robin, it's about that time. I'm really tired." "Yes, of course. Goodnight." At the door she turned to look at him, lying contained within his white, white self.

He was not simple. He was more than she knew. When she rubbed her back raw by rolling with him on the carpet, he joked about "rug burn." But after the sore scabbed he declared it "ugly" convincingly. With what ease he found the right word. How long, she wondered, had he held it ready?

Despite herself, she asked him once, "Do you like the way I look?"

"You're lovely. I told you. And exotic."

"Exotic?"

"You know, like something strange to eat."

While she drank milk from a beautiful glass, he went to the bad part of town for an ethnic meal. *The food's great but don't inspect the kitchen, and don't use the bathroom, whatever you do.* She was sure that in a matter of time she would repulse him, utterly.

When he told her he lost his virginity on a train, she asked, "Where, in the toilet?" and startled both of them with her ignorance of sleepers riding moonlit rails. She spoke too soon, too loud, and her imagination faltered. With a rank air she revealed herself, as though a door had swung open.

"And your first time?" he asked.

"On a bed. In the background I heard radio music. While in your berth you heard the locomotive." Beside him, she lay very still and added, "How romantic."

"I didn't know what I was doing,"

"Neither did I, I pretended."

"Did you fool him?"

"Probably not."

"You didn't know him well?"

"We were classmates. It was nothing, really."

"I don't mean to pry, you don't have to tell me, but

altogether how many?''

So, the flower had been picked and now the leaves, defoliation. "Of course I'll tell you. Let me think,'' Plus one, plus one, plus one . . . She liked to count them off while she walked sometimes; she liked to step on each of them. "Fewer than all my fingers and toes. Enough for a team.''

He laughed at this.

"Now you,'' she said.

"Hmm . . .''

She turned toward the wall and felt desolate for three minutes. "Well?''

"So far twenty-nine.''

"So far? You haven't come to me yet?''

"You were first. From you I worked back.''

Aging, she had gone the opposite route, while he grew younger. "And you're still not sure who thirty is?''

"I just unearthed her. My first year in college. True love! I remember . . .''

Everything but her name, though he remembered other names. He had loved in sets: sisters, roommates, friends. In love, he'd correspond, and he'd saved every envelope and letter. *Dear Peter, with all my kisses.* Love in an attic, a borrowed car, a dormitory room, an unheated cabin. All she thought love would be until she knew better, or did she? She knew he didn't love her.

"Robin, you okay? I hope I haven't said something . . .''

"Of course not. I'm just surprised to hear you're so romantic. Actually, I suspected all along." She laughed. Ugly now, or still exotic? No matter. He was in France again with a woman named Ruth. He couldn't get enough of her. "Was she exotic?''

"Who, Ruth? No, silly, you're exotic. You.''

He fluffed her hair, no longer hair but rainbow plumage. He wasn't kissing, but sampling. How exotic. How peculiar. Occasionally, a taste might develop further, into distaste. *You ate it last week, Peter. I don't understand. All right, all right. If you don't like it, leave it on your plate.*

Similarly, when he decided he did not like where he was living, he moved. "I knew from the start this was temporary, or else I couldn't have stood it. My new place is in the woods. A guest house, rent-free in exchange for doing a little carpentry work in a mansion nearby."

"So you're the kind of person who gets those kinds of deals. I always wondered."

"Now Robin."

"Now Nothing."

"We'll see each other."

He spoke with such certainty that she knew he meant the opposite. "Yes," she said, "We'll see each other."

She stared at his eyes. In a certain light, the outer corners showed their wrinkles: the stamp of a citrus fruit sliced open, radiating lines. Had he suffered? No, he had squinted; through his childhood he'd played outdoors every day in a hot, sunny climate. Now he slid sunglasses from his shirt pocket, unfolded them, and put them on.

Sadness, loneliness, pain. The few times he invoked those words he seemed to be drilling for tomorrow's vocabulary quiz. *Of course you'll feel uncomfortable with these new words, Peter, but you must try to use them just the same.* Rightfully, they did not belong to Robin either.

Her problems? No more serious than her landlord's. Now that Peter was gone, perhaps she should hang a sign around her neck: Vacancy. For Rent.

Sue Miller

Expensive Gifts

Charlie Kelly was her eighth lover since the divorce. He was standing naked in silhouette, as slim as a stiletto in the light from the hall, rifling through the pockets in his jacket for his cigarettes. The sight of him gave Kate no pleasure. She hated the smell of cigarette smoke in her bedroom. She hated the horrible silence that fell between men and women who didn't know each other well after making love, but she hated even more for it to be filled with the rustling little rituals of the smoker.

"I'm afraid there are no ashtrays in here," she said. Her voice was pinched and proper. Five minutes before she had been expelling short, pleased grunts, like a bear rooting around in garbage.

"That's okay," he said, sitting on the bed again, and lighting up. "My wineglass is empty."

"Actually," she said, although she wasn't at all sure of it, "that was *my* wineglass. And I was going to get some more wine." She stood up on her side of the bed and smashed her head on the Swedish ivy. She usually occupied Charlie's side of the bed. She wasn't used to the pitfalls on the other side. He appeared not to have noticed her accident.

"Here," she said, reaching over for the glass. "I'll bring you a real ashtray." He handed her the expensive wineglass, one of her wedding presents. The cardboard match leaned at an angle within it, its charred head resting in a tiny pool of red liquid. Kate felt Charlie's eyes upon her as she walked away from him, her slender silhouette now harshly revealed in the glare of the hall light. Her gait felt unfamiliar to her, awkward.

In the kitchen she threw the match away and set her glass down. She wanted to check Neddie. He always kicked the covers off in the intense, private struggles that dominated his dreaming life, and he had a bad cold now. Kate dressed him for bed in a big sleeper that made a blanket unnecessary, but she still had a mystical belief in tucking him in, in pulling the covers right up to his chin.

The night light was on in his room, a tiny leering Mickey Mouse head that leaked excess light from a hole where its nose had been until Ned had knocked it off with a toy one day. The covers had slid sideways off the bed into a tangled heap on the floor, and Neddie lay on his stomach. His hands were curled into fists, and one thumb rested near his open mouth, connected to it by a slender, almost invisible thread of saliva. His breathing was labored, thick with mucus.

Kate bent over him to tuck the covers in on the far side. Her breasts swung down and brushed his back. He muttered in his sleep, and reinserted his thumb in his mouth. He sucked briefly, his throat working too, in the same thorough way he'd pulled at her breast when he was nursing; but he couldn't breathe. His mouth fell open after a moment, and his thumb slipped out. His face puckered slightly, but he slept on. Kate watched his face smooth out, and stroked his hair back.

She stopped in the kitchen and poured herself a new glass of wine. She looked briefly and half-heartedly for an ashtray for Charlie, and settled, finally, for a saucer. She didn't want to return to her bedroom and make polite conversation with him. She wanted to call Al, her ex-husband, and talk comfortably; to make a joke of Charlie's stylized flattery of her and her own dogged unresponsiveness. But she couldn't have called him. Al was getting married again soon. He'd fallen in love with his lab assistant, a dark, serious woman, and she would be sleeping there beside him.

She had called Al frequently in the two years since he had moved out. Usually it was late at night; often she was drunk. Almost always it was after she'd been with someone else for an evening. Though they had fought bitterly in the year before they separated, the year after Neddie's birth, they were kind and loving during these drunken phone calls; they commiserated on the difficulties of a single life.

"Jesus," he'd said to her. "I can't seem to get the hang of anything. All the goddam rules have changed. Either I'm a male chauvinist pig, or I'm being attacked by an omnivorous Amazon, and I'm always *totally* surprised. No wonder those statistical people remarry so fast."

There was a silence while she thought of Al attacking, being attacked. He was small and slender, with curly brown hair and thick, wire-rimmed glasses that he removed carefully before starting to make love. They left two purplish dents, like bruises, on the sides of his nose.

"Oh, I don't know. It seems to me the main thing to remember is that there just aren't any rules anymore. You just have to do what makes you feel comfortable and good about yourself."

"Oh, Katie. You've been taking those *wise* pills again." She didn't respond. He cleared his throat. "Well, how about you? You feeling good about what you're doing?"

Kate had thought about the evening she had just spent. Her voice rose to a dangerously high pitch as she said "No" and started to cry.

Now she carried her wine and the saucer back to Charlie. In some previous life her bedroom had been a sunporch. Two of its walls were a parade of large drafty windows. As if to compensate, the landlord had installed huge radiators the entire length of one of these walls; they clanked and hissed all winter long, and made her room the warmest in the apartment. Kate had hung the lower halves of the windows with curtains that moved constantly in the free-flowing air currents. She liked to lie in bed and look out of the naked top panes at the sky. It had been a luminous soft gray earlier, and now thick flakes, a darker gray against its gentle glow, brushed silently against the panes.

"Look," she said to Charlie, handing him the saucer. He was lying on his back with the open Marlboro box on his chest, using the lid for an ashtray.

"Yeah, I saw. It's sticking too, and I don't have snow tires. I'm going to have to leave pretty soon."

She looked away so he wouldn't see relief leap into her eyes. "It's so pretty, though. I almost feel like waking Neddie up to show him. He doesn't really remember it from last year. It's all new to him again. Can you imagine that?"

Charlie put out his cigarette in the saucer.

"You must be freezing your ass off." Kate was standing by the windows watching the snow's straight descent. "Slide in here, lady, I'll warm you up."

She turned obediently and got in, but she said, "My father had a dog named Lady once. A collie. Horrible barker. He finally had someone shoot her. She just wouldn't shut up." None of that was true, but Kate didn't like to be called *lady*.

Kate was, in fact, a reflexive liar. She hated to be unpleasant or contradictory, and when she felt that way, a lie, fully formed almost before she began to think about it, fell from her lips. Al had had a knack for recognizing them — he'd said it was as though her voice resonated differently — and he would simply repeat them slowly so she could hear them herself, and then tell him what it was that was making her angry. Once in a fight about whether Al should work less and help her more with Ned, she had cried out "Ned is wonderful because I've given up my fucking *life* to him!" His patient echo had made her weep; her claim seemed at once the truth and a terrible lie.

Now Charlie tried to pull her over to him, but she said Ah, ah, and held up her full wine glass as an explanation. She took a sip. He turned away to get another cigarette.

"The kid all right?"

"What, Neddie?"

"Yeah, is that his name? Is he okay?" He leaned back with the cigarette in his mouth, and exhaled two long plumes of smoke from his nostrils. Kate thought about how the pillows would smell after he'd gone.

"He's sound asleep, but really stuffed up."

"How old is he?"

"He's just three."

"Cute age," Charlie said, tapping his cigarette on the saucer. "I've got two, you know."

"Two kids?" She was surprised. He nodded. "I would never have guessed that about you, Charlie. You're too much the gay blade, the town rake."

He grinned appreciatively. He worked at it, and liked to know his efforts were successful. "They're in Connecticut with my ex-wife."

"Do you see them often?"

"About once a month I guess. She's remarried, so they've got a whole family scene there, really." He shrugged. "It doesn't seem so important anymore. They're pretty much into their life, I'm pretty much into mine, *you* know."

"Yes," she said. They sat in what she imagined he thought was companionable silence. Two used parents. She had an old iron bedstead with a large ornate grille for a headboard. Charlie's head had slipped into the space between two of the white painted rods. They pushed his ears forward slightly. He looked a little like the Mickey Mouse night light in Neddie's room. She smiled. She wondered why she had been so excited about going out with him tonight. When he'd finished his cigarette, he reached for her again She set her wineglass down on the floor by her side of the bed and they made love. Charlie seemed interested in some variations on their earlier theme, but she shook her head no, no, and their love-making was short and somewhat neutral in character. Just as he pulled limply and stickily away from her to find another cigarette, Neddie's agonized shout floated back through the apartment to her. She leaped out of bed, upsetting her half-empty wineglass, but avoiding the plant this time,and sprinted into the light and down the long hallway, pushing her breasts flat onto her chest to keep them from bouncing painfully.

Neddie's eyes were still shut. He had turned over onto his back and tears ran down his cheeks into his ears. The covers were piled on the floor. "Nooo, monkey!" he moaned, and thrashed. Kate picked him up and cradled him close, his wet face pressing on her neck.

"Neddie, it's Mommy. Mommy's here now. *No* monkeys. The monkeys are all gone. You're in your room, Neddie, with Mommy, see?" She pulled her head back to look at him. His eyes were open now, but he looked blank. She walked around the room with him, talking slowly.

"We're at home, Neddie. You had a dream. That wasn't real. That silly monkey was a dream. See, here's Sleazy. He's real." She pointed to Ned's bear, sitting on a shelf. Ned reached for him. "Sleazy," he said, and tucked him in close under his chin, the way Kate held him. She shifted him to her hip now, and went around the room, showing him all his favorite things. Kate was tall and thin. She had down-drooping breasts and flat narrow hips. She looked like a carved white column in the dim light.

"And look, Ned. Look what's happening out here." she carried him to the window. Under the street light outside Ned's room the flakes danced thickly in a sudden gust of wind: a thousand suicidal moths. "Do you know what that is?"

"Dat's da snow!' he said. His mouth hung open and his breath was hot and damp on her breast.

"And it's all piling up on the ground, Neddie, see? And tomorrow we can find the sled that Daddy gave you in the basement, and put on boots and mittens . . ."

"And my hat?" Ned wore a baseball hat every day. He watched her face now to be sure that they were in agreement on this.

"Yeah, your hat, but you have to pull your hood up over it to keep your ears warm. And we can play all day because tomorrow's Sunday. Mommy doesn't have to work."

"Not day care?"

"No, tomorrow we can stay home *all* day. Okay?" They watched the snow together for a moment. Then she turned from the window. "I'm going to tuck you in now." She carried the child to his bed and started to lower him. His legs and arms gripped her tightly, a monkey's grip.

"Stay here, mumma."

"Okay." He relaxed, and let her put him down on the bed. "But Mommy's cold. You move over and make room for me under these covers." He wiggled back against the wall and she slid in next to him and pulled the covers over them both. His face was inches from hers. He smiled at her and reached up to pat her face. His hands were sticky and warm. "Mumma," he said.

"Yes," she said tenderly, and shut her eyes to set a good example for him. Sometime later she woke to hear the front door shut gently, and footsteps going down the stairs. Then dimly, as if at a great distance, or as if it were all happening in some muffled, underwater world, a car started up in the street, there was a brief series of whirring sounds while it struggled back and forth out of its parking place, and then, like a thin cry, its noise evaporated into the night.

When Neddie woke her, the sky was still gray. The light in the room was gray too, gentle and chaste. The snow had stuck in the mesh of the screens still left on the windows from summer and the house seemed wrapped in gauze. It still fell outside, heavy and soft, but from somewhere on the street came the chink, chink of a lone optimist already shoveling.

"Ned. Let me sleep a minute more."

"You already slept a long time Mumma. And I *need* you."

He was standing by the bed, his face just above her

head. He wore a red baseball cap, and his brown eyes
regarded her gravely.

"Why do you need me?"

"You hafta make my train go."

"What, Granpoppy's train?" He shook his head
solemnly. "Oh, Christ!" she swore, and violently threw the
covers back, swinging her legs out in the same motion. He
looked fearful, and instantly she felt remorseful. "No,
Neddie, it's all right. I'm just mad at the *train*. I'll fix it."

Her parents had given Ned the train, an expensive
Swedish model of painted wood. The cars fastened together
with magnets. Occasionally, by chance, Ned would line them
up correctly, but most often, one or two cars would be turned
backwards, north pole to north pole, or south to south, and
the more he would try to push them together, the more they
repelled each other. Her parents' extravagance since her
divorce, their attempts to ease her way and Ned's with things
she didn't want and couldn't use, annoyed her. She must
have bent down to correct the magnetic attraction on this
thing thirty times since they had given it to Ned.

He came and squatted by her. He had laid the track out
and there were miniature pigs and sheep and ducks heaped
up in the tiny open train cars. The thought of his working
silently for so long, trying not to wake her, touched her. As
they squatted together she began to try to explain to him the
idea of polar attraction, turning the brightly painted cars first
one way and then the other, so he could see the greedy pull
at work.

Suddenly his head dipped slightly to look underneath
her and his expression changed. She stopped. "Mumma's
leaking?" he asked, pointing to the floor. She shifted her
weight to one leg and looked on the floor, where she'd been
squatting. Thick drops of whitish liquid, reminders of
lovemaking the night before, glistened like pearls on the
nicked wood. She laughed and got up to get some Kleenex.

"It's all right Neddie. Mommy can clean it up in a

second. See?'' she said. ''All gone.''

She smiled down at him as he squatted, fuzzy and compact in his sleeper, like a baby bear. He turned away and began to pull the toy train, now perfectly attached, around the expensive track.

Edward P. Jones

Island

From her place at the window she watched him, hatless, coatless, lead the mule to the wagon beneath an evenly gray sky. An empty pipe clamped between his teeth, he hitched the mule, and after she came out of the house, having kissed the children goodbye, he helped her up onto the wagon. She took the reins from him and settled herself on a seat of rags. He covered her legs with their oldest quilt, tucking it with care, and his hand lingered on the toe of her boot.

"You think of anything you want?" she asked, looking down at him. Her head was all but concealed in a makeshift woolen scarf, so that only the very tip of her nose could be seen from the side.

He said, "A bad cold snap's comin. Tonight, maybe early tomorrow mornin." He looked east, west, then up at her. He offered a piece of a smile and his eyes squinted and the empty pipe whistled with every breath. "Could be snow."

After nearly eleven years with him she had not gotten used to that way he had of saying something out of the blue or of leaping ahead in their conversations, supplying answers to questions she had yet to ask, or did not want the answers to.

The mule turned his head to stare at them with a look of sad and humble impatience.

"Maybe tis snow," she said. But she did not care if he was right or wrong, though about such things he was usually right.

"Some pipe tobacca . . .," he said. "And some sweets for them children. You know how they are when they ain't brought nothin." He put his hands in his pockets and dug absently in the dirt with his toe.

"Yes," she said.

The mule stamped a hoof.

In the cold their words were puffs of white mist that floated away a few inches and died; their son, her son, called them cold words. About them, in the final days of November, there was barely a sign of life. Each thing — bush, tree, smokehouse, barn — seemed to have contracted, as if to keep within what warmth there was left. Whenever the wind blew, an occasional wood chip or an ugly ball of dry weeds and twigs sailed across the yard, and the peach tree's swing swung with what she told her children was a ghost child.

"I betta get on," she said, leaning down to kiss his mouth so that a part of his face momentarily disappeared inside the scarf. Except when he took his crops to market or went to church, he rarely ventured beyond his own land, but traveling, moving, was something she had discovered over the years was in her blood. Absalom held her shoulder for an instant, then stepped back, and she called to the mule, "Get up!"

Breathing heavily, the mule took her out to the path, and in a long moment she passed from his sight. She knew he would stand there until he could no longer hear the heavy rumble of the wagon. (In warmer weather he would follow her out to the road and watch the dust swallow her up.) Years before, she used to wonder when she pulled away whether he thought that she would not come back, that with that old mule and wagon she would take to the roads and try once more to find her way to New York. . . . Now she did not wonder, and if she had been asked, she would have said that that was the furthest thought from his mind. And if it was, she would have said it was partly because she herself did not think of it anymore. Now they had a shared history of eleven years that bound them together, and she felt his eyes follow her around the bend in the path.

Coming fully into the road, she considered speaking a

soothing word or two to the mule, but in his old age he had grown solitary, withdrawn, and she did not think he would hear her or care for words as he once might have. Once upon a time he had been smart and had enough life in him for three mules, Absalom had told her, but now, his eyes dull, lifeless, the mule kept to himself in his corner, his backside turned to the rest of the barn.

And so she hummed.

It was a back road, the one she was traveling on. The fields that bordered it were worked by people who lived in cabins that bordered more traveled roads. Here and there was an abandoned shack, mauled by the weather and time, its door open to the winds and homeless dogs. A single bird flew over, too high for her to tell what kind, its wings pumping, pumping with all the life it had. "You late," she said to it, "and it'll catch up with you. Tonight or tomorrow, it'll catch you. You late thing."

After a mile or so she crossed the small bridge his father had built. The creek had given up its life and was now still, a mirror reflecting the grayness above. The bridge and the creek gave the area where they lived its name, The Island, though it was far from that. Absalom had lived there alone until the day she came, a day not unlike today. Hungry and cold to the bone, she had pounded at his door until her hand was scratched and bleeding slightly. When he had finally opened the door and she saw him, calm and as expressionless as an egg, she knew he had heard her from the first knock.

"I ain't a rich man," he had said later while she sat shivering before the fire, though she had not inquired about his circumstances. She could see he was not much older than she, but he had the bearing of some old men, that haughty look that seemed to say all time was now in his back pocket and there was no need to hurry. He draped a blanket that smelled of pine wood over her shoulders and handed her a cup of bitter tea. As she drank, he brought in a bucket of warm, salted water for her swollen feet. "I've neva bothered a soul . . ." As she listened, as feeling painfully returned to her feet and legs, she perceived that his was not the sound of complaining about being disturbed, but more a simple stating of what was true and what was not.

Long before she reached the shack near the fork in the road, she saw the black smoke rising, dissipating. She watched it until she was close to the shack, then she saw a small figure wrapped in a blue cape, standing before her in the road. The person pulled back the cape's hood and she saw an old woman, gray hair in plaits, smiling with a mouth full of dark yellow teeth. Calling to the mule, the younger woman stopped the wagon.

"Hi you doin?" the old woman said, hurrying to the side of the wagon. "I was hopin you'd stop. I'm Sally Longwood. Been livin there" — with her chin she pointed to the shack — "for bout a week and you my second company today. The second in all the time I been here." She spoke in quick, anxious spurts, as if there were some danger of something cutting her off at any moment. "Well, really you my first, cause that otha today wasn't no company atall."

"I'm Hortense Stuart. But I ain't come to visit. I'm headed to town, to the sto."

The old woman glanced down the road as if she could see the store from where she stood. "Oh . . . Oh, I see. I knowed I was out here by my lonesome, but when I heard the wagon, I guess I just thought you was comin to see me." She pulled the hood back over her head. "But come in and stop a minute anyway. Why don't you?" She touched Hortense's knee. "Just for a cup a coffee then. That sto ain't goin nowhere, hon."

Hortense shook her head. "I wish I could, but my son's taken with a bad cold and I don't want to leave him for too long. I'm goin in afta some salve and quinine pills."

"A cold?" the old woman said. "Oh, shoot! He'll get ova that with or without you. You know chirren . . . Now come on with yourself." She took the reins from Hortense and secured them, then stepped back with another yellow smile. "A cup of coffee, a word or two, thas all, then you can be on your way."

With a deliberately loud sigh Hortense climbed down. "Just a minute though, then I'll have to be goin."

"A minute's all thas needed tween friends, child."

A thick warmth enveloped her as soon as the old woman pushed open the shack's door. Inside there seemed no space in which to move, to breathe. Furniture and pasteboard boxes from floor to ceiling hid the walls, the lower boxes crushed in places from the weight of those on top. On the boxes were written in a childlike scrawl "china", "lenen", "can goods", "nic nacs." Clothes — dresses, skirts, coats — were draped over expensive-looking high-backed chairs and were hanging heavily from rope nailed to the ceiling, and what must have been two dozen pairs of women's shoes stuffed with rags were lined in neat, shiny rows on boxes and along the floor. Near the center of the room, just to the side of a pallet, a pot-bellied stove showed a small raging orange face.

"I had to give way some a my stuff before I moved here. My otha place caught fire and so they moved me here. You shoulda seen all that I lost in the fire." She pulled two cane-bottom chairs up to the stove. "My people moved me to this place, and I guess it'll do for the time bein." For a good while the old woman looked solemnly at the great mass, and the younger woman watched her. "You just my second company today and I'm so glad to see you, hon."

"Your people?" Hortense said, taking off her coat and sitting down.

"Yes. That is my white people, the ones I useta work for before I got so I couldn't. Lord, if it wasn't for them, I don't know what I'd do." She sat down next to Hortense and put a coffee pot on the stove, then she handed Hortense the prettiest china cup and saucer she had ever seen. On the saucer and the cup was the same decorative rose, which seemed as real to Hortense as any she had seen in life. Its petals were a breathtaking red, promising to the touch a softness unequalled, and curling out from each rose was the same vibrant green stem. And into each cup Miss Sally put a shining silver spoon.

"You say you had some company today?"

"Oh, he wasn't no real company like you, hon," the old woman said. "Just some colored fella in a big blue automobile. He was lost and he wanted darections from me. From *me*, and I as lost in this here place as he is. Said his home was right near here; called the name a the place, but I done forgot. When he found out I couldn't help him he went away. Offered him some coffee, the fire, but he wouldn't stop. Didn't even get out that thing. Said he was in a hurry, so what could I do? Lord, but that automobile was big! Bigga than some parlors I done seen."

Where space allowed along some boxes, ancient photographs were displayed. A host of white people stared blankly out at Hortense: the women with mourning eyes and severe, ax-sharp parts in the middle of their heads, aged-looking children standing stiffly to either side of their elders, and gaunt men in Confederate army uniforms with thick moustaches and heavy beards. There was a more recent photograph propped against a jewelry box at the head of the pallet. Hortense leaned down to the side to see a woman — obviously a younger Miss Sally — in the middle of a group of white children. At her side, his hand in hers, was a small black boy, smiling.

"Thas my oldest. I had five," the old woman said, holding her open hand before her face, "but they all turned on me. Chirren will do that. They forget what you did for em and they turn on you." She poured coffee into their cups. "I have sugar round here somewhere, if you want." Hortense shook her head.

Then they were quiet, sipping and watching the fire. It

cracked, spit. The wind rattled the roof and for a second or two the women look up at the stovepipe, then shyly at each other.

"Where they at now, your children?" Hortense asked.

"Here and there, this place, that place." She pointed to the picture on the floor. "He in Philadelphia. Been there now goin on fifteen years. You know that place, Philadelphia?"

"No, ma'am, I don't."

Miss Sally sighed and set her cup on the floor. "I got anotha boy in Washington, D.C., where the president lives, and my girls they in *De*troit. My youngest son's in Boston, or California, I cain't memba which. The last time I heard, I think it was California." She was a small light-brown skinned woman. Her hair was tied with long, exquisite green ribbons and the skin on her jaws hung down and moved sluggishly whenever she turned her head. She stared into the fire, one hand cupped in the other, her slippered feet tucked demurely under the chair. About her there was an aura of gardenia.

As she drank her coffee, Hortense looked about the room. The more she looked the less impressive everything seemed. Some of the clothes had an ugly dinginess about them, others had colors fading or completely lost. And many of the shoes were badly scuffed with peeling leather and only their shine to recommend them. Even the cup she held had two cracks thinner than hair. She sensed that there was not one person in all the old pictures who was alive, or as alive as she and Miss Sally were now. And somehow that made the pictures — despite the fine wooden frames and the quaint majesty of some of the faces — as unimpressive as the dingy clothes and the cracked cups.

"They thought I treated them betta, but that ain't true. As God is my witness, that ain't true," Miss Sally was saying in a voice plaintive and low.

"Ma'am?"

The old woman said nothing. She looked at Hortense for a long time and touched her hand. "My chirren. They cused me a that, but it ain't true. . . . I been here a week and you my first company. Listen: I neva did what they said. Sometimes I wish God had neva give em to me. Thas bad to say, I know, but thas what it all done come down to: me questionin His work."

"You say they accused you?"

"Yes. Yes," she said. She looked into the face of the fire and it was as if she were speaking to it, as if that was the only way she could speak to Hortense. "Yes, they did. They said I treated the white chirren betta that I brought up, that I gave the white where I wouldn't give them. Gave myself, my time, you see." She folded her arms. "Maybe I did once or twice, but no more than that. No more. A body is human. It happens. Maybe I did." Then, with her eyes intense and one string of a vein prominent in her neck, she seemed to gain strength and become more confident of what she was saying, and she turned to face Hortense. "But it wasn't like they said. I loved my own above all. I know and God knows." She began rubbing her eyes with the palms of her hands. "Maybe you know what I mean. I put my chirren first, first as I could, and I'll say so come Judgement."

"I don't think you should worry, Miss Sally, if you did the best you could."

"I know I did," she said in a whisper, turning back to the fire.

Hortense searched herself for words to give her, but everything seemed small and inadequate when she considered the old woman's loss. Like faces, the boxes and clothes and shoes stared at her. She closed her eyes and wiped the sweat from her brow, from her eyelids.

After several minutes Miss Sally said, "Here, let me show you somethin, hon. I don't show it to just anybody, cause not everybody can preciate it." From a box near the back of the room she brought a stereoscope and several 3-D pictures.

"My white lady gave this to me," she said, handling the objects with the greatest care. "It was her daddy's and she give it to me. Everything in this room just about she gave me. Her son moved me here, the same one I took care of all his life. He nice, but he ain't like her. The livin neva come close to what the dead was, but we learn to make do." She slid one of the double pictures into the stereoscope and handed it to Hortense, who peered into it to see people at a World's Fair. Miss Sally changed the picture and there was a tower-like building with hundreds of windows. She changed it again and a busy city street appeared, then a half-naked dancing woman, then a man in a cowboy suit with guns strapped to his side, sitting on a white horse; all of it — except for the lack of color — as life-like to Hortense as the woman next to her.

"Ain't that nice?" Miss Sally said. "I treasure that. It's like bein right there, don't you think? All them places up close like that. It belonged to her fatha. He was a judge and seen all that, and more besides."

"It's right nice."

Miss Sally placed the stereoscope and pictures back in the box. "I got more pictures, more than you can shake a stick at. You come by some time and see em. We could make a day of it, you and me. A whole day, lookin at pictures and what not."

"Yes, ma'am, maybe I will." Hortense stood up, giving the old woman the cup and saucer.

"Yes, child, do come by." She stood and her hand, far more bone than flesh, held Hortense's, patted it. "But why would God let my chirren leave me floatin out here like this? Why would somebody do that to somebody?"

"Oh, Miss Sally, you shouldn't worry. He always makes a way for us." Hortense opened the door.

"I know I shouldn't worry, but I do. I have to."

Pulling the hood of the cape over her head and putting

her hands in her pockets, she walked Hortense to the wagon. The mule bucked when she got up on the wagon and his ears perked up.

"You'll come back soon, won't you?" Miss Sally asked. "We have a lot to talk about." Hortense nodded. "But now if my people come for me, I won't be here."

"That'd be good," and she wanted to ask why she wasn't with them now, but the old woman turned and went back in the shack. Hortense said good-by and the door shut and the mule pulled her away.

The gray land moved past her and she moved deeper into it. She did not want to think about the old woman, surrounded in that shack by her precious things. She wanted to hum, but her mind would form no tune. She thought of her own children and a sadness took hold of her. If Absalom did not watch them, the boy would be out in the day's cold, dragging along his sister. Hortense saw them vividly in her mind at that moment, standing before the cabin, hand-in-hand as if posing for a picture, their faces and clothes dirtied. The boy had none of Absalom's blood, and the girl, being female, surely had more of her being than his. Yet sometimes — like now, on that cold road — she felt as if they were not hers at all, but belonged completely to him, had been formed from their first second of life in his image, with his ways and nature, so that now as she imagined them standing before the cabin, she felt lost from them. She remembered what a fat revival preacher had said about Mary some long ago summer evening in her childhood: That Mary was only the instrument, the tool, it was Jesus and God that really mattered in the end, "cold and cruel as that might sound to y'all." It could have been any woman, the man had thundered, but there was only one God and could have been but that one Jesus.

There was nothing moving in the town except a stray

dog. He looked up at her with drooping eyes, sniffed the air a moment or two, and hurried away, one hind leg held up from the ground. Even before she reached the store, she could see the blue automobile, bold and shining and alone on the street, parked in front of the store. And standing on the store's porch was a dark-skinned man watching her. She sensed immediately that the car belonged to him, and she remembered the man Miss Sally had said had not stopped. He wore a brown dress hat and a brown overcoat, the expensive kind she saw in South Boston's store windows on white mannequins, and as the mule took her closer she could see that his shoes were as shiny as any of Miss Sally's. He wore a tie which she rarely saw on a colored man in mid-week.

She secured the reins and got down from the wagon. He caught her eye as she walked up the steps, and in that moment she knew that she knew him. She slowed without realizing it, and when she was just past him, the smell of his cologne in her nose, her lips began to quiver until she pressed them tightly together. She reached for the door knob once, twice, missing it each time because it was not where she thought it was. *Say my name. Say my name.*

"You the best lookin thing to walk by me yet," he said and took off his hat. "The only think cept that fool dog. Don't hurry in, stay a while."

She studied the face and slowly took it back through the years until it was not as mature, had no moustache, no glistening, thumb-sized scar on the left cheek. *Say my name.* He came toward her and tilted his head. Then, before long, his mouth opened wide enough for a June bug to fly in. He squinted with a look of gradual recognition, and in his eyes she thought she could see words of familiarity, of remembrance, forming in his mind, preparing to march their way down to his mouth.

He turned his eyes away from her. "It's cold," he said, as if that were the news of the day. "I always been kinda fraid of the cold." He still did not look at her and he began to mumble.

"What you want with me?" She could see herself walking on that road that day, walking away home, from her father and brother, walking all those miles whenever she couldn't get a ride in a buggy or on a wagon, seeing more of the world than she had in all her days. Walking until the fruit and ash cakes she had eaten along the way began to turn her stomach, walking until she found herself standing in Absalom Stuart's yard and looking at his door like it was salvation itself.

"I don't mean you no harm." He spoke softly, smiled nervously, a familiar smile that had not changed as much as the face had. *Say it. Say my name.* "We learned in school — at least I did in my school — bout that ice age, and the teacher said how it was gonna come again. Maybe soon. And every winter since she said that I keep thinkin this gonna be it, that the cold's gonna come and never go away, and I'll be caught somewhere and get turned to a block a ice. Know what I mean? I dream about it sometimes. Nightmares." He gave a small laugh. She remembered the teacher, the lesson, the two of them in that schoolroom with the stove that never worked properly. "I guess if it did happen to me, I'd be good for nothin but bein chopped up and dropped into somebody's glass a lemonade." He seemed to huddle in his coat. *Just say it, thas all.*

When she saw that there were more of the same words about to come from him, she glared at him until a pained look came over his face. Blinking, he merely looked at her and after a bit he lowered his eyes, closing them off to her. Then slowly he seemed to compose himself, his face losing all expression. He straightened his tie, looking into her scarf-shadowed face as if it were a mirror. And when that was done, he smiled boldly, and that smile was not at all familiar. It shook her, and though she knew he recognized her, she knew that he would not say her name, even if he remembered it. She felt the need to sit down, but she steeled herself, commanded her feet to anchor themselves to the porch. She reached for the knob again, and again she missed it.

"What you want with me, I said?" *Yes, walked and walked till my feet swolled and I got dog-tired and almost forgot my own name, trying to get to you in that New York place. And then knockin and knockin till my hand bled.*

"Some friendly talk, is all," he said. "I bought stuff in his store, but he won't let me stand in there out the cold. I shoulda knowed it would be that way when I left home, but bein away from all this you forget. I got tired a bein in that car, nice as it is. So I just stood up here."

"There ain't nothin I can do for you," Hortense said and stepped away from him. She thought of calling him by name to let him know she knew who he was, but when he smiled again, a gold tooth caught her eye and would not allow her to speak.

"But hey now . . ." He came toward her, tall, imposing, blocking out what daylight there was. She opened the door and a little bell tinkled and she stepped into a room that smelled of molasses and pickles.

"Some Vicks salve and quinine pills, please," she said to the old white man half-asleep behind the counter. They were alone in the store. Behind him on the wall was tacked a Coca-Cola calendar with a Santa Claus smiling beneficently at her, a glass of the dark brown liquid in his hand. The year on the calendar was different from the one it was presently.

In her head there were falling leaves, each one so separate from the others that she could count them, each one floating down within its own space of color.

Lucas, I'll be patient.

"Some peppamints, too, please. And pipe tobacca, that kind there in the red can."

Don't count the days, baby, cause there ain't gonna be no need for that. Before you can turn around good the ticket'll be here and you'll be there. Snap! Quick as that.

"Sixty-two cents," the man said. "And there's two extra

pieces for the children."

Hortense nodded, unfolding a handkerchief and giving him one of two crumpled dollar bills.

"I always give extra to children. It makes for business in years to come." She knew this, had heard it dozens of times. But if he had offered, she would have sat down on the flour barrel and listened to it for the rest of her life.

She saw herself sewing in her father's house, saw herself watching the falling leaves.

She thanked the man, walked to the door. The bell tinkled and she breathed odorless air heavy with the threat of snow.

"I'm down to see my mother," the man she knew as Lucas said. He stood partly in front of her and partly to the side, so that if she had wanted she could have walked past him. "I started out way long before sunup. And somethin kept tellin me all the way that I was too late, but the more it said that, the faster I drove." He spoke slowly, almost sadly, and she was reminded of Absalom, giving answers to unasked questions. "I thought I was bein good to her, y'know? I had her up to visit me. I sent down what money and things she needed. But now my aunt that live with her sent me this telegram" — he patted his breast pocket — "sayin she took bad. Dyin. I always sent her money, but I guess money don't buy medicine enough. She deserved a better son, I guess. She deserved that at least." He looked fully at her, taking her whole face in, and came one step closer. Hortense could see his mother, sweating, standing alone in a wide field of tobacco and waving to her, her arm high above her head, her hand open.

"This the only real town around," he said, "the only place where I could get gasoline. I know I can't be no more than fifteen miles or so from where my home is." Rubbing the scar, he paused. "But I ain't been in this part a the world in a lotta years and I guess I got myself lost." She sensed an attempt at something beyond the words and found herself listening and waiting, but then she heard a leaf hitting the ground and the sound was like a scream. "But say now, you live round here?" he said finally, his eyes taking all of her in, his voice reverting to that tone in which he had first addressed her.

"No. And I gotta be goin."

The wagon creaked as she got up. He came down to her, and putting on his hat, he pointed with a gloved hand to the car.

"If you wanna change your mind, honey, that belongs to me. Free and clear. It rides like your own bed: you hardly know you movin. The Packard people guarantee every one a they cars, and I extra-guarantee this one." She stared briefly at him, and it came to her — painfully obvious, like something she had fought a long long time to reject — that she could stand before him forever and he would spend that eternity denying her.

She picked up the reins. The mule took his time, but she managed to turn him around. Then there were no more falling leaves, only a skeleton tree that looked relieved to be free of a burden. The leaves swirled up as if to return, but the limbs shook them away and the wind stopped.

Behind her he was saying something she could not hear.

When she was almost to the edge of the town, out of his sight, she stopped the wagon, got out and looked around the side of a building at him. A white man came up the street and spoke to him. Lucas leaned against the porch post, saying nothing. For a good while the man looked into each window of the car, and after saying something more to Lucas, he walked away. Soon afterwards Lucas took off his hat and coat and got into the car. In a minute or so he was gone.

Say my name. The motor kept saying it until the name was just a vague mechanical sound in the distance that could have been any name.

My pretty gal, thas what I'm gonna call you. My pretty gal. The prettiest gal in all Virginia, in the whole damn south for that matta.

When she got back on the wagon, the mule, sensing home at last, picked up his pace. She began to cry and could not see the road, but the mule knew the way.

She thought of what lay before her — Absalom, the children, home. And once or twice she looked back down the way she had come. Absalom. Whom she had stumbled upon and who had let her stay out of a kindness she had never known before, a kindness she found sharp-edged one moment and bountifully reassuring the next. In those first days he never once asked who she was or where she had come from. When she was going. He seemed to disappear and reappear in the room at will; she would be sitting before the fire trying to tell him how she came to be there, only to look up and find him gone. Gradually, over the weeks and months, most of her adapted. He delivered the child, the boy, because the midwife could not find her way in the snow to The Island. When the child is strong, she kept telling him, I will be gone.

She continued to cry. The reins became slack, and fearful of losing them, she wrapped them tightly around her hands. She watched the mule make his half-blind way over the road and something in her envied him. In the beginning, in that cabin of what was then one room and a kitchen, she and Absalom staked out a separate space for themselves, while the boy was free to crawl wherever he wished. In time, with the sharing of responsibility for the child, the cabin became whole again. Three years after the birth of the boy Absalom delivered his daughter.

Until two years or so after the girl was born, she could not have said she loved Absalom Stuart. She had had his child, but that had nothing to do with loving him. And though she did not think very much about Lucas after the first five or so years with Absalom, a word or something seen would set free a memory and tell her she did not love Lucas any less. But one day in the sixth year, as she stood alone in the kitchen, something touched her mind as lightly as her hand would touch one of the sleeping children, and she stood quiet, first tensing, then relaxing, her mind swimming, and when she had calmed herself, reached the shore, she went without thinking into where he was playing with the children. She touched his shoulder, his neck, and pulled at a twist of his hair, though he did not acknowledge her presence. From that day on she believed she loved Absalom and gave next to no thought at all to Lucas and none to leaving, until that moment she saw him on the store's porch, his blue car parked in front of him, a diamond stick pin in his tie.

* * *

By and by the tears stopped and she hoped Miss Sally would be standing in the road again. She wanted to sit with her before the stove and look into that thing and see the World's Fair and the dancing woman and the cowboy with the shining guns. She wanted to be told again about the old woman's life and how her children had turned on her and how she had come to be in that place surrounded by things and by the memory of the living who might as well be dead.

It pained her deeply to think that she may not have ever loved Absalom.

She looked down the road, hoping for Miss Sally, but it was clear and nothing stood in her path. She was frightened, and knew that if Lucas had only called her name and bowed his head in repentence, she might well have taken his hand and pressed it to herself.

She passed the old woman's shack. The door was shut. The smoke rose in the same black line to the sky where it disappeared. She did not have in her what it took to stop and knock at the door.

Even though she knew she would never see Lucas again, she felt somehow suspended between the two men, suspended without life or will, like a dress hanging alone in the middle of a clothesline. If eleven years was not long enough, she thought, then how long? In her mind she saw Absalom standing before the cabin. Perhaps he had known all along, and that was what was on his mind each time he watched her ride away. Perhaps he cared if she came back and at the same time perhaps he did not, as she herself loved and yet did not love. Who would know or care, except the old woman dying for company, if she spent the rest of her life going up and down the road?

Maybe he would after so long a time.

Reaching home, she drove the wagon into the barn and unharnessed the mule. He went directly to his corner without a sound or a look back.

She found the three of them in the room Absalom had built for the children.

"Mama," the boy said from the bed, sitting up, "I feel all betta. Daddy said he'd see and maybe I can go outside tomorra if the snow ain't deep."

Absalom sat in a large cushioned chair beside the bed and the little girl was nestled in his lap. Reaching up to be kissed by Hortense, she giggled and drew back slightly when she encountered her mother's cold lips and cheek.

"Make it all right?" Absalom said.

"Yes." She gave him the bag and touched his shoulder momentarily.

"See anybody?" he asked.

"No," she said, taking the jar of salve from him. "Oh, wait — there's a old lady down the road a piece. Moved there two weeks ago, I think she said. All by her lonesome in that shack, poor thing. I feel for her."

"She all right?"

"Seem to be. She asked me to come back to see her, and I think I will. But maybe you'd betta see how she doin tomorrow. Bout food and wood and such."

He nodded and handed a peppermint stick to each child. "Now no more before y'all get your suppa, y'hear me?"

The girl smiled and shook her head. The boy bit down

loudly.

Hortense rubbed the salve over the boy's chest, then she covered it with a patch of wool and pulled the blanket up to his neck. She stepped back, watching them, as if through a window. Don't think past what's at hand right now, she told herself. If you do, you'll go all to pieces like some dry leaf. If not eleven years, then . . .? *They shouldna left me floatin out here, hon.*

From a trunk at the foot of the bed Absalom took a Bible as large as the girl's chest and began reading to the children about the baby Jesus, the only story in the Bible, except the creation one, that they would sit quiet for. The girl looked up into his face, following intently the movement of his lips. The boy closed his eyes and rested his hands behind his head.

From a shelf Hortense took down a pair of the boy's pants that needed mending. Quietly, she carried a chair and the pants and her sewing box and sat down against the wall where not much of the lamp light fell. It was a comfortable corner farthest from the hearth.

Sandra Scofield

Trespass

Katie had already made plans to go to Texas with the baby. Her going didn't have anything to do with Fisher hitting her. On the other hand, she wouldn't change her plans, even though her eyes were black in the morning; even though he cried and said he'd sat up all night in remorse, thinking about killing himself (he'd slept the sleep of the dead drunk—she'd heard his snoring); even though she'd have to lie to her mother, and her mother wouldn't believe her, so that she'd end up defending him the way she always had, when he didn't deserve it any more. It was the first time he had hit her, unless you counted a couple of shoves. Once, long before they had married, they had been visiting an army buddy of his in Sausalito, and Fisher had given her a push, out on the deck of the buddy's houseboat, because she was yelling at him not to go off drinking and leave her with the buddy's pregnant super-Christian girlfriend. The push shut her up, and scared her, out there in the dark; it almost made her mad enough to get on a bus and come home alone. But the buddy's girlfriend who had been an acid freak before she tuned in to Jesus on a Christian radio station, said it was just that the guys were still coming down from all those killing vibes, and praying and loving were sure to bring them back. Katie worried about being out on the water without the rowboat; when she thought about it, she realized that the other girl had been thinking longer term. If Katie had had a longer view, too, she might have made the bus, but common sense told her Fisher wouldn't leave her bobbing a hundred yards off shore from a disco, once he'd had enough of whatever he'd gone off to get. Sure enough, he'd made it up to her; he arrived near noon with croissants and eggs, made an omelet and pleaded temporary insanity. He took her out on the deck again—she could remember still the smell of shingles and the water and gull droppings at her feet—and shyly offered her a fat joint. "I'm better with gestures than words," he said," a grin plucking at the corners of his mouth. She gave in to his awkward charm, wishing there were more of it, and that it were real. She smoked a little with him, and then went inside, her heart a caught bird thumping against the back of her ribs.

The next time he struck her wasn't that long ago, which made things seem really bad, because she could see a connection between what had happened then and what had happened now—an escalation of violence she'd have to think about before she'd know what she ought to do. He had come home from a bar where, over a pitcher of Oly, he had heard some real straight-arrow assholes saying the soldiers in Vietnam must have been chicken, and now half of them were turning out crazy too. Some guy had shot his wife and then himself, and the paper ran a series on the syndrome that was supposed to explain it all. Downtown, in a seedy neighborhood near the bridge, some longhaired vets ran a center for their own kind; Katie and Fisher passed it whenever they went to their favorite restaurant, run by a family of Thais. "Fucking everywhere," she heard Fisher grumble as they walked by. He was eight, nine years home from Asia. Those guys in the bar had been in grade school or junior high when he was slogging around in mud up to his knees. "Baby fascists," Fisher said. "They're still wet from their first fucks." She meant to sympathize, to try to feel whatever it was he felt. What did she know about war? She hadn't been in junior high, she'd been in outer space when it was going on. She remembered the demonstrations in the same dim way she remembered July the Fourth and Rose Parades. Pictures from the war were recently remembered and surprisingly clear: burned, screaming children; the little guy wincing as the bullet hit his brain. Those had been famous pictures, or else she wouldn't have seen them. She had never been political; she didn't have time between classes and waitress jobs. And she hated the way students shoved flyers in her face; she always let them fall. The war meant more to her now, because of whatever Fisher had brought home and held on to for so long. She wasn't so strange; she read in *Time* that it took years after a war for the good books and movies to come out. She took that to mean that people who were there were just now figuring it out. She did sympathize, if that meant feeling bad when Fisher did; she felt sympathy welling in her like some deep boiling dread. But she already had such terrible indigestion from the baby in her, she didn't have room inside for any more agitation, and so instead of saying something right, she belched. That was when he shoved her. She fell to the floor like a beanbag, big belly down, and then rolled over with a moan in time to see him out the door. There were no omelets in the morning.

This time, he had punched her. That was that. She had been sitting on a high stool near the stove in the kitchen, nursing the baby, and he came in late and loud and stumbling. She knew well enough not to say anything, not to ask where he'd been or what was wrong, or why he was drunk when he'd said he wouldn't be, when he'd been sober for almost three weeks, ever since the day the baby, Rhea, had been born. She looked up and said, "Hi, Fish," trying on her understanding-wife-and-Madonna-mother pose, and she tried to smile, though she was very nervous. It was late, and she didn't want him to break somethng and alarm the neighbors or the baby. Once she had yelled at him, "Turn your fucking drunk down, Fish!" and he'd thrown a pot off the stove right through the kitchen window. She did smile at him, and he turned and snarled at her. It helped her, later, to remember that she had never seen him quite like that, so that she could believe it was a stranger who had struck her. "What are you grinning about?" he asked. She felt terribly self-conscious, with her heavy warm breast exposed, and so she smiled even more, in compensation, the way she had in school when she was bawled out for reading ahead. Then he hit her, smack, right between the eyes, with his fist. He wasn't standing very far away, and he didn't pull his arm back or take aim or anything. His arm shot out like a rubber band released from tension, and her face happened to be in the way. Later she wondered if he had meant to hit her in the mouth, to wipe the grin off, since she didn't do it herself. My God, she thought, he could have knocked my teeth out. But her memory was clear. He had stuck his arm straight out like a robot, and she was exactly an arm's length minus two awful inches away, just above nose height, just between the eyes.

I'm tired," she said as she came through the gate. Her mother, June, was there, with her aunt Christine. Katie hadn't been home in years. Both women looked different than she remembered them. Her mother, in her designer jeans and nubby sweater, looked prettier. With her hair cut in a skater's precise style, she looked forty instead of fifty. Christine looked older than her sister, though she wasn't. Both of them widowed in recent years, they had gone off in opposite ways, not like Katie had expected. It was Christine who had had the sour husband, the tight budgets, the blank loneliness of no children, yet she had been perpetually chatty, a maker of fancy cookies with frosting. Katie thought she might have bloomed, but here she was, her hair ratted and her stomach bloated, wearing a smile like a ribbon on a crutch. Katie's mother had had the luck of a good husband, and Katie had thought she would wither without him, but no, she was brisk and attractive, as if it had been an amicable divorce instead of a heart attack that had parted her from her husband. Katie handed the baby to her mother. Christine went to claim the luggage.

In the car, Katie told them how she had been going out the back of the house to call Fisher for dinner, and she had gone around the corner just as he came around the other way, carrying a two by four. "It was really stupid of me," she said. Christine wailed in retrospective horror: "Thank God you weren't carrying the baby!" "Seems to me he might have been more careful," said June, grim, both hands on the wheel. "Stop at intersections?" Katie asked tartly. "Honk at corners? It was very unusual for me to go out for him; I could raise the kitchen window and call to him. It was raining. Now that I think about it, I don't know why I went out." She felt her cheeks flush with conviction, as they always had when she argued with her mother. The story fell so easily into place. "The baby was dozing. It seemed I'd been indoors ever since I got home from the hospital. Maybe that's why I went outside." She had shifted the responsibility from Fisher to herself. She felt a little smug, it had been so easy. For the moment, she forgot her dull anger at Fisher, though she had spent her entire day, in planes and airports, chewing on it. It was displaced by the more immediate clash with her mother. They had wasted no time. Her mother drove in silence, but the tension was there, waiting for words. "Terribly tired," was the next thing she said, once they got into the house. The baby was screeching. Katie sprawled on the couch and undid her blouse and bra, and fed the baby. Her mother's old Uncle Dayton sat across from her in a lazy-boy recliner, smiling and nodding from behind his blind frailty. The baby sucked, and Katie lay with her eyes closed. Her whole face throbbed. She knew she had been a shock to see; she looked a little like a raccoon. She thought again about Fisher, and found she hadn't the energy to remember the decisions she had to make about him. She had brought him like luggage, waiting to be unpacked, unless she ignored it and took it back exactly as it had come. She thought of Fisher and found he was as flat in her mind as a photograph. Yes, exactly as a photograph, she saw him perched on the roof of the long metal warehouse where he was working. There would be drizzle; it would be so easy for him to fall. She saw him, like a feather off a pillow on a bed, drifting toward the pavement. She was falling asleep. Unconsciousness would bring her dreams—brilliant, violent ones. She had had them for so many months now they were almost welcome. It was their predictability that made them bearable. She found, more and more, that she wanted things laid out in patterns— meals, and sleep, and quarrels, and baths. Fisher was unobliging. She never knew what was coming from him, or when, and so she had constantly to expect trouble. She was fast assuming a victim's pose. Except, she thought, that she was too smark-aleck to be victimized. Collaborator she was, in their script. It had been better, much better when he— they—had smoked grass, but he didn't like the game he had to play, or the price he had to pay. He said wine was just as good, which of course it wasn't. The wine shut her out: she hated the smell, the taste, the stickiness of it. When they had gotten stoned, they had crawled into a safe place together. Sometimes he had talked to her there. She remembered sitting on their bathroom floor while their friends laughed and yelled at one another out in the kitchen. She and Fisher sat, knees up, eyes floating out toward one another, and he told her the whole war had drifted by on such a cloud, a cloud of mountain shit, he called it. Rain, more rain; bodies—theirs and ours and those you couldn't be sure of; death all colloidal in the choking jungle stench; everything drifting, make-believe, while everybody watched and waited and got old really fast. She remembered the way her throat pulsed while he talked, and how hot the small room was. She lay down on the floor and put her cheek against the porcelain of the toilet, and then Fisher lay down beside her and said, "Some day we'll be really old, and I'll have told you everything."

Someone brought a blanket, and took off her shoes, and set up a vaporizer. Her mother took the baby. "I've got a crib set up," she said. She came back in a few minutes and laid hot cloths across Katie's eyes, and then changed them for cold. Back and forth the cloths went; she felt as if she were dissolving.

They both had had some money when they met. She
had become part of a circle of friends that had been his
before he enlisted. Some of them graduated, and went on to
be social workers and post office clerks and land use planners.
They had children and houses. Others, like her, drifted.
Burly Winston, everybody's confidante, drove a school bus
and then went to Salt Lake to trace his lineage. Katie worked
in a fish and chips place and saved up enough to go to Mexico
in winter. That was when Fisher came home. He had money
left from his tour, where there'd been no place to spend it,
except on the way in and on the way out. He had two cameras
and two radios. He gave her one camera and sold the other.
One of the radios had been gutted and stuffed with hash. He
sold most of that. Then he went downtown and got a drive-
away car. He told Katie, whom he didn't know very well, that
she had a good idea. She liked him for assuming they would
go together; she had thought she'd take buses all the way.
Eventually she realized it had been one of the bolder things
he'd ever done. They drove like idiots, in someone else's car.
They told each other stories about made-up people, and
made-up stories about themselves. It was understood that
this was a lark. What else should I expect from a man just
back from the brink of death? she asked, thinking she was
joking. She thought he probably wanted a lot of sex. It didn't
make much difference to her, one way or the other, except
that she had the idea that a man owed you a little for each
time—a little conversation, a little attention. A little
remembrance, after he left, or you did. At the border,
though, he went into a deep funk and didn't talk at all. He
saw her looking at him, and said he was going to have to get
used to being here instead of there, though he thought it
would help to be in a foreign country again, one that wasn't
stinking with war. They were on a Mexican bus by then and
her curiosity was building. "I'll recover when we see the

ocean," he promised, and then didn't say another word for a day and a half. By then she'd forgotten what she wanted to know. She bought them candy bars and beer at the places the bus stopped, and he took them without looking at her. She thought him exotic, his enervation a come-on. She had been anxious most of the time since puberty, and she didn't know much of anything about depression. The first night in Mazatlan, he snapped out of it. They got a room in a decent hotel and ate lobster and got very high. "Oh lady," Fisher crooned, two fingers in and half the night to go, "your flak jacket's open, dumbshit lady." She thought he was talking out of some dream station, and she didn't care. Communication wasn't very high on her list right then. Everybody wakes up, even from deep sleeps, she thought, thinking of dreams as events, not states. Never thinking that what you take out of a dream might work like erosion on the solid parts of waking. Knowing nothing about war under water.

They took a bus to a village down the coast, and rented a thatched house. They were there for weeks; she thought she was happy. One morning they hiked over a hot hill to a lovely stretch of beach lying below a grove of orange trees. She sat on a towel while he waded into the surf. He had just shouted, "Aren't you coming in?" when she saw the Mexicans at the edge of the grove. They made a line, squatting against the trees. Katie ran down to the water's edge. "Come back!" she cried. "I don't like it here." Fisher mocked her, but she begged him to come out, pointing to the Mexicans who sat like stones. He told her she was stupid, but he went with her up the hill again. As they passed the point closest to the campesinos, there was an audible rush of sound along the line. Then the Mexicans walked away. "What did they want?" Katie whispered. Fisher pushed her onto the hill. "Nothing," he said. She asked him again when the hill was behind them. "The water had a treacherous undertow," he said. "They were waiting for us to drown."

She got diarrhea, couldn't get over it. She took a plane

out of Mazatlan and went to her parents'. It was high season
for her dad's tire store. As soon as she was well, he put her to
work on a phone. She called all the people on the list, people
who had bought tires from him a year and a half ago. She let
the Texan back into her voice, made herself chirpy, sold a lot
of tires. It amazed her. A few people hung up on her, but a
surprising number said heavens, they hadn't realized it had
been that long. Every night her mother made mashed
potatoes. Then Fisher showed up in another car. Katie
bought her mother a blender at the drugstore and left it on
the kitchen counter with a thank you card.

The next day she realized that she and Fisher had no
contract at all. They didn't even know each other's age. He
had hardly looked up to say goodby when she left Mexico
holding her gut. They were on their way now to see some
friend of his who lived maybe in Mill Valley and maybe in
Sausalito. It was crazy. But by then they were in Arizona, and
there was nothing she could do but read the map and keep
the radio tuned. In a roadside park, just past dusk, they
made love on the back seat of the Grand Prix. It made a wet
spot on the dove gray upholstery. She thought it was an
awful thing to have done, a kind of trespass. Maybe nobody
would know. But when you made love—or did hateful
things, at the other extreme—some of you stayed behind.
She didn't know how to explain it; she had never tried to put
it in words. It was another of her ideas. She wondered sometimes if everybody who didn't watch television and didn't
like to read very much had ideas like hers. What was
important about this one was that it helped her make moral
decisions, when she remembered in time. She knew, for
example, that she'd never have made it in a war. Back on the
highway, she kept thinking about it, and she decided that
there probably wouldn't be much of her left anywhere, if it
depended on intensity. On action. She felt a kind of constant
desperation, small and steady like the hum of a cat; it kept
her moving, but it didn't make her especially interesting. She

couldn't imagine what Fisher saw in her, except accessibility, and though she could see that that might have appealed to him, she didn't think it made much of a bond. For her, he was made up of a lot of secrets, and she thought inside them all, his hum might be louder. It wasn't just that he was male; it wasn't that at all. It was that he had been somewhere, somewhere she couldn't even imagine, somewhere he was just making her think about. When he said he didn't mind if they made love during her period, she said she was glad. She didn't say that she imagined sometimes that she could smell blood on him.

She finally got up her nerve and asked him. "What was the worst thing that happened in the war?" She was scared to ask him. He said it was in an Oakland bar, right after he got out. Some drunk navy kid tried to get a guy to fuck him, right there in the bar, and before Fisher could finish his beer, there were cops and MPs both, beating the shit out of this wimpy kid. "Jesus, Fish, what could you have done?" Katie had waited a long time to get up the nerve to ask him. She didn't like being put off. "What about the *war*? She hated ellipses, metaphors, any lies that weren't up-front fantasies. And here she was, a walking ambiguity.

"I just watched," Fisher said. "More or less."

She nursed Rhea again toward morning. Someone laid the crying child in her arms, nudged her: Katie, Katie, the baby's hungry. She was in bed, though she couldn't remember changing or moving. She put her hand down on her hip — she was wearing a flannel gown, probably one of Christine's. Her mother had always worn pajamas. The baby was noisy; for a fraction of a moment Katie felt annoyed to have this creature attaching itself to her body. But then the gargled sucking of the baby shifted into an intense, rhythmic tug; Katie felt it in her breast and neck and groin. Fisher had watched her nurse, had never said anything. As the baby grew less hungry, she stroked Katie's breast, and Katie spread her free hand over the baby's fuzzy soft head. Though the urge was gentle, maternal, Katie felt the fine hint of hostility in her hand. A sharp push down—she shuddered and drew her hand away. She whimpered, lifting the child a little. It was whisked away, and she slept again, not thinking, for once, about the territories of the bed. She slept beneath her dreams. When she awoke, she felt better, but she had no desire to get up. To be a child again, the baby instead of the mother—how foolishly she craved that. Refuge, succor, regression: these were the craved things. When her mother suggested moving the crib into the livingroom, Katie agreed with relief.

Her mother came in and said there was a phone call for her. "It's Fish," she said, looking as if she were holding one. Fish spoke in a low monotone. He didn't have anything to say. Katie knew the call was as close to an apology as she would get, but it was not enough to acknowledge. She wouldn't take over the conversation. He had called. "How's your mother?" he asked. "See me shrug," she answered. Her mother was across the room cutting at the counter. "She's there?" he asked, and Katie said she was. The momentary focus on a third party, one Katie had betrayed in dozens of stories of minor malice, brought Katie and Fisher momentarily closer. "They're crazy for the baby," Katie said, relenting a little. Then she couldn't think of anything else to say. "Do you know how long you'll be?" he asked. She knew it took some courage on his part. At the airport, she had refused to let him touch her. She had told him that, after all this time, she finally saw that it was hopeless. He was a drunkard and a beast. He stood docile as a lap dog while she hissed at him. She wanted him to do something really vile, to fuel her journey, but he was too tired, or too indifferent to her baiting. She had every intention of leaving him. Maybe she had left him already. "We haven't really talked yet," she said. "I don't know how much I'll have to take." The last words had slipped out without censorship; her mother looked up from her dicing curiously, and then looked down again before her eyes met Katie's. Katie suddenly wasn't sure what they were talking about, or even who she was talking to. Oh, why did they always all talk in riddles? "I'll write," she said weakly.

The next day her mother went back to her regular schedule. She owned a small dress shop. She went there in mid-morning and came home around four. She said while Katie was there she would try to come home for lunch, too. Christine took care of the house, and of Uncle Dayton, and of the baby. Katie stayed in bed. She read old magazines and condensed books, and did her nails for the first time in years. She kept thinking she would go back over her marriage, her years with Fisher, and try to make some sense of them, but then it would be time for lunch or a cup of tea or a nap, or time to feed the baby, and she never really got started. She only got as far as that long ride down the length of California in the drive-away car, when they'd laughed so much, and she'd put her head down in his lap while he was driving, to see if she could shock him. Christine came in now and then to talk. She had quilting on her mind. Katie had admired the intricate Texas pattern of the quilt on her bed. Her grandmother had made it, Christine said. She had no talent for it. But she liked the feel of material in her hand, so she made them out of squares, and tied them at all the intersections. She was making one for Uncle Dayton, double-thick with batting, because his circulation was so bad. She showed Katie that the material was polyester, said it would last forever. Katie wondered silently why that would matter.

Her mother came home early and pulled a chair close to the bed. It was like Katie was a patient in a nursing home. Her mother said she wanted to tell Katie about a time when Katie was just an infant, and Christine had come to help out. She said Katie had been very colicky, and that she, her mother, had not managed well. One day she had slapped Katie, hard, while Christine was there. That was when Christine came to stay for a week. "I went to bed," Katie's mother said, "and when I got up, a week later, I was sane again, and mortified at what I'd done. It's a serious thing to hit a tiny baby. I never hit you again." She stopped. Katie waited for the moral. Maybe her mother meant to let her know that she understood the way she was feeling. Or she might be letting her know that one week was enough. But Katie was more interested to know how many times there had been that her mother might have hit her, if she hadn't remembered her blow struck too early. Neither of them spoke for a few minutes, and Katie saw that her mother wasn't going to clear up any of Katie's questions, and Katie knew, too, that she wouldn't ask them out loud. She never wanted anything from her mother that she had to ask for. "You know I never liked Fisher," her mother said. Katie was expressionless. "It's not just that he came through here and collected you without a pause for simple courtesy —." Katie knew quite well that that was one reason. "It's not that you haven't had a home, all these years, or that it was such a long time before you married." "So what was it?" Katie interrupted. Her mother looked at her oddly, with what Katie later decided had been distaste. "It's that your relationship with him has done nothing to change you." "And you think that's his job?" "I think that a good relationship helps you to grow up. Helps you to be a better you. Fisher doesn't seem to have been much good for that. I assume the same is true the other way around." Katie thought for a moment of leaping, cat-like, in an arch, and scratching her mother's eyes out. "While you are here, I want you to think about that," her mother said. "About Fisher's failure to mature me?" "About what you want to be, and what you are." "You are incredible!" Katie spat out. She must have been mad to come. "No," her mother said smoothly. "I am quite normal." Katie, who had risen stiffly from her pillows as her mother spoke, fell back against them with a thud. Damn her; she struck the mattress with a fist. She had wondered what the price of her mother's hospitality would be. She had expected a little advice on mothering. But no, she was to consider alchemy. To be something she was not, when neither of them knew what she was.

The subject of marriage came up between them when they had been together a year. Not their marriage. His. She heard him talking with Winston about a girl in Bangkok, where he had spent four months. The two men laughed about Fisher's "first wife." Paper Lady, they called her, and Blossom Juice, and Dragon Wife. Her name was Chee Sum or Chum See, something like that. Katie tried to ignore it, but she heard them talking about it a second time, and she confronted Fisher with it. He wouldn't tell her anything. He said there had been a girl in Bangkok, yes, but not a wife. There had also been the best restaurants in the world, he evaded, with fish caught that day, and peppers that put your eyes out. She wanted to know what was so funny about the girl. Fisher said she couldn't understand. She hadn't been there. She said Winston hadn't been there, either. But Winston had been in the army; he was stationed in Japan. "Eyes up, eyes down," Fisher laughed. "Forget it." She tried, but then his mother forwarded a letter to him from Bangkok. She came up on him as he was reading it, the slight pale paper of the overseas letter. She cornered Winston and demanded to know what he knew. Winston said there had been a civil ceremony of some sort, to "save the girl's face." Her father wouldn't let her live at home anymore any other way. Her father owned a bus line in Bangkok; there was a nice house on the outskirts of the city. Fisher spent a lot of time there. "Where did he meet her?" Katie wanted to know. Winston said in a whorehouse. The girl wasn't a whore, but a friend of hers was. Katie remembered a story Fisher had told someone about a whore who sat in a plate of mushrooms on the bar. Was it that bar? she wanted to know. "Shit, Katie, how would I know something like that?" Winston hated being put in the middle. Katie thought he owed her more loyalty because she'd know him first; he was a latecomer to Fisher's circle, like her. But he was Fisher's friend now. They drank together. She came home to find them drunk and hateful, surrounded by cans and bottles, take-out boxes and potato chip bags. The girl must have taken the ceremony seriously, she said to Winston. Winston said it had just been for show. But the girl had gone to the army, later, and that was when she found out it really did amount to exactly nothing. A joke on her. Somehow, she'd gotten an address for him. It had taken a year, but here was the letter. Katie didn't think the girl could have managed to get Fisher's address unless she was pregnant. Fisher tore the letter up in front of Katie. "She just wanted a free ride," he said. "Who did?" Katie asked. Some days later—she and Fisher hadn't spoken since the letter—Katie came home to find Fisher gone. Winston was cleaning her kitchen. He said he didn't like the way she washed dishes. "What are you trying to make up for?" she asked, affectionate in spite of herself. Winston said Fisher had gone to B.C. to see friends. Katie begged Winston to stay with her. He was embarrassed. 'I'm not inviting you into bed," she said, amused. "I just want company." They went out for hot Indian food, and washed it down with a lot of beer. "I can't figure him out. I'll never understand him," she whined at the end of the evening. "He contradicts himself. I wish I'd known him when he was in the army, or before he was in. So I'd know what was him, and what was them. So I'd know if he'd change." "Man, I wouldn't count on that," Winston said. He took her home, and slept with her after all. Maybe he did think he owed her. He tried to help her understand. "There were those who thought you laid low." he said. "Shadow grunts. Others said, keep moving. Different schools of survival. Fish—he still hasn't figured out which way he stays alive."

The next time the subject of marriage came up was four years later. She thought she was pregnant, and right away she said she'd rather be married than not, though she didn't make it an ultimatum. He agreed. They signed papers in front of a friend's minister at someone's house. The minister, who was wearing purple beads, couldn't seem to believe that they really didn't want him to say anything. "I could try to remember something from some other wedding," he offered. "Or say some more usual thing." They gave him a glass of Cold Duck. It was flat. Fisher had opened and taken a slug of it early in the morning. It turned out she wasn't pregnant after all.

The night she went into labor with Rhea, Fisher was drunk, and she had to take a taxi. He made his appearance early the next afternoon. The baby was bundled in a rolling crib by her bed, and she was reading. "A divorce would be awful," he said right away. He hadn't even looked at the baby. "All those papers, and a judge; you'd have to do it without me." She blinked. It took her that long to figure him out. The marriage had meant more to him than to her. She had said she wanted to be married so he would know she didn't mind having a baby, didn't mind that it was his. He had thought it was full of promises. Now he felt guilty and was laying their marriage out like a pig on an altar. He *was* guilty. She couldn't even depend on him for a ride to the hospital. "Look at her," she said, placid as a cow, ignoring his contrition. Of course she wasn't going to divorce him. It was too easy a penance. She wouldn't make so neat a trade—his conscience for a baby. She wanted both. The world was full of women who had both. (She ignored the corollary.) He just had a hangover. Besides, he did look at the baby, and then he cried. Like any other father, he cried, and made promises neither of them would try to remember. The promises fell easily, like tears, and she was happy for them. For a few moments, she really was just like anybody else.

"I love you," she told him the next time he called, after she had been at her mother's house two weeks. She didn't have the courage to say she wasn't coming back. She did love him, so it would be hard to explain. She would write him about it. Draw a line down the middle of a page. Write "Love," on one side, and everything else about him on the other. Put it in an envelope and mail it. Getting divorced would be like that, stamps and signatures and a great distance between them. She would stop talking to him. He would be humiliated, his worst doubts about himself confirmed, his self rejected. He would go away from the people who knew them both, and in a while she could go back if she wanted. It would be like he'd never been there.

Rhea lay propped in an infant seat on the diningroom table. Sunlight streamed across the table and across her fat legs. Next to her seat, a big Tupperware bowl of rising dough sat glowing yellow. The wind was blowing across the bare landscape outside. A norther was due, but who could complain? The sun had been bright every day. When Katie's mother came home for lunch, she opened the blinds in Katie's room and pulled back the curtains.

In the afternoon, her mother brought home another baby girl about Rhea's age. It was the child of a friend's daughter. Katie, lying on her bed, but dressed, heard the strange baby crying. She went into the livingroom and saw the two older women, each with a child in her arms. The new baby sounded hungry, and Katie's breast started to leak. Her mother was trying to give the child a bottle. "Is she used to nursing?" Katie asked, taking the baby away from her mother. "Some of each," her mother said. She was quite agitated. "Her mother works part-time. Usually my friend keeps her, but she had to go to the dentist." Katie took the baby over to the couch and undid her blouse. The baby went to Katie's nipple greedily. Katie had wanted to make the baby stop crying, but as the child sucked, she felt a wonderful feeling come over her. It was as if she were in sunshine. She looked up and saw her mother and her aunt staring at her. She smiled. "Milk's milk, isn't it?" she said. To herself, she thought, it's just the same. In the evening, while Rhea was sleeping, Katie went and sat by the crib for a long time, her face against the slats. She looked at Rhea, trying to find something that was uniquely her. Fisher had asked, "Does she look like me or you?" when he called. She had said she looked like herself. Looking at her now, she saw that she just looked like a baby.

In the morning, she woke to a terrible taut pain in her breasts. The front of her nightgown was soaked. She looked out the window. It was late morning; no one had waked her to feed the baby. She went into the kitchen and found her mother giving Rhea a bottle. "I hope you don't mind," her mother said coolly. She had gouged a bigger hole in the nipple, and was giving Rhea a pasty cereal. On the counter, Katie saw the cereal box and a case of formula. Easy as a breast. The oozing cereal ran down the baby's chin and over the front of her bib. Katie stared at her a moment. Then she turned away and poured herself a cup of coffee. Puppies get teat, she thought. Mother rats shred paper for a fresh nest. She poured the cream carelessly; the cup was too full. The kitchen was noisy and bright; things hummed and clicked and bubbled. Katie bent over and slurped from the cup. Then she stirred in sugar.

Her mother came into Katie's room after lunch. The window was still dark. Her mother raised the blinds brusquely and stood at the foot of the bed. Katie saw that the sky had turned gray; it was getting cold at last. "I'll keep the child if you want me to," her mother said, when Katie was expecting a comment about the weather. "I'm not very old, I'm healthy, I have enough money. I'm not desperate for someone else to take care of, I don't think it's a neurotic impulse. I think I'm thinking of the baby, though I must say a child is a sweet commitment in the early years." Katie said nothing. Her scalp seemed to be on fire. In another hour, her mother returned. "If you do leave the child, it has to be something legal. I won't have her for a while. and then have you come through your way to L.A. and take her away."

Katie looked at her mother this time with open, sullen hatred. "Think about it," her mother said, gently.

In the morning, Katie was up and dressed by eight o'clock. Christine fluttered around her, pouring coffee for her, but her mother acted as if it had been that way every day. Her mother was sitting on a chair by the kitchen table with the baby on her lap. "I bought a portable play pen for the shop," she said, more to Christine than to Katie. "I thought Rhea would enjoy being around more people." Katie, out of her own thoughts, said she had been thinking maybe she could help. Her mother looked confused. Katie laughed. "I don't mean with the baby," she said. "I mean with the shop." "I'm busy catching stock this week," her mother said. "You can come down next week. I'd enjoy showing you the store." She stood up and handed Rhea to Katie. "She's been fed," she said, and went off to get dressed. Katie dangled the baby over one arm, and carried her coffee in the other hand, and went into the other room. Uncle Dayton was already in his place in the recliner, dressed in gabardine trousers and a plaid shirt. "Good morning!" he bellowed. Katie didn't know if he knew who had come in. All the vision he had, her aunt had said, was enough to see objects as blocks against the light. "Bring me that little one to kiss," he said, and when Katie did, he was surprised. "Well, it's you, isn't it?" he said. Katie saw how long the days would be, if she started them so early.

The buddy with the houseboat was part Indian. His name was Jake. They called him Kneebone in the army. Fisher called him that when they got tight, and Jake gave a war whoop. After a while, one of them remembered another Indian, Charlie Bird-in-Ground. They cut his balls off and stuffed them in his mouth. In a whorehouse in Saigon. That was the war, Fisher and Jake said. Katie thought they talked about it all as if it were a series of pranks remembered from adolescence. Good ole Charlie no-balls.

There was a picture, not a very good one, of Jake. It hung on the wall of his houseboat. He was wearing a headband made from torn fatigues, the kind with spots all over them. His hair hung lank, silky looking, to his shoulders, as if he'd had a shower and then put back on his dirty clothes. He looked like he was standing in a sepia cloud. Whether it was dust or mist, Katie couldn't tell. He had a smart-ass expression that didn't look like him now. But he must have still had some of those feelings, or he must remember them, or want them, she thought; there was the picture. Fisher looked at the picture, too, and named a place: Tho or Do something. "Right," Jake a.k.a. Kneebone chortled. "Got there after the fucking place went up. It was still smoking. I was always just behind the fireworks. That was my charm." "And I was always in the fucking middle," Fisher said. He flicked the picture with his fingernail. "I was good at drawing fire." He acted like it was funny. "God, Fish," Katie whispered when they were in their sleeping bags, inches away from the couple's bunk. "I don't even know what the two of you are talking about and it scares me. Even when it's all over, and I don't understand what it was about." She could see his face in the glare of lights from the disco, bouncing off the window above her head. The look he gave her was the look you'd give a cat on your lap just before you put it off. "Don't try," Fisher said neutrally. "Stay where you are, dingdong." His voice cracked, as if they were talking over a phone, or over a radio. Across a paddy, maybe, or over a hill, she thought.

Fisher sweated all night, every night. He woke smelling sour and stale. All his shirts were wet in big circles under the arms. For a long time she changed the sheets every day, but it became too much. She lay on a dry place on her side. A girlfriend said it sounded like diabetes. Katie nagged and nagged until Fisher went to see a doctor. He came home really pissed. The doctor found out he was a carpenter, and then he said, "Well, laborers do sweat." There hadn't even

been a blood test. Nothing Katie would say would make
Fisher talk about another doctor.

He dreamed, too. Sometimes he groaned, or cried out,
in his sleep. It didn't seem to wake him, only her. The
dreams went on, year after year. She told him about them.
"You should talk," he said, "with your twitching and
moaning in your sleep." He changed the subject with high
humor. Made an excuse of it, for taking her from behind.
"You wiggle around and get your little ass in my face," he
laughed, and it was clear that he didn't intend to discuss it.
She knew her own dreams drew from his, but his were the
real nightmares. The groans were too deep to ignore. She
learned to sleep over them, like street noise in a city, but she
knew they were there, and they bothered her. And the
sweating—that didn't go away. Sometimes, to prove to
herself that she loved him, she drew close to him, her thighs
recoiling as they touched the cool clammy space between his
body and hers, where he had soaked the sheets.

But there were nights, dark rich nights, plum and apricot, grapes and nougat nights, when they met and slid and
plunged in the juice and acid sweetness. He lay sleeping, and
when the sea of her chest was dry, she wiped her finger across
the top, above the nipples, and licked it, to taste the salt he
had left there. The bed was pungent with the smells they had
made. There was no word for this. Love. Hate. Need. She
lacked a word; it needed six, eight syllables, rolling conso-
nants, resonance, repetition. Perhaps a Russian word would
do, a Bolshevik word, she thought, and didn't even know
what it meant. She who had voted once because a neighbor
ran for city council. She needed a word thick and rich enough
to name what there was with them, some word complex
enough, and sad, if spoken aloud.

He did wake up once and tell her he had dreamed he
was firing into a tangle of thick green vines, and suddenly a
bunch of gooks fell from everywhere, silently, like blossoms
off a tree in a light wind. He saw that she was one of them, a

body rising and folding over before him into the slime. She thought it a loving thing, his telling her, but once he had done so, he shut her out. He seemed to hate her for knowing about the dream; sometimes, in the dark, he would lie with his eyes open, staring at her, until she turned her back to him. He wouldn't tell her anything else. "I tell it to my lady," he mocked, and held up a half gallon of burgundy, settling down for a night on the couch. She started to have more vivid dreams of her own. They were black, crisscrossed with lights. She never knew what was going on; she woke disoriented. He asked her what the hell was going on, and she said, ruefully, that it might just be fallout from his dreams; they'd grown so big in him they'd crawled over into her. "What a dumb cunt thing to say," he said. She agreed, her lips slick with tears. Maybe she didn't have any right to his pain, but they were working on a decade together. There they were, two bodies side by side, wet and dry. Was it so strange that, after so long a time, she should start to share his night terror? She didn't ask for his dreams, she told herself. She had never had patience for dreams. But these? Maybe she did welcome them. It was aggressive of her, to walk into his secret place and steal from him. One night she woke cold with fright, and woke him, too. "I don't know what I'm dreaming," she said. "Help me," she begged. He got out of bed and wouldn't sleep with her for days after. "Surrealistic dildo," he said, carrying the best blankets off the bed.

She found Uncle Dayton's company agreeable. She began to spend most of the day with him. His face had two expressions, and he slid back and forth between them. Sometimes he was benign, listening to the baby gurgle when she was near him, or listening to the game shows on television. Because his hearing was poor, he had a radio that tuned to the television channels. He put them on, both very loud. Katie asked him why he turned the television on at all, since he couldn't see it. "All you do is listen," he said, "it's only half of what's going on." After that, if she was in the room, she would describe some of what was happening. He liked that. At other times, he sat in silence, vulnerability sliding down over him like a fog. His paper skin looked ready to split. "He's scared he won't live to see ninety," Christine explained. Katie couldn't tell what that meant to her aunt, who had taken care of him for so long. She asked her mother what it meant. "Scared of facing payments due on his living," her mother said. Katie looked at the old man in the lazy-boy chair, so thin she could lift him like her child. "What did he ever do?" she asked, but her mother, silent, tightened her lips to a slit.

Katie watched her mother with Dayton. Spoon by spoon, June fed him, catching the occasional dribble of broth before it got to his chin. Her voice cooed and cajoled; her face remained hard and resentful. Katie was fascinated. She supposed she would never know what history bound her mother and her old uncle so hatefully. Her eyes on her mother, Katie doubted all the kind things her mother had done over the years. The generosities.

Katie asked her mother if she had a boyfriend. Both of them smiled at the word. "A friend," Katie amended. "Yes, I do," her mother said. He was a surgeon. "Will I ever meet him?" Katie wanted to know. Her mother said she hadn't thought it was a good idea. "I promise I'll behave," Katie said, trying to sound light. Her mother invited the doctor to dinner. He was pleasant, and Katie saw that her mother liked him very much. She saw, too, that the surgeon liked her mother, and something more. On his face she saw something she had not seen in a long while, the ripe open look of desire. She left the table.

She went to her mother's store. There a blouse caught her eye. It was of Chinese-red silk. Her mother insisted that Katie take it. Katie wore it as a night shirt, with bikini panties. She thought she looked like a Chinese whore, and she wished Fisher could see her.

She had been in Texas a little over two months when she figured out her dream. She had been trying to find herself in it; it came clear when she realized that she was there, but not visible. She had to look at it from inside. She had to decide what to do. The center of the dream was Fisher; she should have known that. But the choices the dream gave her were hers. She could go back, farther into the brush, but she couldn't take Rhea, not knowing what was there. Or she could move out into the clearing toward Fisher, trusting him to wait, to see her face, trusting him not to panic and shoot in fear. She couldn't do that with the child between them.

Either way, she couldn't risk the child.

She got up in the middle of the night. At first she thought she was hungry, but she went into the room where the baby lay, and looked at her. She only stayed a moment.

For the baby, Katie went to bed without touching the downy skull, without tucking a finger into a little fist. Then she put the night between them, waking alone in the morning, lying there in the cold dark, thinking of what to take, and what to leave.

Max Apple

The Eighth Day

I

I was always interested in myself, but I never thought I went back so far. Joan and I talked about birth almost as soon as we met. I told her I believed in the importance of early experience.

"What do you mean by early," she asked, "before puberty, before loss of innocence?"

"Before age five," I said.

She sized me up. I could tell it was the right answer.

She had light blonde hair that fell over one eye. I liked the way she moved her hair away to look at me with two eyes when she got serious.

"How soon before age five?" She took a deep breath before she asked me that. I decided to go to the limit.

"The instant of birth," I said, though I didn't mean it and had no idea where it would lead me.

She gave me the kind of look then that men would dream about if being men didn't rush us so.

With that look Joan and I became lovers. We were in a crowded restaurant watching four large goldfish flick their tails at each other in a display across from the cash register. There was also another couple who had introduced us.

Joan's hand snuck behind the napkin holder to rub my right index finger. With us chronology went backwards, birth led us to love.

II

Joan was twenty-six and had devoted her adult life to knowing herself.

"Getting to know another person, especially one from the opposite gender is fairly easy." She said this after our first night together.

"Apart from reproduction it's the main function of sex. The bibical word 'to know' someone is exactly right. But nature didn't give us any such easy and direct ways to know ourselves. In fact, it's almost perverse how difficult it is to find out anything about the self."

She propped herself up on an elbow to look at me.

"You probably know more about my essential nature from this simple biological act than I learned from two years of psycho-analysis."

Joan had been through Jung, Freud, LSD, philosophy, and primitive religion. A few months before we met she had re-experienced her own birth in primal therapy. She encouraged me to do the same. I tried and was amazed at how much early experience I seemed able to remember with Joan and the therapist to help me. But there was a great stumbling block, one that Joan did not have. On the eighth day after my birth, according to the ancient Hebrew tradition, I had been circumcised. The circumcision and its pain seemed to have replaced in my consciousness the birth trauma. No matter how much I tried I couldn't get back any earlier than the eighth day.

"Don't be afraid," Joan said, "go back to birth, think of all experience as an arch."

I thought of the golden arches of McDonald's. I focused. I howled. The therapist immersed me in warm water. Joan, already many weeks past her mother's post partum depression, watched and coaxed. She meant well. She wanted me to share pain like an orgasm, like lovers in poems who slit their wrists together. She wanted us to be as content as trees in the rainforest. She wanted our mingling to begin in utero.

"Try," she screamed.

The therapist rubbed vaseline on my temples, and gripped me gently with teflon coated kitchen tongs. Joan shut off all the lights and played in stereo the heartbeat of a laboring mother.

For thirty seconds I held my face under water. Two rooms away a tiny flashlight glowed. The therapist squeezed my ribs until I bruised. The kitchen tongs hung from my head like antennae. But I could go back no further than the hairs beneath the chin of the man with the blade who pulled at, then slit my tiny penis, the man who prayed and drank wine over my foreskin. I howled and I gagged.

"The birth canal." Joan and the therapist said.

"The knife," I screamed, "the blood, the tube, the pain between my legs."

Finally we gave up.

"You Hebrews," Joan said "your ancient totems cut you off from the centers of your being. It must explain the high density of neurosis among Jewish males."

The therapist said that the subject ought to be studied but she didn't think anyone would give her a grant.

I was a newcomer to things like primal therapy but Joan had been born for the speculative. She was the Einstein of pseudo-science. She knew tarot, phrenology, and meta-poscopy the way other people knew about baseball and cooking. All her time was spare time except when she didn't believe in time.

When Joan could not break down those eight days between my birth and my birthright, she became, for a while, seriously antisemitic. She used surgical tape to hunch my penis over into a facsimile of precircumcision. She told me that smegma was probably a healthy secretion. For a week she cooked nothing but pork. I didn't mind but I worried a little about trichonosis because she liked everything rare.

Joan had an incredible grip. Her older brother gave her a set of Charles Atlas Squeezers when she was eight. While she read, she still did twenty minutes a day with each hand. If she wanted to show off, she could close the grip exerciser with just her thumb and middle finger. The power went right up into her shoulders. She could squeeze your hand until her nipples stood upright. She won spending money arm wrestling with men in bars. She had even broken bones in the hands of two people, though she tried to be careful and gentle with everyone.

I met Joan just when people were starting to bore her, all people, and she had no patience for pets either. She put up with me, at least at the beginning, because of the primal therapy. Getting me back to my birth gave her a project. When the project failed and she also tired of lacing me with pork, she told me one night to go make love to dark Jewesses named Esther or Rebecca and leave her alone.

I hit her.

"Uncharacteristic for a neurotic Jewish male," she said.

It was my first fight since grade school. Her hands were much stronger than mine. In wrestling she could have killed me, but I stayed on the balls of my feet and kept my left in her face. My reach was longer so she couldn't get me in her grip.

"I'll pull your cock off" she screamed and rushed at me. When my jab didn't slow her, I hit her a right across the nose. Blood spurted down her chin. She got one hand on my shirt and ripped it so hard that she sprained my neck. I hit her in the midsection and then a hard but openhanded punch to the head.

"Christ killer, cocksucker," she called me, "wife beater." She was crying. The blood and tears mingled on her madras skirt. It matched the pattern of the fabric. I dropped my arms. She rushed me and got her hands around my neck.

"I must love you," I said "to risk my life this way."

She loosened her grip but kept her thumbs on my jugular. Her face came down on mine making us both a bloody mess. We kissed among the carnage. She let go, but my neck kept her fingerprints for a week.

"I'd never kill anyone I didn't love" she said. We washed each other's faces. Later, she said she was glad she hadn't pulled my cock off.

After the fight we decided, mutually, to respect one another more. We agreed that the circumcision was a genuine issue. Neither of us wanted it to come between us.

"Getting to the bottom of anything is one of the great pleasures of life," Joan said. She also believed a fresh start ought to be just that, not one eight days old.

So, we started fresh and I began to research my circumcision. Since my father had been dead for ten years, my mother was my only source of information. She was very reluctant to talk about it. She refused to remember the time of day or even whether it happened in the house or the hospital or the synagogue.

"All I know," she said, "is that Rev. Berkowitz did it. He was the only one in town. Leave me alone with this craziness. Go swallow dope with all your friends. It's her isn't it? To marry her in a church you need to know about your circumcision? Do what you want, at least the circumcision is one thing she can't change."

Listening in on the other line, Joan said, "They can even change sex now. To change the circumcision would be minor surgery, but that's not the point."

"Go to Hell" my mother said and hung up. My mother and I had not been on good terms since I quit college. She is closer to my two brothers who are CPA's and have an office together in New Jersey. But, to be fair to my mother, she probably wouldn't want to talk about their circumcisions either.

From the United Synagogue Yearbook which I found in the library of Temple Beth-El only a few blocks from my apartment I located three Rev. Berkowitzes. Two were clearly too young to have done me so my Rev. Berkowitz, was Hyman J., South Bend, Indiana, Congregation Adath Israel.

"They all have such funny names," Joan said. "If he's the one, we'll have to go to him. It may be the breakthrough you need."

"Why?" my mother begged, when I told her we were going to South Bend to investigate, "For God's sake why?"

"Love" I said. "I love her and we both believe it's important to know this. Love happens to you through bodies."

"I wish," my mother said, "that after eight days they could cut the love off too and then maybe you'd act normal."

South Bend was a 300 mile drive. I made an appointment with the synagogue secretary to meet Rev. H. Berkowitz late in the afternoon. Joan and I left before dawn. She packed peanut butter sandwiches and apples. She also took along the portable tape recorder so we could get everything down exactly as Rev. Berkowitz remembered it.

"I'm not all that into primal therapy anymore," she said as we started down the interstate. "You know that this is for your sake, that even if you don't get back to the birth canal this circumcision thing is no small matter. I mean it's almost accidental that it popped up in primal—it probably would have affected you in psychoanalysis as well. I wondered if they started circumcising before or after astrology was a very well developed Egyptian science. Imagine taking infants and mutilating them with crude instruments."

"The instruments weren't so crude," I reminded her. "The ancient Egyptians used to do brain surgery. They invented eye shadow and embalming. How hard was it to get a knife sharp, even in the Bronze Age?"

"Don't be such a defensive Jewish boy," she said. "After all, it's your pecker they sliced, and at eight days too, some definition of the age of reason."

For people who are not especially sexual John and I talk about it a lot. She has friends who are orgiasts. She has watched though never participated in group sex.

"Still," she says, "nothing shocks me like the thought of cutting the foreskin of a newborn."

III

"It's no big deal," Rev. Berkowitz tells us late that afternoon. His office is a converted lavatory. The frosted glass windows block what little daylight there still is. His desk is slightly recessed in the cavity where once a four legged tub stood. His synagogue is a converted Victorian house. Paint is peeling from all the walls. Just off the interstate we passed an ultramodern Temple.

"Ritual isn't in style these days" he tells Joan when she asks about his surroundings. "The clothing store owners and scrap dealers have put their money into The Reformed. They want to be more like the goyim."

"I'm a goy" Joan says. She raises her head proudly to display a short straight nose. Her blonde hair is shoulder length.

"So what else is new?" Rev. Berkowitz laughs. "Somehow by accident, I learned to talk goyim too." She asked to see his tools.

From his desk drawer he withdraws two flannel wrapped packets. They look like place settings of sterling silver. It takes him a minute or two to undo the knots. Before us lies a long thin pearl handled jacknife.

"It looks like a switchblade" Joan says. "Can I touch it?" He nods.

She holds the knife and examines the pearl handle for inscriptions.

"No writing?"

"Nothing," says H. Berkowitz. "We don't read knives."

He takes it from her and opens it. The blade is as long as a Bic pen. Even in his dark office the sharpness glows.

"All that power" she says, "just to snip at a tiny penis."

"Wrong," says Rev. Berkowitz. "For the Shmekel I got another knife. This one kills chickens."

Joan looks puzzled and nauseated.

"You think a person can make a living in South Bend, Indiana, on new born Jewish boys? You saw the Temple. I've got to compete with a half dozen Jewish pediatricians who for the extra fifty bucks will say a prayer too. When I kill a chicken, there's not two cousins who are surgeons watching every move. Chickens are my livelihood. Circumcising is a hobby."

H. Berkowitz blushes. "Shiksas always like me. My wife worries that some day I'll run off with a convert."

"You came all this way to see my knife?" He is a little embarrassed by his question.

I try to explain my primal therapy, my failure to scream before the eighth day.

"In my bones, in my body all I can remember is you, the knife, the blood."

"It's funny," Rev. Berkowitz says, "I don't remember you at all. Did your parents make a big party or did they pay me a little extra or something? I don't keep records and believe me, foreskins are nothing to remember."

"I know you did mine."

"I'm not denying. I'm just telling you it's not so special for me to remember it."

"Reverend," Joan says, "you may think this is all silly, but here is a man who wants to clear his mind by reliving his birth. Circumcision is standing in the way. Won't you help him?"

"I can't put it back."

"Don't joke with us, Reverend. We came a long way. Will you do it again?"

"Also impossible," he says. "I never leave a long enough piece of foreskin. Maybe some of the doctors do that, but I always do a nice clean job. Look."

He motions for me to pull out my penis. Joan also instructs me to do so. It seems oddly appropriate in this converted bathroom to be doing so.

"There," he says, admiringly. "I recognize my work. Clean, tight, no flab."

"We don't really want you to cut it," Joan says, "he just wants to relive the experience so that he can travel back

beyond it to the suffering of his birth. Right now your circumcision is a block in his memory."

Rev. Berkowitz shakes his head. I zip my fly.

"You're sure you want to go back so far?"

"Not completely," I admit, but Joan gives me a look.

"Well," Rev. Berkowitz says, "in this business you get
used to people making jokes, but if you want it, I'll try. It's
not like you're asking me to commit a crime. There's not even
a rabbinic law against pretending to circumcise someone a
second time."

IV

The recircumcision takes place that night at Rev. Berkowitz's house. His wife and two children are already asleep. He
asks me to try to be quiet. I am lying on his dining room
table under a bright chandelier.

"I'd just as soon my wife not see this," Rev. Berkowitz
says, "she's not as up to date as I am."

I am naked beneath a sheet on the hard table.

Rev. Berkowitz takes a small knife out of a torn and
stained case. I can make out the remnants of his initials on
the case. The instrument is nondescript stainless steel. If not
for his initials, it might be mistaken for an industrial tool. I
close my eyes.

"The babies," he says, "always keep their eyes open.
You'd be surprised how alert they are. At eight days they
already know when something's happening."

Joan puts a throw pillow from the sofa under my head.

"I'm proud of you," she whispers, "most other men
would never dare do this. My instincts were right about you."
She kisses my cheek.

Rev. Berkowitz lays down his razor.

"With babies," he says, "there's always a crowd around,
at least the family. The little fellow wrapped in a blanket
looks around or screams. You take off the diaper and one two

it's over." He hesitates . . . "With you it's like I'm a doctor. It's making me nervous all this talking about it. I've been a moel 34 years and I started slaughtering chickens four years before that. I'm almost ready for social security. Just baby boys, chickens, turkeys, occasionally a duck. Once someone brought me a captured deer. He was so beautiful. I looked in his eyes. I couldn't do it. The man understood. He put the deer back in his truck, drove him to the woods and let him go. He came back later to thank me."

"You're not really going to have to do much," Joan says, "just relive the thing. Draw a drop of blood, that will be enough, one symbolic drop."

"Down there there's no drops," Rev. Berkowitz says, "it's close to arteries, the heart wants blood there. It's the way The Almighty wanted it to be."

As Rev. Berkowitz hesitates, I begin to be afraid. Not primal fear, but very contemporary panic. Fear about what's happening right now, right before my eyes.

Rev. Berkowitz drinks a little of the Manishewitz wine he has poured for a blessing. He loosens his necktie. He sits down.

"I didn't have the voice to be a cantor," he says, "and for sure I wasn't smart enough to become a Rabbi. Still, I wanted the religious life. I wanted some type of religious work. I'm not an immigrant, you know. I graduated from high school and junior college. I could have done lots of things. My brother is a dentist. He's almost assimilated in White Plains. He doesn't like to tell people what his older brother does.

"In English I sound like the Mafia, 'a ritual slaughterer'," Berkowitz laughs nervously. "Everytime on all of the forms when it says, job description, I write 'ritual slaughterer.' I hate how it sounds."

"You've probably had second thoughts about your career right from the start," Joan says.

"Yes, I have. God's work I tell myself, but why does God want me to slit the throats of chickens and slice the foreskins of babies? When Abraham did it, it mattered, now why not let the pediatricians mumble the blessing, why not electrocute chickens?"

"Do you think God wanted you to be a dentist," Joan asks, "or an insurance agent? Don't be ashamed of your work. What you do is holiness. A pediatrician is not a man of God. An electrocuted chicken is not an animal whose life has been taken seriously."

Rev. Berkowitz looks in amazement at my Joan, a twenty-six year old gentile woman who has already relived her own birth.

"Not everyone understands this," Rev. Berkowitz says, "most people when they eat chicken think of the crust, the flavor, maybe of Col. Sanders. They don't consider the life of the bird that flows through my fingers."

"You are indeed a holy man," Joan says.

Rev. Berkowitz holds my penis in his left hand. The breeze from the air conditioner makes the chandelier above me sway.

"Do it," I say.

His knife, my first memory, I suddenly think may be the last thing I'll ever see. I feel a lot like a chicken. I already imaging that he'll hang me upside down and run off with Joan.

"She'll break your hands," I struggle to tell him, "you'll be out of a job. Your wife was right about you."

The words clot in my throat. I keep my eyes shut tightly.

"I can't do it," Rev. Berkowitz says, "I can't do this, even symbolically to a full grown male. It may not be against the law, still I consider it an abomination."

I'm so relieved that I want to kiss his fingertips.

Joan looks disappointed but she, too, understands.

"A man," Rev. Berkowitz says, "is not a chicken."

I pull up my trousers and give him gladly the fifty dollar check that was to be his professional fee. Joan kisses Rev. Berkowitz's pale cheek.

The holy man, clutching his check waves to us from his front porch. My past remains as secret, as mysterious, as my father's baldness. My mother in the throes of labor is a stranger I never knew. It will always be so. She is as lost to me as my foreskin. My penis feels like a blindfolded man standing before the executioner who has been saved at the last second.

"Well," Joan says, "we tried."

On the long drive home Joan falls asleep before we're out of South Bend. I cruise the turnpike not sure of whether I'm a failure at knowing myself. At a roadside rest stop to the east of Indiana beneath the full moon, I wake Joan. Fitfully, imperfectly, we know each other.

"A man," I whisper, "is not a chicken." On the eighth day I did learn something.

Mary Peterson

The Carved Table

It was her second marriage and Karen sat at the round table in Marblehead with her new family, listening to their conversation and thinking of what her first husband would see, if he was there. He would notice, she thought, my new mother-in-law's enormous diamond, and he would see this new father-in-law's yachting jacket, and he would be disgusted. Might even say, "What are you doing here? You'll lose your soul to these people."

There were six around the table: she and her handsome husband, his parents, and her husband's spoiled-looking older brother and his glossy wife, who tossed her fine red hair and laughed at the right times and made little asides to the mother-in-law while the men held forth. Karen envied that sharing. She envied her thoroughbred sister-in-law who did not take it all so seriously. She herself took it too seriously and she couldn't shake off the feeling that something was terribly wrong.

She touched the carved wood edge of the table with one hand and with the other she reached toward her husband, rested her hand on his knee. He was always quiet during the cocktail hour, but also he listened with an odd, fixed smile: one of complicity — mesmerized like a twelve-year-old trying to learn the hard lessons of being an adult. When you were an adult you drank a lot; you kept up with your father in the drinking. This was difficult, since his father went to the bar for more bourbon often, and with each new drink he grew louder, and with each he had more to say and less that made sense. The man was well educated, she reminded herself, and certainly he knew much about banking, airplanes, and stocks. But also, he believed children on welfare should be allowed to die, so that we could purify the society. He believed in capital punishment. He believed we should step up the arms race and show more muscle abroad. Wars are different now, she wanted to say. We have nuclear weapons. We need a different set of rules. She did not say these things. Neither did she say that his capitalism created in the minds of the poor a need: they saw the television advertising, they saw the consumption of goods. How could they have any dreams but the ones he himself had? No wonder, she wanted to say, the Cadillac sits outside the tenement, and at the market people buy junk food with food stamps. What do they know about beans and meat? They know what they see on television, in the magazines; they know the Mercedes they see *him* driving. Your capitalism, she wanted to say, is educating them in desperate ignorance. Your free enterprise system.

She did not say any of it.

Her first husband would be thinking and maybe saying these things. He would know that the people around the table were the enemy, the very same she and he had fought when they lived in Chicago and worked against the war in Viet Nam. The same they had studied during the terrible sixties, the one they had hated.

"You're so quiet," her husband said, leaning toward her, giving her his hand. He was handsome and gentle and he didn't pontificate like his father and she loved him in spite of a score of things, and for a hundred others: not the least of them his stability, his good sense, his ability to be socially at ease with people, his open affection with her, the pure security of him.

"I was wondering," she said, "about the carving around this table." She tried to say it quietly, so the others wouldn't hear. "I know one of the wooden scallops was added, because one was broken, and I've been trying to guess if any of these —" and she ran her hand along the perimeter of the table ''— is the new one. To see if it really fits so well.''

"None have been added," he said. He seemed confused.

"You told me one was new. I remember."

"Karen's right," his father said. "One is new. I can't find it, either."

The other daughter-in-law and the mother had begun to play backgammon. They used an inlaid ebony board and when the dice were thrown they clicked like teeth. Her husband's brother had taken out an expensive cigar and was lighting it with great ceremony. He looked rich. His haircut looked rich and exactly right and his three-piece suit matched his shirt and tie exactly. He had a bored rich face and a sullen lower lip. You could not ask him a question because he would never answer it; he made light of everything.

The mother-in-law was beautiful and smooth-skinned and Karen had often watched her play with her grandchildren. She was the best of the family, but even in the best there was this other thing. In one game, the woman lined the children up to race. When they were ready, she broke away before she'd finished counting — she always won. "Your Grandmother lies," she told the children, laughing. One grandchild cried the first time she did it. The next time, the child who cried — a little girl — broke away early too.

Her first husband would have seen and understood all this, and although she didn't love him and didn't miss him, she respected his intelligence and he was more like her — shared with her a way of seeing. He would have observed her new husband's expensive suit, and her own diamond, and her own good haircut. But he's gone, she thought, and that's over. She released her new husband's hand. I'm seeing with my own eyes, she thought, and I mustn't blame it on anyone else. So now I must decide what to do.

Richard Wertime

Moonlight

In the memory, he was six. Maybe five, maybe seven. But it wasn't a memory he'd invited; it had stepped up to him as unexpectedly and indifferently as — as what?

The thought faltered.

Here was the memory in any event, so clear because it was unsolicited; it hung before him as detached as the cold September moonlight slanting into the loft. He couldn't remember ever seeing light this cold before. He himself was warm enough, though. He lay in his T-shirt with the sheet pulled up; the single blanket sprawled at the foot of the bed. No, the cold was purely visual: it flattened every object into a slab, a ghost-image lacking resonance or dimension.

In his sudden recollection, he was standing before the full-length mirror fixed to his closet door, young, unclothed, pink of skin. The rest of the family was off somewhere. Had it been, he wondered, his way of celebrating the privacy he got in such skimpy portions? He'd begun by undressing in a ceremonious fashion, watching his nakedness take shape in the pleasing pool of his own reflection. Shoes and socks, pants and underwear, his shirt, always, last. What followed then were a child's clownish antics, absurd from any point of view. He found it difficult to remember all of the elaborate contrivings which had gone into those rituals — or was it, rather, the accessory feelings that eluded him so shyly? Either way, the memory was pleated: parts of it hid behind others. What had caused him to do those things? And just how far back into his childhood did those episodes actually reach? He could answer neither question, two of the many he couldn't answer. What he did have, however, was a sharp sense of function: what he had done was not random.

He could hear the man returning; the rickety steps fussed beneath him. A bar of flat cold moonlight struck across the man's midsection as he came toward the bed. The hair on his abdomen was a swirl that made Mark think, for a second, of flames.

The bed rocked. Mark wondered if closing his eyes was the thing to do. He had closed them without thinking, and lay now tensely staring up into the busy net of fibers which his eye nerves slung before him. To be left alone now: it was all that he wanted. No talk, no aimless stirring.

The man made adjustments at a careful distance from him. It seemed he wanted something. Talk? Privacy to think? Sleep? Mark couldn't tell. He didn't much care, really; he had given what he was giving.

He smiled at the thought: he had given what he was giving. And what, in turn, had he got? This hard cold slice of September moonlight — that was one of the things. As well as a curious mental clarity: cool, detached, amused, ironic. He had never seen himself with such lucidity before, had never found it so easy to lay aside his infant swaddlings, the murky self-deception, the habitual self-pity. This evening, for once, at least, he knew exactly who he was, could calibrate with calm precision the results of his actions. He had rumpled his future. That he would be a long time paying was as logical to him as the fact that his jarred mind had sought to stretch itself backwards, moor itself to his earlier life. As if, untethered, it would wander into pools that were harmful to him.

And the fish, downstairs, packed away in the refrigerator: his big prize for the day. What they'd come here for in the first place . . .

Smiling again, he opened his eyes. Fish. A trio of handsome largemouths, averaging eighteen, nineteen inches. He had known how he would pay for them the instant the first one had hit the lure that he was playing, a small red and white Flatfish. He'd watched the bass drift in, a small torpedo, stiff-tailed, lethal. He had known how he would pay — had known it later, too, downstairs, when they were packing the fish away, all cleaned, in wax paper. The irony had struck him then a short, hard slap which brought the anger into his cheeks. His host (enormous and yet remote there on the pillow an arm's length from him) had gone about preparing their supper on a tiny portable gas stove with a hoarder's insulting caution.

He closed his eyes experimentally. Again he let them open. Galaxies shattering into nothing. The man had turned away, and dipped, now, down into his lungs and fetched up light shreds of sleep. Mark surveyed how he felt. Alert. Stunned. Thoughtful. Calm. His feet seemed to belong to someone other than himself.

And the loft: he looked about him. Moonlight drilling in through the window like a bit into coal. Glints of metal: the iron bedstead, something hanging from the rafters. By the stairs stood a .22, perhaps placed there as a kind of prompter or talisman against intruders. The man and he, this after-noon, had walked out into the scrubby meadow to do some shooting beyond the farm-pond. Mark recalled the jerk of the rifle: a single heartbeat squeezed from silence. Like the sudden pulse he'd felt when each of the three bass had struck — an electric jolt, an enlivening current. But his aim had been off; he hadn't hit a single one of the old cans and bottles they'd set up on the hillside. And the man, assuming him to be untaught in the use of a rifle, had begun giving him pointers.

He let his vision prowl above him. The beams cast shadows which were sharp-edged yet ambiguous, inacces-sible. Pleated. . . Another piece of the memory: his old rituals had always ended in the same exact fashion. A strange, disquieting finale. He would step into the closet, the one whose door supported the mirror, and wrap a cord (or belt, no matter) around the bar from which his clothes hung. This he would wrap around his neck. Then he'd lift his knees up to make his throat take the weight, as much as his spine could possibly bear. His neck would feel close to snapping, his gorge would rise toward nausea. And all the while he'd be busy with himself down below in his child's comical fashion.

Why this added memory now? Perhaps because of whatever it was that hovered up beneath the rafters. Mark's eye had met it and swerved away. There was something sinister in its formlessness, its lack of legibility.

Beheaded: the word that best suited. These last several hours had sheared away the tops of things: proper names, decent futures, pride, trust, the peak of joy. Of course, they hadn't, not really; he was aware of who he was, knew who this man was. He knew their names, his parents' names, the names of this county and state, this region. Yes, and the several states they'd entered, crossing boundaries in a scribble of evasions, lies and stories. He had got what he'd wanted. They had each got what they'd wanted.

And the moonlight: strict; unfiltered. A piece of it gripped the foot of the bed now. It blanched the metal. Mark rolled over. He had a thought which struck him as funny. He opened his eyes to relish it better, but his vision snagged on the barrel of the upright .22. *Had* it been placed there to serve as a hint, a breath of persuasion? If so, how sad, unnecessary. Some were born to be taken captive. Fish for catching. Things for shooting.

Still this moonlight. Cold. September.

Sharyn Layfield

The Coggios

It is spring, and flamingoes return to the Coggios' lawn, along with the virgin in her sky-blue robe. Inside the miniature picket fence, daisy pinwheels are spinning; a pair of young deer graze and listen. I listen too, imagining the voices of the Coggios calling to me from out behind the house where they take their afternoon leisure.

The Coggio house is lemon yellow, large but not too large. Mr. Coggio is old and bowlegged, and he wears a straw hat when he works outside. In the early days of spring, two of his boys are out with him, hauling manure, mowing and raking while Mr. Coggio, on his hands and knees, trims the edges and collects clippings, talking softly to himself or maybe to the ground. You never see a dandelion on the Coggio property. No clover, no weeds. The grasses are plush, untangled, as tempting to walk on as those golf courses you see.

As lunchtime approaches, two large Coggio daughters emerge from the house carrying first rags and buckets of soapy water, then linens, china and silverware. They move across the lawn through sunlight and shade to the screened-in picnic pavilion which has the same yellow roof as the house and birdhouses, perched high over the garden on long poles. Daughters scour the picnic table, the benches, the cement floor. Now they lay out a clean white linen table cloth. The cloth and the table may be ten, twenty, thirty years old. It's hard to tell the age of things the Coggios own, because they take such good care of them. The white cloth, for instance: if anything is spilled on it the women run boiling water through the stain, soak it, scrub it, and hang it on the clothes line in the sun. I have seen them circle the yard in the evenings gathering up garden tools, lawn chairs. Their knives are sharpened on a stone, their tools oiled, paint brushes rinsed and rinsed. Rust never forms on the hedge clippers. Nothing is left out in the rain or snow.

It is time to eat, and Mrs. Coggio steps grandly out of the house carrying before her a deep dish pie with an intricate lattice-work crust on top. The ruffles on her flowered apron, stiff and shiny with starch, are unmoving in the breeze. All the Coggio clothes are crisp, their colors bright with bluing, ironed with great patience by daughters on the sunporch. Tuesday afternoons they take turns at the ironing board, singing with the radio and sipping lemonade while they work. When they sweat, they pat their faces with real handkerchiefs.

The Coggios have settled at the table, crossing themselves and saying the words. Plates are passed and napkins raised and lowered. The boys and their father eat fast, buttering rolls and popping them into their mouths. The women chew steadily, rhythmically, watching the youngest boy as he talks. Mr. Coggio listens but does not look up from his plate.

The ceremony reverses itself, and the women rise to collect remnants of the meal, returning to the house in a silent procession. Now that I know them so well I can almost see the Coggios through the walls of their house, working in the kitchen. They are placing empty soda bottles under the sink in order of size. They are twisting the tops of large plastic trash bags. Someone is bent over the oven replacing the perfectly clean tin foil liner. I can see white, gold-flecked formica countertops, gleaming chrome and stainless steel, a toaster cover made to look like a cat.

Outside Mr. Coggio takes up his bag of clippings. The boys poke each other, returning to their rakes. Then there are sounds: dishes tinkling, a bird that alternates melodies, one high shrill call followed by another that sounds like a crow. The oldest Coggio boy is smoking a cigarette behind the shed, leaning against the wall and staring off into the woods.

It is late afternoon. I can see them from here, taking the

sun out back. The girls sit across from one another in the swing, the sun in their hair. The Mr. and Mrs. sit close by in lawn chairs. She knits and he, like his son, gazes toward the woods, smoking his pipe. The girls talk softly. Mr. Coggio nods, is sleepy. The pipe in his lap, he sleeps. The girls whisper. Nothing is moving but the wisps of loose hair that flutter around the faces of the women in the sunlight. This is my favorite way of seeing them.

I survey the house, the grounds, and imagine the Coggios' future. I know the girls will never marry. Why should they? But the boys are restless. They will go, and come back with women carrying babies in white baptismal clothes, and the Coggios will add a high chair, swing sets and a wading pool to their collection. Sunday afternoon gatherings will be bigger and louder. The girls will play with toddlers in the green grass, first urging them to walk, then holding them back as they chase one another in and out among the adults, screaming happily.

At this hour of day, when the sun is low and strong, the Coggios will stand at the end of the driveway waving and smiling as the sons and wives and children back away from them onto the highway and disappear. It is then they will see me. I am patient, knowing that if I wait long enough I will be welcome in this yard. I will be ready, having learned their cleanliness and their order; ready, when I hear them call me from across the yard.

Come to us, the women will sing sweetly. Come, come! The old man will speak roughly but with a hint of a smile. Mrs. Coggio will hold up a peach pie for me to see.

I'm coming! I'll call back, and stepping lightly onto the grass, past the pinwheels, past the virgin and the flamingoes, I will take my place.